Praise for The End c

"Ansolabehere and Snyder combine suspens
hard numbers of political science to show th
one-vote revolution in the past 40 years of A.
—Andrew Gelman, Columbia University

"Using new documentation and measurement in this fine work, Ansolabehere
and Snyder breathe new life into the redistricting revolution of the 1960s."
—David R. Mayhew, Yale University

"Today, the rule of one person, one vote is taken for granted. *The End of
Inequality* reminds us that it was not always this way, that the battle was hard-
fought, and the payoff in terms of equality of representation is very real."
—Robert S. Erikson, Columbia University

"More than merely a retrospective, *The End of Inequality* shows how courts can
remedy defects in American democracy and engages current debates concerning the impact of gerrymandering on political competition and representation."
—Nathaniel Persily, Columbia Law School

"[Ansolabehere and Snyder] weave a tapestry of American politics in which
the origins and profound effects of *Baker v. Carr* are given a central place. This
is an extraordinarily fine piece of political history and social science."
—Kenneth A. Shepsle, Harvard University

"A dazzling, sophisticated account of the hard-fought battle for what is seemingly the most basic of democratic values: the equality of each citizen's vote."
—Samuel Issacharoff, New York University School of Law

THE END OF INEQUALITY

ISSUES IN AMERICAN DEMOCRACY

Inspired by the legacy of mid-twentieth-century landmark books in political science by such leading figures as V. O. Key Jr., David Truman, E. E. Schattschneider, and Robert Dahl, this series crosses boundaries of substance and method to explore significant questions about politics and policy in the United States. It uses the range and scope only book-length studies can offer to probe the role of government, to ask how the country's institutions are performing, to inquire about the character of decision making, and to identify the role of government in shaping issues of might, equality, liberty, security, and membership.

IRA KATZNELSON
Series Editor
Ruggles Professor of
    Political Science and History
Columbia University

THE END OF INEQUALITY

One Person, One Vote and the
Transformation of American Politics

Stephen Ansolabehere
MASSACHUSETTS INSTITUTE OF TECHNOLOGY

James M. Snyder Jr.
MASSACHUSETTS INSTITUTE OF TECHNOLOGY

ISSUES IN AMERICAN DEMOCRACY
Ira Katznelson, Series Editor

W. W. Norton & Company
New York   London

W. W. Norton & Company has been independent since its founding in 1923, when William Warder Norton and Mary D. Herter Norton first published lectures delivered at the People's Institute, the adult education division of New York City's Cooper Union. The Nortons soon expanded their program beyond the Institute, publishing books by celebrated academics from America and abroad. By mid-century, the two major pillars of Norton's publishing program—trade books and college texts—were firmly established. In the 1950s, the Norton family transferred control of the company to its employees, and today—with a staff of four hundred and a comparable number of trade, college, and professional titles published each year— W. W. Norton & Company stands as the largest and oldest publishing house owned wholly by its employees.

Editor: Aaron Javsicas
Managing Editor—College: Marian Johnson
Associate Managing Editor—College: Kim Yi
Director of Manufacturing—College: Roy Tedoff
Series Design by Anna Oler
Composition by Binghamton Valley Composition
Manufacturing by Courier

Library of Congress Cataloging-in-Publication Data
Ansolabehere, Stephen.
The end of inequality : one person, one vote and the transformation of American politics / Stephen Ansolabehere, James M. Snyder, Jr. — 1st ed.
p.   cm. — (Issues in American democracy)
Includes bibliographical references and index.
ISBN 978-0-393-93103-7 (pbk.)
1. Apportionment (Election law)—United States.   2. Apportionment (Election law)—United States—History—20th century.   3. Proportional representation—United States.
4. Election districts—United States.   5. United States—Politics and government—20th century.   I. Snyder, James M.   II. Title.
KF4905.A96 2008
342.73'053—dc22   2007045605

W. W. Norton & Company, Inc., 500 Fifth Avenue, New York, NY 10110
www.wwnorton.com

W. W. Norton & Company Ltd., Castle House, 75/76 Wells Street, London W1T 3QT

1   2   3   4   5   6   7   8   9   0

To Laurie Gould and Julia Corbett

Contents

Acknowledgments

This book began with an after-dinner conversation. One of us—Steve—made a presentation to the Boston Chapter of the MIT Alumni Association in 2002 on a topic completely unrelated to this book. The woman seated next to him asked what projects he was working on, and he described his recently published article (which eventually became chapter 9 of this book) on how reapportionment following *Baker v. Carr* altered the distribution of public finances. She demurely commented in the sweetest Southern accent, "My daddy was the city's attorney in that case, and we heard all about it growing up. He would love to talk to you." Within the month Steve was on his way to Nashville to meet Harris Gilbert. This was the beginning of a fascinating search to discover how and why America ended its long history of political inequality.

Many people helped us in our explorations, and we would like acknowledge our gratitude to them. First and foremost are Harris Gilbert and Roy Schotland, who served as our able guides through the rings of history. There is no way we could have completed the research here, especially in piecing together the tale of the case itself, without their wisdom and insights. They also introduced us to many people who added to their knowledge. We are especially grateful to Maclin Davis, John Seigenthaler, and John Jay Hooker for taking the time to discuss the case and its political context with us, and to Stephen Barnett, Jerold Israel, and Frank Michelman for pointing us in useful directions and validating Court documents.

Jonathan Woon wrote with us on our first foray into this subject, a conference paper on the California electorate's odd decision to approve an unequal apportionment plan, and Alan Gerber, our colleague and friend at Yale, collaborated on the research article that appeared in the *American Political Science Review* in 2002. Both helped shape this book in ways they do not fully know. Many other colleagues, especially law professors, have educated us about the meaning of the case and its ramifications for contemporary politics. We are especially grateful to Sam Issacharoff, Nate Persily, Gary King, Mark Hansen, Dan Lowenstein, and David Brady.

An army of research assistants, scattered throughout the country, helped us assemble the state legislative election returns. Looking at the six filing cabinets—not drawers, cabinets—that they pulled together, we are in awe of the amount of time and care they took in this endeavor. Chief among those to whom we owe our deepest thanks is Philip Burrowes, data maven extraordinaire. Others who made substantial contributions to this effort include Andrew Reeves, Michiko Ueda, Wilmer Fiorentino, Gillian Harding, John Bruner, Matt Williams, Meghan O'Kane, Tony Hill, Caroline Fu, Sarah Sled, Laura Feiveson, Paul Staniland, Alexandra Coso, Alex Theodoridis, Dusti Miller, Karen Shafer, as well as the librarians at MIT, Harvard University, University of Chicago, Yale University, University of North Carolina at Chapel Hill, the Library of Congress, and state librarians and archivists across the country. Financial support came from the Carnegie Corporation (thanks Pat), the National Science Foundation, and MIT.

Throughout we have benefited from the critical eye of Laurie Gould, who read the very first draft of the first chapter and every alteration in the text since. Ira Katznelson, the editor of this series, helped us to sharpen the book and draw out its larger lessons; Ann Shin and Roby Harrington championed this project at Norton, and Aaron Javsicas provided invaluable editing of the final manuscript. John Lovett proofread the entire manuscript and helped us manage the project, especially in the final months of writing.

Finally, we wish to thank our wives for their support and patience. This book is dedicated to them.

THE END OF INEQUALITY

1

A Quiet Revolution

Harris Gilbert, John Jay Hooker, and Tommy Osborn arrived in Washington, D.C., an unlikely revolutionary troika. The Kennedy administration was just one month old, and entering its honeymoon with America, after the bitter and controversial 1960 election. John Jay Hooker had arranged meetings with Robert F. Kennedy, the new attorney general of the United States, and with Archibald Cox, the solicitor general, with whom he had worked on John Kennedy's presidential campaign. Hooker, the scion of one of Nashville's most distinguished families, was a friend of Robert Kennedy and had worked with Cox on John Kennedy's presidential campaign. Hooker's meetings now, however, were not social calls.

Hooker had brought with him two attorneys from back home, from Nashville. Tommy Osborn, a fiery, brilliant trial lawyer, was, at age forty-two, emerging as a star in the state's legal community. Harris Gilbert, an attorney working for the City of Nashville, was fresh out of law school. Hooker, Osborn, and Gilbert were also in the vanguard of a new generation in Tennessee politics and in the nation. A decade earlier, Estes Kefauver and Albert Gore Sr. had captured Tennessee's U.S. Senate seats, defeating the handpicked candidates of the state's political establishment. The Kefauver and Gore victories began the slow unraveling of the political machine that ruled the state's Democratic Party. The young Turks followed into the breach. They now sought to dismantle the structure on which political power in the state rested—the overrepresentation of rural counties in the state legislature—and they had come to Washington, D.C., to enlist the Kennedy administration in their cause.

The state legislature had not redrawn district boundaries to adjust to shifts in population since 1901, despite the state's constitutional requirement for equal population representation. It was now 1961. Severe inequalities in legislative district populations guaranteed rural areas a majority of seats in the Tennessee assembly and senate, even though these areas contained a minority of the state's residents. The legislature had once again turned back efforts by the representatives of Nashville to draw new districts that would comply with the state's constitution. The State Supreme Court of Tennessee had denied their complaint, citing a lack of jurisdiction over legislative matters. In April 1961, in just two months' time, the U.S. Supreme Court was going to hear their complaint, the case of *Baker v. Carr.* The High Court was their last hope, and Gilbert, Hooker, and Osborn needed all the help they could get.

The Tennessee lawyers knew the importance of the administration's potential support for their case. The solicitor general of the United States is granted special privileges to argue cases before the Supreme Court. Bringing the solicitor general on board would underscore the importance of the complaint and its far-reaching implications for the nation. It would provide expertise on the merits of the case and the intricacies of the procedure, and it would guarantee a longer period of argumentation for the lawyers' cause.

Archibald Cox himself had vast knowledge of the inner workings of the Court. He understood the subtleties and politics of the Court well, and he had personal ties to one of its most respected and most senior members, Justice Felix Frankfurter. Frankfurter had been one of Cox's professors at Harvard Law School, and Cox was a particular favorite of the august Harvard professor. Frankfurter considered Cox his protégé.

The case faced an uphill battle. The Supreme Court had dismissed a similar suit that Tommy Osborn and a group of political activists had brought six years earlier. Standing in their way was Justice Frankfurter's famous dictum that the courts ought not to enter the "political thicket." The Court had set aside Osborn's earlier efforts without comment. In 1961, Frankfurter still anchored the conservative bloc on the Court. Justices John Marshall Harlan, Charles Evans Whittaker, and Thomas Clark nearly always sided with Frankfurter on questions involving political rights.

But this time there was reason for hope. The Court had changed since 1946, when Frankfurter warned the Justices to steer clear of questions of legislative reapportionment. Chief Justice Warren had replaced Chief Justice Vinson in 1953. Justice William J. Brennan had replaced Sherman Minton. Warren and Brennan, along with Justices Hugo Black and William O. Douglas, formed the vanguard of the rights revolution. Warren's Court had set out dramatic new directions in civil and political rights, exemplified by *Brown v. Board of Education.*

In the 1960 term, just one year earlier, the Supreme Court had overturned the racially based gerrymander of the city of Tuskegee, Alabama. Alabama's state legislature had redrawn the boundaries of the city of Tuskegee so as to dilute the voting power of blacks, especially those at the Tuskegee Institute, in city and county elections. William Gomillion, a sociology professor, sued, charging violation of his political and civil rights. Frankfurter himself wrote the opinion in *Gomillion v. Lightfoot*, though he carefully distinguished that case from his earlier dictum. The Tuskegee case had clearly violated the voting rights of African Americans guaranteed by the Fifteenth Amendment.

The Tennessee complaint asserted a broader right, a right of equal political representation for all—one person, one vote. The idea was certainly not foreign. Most state constitutions required representation of population in least one chamber of the state legislature. However, most states were not in compliance with their own laws. Tennessee was typical. The state legislature would not or could not come to an agreement about the apportionment of its seats. Rural areas lost population, first to cities, then to suburbs. Complying with the state constitutions meant giving away political power. The rural majority in the legislature would have to create more urban and suburban constituencies and reduce their own numbers. It was easier to do nothing. Gradually, with the movement of people off farms and into cities and metropolitan areas, malapportionment in the state legislatures progressively worsened. One political commentator at the time observed that "places with more cows and sheep than people often had as many votes in the state legislature as the large cities."[1]

Therein lay the political risk for the Supreme Court. *Baker v. Carr* could affect every state legislature in the country, angering political leaders not just in Tennessee but throughout the country. State legislatures from California to Connecticut, from Florida to Michigan, had severe inequities in legislative representation. If the Court insisted that the state legislatures reapportion, it was asking for trouble. The Court was already embroiled in the midst of fiery battles over desegregation. *Brown v. Board of Education* had proved particularly difficult to implement from the bench. Southern political leaders, from governors down to local sheriffs, openly and at times violently opposed the integration of schools and other public facilities. Reapportionment risked just such opposition, but on a much broader scale. The reapportionment case would hit state politicians where they lived, and the courts would have to rely on the state legislators themselves—the very people affected—to implement the ruling. A show of political will and support from the president might blunt some of the political concerns surrounding the case.

---

1. David Brady and Douglas Edmonds, "One Man, One Vote—So What?" *Trans-Action* 4 (1967): 41–46.

The suit posed political risks for the administration, too. President Kennedy had failed to rally Tennessee's Democratic Party behind his campaign in 1960. The Tennessee Democratic Party had fractured in the 1950s, with New Democrats from Nashville warring with rural Democrats and the remnants of the Memphis political machine. Governor Bufford brought the Tennessee delegation to the Democratic National Convention in 1960 committed wholeheartedly to Lyndon Johnson for president. Johnson's presence on the ticket added some appeal for the traditional Democrats, who constituted a majority of the state's elected officers, but the traditional Democrats' support for Kennedy was, at best, lukewarm. The rift between the state and the administration took on a personal flavor as well. The rival for the 1956 vice-presidential nomination of Senator Estes Kefauver, the leader of the state's New Democrats, had been none other than the junior senator from Massachusetts, John F. Kennedy. In his bid for the presidency in 1960, Kennedy lost Tennessee, barely. The administration clearly needed to mend fences in the state if it hoped to win there in 1964.

The potential political pitfalls involved in the Tennessee reapportionment case might have made Robert Kennedy reluctant to meet with Tommy Osborn, John Jay Hooker, and Harris Gilbert. But the men shared intense personal ties. John Jay Hooker was a close friend of the Kennedys, especially Bobby, and he had worked tirelessly on the 1960 campaign. There was also another Tennessee connection to the Justice Department. John Seigenthaler, a reporter for the *Nashville Tennessean* whose investigation of union corruption brought him national prominence, had also joined the attorney general's professional staff. Hooker's personal ties helped attract the attention of Robert Kennedy, but Seigenthaler's presence would also prove crucial.

The meeting with the attorney general never happened. On the day that the Tennessee lawyers were scheduled to see Robert Kennedy, an intense snowstorm engulfed the nation's capital. Four or five inches had fallen by midmorning. The attorney general was tied up in meetings when Tommy Osborn, John Jay Hooker, and Harris Gilbert arrived at his office that morning. They saw John Seigenthaler and met with the deputy attorney general, Byron White. While they waited to meet with the attorney general, John Seigenthaler took them in to see Archibald Cox. By the time that meeting had ended, it was early afternoon. Bobby Kennedy had gone home early to avoid being stuck in his office while the city dug out from the storm.

Archibald Cox, however, met with the Tennessee attorneys at some length. John Jay Hooker had worked closely with Cox on the campaign, and Hooker approached the meeting with the same informality one encounters on the campaign trail. Harris Gilbert recalled the meeting years later. "The Solicitor

General's office had high ceilings, oriental rugs, and a beautiful mahogany desk. John Jay made himself at home. He leaned back in a chair with his feet propped up on the desk, while Tommy Osborn explained the case. The Solicitor General listened intently, and asked one or two questions. From the questions he asked you could tell he understood the subtleties of the case immediately."[2]

The Tennessee lawyers left Washington, D.C., empty-handed. They had even met with the attorney general, and Cox offered no commitment to their cause.

But the solicitor general was hooked. The circumstances that Osborn described sounded like a perfect case to test Frankfurter's political thicket doctrine and an opportunity to put before the Court a new theory of representation founded on the principle of political equality.

"Within the next day or two," Cox recalled in an interview with Gene Graham several years later, "I was in the Attorney General's office and I remarked to him that his friend John Jay Hooker had been in and sent his regards. The Attorney General asked what he wanted, and I told him that he wanted us to file an amicus brief in *Baker-Carr*. The Attorney General asked whether I was going to do it, and I said, well, I thought I would unless he saw some strong objection. The Attorney General said, 'Well, are you going to win?' I said, 'No I don't think so but I think it would be a lot of fun anyway.'"[3]

But win they did.

BREAKING POINT

The Tennesseans' suit ignited an intense year-long debate. From March 1961 through March 1962, the Supreme Court grappled with one of the most difficult cases of Chief Justice Warren's tenure. The Justices would hear oral arguments on the case not once, but twice. The brethren would meet repeatedly on the matter in formal conferences, and countless times in private, as the great case preoccupied the Justices. William Brennan and Felix Frankfurter—one in support of the Tennesseans' complaint and the other opposed—spent months writing and rewriting their opinions to win the votes of the other, ambivalent Justices.

Out of their deliberations would come a wholly new vision of the role of the Court in American politics, and the solicitor general would prove instrumental in guiding the justices through the most troubling questions the Warren Court

2. Harris Gilbert, interview by Stephen Ansolabehere, April 15, 2002.
3. The definitive history of the case remains Gene Graham, *One Man, One Vote*. Little, Brown: Boston, 1972. Some of the material in this chapter and chapters 5, 6, and 7 draw also on Stephen Ansolabehere and Samuel Issacharoff, "The Story of *Baker v. Carr*," in *Constitutional Stories*, Michael Dorf, ed., Foundation Press: New York, 2004.

would face. At issue were the central precepts of democratic government in the United States and the legitimacy of the courts themselves. Did democratic representation require equal representation? If so, what did that mean, and could the courts ensure equality without irreparably damaging their own political power and the Constitution itself? In the end, though, the Tennessee lawyers prevailed. The U.S. Supreme Court opened the doors to the leveling of American politics.

Six Justices—Earl Warren, Hugo Black, William O. Douglas, William Brennan, Potter Stewart, and, surprisingly, Tom Clark—decided that the courts indeed had jurisdiction over questions involving representation. The majority opinion, written by Justice Brennan, threw over a principled caution that steered the courts away from the tricky issues of legislative districting and a potential conflict between the courts and the legislatures. Brennan's opinion did not offer a solution; it merely sent the case back to the Tennessee courts for a resolution. The decision, however, did put the courts squarely on track for a collision with the legislatures.

Felix Frankfurter and John Marshall Harlan stood alone in their dissent. Stewart and Clark had broken ranks. Justice Charles Whittaker, overworked from other responsibilities and suffering stress from Frankfurter's unrelenting pressure on *Baker*, took ill shortly before the decision was to come down. Recuperating at the time of the decision, he asked to be recorded as not taking part. Throughout the Court's two-year struggle over the case, he had voted consistently with Justices Frankfurter and Harlan; but Whittaker also expressed considerable ambivalence about the case, and his departure from the Court tipped the balance of votes on the Court decidedly in the direction of the liberals.

This was a subtle but profound shift in the politics of the Court and the nation. Frankfurter and Harlan defended a principle of judicial restraint, the notion that courts must stay out of political matters because courts cannot fashion solutions to political problems. Judicial restraint is a fundamental principle of American jurisprudence. It argues for self-control and conservatism. According to this view, judges only risk lessening their own authority and the legitimacy of the Constitution when they confront political issues and take on the legislative function of writing public policy so as to balance competing interests. In 1961, the Justices needed to look no farther than the school desegregation cases to see the potential backlash that their involvement in political questions could spark and the difficulties that the judges had making law from the bench.

Frankfurter's political thicket doctrine had even more force in the area of legislative districting. Frankfurter had argued in *Colegrove v. Green* in 1946 that few actions that the government must take are more political than the act of drawing districts. Electoral constituencies must reflect the complex of political, social, and economic interests of the society. The courts, at least as Frankfurter saw it, could never serve that role, which is, after all, the function of the legislature. The inevitable conclusion, it seemed, is that courts should stay out of the area of political districting entirely. Moreover, Frankfurter warned, if the Court ruled on questions of districting, the Justices risked creating a constitutional crisis. A conflict with the legislatures seemed inevitable if the Justices stepped into this matter, and in such a conflict the courts would surely lose. The courts' best approach was to be calm, cool, and conservative—to do nothing, even when constitutional principles might be at stake. The principle of judicial restraint, a long-held presumption of the Justices, had stayed the hands of courts throughout the country. The judges had steered clear of political matters in general, and few questions were more political than the crafting of legislative district boundaries.[4]

The Tennesseans' suit would prove the breaking point for those who preached political caution. The principle of judicial restraint had been severely tested since the 1930s. Felix Frankfurter had championed the traditional approach and often found himself locked in legal combat against the poster boy of judicial activism—William O. Douglas. Frankfurter and Douglas were appointed within months of each other in 1937, less than two years after Franklin Delano Roosevelt's failed effort to pack the Court with judges favorable to the New Deal program. The political and philosophical differences between Frankfurter and Douglas defined the Court for the quarter-century leading up to *Baker*. For much of the 1950s, the balance tilted in Frankfurter's favor, but by the end of that decade the Frankfurter and Douglas camps divided the Court. Justices Felix Frankfurter and John Marshall Harlan anchored the conservative wing, which counseled judicial restraint and traditionalism, while Justices William O. Douglas, Hugo Black, and Earl Warren pushed the Court to become more active. The challenges of racial conflict, the blacklisting and red-baiting of Senator Joseph McCarthy, demands for free speech and press, inequities in the legal system created by poverty and violations of rights of accused—all made it difficult for the Court to sit idly by, and the ground beneath the doctrine of restraint began to give way. With *Baker*, the stalemate between the two extremes had at last tilted in favor of Douglas, Warren, and the liberal activists.

Felix Frankfurter and John Marshall Harlan did not roll over without a fight. They struggled valiantly to reinforce the great principle of self-restraint.

4. Anthony Lewis, "Legislative Apportionment and the Federal Courts," *Harvard Law Review* 71, no. 6 (April, 1958): 1057–98.

Together, Frankfurter's and Harlan's opinions in *Baker* totaled over one hundred pages. They raised the dismissal of Osborn's earlier suit as precedent. They cautioned against issuing a ruling for which the Court had no remedy. They cited the sovereignty of the states and the need to balance urban and rural interests. They descried the coming dominance of large urban interests over politically eviscerated rural populations. They warned of the coming political battles between the courts and the state legislatures. They prophesied the Supreme Court's loss of legitimacy. They wrote for naught. They were just two voices holding out against a majority of six that wrote with a new voice and newfound confidence. The Court had entered the political thicket.

THE END OF INEQUALITY

A half-century later, the decision itself reads as quite limited. The majority opinion stated that voters had the right to sue under the Fourteenth Amendment and that the courts could entertain such cases. But it offered no solution, no remedy, no path forward for other plaintiffs or other states. The ruling merely sent the case back to the Tennessee courts to be decided in a way consistent with state law. That, however, was enough. Brennan's opinion set in motion a chain of events and decisions that would lead to one unavoidable conclusion—that all legislative districts must have equal populations. The only questions were how quickly the transformation would occur and how painfully.

The rapidity of the revolution surprised even its architects. Within a year, the Justices established a new interpretation of the Fourteenth Amendment to the Constitution.[5] Equal protection before the law requires equal representation—one person, one vote. One more cycle of the Court's calendar would pass before the meaning of the *Baker* decision would finally come clear. On June 15, 1964, the Supreme Court handed down six decisions requiring the states to apportion both chambers of the legislature so that all districts had equal populations; a week later, the Court declared unconstitutional state legislative apportionments in a dozen other states. Every legislative chamber in every state had to comply with the new standard of mathematical equality. No exceptions were permitted. By 1970, all states had brought their legislative and U.S. House district boundaries into alignment with the new legal criteria. Only the U.S. Senate was beyond the scope of the line of cases following *Baker v. Carr*, and that was because the Senate enjoys special protection in the

---

5. The case was *Gray v. Sanders*, 372 U.S. 368 (1963). It concerned the county unit-vote in the selection of Georgia's governor, not its state legislature.

Constitution.[6] *Baker v. Carr* led in short order to the equalization of voting power in the U.S. House, in every state legislature, in every city council. The Court's success was immediate, complete, and stunning.

Earl Warren later wrote in his *Memoirs* that *Baker v. Carr* stands as the most important decision of the U.S. Supreme Court in his fifteen-year tenure as its Chief Justice[7]—more important than *Gideon v. Wainwright* and the cases protecting the rights of accused in the criminal system; more important than *New York Times v. Sullivan* and the cases that redefined the First Amendment rights of the press; more important even than *Brown v. Board of Education* and the subsequent decisions that forced American society to end racial segregation of schools and other public facilities. Like these other landmark cases, *Baker v. Carr* would ultimately establish a fundamental right—the right to an equal voice in representative government—and it asserted the authority of the Court in protecting that right. But more than any other modern Supreme Court case, *Baker* profoundly altered the balance of political power in the United States.

Here was a brilliant solution to one of the oldest and most vexing problems of representative democracy. For centuries, political theorists have pointed to legislative districting as one of the fundamental flaws of self-rule.[8] The legislature expresses the will of the people and, as such, acts as the sovereign that determines the laws governing the society. The problem arises because the legislature, as the sovereign, writes the laws that govern elections. An obvious conflict of interest arises: the sitting legislature determines the rules of elections, especially the districts, under which future legislatures will be chosen. And district boundaries must change; they cannot remain static. As populations move, legislative district boundaries must accommodate the changing demography, or representation will become skewed. Inevitably, the responsibility falls to the legislature to craft new constituencies. This moment—the moment at which districts are created—turns democratic representation back upon itself, because at this moment the legislators choose their constituents rather than the constituents choosing their legislators.

It is a fundamental law of politics that those in power will do what they can to remain in power. Nowhere is the impulse and opportunity for self-preservation

6. Article 5 of the Constitution states that "no state, without its consent, shall be deprived of its equal suffrage in the Senate." The provisions for constitutional amendments stipulate that no amendment can change the representation of the states in the Senate. This proviso protected the Connecticut Compromise, a political deal struck by Roger Sherman of Connecticut to satisfy smaller states, which wanted to keep the equal representation of states under the Articles of Confederation, and larger states, which wanted representation of population. Without this compromise, it seems doubtful that the U.S. Constitution would have been ratified by Congress. (See also Chapter 3, p. 45.)

7. Earl Warren, *The Memoirs of Earl Warren* (Garden City, NY: Doubleday, 1977), 306.

8. The problem dates back at least to 1690 and was described by the great English philosopher John Locke in his *Second Treatise on Government*, chap. XIII, sec. 157.

greater than in the creation of election districts. Districting becomes a tool through which the sitting legislators can sustain themselves in office, even long after they no longer represent the majority of the people. England, from which the United States inherited its electoral institutions, labored under this malady for centuries. America adopted the English system of representation with all of its strengths and flaws. By the middle of the twentieth century, malapportionment had become acute in the American states as well.

The U.S. Supreme Court broke the vicious legislative cycle that sustained unequal representation. The Justices asserted a new right to an equal vote and their own authority to check the power of the legislature. The Warren Court has been criticized for anointing itself chancellors, "guardians of American democracy."[9] However, the solution that Brennan fashioned worked precisely through the means that Frankfurter desired, by allowing—no, forcing—the normal political process to work. The judges did not draw the lines. Rather, they put the onus on the legislature to accomplish the task of forming new districts subject to the requirement that districts have equal populations.[10]

On its face, the requirement that all districts have equal populations seems like a simple and not very restrictive rule. However, in order to comply with the rule, state legislatures have to alter the boundaries of nearly every district with each decennial census. Americans move—a lot. As a result, districts must be adjusted merely to accommodate such shifts in population. Most districts experience relatively small net changes in population, but some have two to three times as many people as they ought to, and in others the population either fails to keep pace with overall state population growth or even shrinks. Redistricting would be an easy task if one could reallocate people from one district to another or change just one line to fix population inequities. But a change in one boundary has a ripple effect. The populations of neighboring districts change, and alterations in those districts' boundaries, in turn, affect other districts' populations. Changes in populations also affect the balance of partisans in the districts, leading state legislators to demand further jiggling of the lines to replace the supporters they lost. Compliance with one person, one vote, then, forces the state legislatures to craft a completely new set of district lines.

The new districting process is politics at work. Legislative leaders must accommodate the interests of individual incumbents, of parties, of factions and

9. Ward E. Y. Elliott, *The Rise of Guardian Democracy* (Cambridge, MA: Harvard University Press, 1974).

10. England solved the conundrum only with the intervention of the king in 1832. Even then, the effort to right representation in the House of Commons took nearly one hundred years, and it altered the constitution of the British government, contributing to the decline of the House of Lords. Charles Seymour, *Electoral Reform in England and Wales: The Development of the Parliamentary Franchise, 1832–1885* (New Haven: Yale University Press, 1915).

interest groups, and of disparate communities and disadvantaged minorities. They must also, in the end, satisfy the courts. The Supreme Court's decisions in the reapportionment cases have, by and large, spared the judges from actually performing the legislative role. Unlike the school desegregation cases, in which the courts have had to write plans for school busing and, in some extreme instances, decide which students go to which schools, the judges have, by and large, not had to draw district boundaries. The legislatures have now taken up that responsibility, one that they had avoided for decades.

Therein lies a great irony of the *Baker* decision. The majority's decision turned Felix Frankfurter's political-thicket doctrine on its head. Justice Frankfurter reasoned, rightly, that the legislatures must draw the lines, as only they can balance the many competing interests. Only the push and pull of a political process could lead to proper districts. It was on that basis that Frankfurter argued that courts ought not enter the political thicket. The flaw in his argument, though, was that politics were not happening. Legislatures simply failed to reapportion, even when their state constitutions required it. Nothing could force the legislatures to act, and the political-thicket doctrine removed a critical check on the legislature— the courts. The majority's ruling in *Baker* allowed the normal politics to work. Court-ordered reapportionment forced legislatures to find a political solution to the districting problem. In the process, the Court opened a new era of political equality in the United States, one founded on the simple principle of one person, one vote and the periodic renewal of that idea through regular redistricting.[11]

THE TRANSFORMATION OF AMERICAN POLITICS

This was the beginning of a great transformation of American politics. Court-ordered reapportionment swept aside decades-old, and in some states centuries-old, political deals grounded in a society that no longer existed. For most of American history, legislators served towns and counties. This arrangement made sense in a nation where almost all people lived on farms or in small towns, and counties contained fairly similar populations. Agrarian America, however, faded fast as the nineteenth century gave way to the twentieth. By 1920, just over half of all Americans lived in urban areas, and by 1960, seven in ten Americans lived in urban and suburban communities. Rural counties and towns, however, held a majority of the state legislative seats in every region of the country, and they were unwilling to surrender power. Most state legislatures, dominated by rural interests, followed the path of least resistance. They left old boundaries in

11. See Bruce Cain, "Assessing the Partisan Effects of Redistricting," *American Political Science Review* 79, no. 2 (June, 1985): 320–33.

place, with the result that enormous inequities in representation worsened as metropolitan areas continued to grow.

Baker v. Carr forced the states to plough under long-established legislative districts and with them the ancien régime. By 1967, just five years after the decision, nearly every state had complied with the Supreme Court's edicts.

With the reapportionment revolution, the era of rural political power receded. Rural politicians, many of whom had dominated state politics for decades, saw their base of political power evaporate as the courts' edicts eliminated thousands of rural legislative seats and gave them to the densely populated metropolitan areas. Long muted by malapportionment, city and suburb enjoyed a newfound political voice, and a new generation of urban and suburban politicians emerged in American politics. They would prove effective advocates of the interests of their constituents and would shift the balance of political power decidedly toward the metropolitan areas.

Reapportionment reshaped the ideological topography of American governments. It raised up political interests and ideas weighed down by malapportionment, and it leveled those whose popular base had long since eroded but who had held on simply from the inertia of the past. Within the legislatures and within the political parties, the centers of political gravity shifted to the left or right, depending on the circumstance. Democrats emerged as a party firmly rooted in urban America, while Republicans shifted away from their rural base and toward the suburbs. The effects differed markedly across the regions of the country, creating new political divisions in the nation.

In the Northeast and Midwest, malapportionment heavily favored the Republicans, especially rural Republicans. Malapportionment inflated the number of state legislative seats won by Republicans across a wide swath of the United States, from Maine and New Jersey to North Dakota and Kansas, and in these states the majority of Republicans represented rural counties. One person, one vote decimated the ranks of rural Republican legislators and shifted the party toward a new type of Republican voter, ones living in the rapidly growing suburban fringe around major cities. This shift also recast the ideological orientation of the Republican Party, as its rural base consisted of its most conservative voters. Reapportionment, then, cost Republicans in the Northeast and Midwest, and it replaced conservative rural Republicans with moderate suburban Republicans.

Across these regions, urban Democrats ascended to power. By 1960, northeastern and midwestern Democrats already drew a majority of their support from those in cities, and northern urban Democrats were the most liberal voters in the country, strong supporters of unions, economic regulation, and expansions of welfare spending and economic redistribution. Reapportionment pushed the Republicans out of their majority status throughout the Northeast and Midwest and either made these regions highly competitive or brought Democrats to power. The net effect was to move politics in the Northeast to the left.

The shift in the South ran along a parallel cleavage, but in the opposite direction. Democrats dominated public life in the South. Unlike their counterparts in the North, the southern Democratic parties were rooted in the staunchly conservative rural areas. The conservatism of southern Democrats concerned civil rights more than economics, though they also disliked unions and expansion of federal powers generally. Reapportionment eliminated large numbers of rural Democratic seats and gave them to urban Democrats, dramatically changing the face and ideology of the Democratic parties in southern state legislatures. The loss of rural seats was not enough to hand majorities to Republicans in the short term, but it likely contributed to the steady decline in the Democratic Party in the region. As the new urban Democrats pulled the party to the left, new opportunities emerged for the Republicans.

Reapportionment gave Republicans an important political foothold in the southern state legislatures. Republicans had little presence in South before the 1960s. They won precious few seats in southern state legislatures, but their strongest support came from cities and the socially and economically conservative suburbs. Reapportionment created, overnight, several dozen suburban Republican seats scattered throughout the region. As suburbanization expanded in the South, these seats grew in number and importance, and the Republican Party in the South and in the nation found in them a new political base that, by the 1990s, would supplant the more moderate northeasterners as the bedrock of Republicanism.

From local school boards to the U.S. Congress, the principle of equality became the foundation for a new political landscape. Huge inequities that once defined American government were leveled. The Tennessee lawyers—Osborn, Hooker, and Gilbert—who led the Court and the nation to raze inequities in district population sought an equal voice in their state's government. They wanted their fair share of money for schools, roads, hospitals, and other government services, and they wanted to shake up the ruling Democratic Party in their state, their own party. By all accounts, they succeeded. As the tumultuous 1960s gave way to the 1970s, the revolution that that Tennessee lawyers incited was complete, and it had come off quick, quiet, and bloodless.

A NATURAL EXPERIMENT

Our interest in the Warren Court's greatest case arose four decades after the decision—long after the Court had settled the web of legal questions and the lawyers and judges involved had retired or passed on. Our interest arose out of a desire to understand some of the most fundamental questions about democracy: What is the value of the vote? What does truly democratic representation achieve? Does it equalize the voice and power of the many interests in society, or do wealth, social standing, and concentrations of interests squelch those who lack such resources?

Today, it is easy to be skeptical about the value of the vote and the importance of the principle of equality. Half of the adult population, after all, chooses not to vote. If you (and only you) were not allowed to vote, surely nothing would change. But what if everyone on your street, or in your neighborhood, or in the city where you live, lacked the franchise? Would government ignore the needs of your community? Would the political parties align themselves more closely with the beliefs and interests of others? How much would we lose if our votes were diminished, and how much would others gain? We are taught from grade school onward that self-rule is the best form of government, that democracy makes government respond to our needs, and that political equality is the purest expression of the democratic principle. These are statements of belief, the American creed, but do equal rights lead to equitable outcomes?

The answers to these questions were laid bare in dramatic relief here in the United States by the reapportionment cases of 1960s. The political inequalities that marked the American electoral landscape before *Baker v. Carr* distorted democratic representation and skewed political power strongly toward those areas and interests that were overrepresented in American legislatures. One person, one vote led to a rapid leveling of our politics and a shift in political power of a magnitude rarely seen in any society.

The reapportionment revolution, then, is for political scientists what an earthquake is for geologists. Most of what we see lies only on the surface and reflects the gradual shifts that occur naturally over time. Typically, it is hard to detect the fundamental forces at work. Upheavals lay bare the raw structure and reveal how the thing itself operates.

Such is the case with the reapportionment of American legislatures in the 1960s. The sudden, surprising shift in representation exposed the simple mechanics of democratic politics. Some voters saw their voting power greatly reduced, while others were raised up. The country moved from a system of unequal representation rooted in old state constitutions to equal representation, enforced by the courts and implemented by the legislatures. This transformation—from unequal to equal—allows us to see in clear relief how representation shapes political power. Revisiting the political history leading up to the decision and the years following speaks directly to one of the most fundamental questions concerning representative democracy: what is the value of the vote?

Two basic and fundamentally different theories of political power in democratic societies clashed in the great debate over *Baker v. Carr.*

Behind the Tennesseans' complaint and the rationale of the Warren Court lay a simple equation: votes equal power. The bargaining that happens within the legislature, however complex, yields outcomes roughly proportionate to people's representation. Those with more power will get more from government, and equal political rights produce fair divisions of the public weal.

Those who defended the ancien régime set forth a very different view of political power: the large and wealthy interests will dominate the small. If given their proportionate representation, the large cities and the interests that govern them will find common ground and create a formidable voting bloc that the diffuse rural voters could not resist or ward off. Those with greater wealth or concentrated interests will dominate the poor or those with diffuse and unorganized interests. Such fears found voice in the writings of a wide spectrum of political theorists of the day—conservatives,[12] pluralists,[13] and radicals[14] alike. Only mixed representation or overrepresentation of rural areas would combat the tyranny of the majority—or worse, the tyranny of urban wealth and organization.

The conflict between these two views of power cuts to the core of our understanding of democratic representation. If the levelers were right, then equalizing representation in the state legislatures would equalize the political power of all voters, regardless of what sort of community they lived in. As a consequence, reapportionment would bring public policy in line with the electorate's wishes. However, if the liberals held a naïve and incorrect understanding of political power, they would permanently empower wealthier and more concentrated urban interests at the expense of the nation's poorer rural areas, magnifying further social inequalities. History, in the end, would prove Warren and the liberals on the Court right.

The effects of reapportionment on these different aspects of politics all point to a singular conclusion: equal votes mean equal power. The equalization of representation led directly to an equalization of the distribution of public expenditures—who got what. It also restored the political balance among competing ideologies and drew state policy back in line with the wants of the

12. Oliver Wendell Holmes, cited in Elliott, *Rise of Guardian Democracy*, 67.
13. Robert Dahl, *A Preface to Democratic Theory* (Chicago: University of Chicago Press, 1963).
14. Alfred deGrazia, *Apportionment and Representative Government* (New York: Praeger, 1962). See Robert Dixon, *Democratic Representation: Reapportionment in Law and Politics* (New York: Oxford University Press, 1968), for a thorough discussion of the competing arguments surrounding the reapportionment cases.

typical voter, who was in most states moderate. Votes equal power. This simple equation emerges in full from the great transformation produced by the reapportionment cases, and it carries broad lessons for democracies throughout the world, including our own.

The reapportionment revolution reveals the value of the vote in two distinct and important domains of government: money and ideology. The first of these—money—is the crudest but most direct indicator of power. Power, in Harold Laswell's famous definition, reduces to who gets what, and distribution of public money has long served as the metric of the ability of various interests and constituencies to get their way in the political arena. Every constituency pushes for its own share of the public weal; party or ideology plays little part. Constituencies who have more representation than they would under an equitable apportionment have a greater chance to win in the complicated bargaining over the division of public money. The second—ideology—is more subtle. Most laws reflect the balance between competing views of the role of government—the balance between left and right, Democrat and Republican. Constituencies who have more representation than they would under an equitable apportionment have a stronger voice in determining the overall ideological balance of the legislature. Reapportionment brought the laws the legislatures passed into closer alignment with the beliefs of the typical voter.[15]

In this book, we exploit the dramatic changes in representation that occurred in the wake of the *Baker* decision to observe directly how votes translate into political power. We carefully reconstruct the electoral history leading up to the *Baker* decision and trace the changes in government spending, public policies, and party competition that evolved over the half-century since. Drawing out the link between representation and political outcomes required that we reconstruct the electoral and legislative histories of the states and that we dig still deeper down to the counties. It is at the most local levels of government, the towns and counties, that we can see most clearly how changes in representation from the 1940s and 1950s through the tumultuous 1960s and down to the present time reshaped the distribution of money in the states. It is at this level that we discover where the Democrats and Republicans, the liberals and conservatives lived. We show that inequities in district populations magnified the voice of some partisans and muted the voice of others. Unequal representation pulled public policies away from the preferences of the great majority in the states. Reapportionment restored the natural balance between the parties and among competing ideologies and interests.

---

15. Anthony Downs provides the classic characterization of ideological politics in *An Economic Theory of Democracy* (New York: Harper, 1957).

One final lesson from this grand natural experiment concerns the agent of change, rather than the outcomes. The equalization of representation in the United States was brought about not by popular rule or through the legislature, but by the least democratic branch of government—the courts. The *Baker* decision ultimately led to a new districting process, one that requires the state legislatures to redistrict periodically under the watchful eye of the courts. The political cognoscenti overwhelmingly dislike this new process, and they blame the courts for making the electoral process even worse than before the 1960s; indeed, many legal scholars and even some Justices now echo Frankfurter's sentiment—that the judges should stay out of political matters.[16]

Looking back over the span of decades before *Baker* and across the nearly half-century since, we can assess whether the Court's intervention in fact aggravated other political problems. The provocative answer, we offer in Chapter 11 of this book, runs completely contrary to the received wisdom. It is certainly the case that the Court succeeded in its immediate aim, of eliminating population disparities in legislative districts. The new districting process also appears to have lessened other forms of political manipulation, especially partisan gerrymandering. The great lesson of *Baker v. Carr*, then, is not just the tremendous value of the vote, but also the power of the American political process, when engaged to the fullest extent, to yield fair outcomes.

The story unfolds in three broad sweeps in the pages that follow. Part I of the book describes the old order. Great inequities in voting strength accumulated gradually with the shift in population from farm to city and were sustained by those in power and those mistrustful and envious of modern, urban society. Part II tell the story of the Court's decision to end malapportionment. *Baker* and later *Reynolds* acted as the deus ex machina that drew to a close the long history of inequality in political representation in the United States. Paradoxically, the least democratic branch of government was needed to save democracy from its fatal flaw. Finally, Part III traces the resulting dramatic changes in political power and public policies that resulted from the Court's decisions. Reapportionment reshaped who gets what from government and made for a more equitable division of the public expenditures on schools, hospitals, roads, and other essential services. It also shifted the balance among competing ideologies or public philosophies, and it restored the balance of majority rule. Equalization of votes resulted in the equalization of political power for the geographic areas of the country. That consequence and the

16. Alan Ehrenhalt, "Frankfurter's Curse," *Governing* (January 2004), www.governing.com/archive/2004/jan/assess.txt. James A. Gardner, "What Is 'Fair' Partisan Representation, and How Can It Be Constitutionalized? The Case for a Return to Fixed Election Districts," *Marquette Law Review* 90, no. 3 (Spring 2007): 555–92. *Vieth v. Jubelirer*, 541 U.S. 267 (2004).

Court's power to reform the American political system stand as the great lessons of Earl Warren's greatest case.

Baker v. Carr stands as more than a faded page in American history. It is as apt today as it was forty years ago.

Malapportionment is common in the world's democracies today. The emergence of democracy across the globe in the last half-century has not come with an attendant embrace of political equality. Countries worldwide have borrowed American institutions. In Europe, Latin America, and Asia, legislatures represent area as well as population. As a result, many countries, such as Brazil and Japan, suffer from malapportionment and struggle to find a way out of the conundrum. Even the European Union is heading down the path of political inequality, as those who have conceived of the new governing organizations that span the Continent have chosen to represent countries more than people.

America's reapportionment revolution points the direction to a way out of the inevitable problems attendant to malapportionment. Democracies must embrace the principle of equality, and the courts must protect the right of all to have their votes counted equally. The story of *Baker v. Carr* reveals how difficult it will be to achieve political equality, especially where it is not written into nations' constitutions.

Inequalities in representation continue in the United States, too. Since the 1980s, the issue of malapportionment and unequal voting weight has morphed into questions involving partisan and racial gerrymandering and violations of voting rights. The Court did not eliminate the desire of those in power to write the laws so as to stay in power; it merely asserted a check. Devious new ways to dilute the votes of some and magnify the power of others have evolved over time. *Baker v. Carr* made the courts available to those seeking to end such practices, although today the courts are increasingly reluctant to hear cases involving partisan gerrymandering. It is vitally important that the courts remain open to appeals in cases involving political representation, as difficult as it may be to resolve the claims. The threat of judicial intervention hangs above the legislatures like the sword of Damocles. Removing that threat only invites those in power to do what they can to stay there.

Even more important than the judges are the men and women willing to take on the abuses and inequities they see around them. Courts are passive; they merely decide what is brought before them. It was the Herculean and heroic efforts of those who challenged malapportionment that ultimately opened the era of equality in American politics, and new generations of levelers have followed the path cut by Harris Gilbert, John Jay Hooker, and Tommy Osborn.

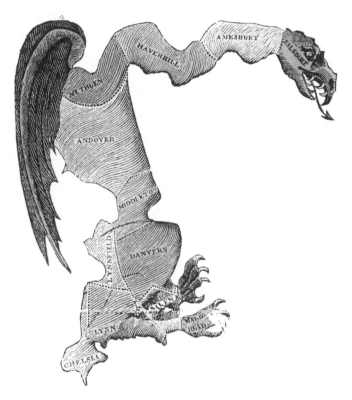

*"**The Gerry-mander:** A New Species of Monster, which appeared in Essex South
District in January last."*
Source: Bettman/Corbis.

PART I

The Old Order

2

Unequal Votes

Felix Frankfurter was right. The *Baker* case opened a path that led into the thick of legislative politics. The Tennessee lawyers sought to raze disparities in political representation; they also sought to shift the balance of power in their state's legislature and throughout the nation. A fair apportionment would give Memphis and Nashville representation commensurate with their populations, but that transformation could only come at the expense of rural counties. In Tennessee, and most other states, rural counties held legislative seats well out of proportion to their populations, and, as a result, representatives from rural counties dominated the decision making and positions of leadership within the state legislatures. Judicial involvement in this matter risked a standoff with nearly every legislature, including the U.S. Congress, which could permanently damage the Court's credibility in American society.

Against that profound political concern weighed the facts of the case. Political equality is one of the fundamental values of American society and government. But midway through the twentieth century, legislative representation in the American state and national governments was anything but equal.

The plaintiffs put the situation in the state squarely before the Court. Attached to Charles W. Baker's complaint came a sizable brief from the City of Nashville containing approximately one hundred pages of facts and figures that Harris Gilbert had compiled.[1] The city's brief showed the populations of each

---

1. Nashville (Tenn.) Office of the Mayor, "Legislative Apportionment: The Denial of the Equality of Voting Rights in Tennessee (report prepared by City of Nashville, Ben West, Mayor, Nashville, 1960).

county in the state according to the 1960 Census and the number of seats each county had in the state legislature. Gilbert calculated the ratio of representatives per person that each county enjoyed, and the plaintiffs rank ordered the counties from those with the least representation to the most. They also presented the amounts residents in each county paid in state taxes and the amounts they got back from the state in its allocation of school and highway funds.

The inequities were striking. The Tennessee Legislative Apportionment Act of 1901, which was still in force in 1961, gave six seats in the state's House of Representatives to Davidson County, which encompasses Nashville, and eight seats to Shelby County, the home of Memphis. The U.S. Census counted 400,000 people in Davidson County in 1960, or 67,000 people per legislative seat, and by 1960, Shelby County had grown to 630,000 residents, or almost 80,000 people per representative. Combined, these two counties contained 30 percent of the state's population, but the Apportionment Act allotted them less than 15 percent of the seats in the state assembly and senate. By contrast, the typical county in the state had approximately 20,000 people and one representative. Bedford County, with 23,000 people, chose a member of the assembly, as did the 14,000 people in Overton County, the 12,000 people in Smith County, the 10,000 people in DeKalb County, the 8,500 people in Cannon County, the 8,000 people in Stewart County, and the 3,400 people in Moore County. The people in some counties had three, five, ten, and in some cases twenty-five times as much representation per person as the people of Davidson and Shelby counties.

Numbers gave life to the enormous inequalities ingrained in Tennessee's politics. Voters in a typical county had three times as many legislators as voters in Davidson and Shelby counties. They had three times as loud a voice in public discourse and three times as much input in making state government decisions.

The City of Nashville's brief made the point even more forcefully. Representation translated directly into political power. Memphis and Nashville ranked among the areas with the least representation in the state legislature, and they ranked at the bottom in per capita expenditures on highways and schools. The typical county received $65 per capita for schools and roads. Davidson and Shelby counties received less than $42 per capita.

Such enormous inequities in representation immediately presented twin challenges to the American conception of democracy. First, and this was the idea tested by the plaintiffs in *Baker*, residents of underrepresented areas did not enjoy equal protection before the law, as guaranteed by the Fourteenth Amendment to the Constitution. A voter in Nashville or Memphis had much less voice and counted much less in the legislative process than did a voter in a typical county. The populations of these cities were subject to laws in the making of which they did not have a fair say. Consent to be governed democratically rests, in part, on the notion that everyone has an equal say. Gross inequalities in state legislative district populations threatened the legitimacy of the laws passed by those very legislatures.

Second, Tennessee faced the very real possibility of minority rule. The idea behind majority rule is simple enough. If at least half of a community approves of a law, then the laws will reflect, however imperfectly, an expression of the public's will. American democracy offers various points at which legislative action may be blocked in order to protect less numerous factions from tyranny of the majority. However, democracy does not mean that a minority should constitute a majority of the legislature. Yet in Tennessee, legislators representing just 35 percent of the population could form a majority inside both the state house of representatives and senate.

Tennessee's state constitution of 1891 required equal representation of populations. Harris Gilbert's brief showed how far the state had veered from that objective. Two academic studies conducted in the late 1950s documented for the nation what the Nashville attorneys had documented for Tennessee. These studies, one by Paul David and Ralph Eisenberg of the University of Virginia and the other by Manning J. Dauer and Robert G. Kelsay of the University of Florida, revealed the tremendous amplitude of the inequalities and the wide sweep of malapportionment in the 1960s. Their studies became part of the public discourse about the growing political inequalities of the time and were even drawn into *Baker*. Today, they provide a comprehensive map of the contours of political geography and representation before the Court forced the states to reapportion. As bad as the situation looked in Tennessee, the inequalities there paled in comparison with those in most other states.

INEQUALITY IN AMERICA

How unequal was democracy in America?

The question begs a comparison between *what is* and *what ought to be*. Such comparisons are usually quite difficult to make because it is hard to say what ought to be. However, in this case, the comparison is straightforward. Under the notion of equality embodied in the constitutions of most states and in the Constitution of the United States, every person should have an equal say in choosing his or her representatives. If one aggregates individuals into areas—such as districts, towns, or counties—then the share of a state's representatives apportioned to each area should equal that area's share of the state's population. Discrepancies between the share of legislative seats that an area actually had and what it ought to have had under an equal apportionment gauges the extent to which the people in an area are under- or overrepresented.

In their study, David and Eisenberg held up each county's actual representation per person against the ideal of equality.[2] They counted the number of legislative seats that represented each county in each state. They then computed the fraction of seats held by each county relative to that county's fraction of the state's population. This ratio provides a handy measure of each county's relative representation, or what we call the Relative Representation Index.

We reconstructed their analysis beginning at the level of each legislative district in 1960. Using information from the Bureau of the Census and the official election reports of each state, we computed the population of each district in each state. Table 2.1 presents the populations of the smallest, largest, and

TABLE 2.1. *Legislative district population disparities by state, 1960*

State	Lower house			Upper house		
	Smallest	Largest	Average	Smallest	Largest	Average
Alabama	6,731	104,767	30,809	15,417	634,864	93,335
Alaska	1,496	8,569	4,837	2,402	41,648	9,674
Arizona	1,220	38,622	16,272	3,868	331,755	46,506
Arkansas	4,927	31,686	17,863	35,983	80,994	51,045
California	72,105	443,892	195,478	14,294	6,038,771	392,928
Colorado	7,867	63,760	26,982	17,481	127,520	50,113
Connecticut	192	81,096	8,622	21,627	175,940	70,423
Delaware	1,643	58,228	12,751	4,177	64,820	26,252
Florida	2,868	311,682	52,226	9,543	935,047	130,302
Georgia	1,876	185,442	19,235	13,050	556,326	73,022
Hawaii	5,030	23,780	12,407	8,518	63,602	25,306
Idaho	915	23,453	11,308	915	93,460	15,163
Illinois	34,783	126,919	56,872	53,502	569,600	173,810
Indiana	14,804	137,838	46,463	39,011	171,090	93,250
Iowa	7,468	133,158	25,533	17,756	266,315	55,149
Kansas	2,069	88,533	17,421	16,083	343,231	54,446
Kentucky	11,364	188,399	30,373	45,122	288,703	80,077

2. Paul T. David and Ralph Eisenberg, *Devaluation of the Urban and Suburban Vote*, (Charlottesville: Bureau of Public Administration of Virginia, 1961).

State	Lower house			Upper house		
	Smallest	Largest	Average	Smallest	Largest	Average
Louisiana	6,909	120,205	32,248	31,175	248,427	83,513
Maine	2,298	15,211	6,373	16,147	45,688	29,371
Maryland	6,541	82,071	25,234	15,481	492,428	107,030
Massachusetts	3,559	49,478	21,339	85,349	176,716	127,405
Michigan	34,006	188,478	71,127	55,806	690,583	230,118
Minnesota	3,942	242,068	26,082	4,896	359,982	50,368
Mississippi	3,576	71,124	15,558	14,314	126,502	44,452
Missouri	3,936	149,200	27,400	82,140	288,317	126,559
Montana	894	12,537	7,178	894	79,016	12,049
Nebraska				18,824	100,826	32,822
Nevada	568	17,829	6,070	568	127,016	16,781
New Hampshire	604	3,783	1,581	11,404	46,445	25,285
New Jersey	48,555	224,499	101,112	48,555	923,545	288,893
New Mexico	1,874	29,133	14,394	1,874	262,199	29,719
New York	14,974	314,721	108,272	166,715	650,112	280,013
North Carolina	4,520	82,059	37,969	45,031	272,111	91,131
North Dakota	2,812	20,514	5,584	4,698	42,041	12,877
Ohio	10,274	148,700	69,830	154,032	456,931	255,443
Oklahoma	4,496	62,787	19,242	13,125	346,038	52,912
Oregon	13,108	42,487	29,472	26,523	92,237	58,956
Pennsylvania	4,485	139,293	53,861	51,793	553,154	226,380
Rhode Island	486	27,806	8,505	486	68,504	19,501
South Carolina	8,629	27,012	19,206	8,629	216,382	51,796
South Dakota	3,531	16,688	9,074	10,039	58,195	19,443
Tennessee	3,454	82,064	36,031	39,727	237,905	108,094
Texas	23,062	155,393	63,956	131,970	1,243,158	309,015
Utah	1,164	32,380	13,900	9,408	64,760	35,629
Vermont	24	35,531	1,585	2,927	18,606	12,996
Virginia	18,680	142,597	39,615	48,574	285,194	97,928
Washington	12,399	57,648	28,527	20,023	145,180	57,636
West Virginia	4,391	39,615	18,600	37,192	126,463	58,138
Wisconsin	19,651	87,486	39,518	74,293	208,343	119,690
Wyoming	2,932	10,024	5,886	3,062	30,075	12,206

Note: Nebraska has a unicameral legislature.
Source: Compiled by the authors using population figures from the
Bureau of the Census and state statutes defining districts.

average districts in the upper and lower chambers of every state legislature in 1960. The table displays the population disparities that existed in every state legislative chamber immediately before the Court took on the Tennessee case. These are the data that David and Eisenberg aggregated to the county level. Throughout the remainder of this book, we will focus on the representation of counties and towns.

Today, the focus on counties seems anachronistic, even problematic. The complicated district boundaries drawn for contemporary legislative elections run helter-skelter across traditional political jurisdictions. They cut across city and county lines and often combine portions of many counties in a single legislative district. Current district lines wind along town and city streets, down to house addresses; they follow highways, waterways, and even rail tracks. With such byzantine districts, there may just as likely be inequalities within counties and municipalities as between them. Indeed, one needs the Census data at its lowest levels of aggregation—the census block and tract—to construct modern legislative districts and calculate their populations and other demographic features. Things were much simpler before the reapportionment revolution.

Before *Baker v. Carr*, the county—or, in the New England states, the town— was the basic building block of state legislative districts. Counties and towns are an ancient form of local government, dating back to early English politics.[3] They were central to the administration of elections and other government activities in 1960, including the distribution of public expenditures and the reporting of demographic data by the Census Bureau, and they remain so today. As late as 1960, almost all states tied representation to counties and, in New England, towns. Districting practices usually forbid drawing lines that cut across other political boundaries, such as county lines, and the large majority of states used the towns and counties themselves as the districts. Counties and towns, then, are the natural level at which to study political inequalities in the United States, especially before the reapportionment decisions.

There was a further, political reason for the focus on counties. The great debate over malapportionment and equal representation emerged out of the rising tensions in American society between rural and metropolitan areas. Urban populations concentrated in a small number of counties, while rural populations dispersed across a large number of counties. Those advocating reapportionment pushed for greater political power for the cities and their surrounding suburbs. Indeed, David and Eisenberg titled their report "Devaluation of the Urban and Suburban Vote," even though districting practices underrepresented many

---

3. Charles Seymour, *Electoral Reform in England and Wales: The Development of the Parliamentary Franchise, 1832–1885* (New Haven: Yale University Press, 1915).

rural counties as well. With few exceptions, the division of the population into urban, suburban, and rural areas mapped fairly cleanly into counties.[4]

David and Eisenberg's Relative Representation Index provided strong evidence to those involved in the *Baker* case that the nation's legislatures deviated far from the ideal of equal representation. That index is a simple ratio. It compares the representation that the voters in any town or county have relative to what they would have under an equal apportionment—what Is versus what Ought to be.[5] If the ratio equals 1, then the county's representation reflects its population: one person, one vote. If that ratio falls below 1, then the county receives less than its fair share of seats in the legislature. A ratio of .5, for example, means that the county had half as many seats as it deserved based on its population. And if that ratio exceeds 1, then the county elects more legislative seats than it would under an equal population apportionment. A ratio of 2 means that the county chooses twice as many legislatures as it deserves. The ratio of any two counties' share of representation captures their relative voting weight. If one county has twice as much representation as it deserves and a second county has half as much, then the first county has four times as much representation as the latter. Almost all states had steep inequities in their legislative district populations.

A simple example demonstrates the calculation and interpretation of the index. Consider a state with nine counties, each of which has one legislative seat. Suppose that Washington County (to give it a name) has 44 percent of the population, and the other eight counties have 7 percent each. Washington County would have one-ninth of the seats but deserved four-ninths. It received one-quarter of what it deserved and would, therefore, have a value of .25 in David and Eisenberg's measure. The other eight counties also received one-ninth (or 11 percent) of the seats each, but they only deserved 7 percent, so they received almost 60 percent more than they deserved (11 divided by 7). The value of the Relative Representation Index for the smaller counties is nine times larger than the value for the larger counties. The populations of smaller counties, in this example, have nine times as much influence as the residents of the larger counties. This simplified example is not far off from the realities that existed in most states.

To give this hypothetical construct flesh, consider the state of Kansas.

---

4. The exceptions lie in the western states, where cities like Phoenix and Los Angeles constitute a relatively small fraction of the land area of their counties, and the counties that they lie in also contained substantial rural populations in 1960.

5. David and Eisenberg called the index the Right To Vote Index. We prefer the term Relative Representation Index, introduced in Stephen Ansolabehere, Alan Gerber, and James M. Snyder Jr., "Equal Votes, Equal Money," *American Political Science Review* 96, no. 4 (2002): 767–77. Right To Vote presumes a certain right and carries a normative connotation, while Relative Representation captures the nature of the comparison implicit in the measure.

According to the Census Bureau, slightly more than two million people lived in the state in 1960. Four of the state's 105 counties accounted for roughly 40 percent of the state population. Sedgwick County, home to Kansas City's suburbs, contained 350,000 people; Wyandotte County had 185,000 residents; and Johnson and Shawnee counties had 150,000 people each. The state's 1909 apportionment law gave every county one seat in the 125-seat house of representatives and divided the remaining twenty seats among the larger counties. That law changed little from the time it was enacted. Sedgwick, Shawnee, and Wyandotte were allotted five seats each, and Johnson was given four. As a result, Sedgwick and Kansas City had 16 percent of the state's population but received only 4 percent of the legislative seats. That county, then, had only 25 percent of the representation in the Kansas house of representatives that it deserved; David and Eisenberg's index of relative representation assigns this county a value of .25. Johnson, Shawnee, and Wyandotte had roughly one-third as many seats as they deserved. At the other extreme, counties such as Greely, Stanton, and Wallace, with 2,000 people each, deserved to have one-ninth of a seat but received a seat apiece. These counties had more than eight and a half times as many seats as they would have had under an equal population apportionment. David and Eisenberg's measure assigned these counties values of 8.5. The Kansas legislature operated as if the residents in counties like Greely and Wallace got to vote 330 times for every time a resident in Kansas City voted.[6]

Every state had substantial inequalities. The peaks and valleys of representation are shown in sharp contrast in Table 2.1, which presents the populations of the smallest, the largest, and the average district in every legislative chamber in the United States. Massachusetts, Oregon, and Wisconsin ranked as the states with the least inequality in the nation. The largest district in Massachusetts's upper house had roughly twice the population as the smallest district (176,000 people versus 85,000 people). In Oregon's lower chamber, the most populous district had slightly more than three times as many people as the least populous district (42,000 versus 13,000). Wisconsin's upper chamber showed a similar threefold difference in population between the smallest and largest districts. These were the most equal apportionments at the time of the *Baker* decision, and even in these situations some voters had two to three times as much representation as others. Things only got worse from there, much worse.

In the typical state, the relative inequalities in representation were on the order of 20 to 1 in at least one chamber. Half of the states granted some voters between 3 and 20 times the voting power as other voters, but in the other half of the states,

6. See Thomas Page, *Legislative Apportionment in Kansas*, Bureau of Government Research Series, 8 (Lawrence: University of Kansas Publications, 1952).

the legislative apportionment created even greater inequalities. Inequalities in Indiana exceeded 50 to 1. In Tennessee, Arizona, and Montana, the inequities in the apportionment scheme created differences in representation of at least 80 to 1. Idaho, Florida, Georgia, New Mexico, and Rhode Island gave some counties (or, in Rhode Island, towns) at least 100 times the voting weight of others. One county in Nevada had more than 200 times as many seats per person as another; in California that ratio reached 400 to 1, and in Connecticut it exceeded 600 to 1.

The U.S. Congress was no exception either. The most populous U.S. House district in 1960 had over one million people and the smallest approximately 175,000 people—those in the smallest district counted six and a half times more than those in the largest district. The U.S. Senate showed even more dramatic malapportionment, with the largest state having approximately eighty times as many people and thus one-eightieth the voting strength of the smallest state.

To put matters bluntly, America in the middle of the twentieth century had the most unequal representation of any representative form of government in the world. Inequities in state legislative district populations dwarfed the differences even in the U.S. Senate or those seen in developing countries today.[7] From Atlanta to Los Angeles, from Vermont to Arizona, from Florida to New Jersey to Michigan to Washington, extreme discrepancies in representation characterized the highly uneven terrain of American political geography.

And the picture was getting worse. Over the course of just fifty years, the inequities in representation had widened substantially. In 1910, in the typical state, the most overrepresented county had approximately six times as much representation as the most underrepresented county. That ratio—of the county with the most representation per person to the county with the least representation—grew from 6 to 1 in 1910 to 20 to 1 in 1950, and then to 35 to 1 in 1960.[8]

MINORITY RULE

The enormous inequalities in legislative district populations set the stage for minority rule in the American states. Some districts had very small populations, while others had large populations. As a result, a relatively small portion of the population elected a majority of seats in most states.

7. See David Samuels and Richard Snyder, "The Value of a Vote: Malapportionment in Comparative Perspective," *British Journal of Political Science* 31 (2001): 651–71.
8. These figures are the average of the ratio of the values of the Relative Representation Index (RRI) of the county with the highest RRI to the county with the lowest RRI in each state in a given decade.

Consider, again, the simple example constructed above. Nine counties elect nine seats in the legislature; the most populous county contains 44 percent of the population, while the other eight counties have 7 percent each. Any five of the small counties could form a majority of the legislature, because they would have five of nine seats. That coalition, though, would represent only 35 percent of the population. A coalition of five legislators that included the representative from the most populous county, so-called Washington County, would encompass 72 percent of the population. The principle of majority rule representation holds that a majority of people elect a majority of seats. The situation described in this example clearly deviates from that principle. Any coalition that contains a bare majority in the legislature either would represent more than 70 percent of the population or would represent a minority of the people.

Although hypothetical, this example exhibits the flavor of legislative politics in the middle of the twentieth century. Typically, legislators representing one-third of the population, sometimes less, could constitute an outright majority in the state legislature.

The first evidence of such discrepancies occurred in the 1930s. Henry Stoner of the International Ladies' Garment Workers' Union (ILGWU) sought to measure the extent to which the states had veered from majority rule by calculating the smallest population that could elect a majority in each chamber of each state. He studied districts rather than counties because some districts within cities had unequal populations. Stoner determined the populations of each legislative district, and, for each chamber in each state, he ordered the districts from smallest to largest. He then took the smallest districts needed to elect a majority of seats in a chamber and totaled their populations.[9]

In 1937, only three states approached majority rule. Half of the population elected half of the seats in both houses of the Massachusetts and New Hampshire legislatures. Just over 45 percent of the population elected a majority of seats in Nebraska's unicameral legislature. At least 40 percent of the population elected half of the seats in both chambers in another ten states: Arkansas, Colorado, Maine, New York, North Dakota, South Dakota, Utah, Virginia, Washington, and Wisconsin. In the remaining thirty-five states (Alaska and Hawaii were not then states), less than two-fifths of the population elected a majority of seats in the legislature. The situation in some states was dire. In the Connecticut house and the Rhode Island senate, districts containing less than one-tenth of the people elected a majority of seats. In the California and New Jersey senates, less than 15 percent of the people elected a majority of seats. In the lower houses in Delaware, Florida, Idaho, and Nevada, fewer than one in four

9. See Gus Tyler, "The Majority Don't Count," *The New Republic* (August 1955): 13–15.

voters chose over half of the assembly. In the typical state, just 37 percent of the population elected a majority of seats in at least one chamber.

Stoner's work received little comment for much of the next two decades. However, increased attention to the problem from organizations such as the National Municipal League and the American Federation of Labor (AFL), a spate of lawsuits, and criticism from, of all places, the Eisenhower White House highlighted the need for a careful assessment of the state of majority rule in the American states.

Building on Stoner's work, Manning J. Dauer and Robert G. Kelsay of the University of Florida documented the extent to which the states deviated from majority rule in 1955, at the time of the report of the Commission on Intergovernmental Relations. Like Stoner, Dauer and Kelsay determined the population of each legislative district in each chamber in each state. They then computed the smallest population that could elect a majority of seats. The patterns looked very similar to apportionments twenty years earlier, but the prospects for majority rule in the states had worsened.[10]

By 1955, no state approximated majority rule. In 1937, approximately 45 percent of the population elected majorities in three states' legislatures—New Hampshire, Nebraska, and Massachusetts—and those were the best cases. Two decades later, no state cleared that threshold. Of the three highly representative states from the 1930s, New Hampshire slipped the most. Exact majority rule held in both chambers of the New Hampshire legislature in 1937, but just 37 percent elected a majority of seats in that state's upper house in 1955. New Hampshire had fallen to the average of all other states by around 1937. In 1937, at least 40 percent of the population elected a majority of the legislature in ten states. Two decades later, just four states—Massachusetts, Nebraska, Virginia, and Oregon—cleared that threshold. The situations in Massachusetts and Nebraska had gotten somewhat worse since the 1930s. Virginia had changed little.

Reapportionment in several states improved matters noticeably. Kentucky and Oregon improved the apportionments in both of their legislative houses. Idaho, Illinois, Michigan, Rhode Island, and Nevada enacted districting plans between 1936 and 1954 that reduced the prospect of minority rule in the lower houses. Missouri, West Virginia, and Wisconsin adopted apportionments that approached majority rule for their upper chambers. Even these states fell short of equality. Oregon, perhaps the most equitably apportioned state in 1960, adopted a new apportionment plan in 1952, resulting in substantial reductions in inequalities in district populations. Forty-five percent of Oregon's population

10. Manning J. Dauer and Robert G. Kelsay, "Unrepresentative States," *National Municipal Review* 46 (December 1955): 571–75.

elected half of its lower house seats and 42 percent elected half of its upper house seats in 1955, compared with just 40 and 32 percent, respectively, two decades earlier.

For every chamber that showed noticeable improvement, three got worse. Missouri and West Virginia improved their upper chambers, but they let their lower chambers slide. Idaho, Illinois, and Nevada made their lower chambers more equal, but the apportionment in their upper chambers worsened significantly. In Illinois, 30 percent of the people elected a majority of the upper chamber; in Idaho, just 20 percent did so; in Nevada, the figure had dropped to just 12 percent. Connecticut's upper chamber, one of the fairest in 1937, went from approximately majoritarian to one in which one-third of the people elected a majority of seats. One-third of Vermont's population chose one-half of its lower house seats in 1937; two decades later, just one-eighth of the Vermont population elected a majority of that state's House of Representatives. The imposition of the county unit-rule on state senate elections in Georgia reduced the percentage of the population that elected a majority of seats from 36 to just 6 percent. The list goes on. By 1955, two-fifths of the people elected a majority of the people in 44 out of the 48 states; one-third of the people elected a majority of at least one chamber in 32 of the 48 states; and less than one-quarter of the population elected a majority of at least one chamber in 19 states.

The Dauer and Kelsay study of minority rule and the David and Eisenberg study of voting inequality revealed the extent to which the Tennessee apportionment case would alter the contours of political representation throughout the country. Unlike the battles then being waged over racial integration in the 1950s and 1960s, this was not a "Southern problem."[11] Many of the key reapportionment court cases came from southern states—Tennessee (*Baker v. Carr* in 1962), Georgia (*Gray v. Sanders* in 1963), and Alabama (*Reynolds v. Sims* in 1964)—but tremendous political inequalities ruled in every region of the country. In nearly every state, voters in some counties had five, ten, and in extreme cases one hundred times as many legislative seats per person as voters in other counties. As a result, small minorities of the populations in most states elected majorities of legislative seats.

BICAMERALISM RUN AMOK

The defense of these inequities turned to the U.S. Constitution and the arguments of the Founders. The *Federalist Papers*—the writings of Alexander

11. "See V. O. Key, *Southern Politics* (New York: Vintage, 1949), 3.

Hamilton, John Jay, and James Madison urging adoption of the Constitution—put forth a novel and clever defense of the mixed system of representation embodied in the proposed Congress. Representation of the people in the U.S. House and states in the U.S. Senate, the Federalists argued, extended the grand principle of the separation of powers and checks and balances. Any faction that gained control of one chamber would have a difficult time gaining control of the other since the two chambers represented different constituencies: people in the case of the House, and states in the case of the Senate. Inequalities, to use Robert Dahl's expression, would not "cumulate."[12]

Many state politicians, fending off the assault on malapportionment, embraced the idea that their districting schemes were smaller versions of the federal system. California even called its apportionment, which represented population in the assembly and counties in the senate, "the Federal Plan" when it was adopted in 1926. Gross inequalities in one chamber might be tolerated if the other chamber had equal representation. Reality, however, veered sharply from the principle espoused.

Just eleven states resembled the federal system, with equal representation in one chamber and unequal representation in the other.[13] Having equal representation of population in one chamber often corresponded with extreme inequities in the other chamber. In Vermont, 12 percent of the people elected a majority of seats in the lower chamber, but 46 percent of the people elected a majority of seats in the upper chamber; in California, 35 percent of the population elected a majority of seats in the lower chamber, but just 10 percent chose the majority of seats in the upper chamber. Even in these situations, however, one could not readily extend the federal analogy. California, Illinois, and South Carolina resembled the national model, where representation approximated population in the lower chamber and regions in the upper chamber. The other eight states that supposedly fit the federal model represented towns and counties in the lower chamber and population in the upper chamber. The smaller number of people in the upper chamber, as James Madison, Alexander Hamilton, and John Jay argued in the *Federalist Papers*, would make for more deliberation, and its members were envisioned as the most respected people from each of the states. Most states that used mixed representation broke with the federal analogy precisely because they represented people in the smaller upper chambers and places in the larger lower chambers.

---

12. Robert Dahl, *Who Governs?* (New Haven: Yale University Press, 1961), chap. 1.

13. These were Connecticut, Vermont, Missouri, Arkansas, Wisconsin, West Virginia, Kentucky, New Hampshire, Illinois, South Carolina, and California.

Often, the mix of representation of counties and of people only served to magnify the representation of some places, especially smaller rural counties. The California state senate granted each county one seat in the chamber, and as a result it had one of the most unequal apportionments of any legislative body.[14] The six million people of Los Angeles County chose one state senator, and the fourteen thousand people of Amador County chose one state senator. In comparison with the upper chamber, the California assembly had a very fair apportionment, but the largest assembly district still contained five times as many people as the smallest—hardly equal. And the areas with the highest assembly representation tended to be the smaller counties.

Most states made no pretext of mirroring the federal government's plan of representation in their bicameral legislatures. Apportionment plans often had similar inequities in both the upper and lower chambers. Florida was perhaps the most egregious case. The apportionment of Florida's lower house was just as skewed as its upper house. In 1960, the one million residents of Dade County had one-seventh the legislative seats they would have received under an equal population apportionment in each of the state legislature's houses, while counties with less that three thousand people had as much as 18 times the representation they deserved. As a result, some of the small rural counties elected 100 times as many legislators as Dade—they had 100 times more power in the legislature.

Bicameralism in most states worked as it did in Florida. If a county had more seats than it deserved in one chamber, it was very likely to have more representation than it deserved in the second chamber. If a county was underrepresented in one chamber, it was almost surely underrepresented in the other chamber. The correlation between a county's Relative Representation Index in the two chambers provides a simple measure of the extent to which a county's representation in one chamber relates to its representation in the other chamber. No state showed a negative correlation: in no state did the representation in one chamber offset inequalities in the other. Only four states—Kansas, Massachusetts, South Dakota, and Ohio—exhibited weak correlations between counties' representation in the two chambers. In three-quarters of the states, the correlation between a county's representation in one chamber and its representation in the other chamber exceeded .5, and in four out of ten the states, the correlation exceeded .7. The upper and lower chambers did not serve as counterweights to one another, as is argued about the relationship between

---

14. California's actual apportionment scheme was more complicated still. The law stated that no county could have more than one Senate seat. There were fifty-eight counties and forty seats, so some of the smaller counties were combined into single seats. Still, the differences in Relative Representation were enormous.

the U.S. House of Representatives and Senate. Rather, bicameralism cumulated and magnified inequalities in representation within the state legislatures. The more seats a county had in one chamber, the more it had in the other.

Bicameralism only served to magnify minority rule. In forty of the fifty states, minority rule cumulated across chambers. In the vast majority of states, a minority of the population elected a majority of seats in both chambers of the legislature. Fully half of the states elected a majority in both chambers with less than two-fifths of the population. And in extreme cases—Alabama, Delaware, Florida, Georgia, Nevada, Oklahoma, and Ohio—less than one-third of the population elected a majority of seats in both chambers of the legislature.

The federal analogy amounted to little more than a convenient excuse to rationalize inequality. The Founders imagined that a bicameral legislature with mixed representation would offer a set of checks and balances. That system, if it ever really operated in the American states, had completely broken down by the middle of the twentieth century. Only a handful of states in fact used the system of mixed representation embodied in the U.S. Constitution, and those that did had substantial inequalities in district populations, even in the popular chamber. In the great majority of states, both chambers of the bicameral legislatures reflected the same inequalities.

Throughout the 1950s, the American states continued their slide toward greater inequities in representation. By 1962, when the Court decided *Baker v. Carr*, only two states approximated majority rule in their state legislature. In the typical state legislature, one-third of the people elected a majority of the seats, and bicameralism only compounded the problem. An editorial in the *The New Republic* summed up this state of affairs quite bluntly: "The Majority Don't Count."[15]

15. Tyler, "The Majority Don't Count," 14.

3

The Origins of Malapportionment

Today, forty years after the reapportionment revolution, the scale of political inequality in the American states in 1961 seems unfathomable. Voters in some counties had hundreds of times more say in the representative system of government than voters in other counties. Minorities of voters could easily constitute majorities of legislative seats. Inequality reigned in the American states.

It did not begin that way. Every state had its own history, culture, and institutions from the decades, sometimes century, before it joined the United States. But almost every state at first embraced the principle of equal representation of population. The original constitutions of forty-one of the fifty states required that in at least one chamber the districts have equal populations, and twenty-three states required equality in both chambers of their legislatures in their founding documents. In 1960, only a handful of states could be said to approximate equal representation of the population in one chamber, and no state came close to that standard in both chambers. Many of the states changed their constitutions to impose a different standard of representation; others simply chose not to comply with their own laws.

How did this state of affairs come about? How did political inequality take root in the American states?

Unequal representation in the American states rose out of the tension between an increasingly urban society and political rules that tied representation to places and to the past. Over the course of its history, the United States has transformed itself from a rural society to an urban nation. The history is familiar enough and has been told repeatedly. The textbook account goes something like the following. At the time of its founding, the United States had an agricultural economy and rural society: nearly all people lived on farms and in small towns. This was era of the yeoman farmer idealized by Thomas Jefferson and chronicled by Alexis de Tocqueville. It lasted forty to fifty years, until the Industrial Revolution spilled over from Europe. Technological innovations fundamentally altered the economy and geography of American society. Industrialization created new sources of wealth and new employment opportunities concentrated in areas that rose up into great cities. Improvements in transportation increased commerce further by lowering the cost of shipping goods and increased the mobility of people around and between cities. The rising demand for industrial labor was met through immigration of people to the United States, especially from Europe, and migration of Americans from farms and towns into the cities.

Movement of population into cities was a constant of American life for two centuries. The first U.S. Census put the portion of Americans living in urban areas at just one in twenty—5 percent. Industrialization in the Northeast took hold in the 1830s and 1840s and spread throughout the United States as the ninetieth century progressed. As a result, the percentage of the population living in urban areas climbed steadily—from 7 percent in 1820 to 11 percent in 1840 to 25 percent in 1870 to 40 percent in 1900. The rise of the manufacturing and service economies spurred further urbanization in the twentieth century. In 1920, for the first time, the Census counted more people in cities than in farms and rural towns. In 1960, 63 percent of the American population lived in cities and their surrounding suburbs.[1] Today, the Census estimates that three out of every four Americans reside in metropolitan areas.

The rise of cities exposed a fundamental flaw with the practice of democracy in America. Political representation in the United States is accomplished through legislative districts—geographic areas from which citizens elect people to do their bidding within the government. Many state constitutions provided that individual towns and counties serve as districts. Other states charged the legislature with the responsibility of drawing new district boundaries after each decennial census in order to accommodate shifts in population. It mattered relatively little whether one represented towns or population at the time of the American founding because the population was distributed relatively evenly across the land. The continual, and at times rapid, shift of

---

1. The Census defined urban before 1950 as "all territory, persons, and housing units in incorporated places of 2,500 or more persons, and in areas (usually minor civil divisions) classified as urban under special rules relating to population size and density." In 1950, an alternative measure of urbanness was proposed. That measure increased the percentage urban in 1960 to seven in ten people, and today over three-fourths of Americans live in urban areas. See www.census.gov/population/censusdata/urdef.txt.

population toward cities created a highly uneven distribution of people across areas. Population migration, in turn, had two effects on political representation in America.

The first was a simple mechanical effect: because districts are static but populations are not, as communities expanded or declined the districts already in existence developed unequal populations. In many states, the constitution defined districts as places—towns and counties. Nothing short of a constitutional amendment or convention could correct the inequities that arose as a result of urban growth. Other states required that the state legislature adjust district boundaries following each decennial census to ensure equal representation of population. Even periodic redistricting could not keep up with the continued urban and suburban growth. As a result, state legislative district boundaries always lagged behind the changing demography of the United States.

The second effect was political: the self-interests of legislators and voters further exploited and compounded the mechanical shift in representation that resulted from the rise of cities. Shifting populations threatened to destabilize the balance of political power between urban and rural areas. Rural state legislators, seeing the threat to their political positions, acted to hold on to power as long as possible. Complicating matters further, urban areas often could not find common ground. Rivalries between cities—Buffalo and Rochester against New York City in New York, Nashville against Memphis in Tennessee, San Francisco against Los Angeles in California—led urban political leaders to undercut one another, and smaller cities often coalesced with the rural factions to oppose the growing might of the largest cities. In most states, rural-dominated legislatures anticipated the eventual shift in power to the cities and adopted new rules for representation that tied legislative seats to area rather than to numbers of people. In other states, legislators refused to abide by constitutional requirements for decennial redrawing of district lines. As long as no other branch of government would or could force the legislatures to draw new districts, they wouldn't. This second, political effect prevented state government from reflecting shifts in population.

In short, malapportionment was the winners' curse. Areas that succeeded economically suffered politically. Industrialization created great wealth concentrated in financial and manufacturing centers and drew people away from rural America and into cities. As the farm population fell, those areas automatically gained political representation, and they were able to hold on to their seats for generations because their representatives could not be forced to give away their own political power.

The forces that generated malapportionment in the United States were not new, nor were they unique to America. Every representative democracy faces the same tension. Societies change constantly, but political institutions change rarely. The problem is as old as representative government itself, and it has vexed those seeking an equitable and just method of choosing the legislature. In 1690, the great English philosopher John Locke considered the conundrum that rotten boroughs and town representation in England presented even then. In *The Second Treatise on Government*, Locke describes so perfectly the forces driving malapportionment that it is worth considering his assessment at length:

> Things of this world are in so constant a flux, that nothing remains long in the same state. Thus people, riches, trade, power, change their stations, flourishing mighty cities come to ruin, and prove in times neglected desolate corners, whilst other unfrequented places grow into populous countries, filled with wealth and inhabitants. But things not always changing equally, and private interest often keeping up customs and privileges, when the reasons of them are ceased, it often comes to pass, that in governments, where part of the legislative consists of representatives chosen by the people, that in tract of time this representation becomes very unequal and disproportionate to the reasons it was at first established upon. To what gross absurdities the following of custom, when reason has left it, may lead, we may be satisfied, when we see the bare name of a town, of which there remains not so much as the ruins, where scarce so much housing as a sheepcote, or more inhabitants than a shepherd is to be found, sends as many representatives to the grand assembly of law-makers, as a whole county numerous in people, and powerful in riches. This strangers stand amazed at, and every one must confess needs a remedy; tho' most think it hard to find one, because the constitution of the legislative being the original and supreme act of the society, antecedent to all positive laws in it, and depending wholly on the people, no inferior power can alter it. And therefore the people, when the legislative is once constituted, having, in such a government as we have been speaking of, no power to act as long as the government stands; this inconvenience is thought incapable of a remedy.[2]

Locke's description of England in 1690 just as aptly characterizes America in 1960 or any number of countries today. The rise of cities meant that old district lines became increasingly obsolete and political representation increasingly unequal. The politics of representation and reapportionment, however, meant

2. John Locke, *Second Treatise on Government* (1690), chap. XIII, sec. 157.

that the legislature would preserve these old social alignments, at least as long as it was in the interest of the majority of the legislature.

This, then, was democracy's flaw. Democratic governance places responsibility for the determination of legislative districts in the hands of the legislature. That, after all, is the highest expression of democracy: to determine your own rules of government. Legislators and voters could pass whatever laws they needed to, even amend their constitutions. Unconstrained by an outside power, though, they chose rules for districting that served their immediate political interests rather than the principle of equality. The powerful did what they could to remain so.

PEOPLE OR PLACES?

The mechanical effect driving malapportionment reflected the legal institutions governing the legislative districts. State constitutions and statutes defined the districts themselves, the number of seats elected from each district, and how, when, and by whom the boundaries could be altered or redrawn. The most fundamental aspect of the rules governing elections is whether the constituencies represent people or places. That choice was typically made in the states' original constitutions, and it had tremendous consequences for political inequality in America that compounded over time.

The democratic ideal has deep roots in American culture and its political institutions, dating back to the first colonial charters. The 1644 charter of Massachusetts Bay Colony created a General Court, divided into two bodies, chosen by the freemen. William Penn's first charter for his colony created a council to advise the governor and provided that the council consist of "respected men drawn from the Penn's colony to serve a term of two years."[3] Following the examples of Pennsylvania and Massachusetts, the Virginia colonies, Connecticut, Rhode Island and Providence Bay colony, New Jersey, and New York all opted for colonial assemblies and councils elected by the taxpayers or freemen of the towns and cities.

The practical challenge lies in making popular representation work. Even this most basic democratic procedure requires rules to govern how legislators are chosen. Every state constitution established the nature of its legislative districts; many even set the district boundaries themselves.

3. Lester K. Ade, *The Charter of King Charles II of England and William Penn's Frames of Government for Pennsylvania* (Harrisburg: Commonwealth of Pennsylvania, Department of Public Instruction, State Library and Museum, 1939); Richard L. Perry, ed., *Sources of Our Liberties: Documentary Origins of Individual Liberties in the United States Constitution and Bill of Rights* (Chicago: American Bar Federation, 1959), 80–81.

Early American constitutions defined districts in two very different ways. One approach defined constituencies as towns or counties; the other required equal representation of persons, typically taxable residents. Both options were viewed as democratic; they were simply different ways of accomplishing popular rule. Most American states opted to tie representation to places rather than people as a matter of convenience and tradition.

The early American governments turned to the familiar model of the English Parliament, whose members were chosen to represent towns, boroughs, and cities.[4] As in England, American towns and counties during the seventeenth and eighteenth centuries performed most of the administrative tasks of government. They were responsible for revenue collection and counting population. They built roads and improved waterways. To the extent it existed, they provided for public education and public welfare. Towns and counties were governed by their own councils, and these councils expressed the preferences of the local areas to the colonial governments.

Legal and philosophical justification for representation of towns derived from the fact that towns themselves created many of the colonies. The social compacts of many colonies were agreements among towns. Connecticut, for example, arose from the merger of disparate towns along the Connecticut River valley and Atlantic seaboard in the farthest reaches of the Massachusetts Bay Colony. Seeking more immediate government, these towns formed Connecticut Colony. Consent from among the towns, then, gave flesh to the philosophical notion of the day that government arose out of a social compact. The towns created the colonies, and the colonial government granted the towns political voice.

The same argument justified the representation of states in the first Congress of the United States and, eventually, the United States Senate. The United States formed as a confederation of equal states. Each legislature consented to join the confederation, and because the government formed out of the consent of each state, each state deserved representation in the legislature. As a result, the Articles of Confederation, the United States' first constitution, gave each state a single vote.

Practical considerations also drove the choice. Allowing towns to send representatives to the colonial assemblies did not require the colony—and, eventually, state—to determine local area populations. The towns themselves were the natural administrative unit to run elections; they continue to do so today. The electors were white male property holders; such qualifications could be readily checked only at the town hall. Elections were held in public meetings at

4. Perry, *Sources of Our Liberties*, 80–81.

town halls in which candidates literally stood for office, and electors made their preferences known publicly. But perhaps most important, town elections were familiar.

For most of the early American states, then, popular rule was expressed through the representatives chosen by the town or county. Several state constitutions simply gave each town or county an equal say in the state legislature: "one county, one vote." Each of the three counties in Delaware chose three senators and seven representatives; each county in New Jersey chose one senator and three representatives; in Georgia and North Carolina, each county elected one representative to the state senate. Vermont joined the United States in 1791 and formed a unicameral legislature to which each town sent one delegate. Other states, wishing to recognize differences in populations, allotted one seat to each town or county but additional seats to more populous areas. Georgia, Maryland, New Hampshire, North Carolina, Rhode Island, and Virginia followed this practice in at least one chamber, and in some cases both. The practice accommodated population differences across areas, but it preserved place as the basis of representation and guaranteed a minimum level of representation for each town or county.

Out of the original state constitutions, though, there came a truly radical and egalitarian idea. In 1777, Massachusetts and New York adopted constitutions that required popular election of members of both upper and lower chambers of the legislature from districts as nearly equal in population as possible. They threw over entirely the English tradition of the representation of towns, cities, and boroughs. Connecticut, New Hampshire, Rhode Island, South Carolina, and Virginia also required equal population representation in one chamber of the legislature, but they kept representation of place in the other.

The idea of popular representation faced very practical difficulties. There was no model for how to create districts on the basis of population, and no experience in doing so—England had not drawn new districts since 1714. To make matters worse, the states had no mechanism to count people.

One solution lay in the election of all state legislators in at-large elections. Connecticut's upper chamber consisted of twelve members elected at-large from the state as a whole, as were Rhode Island's ten "assistants" to the governor. In an at-large election, each of the top vote-getting candidates statewide—twelve in the case of Connecticut and ten in the case of Rhode Island—wins a legislative seat. This was not a system of proportional representation. The idea of proportional representation, in which each party receives seats in direct proportion to votes it receives, emerged some fifty years later, in the middle of the nineteenth century. The problem with at-large elections is that any faction that constitutes a bare majority can win all of the seats, effectively locking out of the legislature minority parties and interests.

The alternative to at-large elections was to create districts based on population and to alter district boundaries regularly so as to account for shifts in population. This approach kept the English institution of legislative districts, but it broke with the ancient English institutions that gave direct representation to the landholdings of the gentry or to the county system that evolved under the Church of England. This new American idea was to make districts to reflect the people.

Unfortunately, no administrative apparatus for counting people and drawing district boundaries existed. Several states relied on taxes to count the electorate. Massachusetts, New Hampshire, and North Carolina apportioned seats on the basis of total taxes paid. After all, the eligible electorate two hundred years ago consisted of white male property holders. Pennsylvania devised a truly novel solution. Pennsylvania's constitution of 1776 gave each county one seat in the legislature and the city of Philadelphia six seats. However, it required the state legislature to conduct an enumeration of taxable inhabitants for the purpose of determining the legislative districts that would ensure representation in proportion to population—in other words, a census. One year later, New York developed a hybrid of the Massachusetts and Pennsylvania plans, one that would create truly popular representation. New York's constitution defined the districts for the first legislature to be elected under the constitution, and it stipulated that the legislature draw new boundaries every seven years on the basis of a periodic enumeration of population.

This idea—the New York model—would eventually become the primary method of ensuring representation of population in the state and federal legislatures. Its chief features were the creation of an enumeration of population, a census; the requirement of periodic adjustment of district boundaries; and the empowerment of the legislature as the originator of the district boundaries. Representation was essential to the functioning of democratic government, and only the democratic branch of government could express the people's will on such matters.[5] The legislature, and only the legislature, could legitimately draw districts and apportion seats.

New York and Massachusetts had developed a practical solution to the problem of popular sovereignty. This was a true alternative to the English Parliament, which rooted representation in places. For the new national government in the United States and for every state, there was now a real choice: representation could be tied to places, or it could be apportioned according to population.

---

5. See Frankfurter's opinion in *Colegrove v. Green*, 328 U.S. 549, 553–54 (1946).

The U.S. Congress would be a mix of the two, as would most of the new states. The debate over representation at the federal level played out the same ideas and interests expressed in the states. The Articles of Confederation, which governed the Continental Congress throughout the revolution, gave every state one vote. At the Constitutional Convention, the Massachusetts, Virginia, and New York delegations, representing three of the four largest states, moved to replace "one state, one vote" with popular representation. While many states already had popular rule, in at least one chamber, the move would mean acceding power to the larger states in the new national Congress. The division of the Congress on this question was a matter of interest rather than principle. The Virginia delegation, whose legislature gave equal votes to towns in the upper chamber, supported the equal population representation wholeheartedly. Rhode Island, even though its state government represented population, opposed the plan bitterly. Massachusetts, Virginia, New York, and Pennsylvania contained the majority of the new nation's population, but they only had four of thirteen votes at the convention. The convention reached a deadlock on their proposal.

Roger Sherman of Connecticut found a compromise. Rather than a unicameral legislature that represents the people, Sherman proposed that the nation have a bicameral legislature that represented both people and place. One chamber represents the states—the places that joined together to form the social contract—and one chamber represents the people. The constitution further provided that the national government conduct a census of the country's population for the express purpose of determining the apportionment of U.S. House seats among the states.

The Connecticut Compromise made voting power more equitable than it was under the Articles, but it cemented malapportionment in the federal constitution in two ways. First, and most obvious, U.S. Senators serve states, rather than equal population districts, a fact that cannot be changed even by amendment. Second, the apportionment of the U.S. House of Representatives guarantees each state at least one seat in the lower chamber. Typically, the smallest state in the nation has too few people to merit a House seat. Today, Wyoming has just shy of 500,000 people; a House district requires 650,000 people, 30 percent more people than the state of Wyoming contains.

The state constitutions and laws adopted variations on the same themes, mixing representation of people and places. The New York plan provided the model for popular representation, though some states also used at-large elections. The long-established constitutions of the colonies and then the states served as the models for the representation of counties and towns. Representation of places was manifest in a wide variety of ways, but three broad methods deserve emphasis.

First, most states guaranteed a minimum level of representation for each county. Twenty-seven of the fifty states provided that each county receive at least one seat in one of its chambers. More populous counties received additional seats based either on the share of the population or on a set formula. For example, Florida allocated seats in its lower chamber as follows: 3 members from the 5 most populous counties, 2 from each of the next 18 most populous, and 1 from each of the remaining counties.

Second, counties with more than one legislative seat elected their state legislative representatives to countywide seats, which typically took the form of at-large seats. An apportionment plan would assign a county a number of seats, say 10, and the 10 candidates who received the most votes countywide would each win a seat. In some states, such as Texas, candidates in counties with multiple legislative seats would run for posts. Each post operated as a single member district that represented the entire county. Candidates had to specify which post they sought, and voters could cast one vote in each of the posted races.[6]

Finally, and perhaps most important, many states represented counties and towns directly in at least one chamber—one county, one vote. Following the analogy of the U.S. Senate, eleven states (Arizona, California, Georgia, Idaho, Iowa, Maryland, Nevada, New Jersey, New Mexico, South Carolina, and Texas) allocated equal representation to counties. Most of these states apportioned one seat to each county. California, Iowa, and Texas provided that no county had more than one seat. As a result, most counties received exactly one seat and some of the smaller counties were combined into single member districts. The six New England states follow a tradition of town government. Maine and Massachusetts represented population in both their upper and lower houses, but Connecticut, New Hampshire, Rhode Island, and Vermont kept long-standing constitutional rules that granted each town a seat in at least one of the chambers of their state legislatures.[7]

Counties provided the basis for elections to other offices as well. The most notable example is the unit-rule used in primary elections for statewide and federal offices in Georgia.[8] In 1917, Georgia passed the Niell Primary Election Act, which created an electoral rule for gubernatorial and U.S. Senate elections

6. One of the more peculiar districting practices existed in Massachusetts. The state legislature apportioned seats to counties on the basis of population and county boards; then it created state legislative district boundaries.
7. The New England states differed in the use of town representation. Rhode Island, parallel to the U.S. system, had one-town, one-vote for its Senate. Connecticut represented towns in its lower chamber, and Vermont represented towns in both chambers.
8. Maryland also used the unit-rule for primary elections for statewide offices. In addition, some states, such as Rhode Island and Connecticut, provided that the legislature would decide the gubernatorial election if no candidate won a majority in the general election, allowing the malapportioned legislature to leave its imprint on the executive.

akin to the presidential Electoral College. Each county was apportioned a number of votes, called unit-votes. The eight most populous counties cast six unit-votes; the next thirty most populous counties cast four unit-votes; the remaining 121 counties each cast two unit-votes. The candidate who won the plurality votes in a county received all of that county's unit-votes. The candidate with the most unit-votes won the election.[9] In 1950, the state of Georgia extended the county-unit system to all statewide offices, from attorney general to utility commissioner to justices of the state supreme court. Because winning the Democratic primary was tantamount to winning the general election, the Niell Act effectively created a county unit-rule in the election of candidates for statewide and federal office in Georgia.[10]

Further variations on the theme of representation of place involved creative mixing of counties into districts and unusual allocations of seats. Neighboring rural counties might be combined into a single district, with the result that those rural counties combined into one district had less representation than a similar-sized rural county that elected its own member to the state legislature. In this way, Tennessee's apportionment plan diluted the vote of those living in the Republican-leaning counties of the eastern third of the state. In addition, state apportionment laws attached some rural counties to an urban district, usually resulting in the depression of the voting strength of the rural area as well as the urban county. An extreme example is a floterial district. Tennessee and Indiana granted a number of districts to urban counties and then created an additional district that consisted of the entire urban county plus a neighboring small county. Small counties unlucky enough to be in floterial districts had some of the least representation in their states. More bizarre still were fractional or part-time seats, such as New Hampshire used. Some towns elected a representative only every third session of the legislature: these towns would have representation for two years and then none for four years.

9. Because political parties often operate as private clubs, the unit-rule had in fact been in operation before the Niell Act, but information about the exact dates of its use is hard to find. According to official vote tallies, it was in use for at least a decade before the Niell Act.

10. Local governments also apportioned representation on the basis of counties and towns. The most famous was the New York City Board of Estimate, which controlled, among other functions, zoning in the five boroughs of the City of New York. In the 1920s and 1930s, Fiorello LaGuardia used the Board of Estimate to consolidate political power, bypassing the city council. Under his mayoralty, the Board emerged as the government of the City. The mayor and each borough president had a seat on the Board of Estimate. The mayor cast two votes; the borough presidents cast one vote each. Two additional members were elected at-large and cast two votes each. In 1989, the U.S. Supreme Court declared the representation of boroughs in violation of the principle of one person, one vote. Because this system of representation was integral to the constitution and operation of the Board of Estimate, the Court's decision ultimately led to the dismantling of the Board. See *Board of Estimate of the City of New York v. Morris*, 489 U.S. 688 (1989).

Counties and towns constrained district structure even where popular representation was the rule. Most states forbade the sort of line drawing that occurs today; district boundaries could not cross county lines. Several counties could be combined into one district, or a single county could be divided into districts, but very few states allowed district lines to cross county lines or even city and town boundaries. Illinois would not allow districts that represented the City of Chicago to include parts of neighboring towns and cities within Cook County. The city had its districts; the rest of Cook County had theirs.

We provide a rough classification in Table 3.1 of the formulas used by the states in their original constitutions and in 1960. Most states that represented place either used the English system, in which each town or county elected the same number of legislators, or provided minimum representation for each county. Some states, such as Georgia and Hawaii, created a mathematical formula that defined the number of voters a county needed in order to have an additional representative. A handful of states set a maximum number of representatives. Pennsylvania allowed no county to have more than one-sixth of the seats, capping Philadelphia's power. Alabama and California eventually allowed no county to have more than one seat, and some counties could be combined into districts. Virginia distributed seats across its regions but provided for population representation within region. And by 1960, several states had chosen simply to fix the districts in their constitution. All of these are ways in which states represented place in their constitutions.[11]

Half of the states, in their original constitutions, followed the lead of New York, Pennsylvania, and Massachusetts. The original constitutions of twenty-five of the fifty states provided for equal representation of population for both their upper and lower chambers in their original constitutions. The other half tied representation to towns or counties in at least one chamber.

Over time, however, the states moved toward representation of place, rather than people. By 1960, thirteen states abandoned population-based representation in favor of some form of representation of area in their lower chambers; another eighteen states moved from population-based representation to representation of area in their upper chambers. Only two states changed their constitutions to provide for representation of population for their lower chambers, and just three did so for their upper chambers. At the time of *Baker*, fully two-thirds of state constitutions provided that the legislature represent counties or towns in at least one chamber, and nearly all of these provisions took the form of "one county, one vote" or minimum county representation.

---

11. Our classification is based on the analysis of each state's legal requirements provided by Robert McKay, *Reapportionment: The Law and Politics of Representation* (New York: Twentieth Century Fund, 1965), 273–476.

TABLE 3.1 *State legislative apportionment rules and minimum percentage of population that elected a majority of seats*

State	Lower house apportionment			Upper house apportionment		
	Original	1960	DK[a]	Original	1960	DK[a]
Alabama	Min County	Min County	23	Population	Population	25
Alaska	Population	Population	31	Formula	Population	28
Arizona	Min County	Min County	29	Min County	County	11
Arkansas	Min County	Min County	33	Population	Fixed	44
California	Population	Population	35	Population	County	10
Colorado	Population	Formula	32	Population	Formula	29
Connecticut	County	County	12	Population	Population	32
Delaware	County	Formula	18	County	Formula	22
Florida	Min County	Formula	13	Population	Min County	12
Georgia	Formula	County	22	County	County	23
Hawaii	Formula	Min County	37	Formula	Formula	18
Idaho	Population	Min County	27	Population	County	17
Illinois	Population	Population	40	Population	Fixed	28
Indiana	Population	Population	34	Population	Population	37
Iowa	Population	County	27	Population	County	31
Kansas	Min County	Min County	18	Population	Population	27
Kentucky	Population	Population	34	Population	Population	41
Louisiana	Population	Min County	28	Formula	Population	30
Maine	Population	Population	37	Population	Population	37
Maryland	County	Population	23	Region	County	14
Massachusetts	Population	Population	39	Population	Population	47
Michigan	Min County	Population	34	Population	Fixed	30
Minnesota	Population	Population	26	Population	Population	31
Mississippi	Min County	Min County	28	Population	Formula	31
Missouri	Min County	Min County	20	Population	Population	41
Montana	Population	Population	34	County	County	16
Nebraska	Population	(unicameral)		Population	Population	36
Nevada	Population	Min County	19	Population	County	8
New Hampshire	Min County	Min County	31	Population	Population	41
New Jersey	County	Min County	37	County	County	19
New Mexico	Population	Min County	29	Population	County	15
New York	Population	Min County	33	Population	Formula	41
North Carolina	County	Min County	27	County	Population	37

	Lower house apportionment			Upper house apportionment		
State	Original	1960	DK[a]	Original	1960	DK[a]
North Dakota	Population	Min County	35	Population	Fixed	32
Ohio	Population	Min County	29	Population	Population	43
Oklahoma	Formula	Formula	26	Population	Population	24
Oregon	Population	Population	43	Population	Population	41
Pennsylvania	Population	Min County	37	Population	Max County	33
Rhode Island	County	Max County	29	Population	County	16
South Carolina	Population	Min County	43	County	County	23
South Dakota	Population	County	38	Population	County	38
Tennessee	Population	Min County	25	Population	Population	27
Texas	Population	Population	33	Population	County	30
Utah	Min County	Min County	33	Population	Population	21
Vermont	(unicameral)	Town	12	Town	Min County	43
Virginia	County	Region	36	Population	Region	38
Washington	Population	Population	37	Population	Population	34
West Virginia	Min County	Min County	39	Population	Population	47
Wisconsin	Population	Population	40	Population	Population	42
Wyoming	Min County	Min County	34	Min County	Min County	27
U. S. Congress	Min State	38			State	17

Note: The figures in this table were calculated by the authors using information on the population of every state legislative district. The figures differ from Dauer and Kelsay's original data, as that study calculated all results for counties.

[a]DK refers to the Dauer-Kelsay index of minority rule.
Source: Based on data in Manning J. Dauer and Robert G. Kelsay, "Unrepresentative States," National Municipal Review 46 (December 1955): 571–75.

To be sure, there were advantages to these practices. Counties and towns lent a degree of rationality to the geography of American politics. The districts were easy to understand. The technical apparatus for drawing equal population districts—demographers, cartographers, and lawyers—were unnecessary, and electoral administration, then and today, rested in the hands of county and town governments. The arrangement of counties and towns into districts also reflected the vertical connections of federalism. When states disburse funds for schools, highways, hospitals, welfare, and other functions and services, they usually transfer the money to the counties and towns, which then implement the specific programs. County representation also stood on the strong analogy to the U.S. Congress: the lower house should represent people; the upper house, places. Counties seemed the natural level to aggregate the geographic distribution of interests, and many states followed exactly this formula.

Tying legislative districts to counties and towns led inevitably to unequal representation. The United States has approximately 3,200 counties, most of them sparsely populated. The great mass of the population lives in a few dozen metropolitan areas. In 1960, over half of the counties had fewer than 20,000 people and a quarter of all counties had extremely small populations—fewer than 10,000 residents. Although rural counties constituted a majority of all counties, they contained only about one in twelve people—only 17 million of the United States' 190 million people in 1960. A very small number of urban counties, on the other hand, contained the majority of the people. Almost 100 million people, over half of the 190 million people living in the United States in 1960, resided in just 125 counties.

Guaranteeing every county or town at least one seat in the legislature, as most state constitutions did, inevitably inflated the voting power of those who lived in rural counties and towns and devalued the votes of those in urban and suburban areas. Georgia offers one such example. That state's constitution allocated two seats in its lower house to each of the 37 most populous counties and one seat to the remaining 95 counties. Echols County, with 1,900 people, elected one representative to the state house; Fulton County's 556,000 residents, nearly all of whom resided in the city of Atlanta, elected just two. Although severe, such inequities were common wherever counties and towns served as constituencies for state legislative districts.[12]

Indeed, much of the variation in malapportionment traces directly to provisions in state constitutions that required representation of place rather than people. This fact is borne out in the basic statistics of representation compiled by Manning Dauer and Robert Kelsay, which we introduced in chapter 2. Alongside the apportionment rules, Table 3.1 presents the Dauer-Kelsay index of minority rule in the columns labeled DK. These figures correspond to the smallest percentage of the population that could elect a majority of seats in each chamber. As we noted in chapter 2, one-third of the population elected a majority in the average state upper chamber and in the average state lower chamber. But that was just the overall average.

Direct representation of population resulted in the most equitable elections,

12. Paul T. David and Ralph Eisenberg, *Devaluation of the Urban and Suburban Vote* (Charlottesville: Bureau of Public Administration of Virginia, 1961), 2, table 1.

though these cases also fell short of the ideal. In the twenty-two lower chambers that represented population, the average value of the Dauer-Kelsay index equaled 39. In other words, approximately 40 percent of the people elected half of the seats in these legislative chambers. In the eleven upper chambers that required representation of population, 37 percent of the people elected a majority of seats. In both circumstances, this was far from equality, but these legislatures approximated popular rule much better than those that defined counties as the legislative constituencies.

Somewhat worse were those chambers that used a mix of geography and population. States that required minimum county representation or that used a formula to assign seats based on population ratios fall into this group. On average, 30 percent of the population elected half of the legislative seats in states that required districts to follow population and geography. The U.S. House of Representatives, which also requires minimum state representation, had a fairly equitable system: it took at least 38 percent of the population to elect a majority in 1960.

By far the least representative legislative bodies were those that gave each county or town a seat. Twelve states used this method to select their upper chambers, and four states used it for their lower chambers. Among the states using "one county, one vote" in 1960, on average only 20 percent of the population—one-fifth of the electorate—elected half of the legislative seats. The U.S. Senate appears typical of this sort of representation. In 1960, the twenty-five smallest states, containing just 17 percent of the population, elected a majority of the U.S. Senate seats.

Just as troubling as the degree of inequality produced by the constitutional and statutory requirements that constituencies represent towns and counties was the requirements' apparent irrationality. Most of the inequities in district populations reflected the sizable differences in counties' populations; however, many of the district definitions simply defied reason.

The Tennessee lawyers brought to the Supreme Court's scrutiny perhaps the least coherent districting map in the country. As elsewhere, the districts obeyed county lines, but the state could not defend the plan as based on representation of the size of place or the type of community. Similar-size rural counties in western and eastern Tennessee had markedly different amounts of representation. Frequent use of floterial districts made it a confusing plan to describe, let alone justify, and meant that some rural counties were as badly represented as the urban areas that gave rise to the suit. Gross inequities abounded, and no rationale could be found for them—not race, not party, not population, not economic interest. As Justice Tom Clark concluded, the Tennessee legislative district map was just a "crazy quilt."

Broadening the scope from Tennessee, the entire nation was a crazy quilt. Every state had developed its own scheme of representation. All gave excess numbers of seats to rural areas at the expense of urban and suburban areas, and many states, like Tennessee, treated apparently similar counties differently. Across states, those differences became even more acute. How much your vote counted depended on where you lived. That fact would prove very difficult to defend against the notion that all Americans have the right to equal protection of the laws.

THE GERRYMANDER

State constitutions produced one force that generated malapportionment; legislative politics acted as a second.

It is a truism of politics that those in power do what they can to stay in power. Nowhere is that more evident than in the struggle to form legislative districts. Any new district map must be approved by a majority of the legislature because it is a statute, a law of the people. As a consequence, the sitting legislatures can influence the rules that will govern their own reelection. Districting, then, presents legislators with an opportunity at which they will, and should, pursue their own interests. They can attempt to move district boundaries to improve their own personal political fortunes or the fortunes of their party, an activity derisively called gerrymandering.

Legislators today face numerous political constraints on gerrymandering. The courts, independent districting commissions, and the executive branch at both the federal and state levels—all have a hand in crafting or approving any new districting plan. Before *Baker*, the responsibility for legislative districting rested solely with the state legislatures themselves. The sitting legislators—those in office—had complete control over the contours of their constituencies. They alone drew district maps and determined if and when a new apportionment plan would be put in place

If gerrymandering was the genus, malapportionment was the species—and before 1965, its most powerful and common kind. Malapportionment, as a form of gerrymander, manifested itself in three ways. First, legislatures crafted districts with unequal populations. Malapportionment offers a blunt, effective gerrymandering technique: give your opponents so few legislative seats that they can never hope to win a political majority. Without the constraint of equality, it was relatively easy to construct a districting map that benefited both a majority of sitting legislators and the majority party. Second, legislatures changed constitutional rules to suit their objectives. Rural legislators seeing their potential decline in political power often altered constitutional apportionment criteria to bind future legislators. Third, and perhaps most invidious, legislatures ignored their constitutional responsibilities and left in place old lines. Over time, as district populations became more unequal, it became increasingly difficult to find any proposal that a majority within the legislature would support and that would rectify malapportionment. Simply by taking no action, the sitting legislators could further their own interests.

From the very first, districting became a tool of political power. As Massachusetts, New York, and other states attempted to draw new maps in line with population, the political problems of their new egalitarian constitutions became evident. Drawing new maps every ten years meant that those in office could craft lines for personal and partisan advantage.

State constitutions offered few guidelines or principles. Most of the states that opted for representation of population provided for a census of population or of taxpayers so that the sitting state legislature would reapportion in accordance with population. Some states prohibited district lines from crossing county or city boundaries. Beyond that, little restrained those who would draw district maps. Nor was it clear how to reapportion. Districting and apportionment had not been practiced under the colonial governments. No one had experience with this new manner of representation, and there were no established practices or rules of thumb to serve as guides. England had not passed an apportionment law since 1714, and its laws did not embrace the radical egalitarian idea of representation of population. The legislatures would have to determine the rules of districting themselves.

State legislators worked on a blank slate. They were unconstrained by the past or other institutions. The great latitude open to them was to create a new problem—the legislative manipulation of electoral maps, or gerrymandering.

The problem became immediately evident in Massachusetts, the state that gave rise to the very idea of representation of people. It was here that the gerrymander was born. The story has been told and retold, certainly with embellishments. One grim winter day in 1812, Gilbert Sullivan, Boston's eminent painter of the Federalist era, visited his friend Benjamin Russell at the offices of the *Boston Sentinel*. Russell, a Federalist and the editor of the *Sentinel*, was in a snit about the great injustices that the Democratic legislature had foisted upon the people. He had hung on his wall the new map of the Commonwealth's political boundaries, and he had highlighted on the map a particularly egregious house district that snaked from Chelsea and Lynn just north of Boston through Salem, Marblehead, and Andover, and up to the New Hampshire border. It encircled the towns of Cape Ann and stretched. It was the work of Governor Elbridge Gerry and the Democratic-controlled Massachusetts legislature. Making light of the map, Sullivan drew the head of a giant reptile on Salisbury, wings sprung from Andover and Methuen, and claws on Marblehead and Salem. Chelsea became the beast's tail; Lynn, Danvers, and Lynnfield, its hauches. The great artist likened the district to a great salamander. "Salamander!" the editor cried in response, "Call it a Gerry-mander." On March 26, 1812, Russell published the cartoon on page 2 of the *Sentinel* with the caption: "The Gerrymander: A New Species of Monster, which appeared in Essex South District in January last." Its many progeny forever bear Elbridge Gerry's name.

The gerrymander laid bare a more general problem: the sitting government could shape its own fate. The options open to the legislatures went well beyond periodic districting. The legislature could alter the state constitution itself, giving permanence either to a particular set of districts or to a new set of rules that would constrain future legislatures. As tensions between urban and rural representation grew, state legislatures throughout the nineteenth century called constitutional conventions to address the problem. In this regard, legislatures followed the rules exactly. This was a procedure specified in their original constitution for making amendments. However, representation in the conventions followed that of the legislature or, worse, represented each town or county.

Massachusetts held tight to political equality and fairness in principle, if not in practice. Over its 200-year history, that state kept its constitutional requirement of representation of population. That constraint, although bent and twisted by the creative cartography of the legislature, proved of lasting importance. By 1960, Massachusetts had one of the most representative legislatures in the country. But even here, just under 40 percent of the population could elect a majority of seats.

The other exemplar of popular rule was New York, which followed a very different path. Rising tensions between the New York City political machines and the upstate area, especially Buffalo, led to the first of New York's seven constitutional conventions. Each convention imposed successively more restrictions on representation, especially the voting rights and districts of those in New York City. In 1821, the political leadership of New York convened to address a wide variety of problems exhibited in the new constitution, especially issues of home rule for the cities, executive powers of the governor, and the question of representation. At this time, the state also restricted the vote of immigrants, who had previously been allowed an equal franchise, and it set out a new apportionment formula that gave the cities less than their fair share of seats. These constitutional changes altered the politics of districting in New York for the next two centuries.

The rapid growth of New York City and Buffalo in the 1820s and 1830s made obsolete the deal struck in 1821. In 1840, a new convention was called to deal with the problems of the cities, but the new convention reflected the representation in the legislature, in which the cities held a minority of seats. It was at this time that the state chose to impose a minimum level of representation for each county: every county received one seat in each chamber; counties and boroughs received additional seats according to population. Every later constitution—in 1867, 1894, 1915, and 1946—reaffirmed that arrangement, which would prevent the cities from gaining a majority of legislative seats as the rural population dwindled to a small minority.

In the latter half of the century, malapportionment and other forms of gerrymandering became tools of partisan politics. Control of the government swung between the parties in this evenly divided state as national political tides repeatedly swept Democrats and Republicans into and out of power. The Democrats were lucky enough to hold the governor's mansion and the legislature during the districting process in 1883 and 1891. Republicans charged that the Democrats, dominated by Tammany Hall, severely gerrymandered the state. It took the elections of 1892 and 1893, which produced catastrophic losses for the Democratic Party nationwide, to knock that party out of power in Albany, and the Republicans quickly moved to call a constitutional convention. Legislative districting was the main issue of the day. The 1894 convention, passed by the legislature and through popular vote, set into the state's fundamental law a plan that badly malapportioned the state and severely gerrymandered its cities. Rural counties, where Republicans held the vast majority of seats, kept the balance of political power, and the urban districting maps squeezed even more Republican seats out of the Democrat-dominated New York City. By the end of this succession of constitutional conventions, New York had perfected the art of gerrymandering and had utterly abandoned the principle it had championed at the founding, equal representation of population.

The reasons for New York's transformation are at once simple and complex. They are also typical of other states.

Making good on the promise of equal representation was to prove politically difficult. From 1790 to 1820, New York's urban population hovered around 13 percent of the total state population. The urban areas' share of population more than doubled again between 1820 and 1840, rising to 25 percent of the state population. It was at this moment—in 1840—that the state's convention imposed minimum county representation. The social change under way was painfully obvious; by 1860, the urban areas would contain 60 percent of the state's population. Rural legislators refused to abide by the state's constitution of 1777, which required representation of population in both chambers, as that would mean giving up their own seats, and rural voters feared the consequences of the growing power of New York City. The state's political leaders and thinkers, however, found themselves at a loss for a justification for malapportionment. By the end of the nineteenth century, a new rationale, a new theory, had emerged to justify the inequities of representation.

Unequal district populations it was argued were needed to make political power equal. Elihu Root—one of America's great political and legal minds of the turn of the century, a U.S. senator, secretary of war, and recipient of the 1912 Nobel Peace Prize[13]—eloquently articulated this new idea at the 1894 New York Constitutional Convention:

> In almost every State which has had to deal with the problem of a great city within its borders, and the relations of that city to an agricultural community, that the problem which they have had to deal with shall be dealt with by us upon the same principle; that the small and widely scattered communities, with their feeble power comparatively, because of their division, shall, by the distribution of representation, be put upon an even footing, so far as may be, with the concentrated power of the great cities. Otherwise we never can have a truly representative and a truly republican government.[14]

Cultural, social, and political differences between cities and rural areas made that inevitable shift in political power all the more daunting. Not only were cities growing much faster than towns and rural counties, but they were attracting a different sort of population. The cities were filling not just with migrants from rural areas, but with immigrants from overseas—English, French, Dutch. Behind them came Germans, then Irish, followed by eastern and southern Europeans. Cities were crowded and unsanitary; disease was rampant. Very few of those in cities owned property; therefore, they paid few taxes to the state governments. Rural residents distrusted and feared the immigrant vote in the cities; so too did many in the cities themselves. Advocates of representation of places emphasized the lowly character of the city population. The primary change in the representation provisions in the New York constitution of 1821 imposed citizenship requirements on voting, which did not exist before then. The spectre of the immigrant reappeared in the convention debates in 1840, 1867, and 1894, and each time the conventions reinforced the disenfranchisement of immigrants so as to limit the political power of the urban machines.

In addition to social and cultural considerations, there was party. The importance of party was nowhere more evident than in the 1894 constitutional convention. Republicans packed that convention following the 1893 election. The convention represented delegates from every legislative seat as well as two

13. See nobelprize.org/nobel_prizes/peace/laureates/1912/root-bio.html.
14. *Revised Record of the Constitutional Convention of the State of New York*, vol. III (September 6, 1894): 1226.

dozen at-large. Republicans held every at-large seat as well as a majority of the delegates chosen in legislative districts. New York City, a Democratic stronghold, was badly overmatched. The convention defined new districts, giving Republican Buffalo its fair share of seats at the expense of the New York City. In addition, the convention crafted district boundaries within the City, ensuring at least four new Republican seats. One district connected Wall Street to the Upper West Side, two highly Republican areas, and ran through Hell's Kitchen and other immigrant neighborhoods that contained many people but few voters. The result was a safe GOP seat and a district four blocks wide and eighty blocks long. The vote on the apportionment plank at the convention divided perfectly along party lines. The handful of Republican delegates from New York City went along with their party's plan, even though the new apportionment plan would reduce substantially the City's political voice and power.

New York was not alone in abandoning the principle of political equality in its constitution. Across the country, state legislators saw that the trends in urban growth meant that they would eventually lose political power, and they changed their state constitutions to slow or even stop that eventuality. Rhode Island dropped its at-large system in favor of direct representation of counties. Pennsylvania granted every county at least one seat in the lower chamber and allowed no county more than one-sixth of the seats in the upper chamber, handicapping the political pull of Philadelphia. Ohio imposed minimum county representation in 1903, as its population pivoted between majority rural and majority urban. Nevada's constitution of 1864 also required population-based representation. The legislature amended the constitution in 1950, just as Reno and Las Vegas were on the verge of becoming the urban majority. The list went on—Arkansas, Florida, Illinois, Iowa, Mississippi, New Mexico, Tennessee, Texas. All told, constitutional amendments changed thirty-three of the ninety-nine chambers from population-based to geographic representation; only four went the other way.

Constitutional constraints on the districting process made it impossible to achieve equity. The state constitutions defined the districts under which the first state legislative elections were to be conducted and, then, stated that the legislature would create new boundaries some years hence (usually five or ten years) in accordance with the state or federal census. Some states imposed further restrictions on how new districts could be formed in order to bind the hands of future legislatures. While such requirements sought to prevent partisan gerrymanders in the future, they made it nearly impossible to make any changes. Such constraints led to stasis.

Ohio provides one such example. Ohio's 1851 constitution allowed for reapportionment based on population, but only if reapportionment did not produce redistricting. Senatorial districts consist of whole counties. Every county initially received one seat in the 35-member senate, except Hamilton, then the largest county and the home of Cincinnati, which got three seats. A county could get a second seat only if any shift in the apportionment of seats could be accomplished by recombining contiguous counties. This seemingly beneficial constraint, however, meant that Ohio's senate districts were very long-lived. In the 110 years from the creation of the Ohio constitution to the courts' intervention in legislative districting, this occurred exactly once, in 1901.[15] Ohio had prevented one form of abuse, but it led to another: inaction.

Even where states kept constitutional rules requiring representation of population, finding the political will to do the right thing proved nearly impossible. Equal population districting meant that boundaries would have to change substantially. Many politicians would have to face massively different districts and likely risk electoral defeat; some would lose their districts altogether. How could the legislators choose who would stay and who would go? It was easiest simply to do nothing.

When the Court weighed the Tennessee complaint in 1961, that state had not reapportioned since 1901. Alabama also had not drawn new districts since 1901. Washington and Wisconsin were both in violation of their state constitutional requirements for decennial redistricting. Minnesota failed to draw new districts between 1913 and 1959; Michigan left its districts substantially unchanged from 1900 to 1952. Maryland's constitution of 1867 prescribed a set of districts, and these were still in force in 1962. Florida had last reapportioned in 1924, Indiana in 1921, Kansas in 1883, Kentucky in 1918, Nebraska in 1935, and Oklahoma in 1907. In these states, legislative districts had ossified into permanent institutions, and all were in violation of their own state constitutions.

These state legislatures repeatedly tried to reapportion, but failed. Each new decade brought a new census and a new call for redistricting. Drawing new lines, however, meant that a large number of districts would have to change to accommodate population shifts. A political solution eluded these states. In some, such as Florida, the governor kept continual pressure on their legislatures, only to be rebuffed. The political stalemate that arose fed on itself. Each new census showed that the state needed to make even greater adjustments, and a possible reapportionment agreement moved farther away. The more a state's districts deviated from population, the less was the incentive facing the legislature to change and the more difficult it became to build political coalitions to

15. That event prompted the state to pass the Hanna Amendment, requiring that every county receive one seat.

reapportion. Over time, districts became more firmly entrenched and more deeply ingrained in the states' politics. They became the ancien régime, and they bore as little relationship to population as towns and counties did.

Redistricting, changing constitutional rules, and inaction—all resulted in malapportionment, and all were forms of gerrymandering. Dauer and Kelsay's index makes clear the political consequences.

Those states that required population representation and regularly drew new district lines had the most equitable representation. Twelve lower chambers and fifteen upper chambers actively and regularly drew new district maps. In these legislative bodies, on average, 37 percent of the population elected a majority of seats. This was a far short of what their constitutions required, and it reflected the fact that in the process of drawing district lines, states created massive malapportionment and political inequalities.

Inactivity further worsened this state of affairs. In nine states, the legislature refused to reapportion. And in those states, just 30 percent of the population elected a majority of the legislature in 1960. This was identical to the degree of representation attained in states that imposed geographic constraints on the representation of population, such as minimum county representation in New York and Ohio.

By far the most inequitable representation arose in states that had changed their constitutions to represent towns and counties directly. In these states, it only took one-fifth of the population to elect a majority of the legislature. It did not matter whether such rules were part of the state's original constitutions, as in Vermont, or were added in reaction to population changes, as in Florida. The state legislatures had no incentive to change their constitutions or even their laws. State constitutional conventions, many of which were called to address the inability of the legislature to reapportion, failed in their charge. Indeed, most made matters worse. Reform from within the legislative system was not only impossible, it was the source of the problem.

THE STRANGE CASE OF CALIFORNIA

Progressive groups, such as the League of Women Voters and the National Municipal League, urban economic organizations, especially unions, and even urban legislators tried to circumvent the legislatures. They would take the issue to the people directly. The political calculation looked simple enough. Urban voters, although they did not have their fair say in legislative decision making, outnumbered rural voters in most states. Putting reapportionment on the ballot in states that allow for direct democracy through the initiative and referendum seemed like a natural way to correct the problem. Surely, the majority of voters would support equality; even the threat of the initiative, some argued, would be enough to keep the legislature in line.[16] The ballot, however, would prove to be a giant step backward.

Eighteen states provided for initiative and referenda to pass laws or amend state constitutions. In these states, the people themselves could, through their own initiative, put a new law or constitutional amendment on the ballot (hence the term *initiative*), or the legislature could refer a proposal to the people (hence the term *referendum*). South Dakota was the first; it introduced initiative and referendum in 1898. Over the next decade Arkansas, Maine, Michigan, Missouri, Montana, Nevada, Oklahoma, and Oregon adopted direct democracy, and by 1920 Arizona, California, Colorado, Idaho, North Dakota, Nebraska, Ohio, Utah, and Washington followed suit. No other states added the initiative until 1968.[17]

Curiously, the initiative states were as likely as others to deviate from equal population representation. The legislatures either drafted inequitable maps or changed apportionment laws or constitutions to prevent the inevitable shift in political power from urban to rural areas. The state constitutions of Maine, Missouri, Nebraska, Oklahoma, Oregon, South Dakota, Utah, and Washington required representation of population and frequent reapportionment. Some of these states managed to draw new lines, though others neglected the duty. Legislative district populations deviated significantly from equality in these states. State legislatures in Idaho, Montana, Nevada, North Dakota, Ohio, and South Dakota amended their constitutions, dropping requirements that districts represent populations and imposing representation of place.[18] These were familiar maneuvers. Legislatures and constitutional conventions elsewhere had taken similar actions. But at least in these states, the initiative offered another way to enact change.

Unfortunately for reformers, the initiative states were a distinctly rural set. The western states had the least urbanized populations in the nation at the beginning of the twentieth century, and every western state but New Mexico had the initiative. The states with the highest concentrations of people in urban areas lay in the Northeast and Midwest, but only three midwestern states and

---

16. See Ward E. Y. Elliott, *The Rise of Guardian Democracy* (Cambridge, MA: Harvard University Press, 1974), 13–16; Robert G. Dixon Jr., *Democratic Representation: Reapportionment in Law and Politics* (New York: Oxford University Press, 1968), 401; and Justice Clark's dissent on *Lucas v. Colorado General Assembly*, 377 U.S. 713, 742 (1964).

17. Florida, Illinois, Mississippi, and Wyoming implemented direct democracy after 1968.

18. The most subtle change occurred in South Dakota in 1948. An amendment to the constitution in that year dropped the clause dating from 1889 that "the legislature shall apportion the senators and representatives according to the number of inhabitants." See McKay, *Reapportionment*, 423.

one eastern state provided for direct democracy. Arkansas was the sole southern state with the initiative. In only four of the states with the initiative, California, Michigan, Ohio, and Washington, did a majority of the population live in urban areas as of 1920. But even by 1960, half of the states with the initiative had populations that were either majority rural or evenly divided between urban and rural areas.

Here, then, lay the principal difficulty with the ballot. Initiatives and referenda were available precisely where those pushing equal representation of population did not have the votes. In those states that allowed initiatives and referenda, the populations tended to live in rural areas and actually benefited from malapportionment.

The ballot, then, could not check the state legislatures. Ten of the initiative states never put apportionment questions before the voters in the first sixty years of the century. Those that did almost always rejected measures to apportion legislative districts in line with population. Eight states voted down ballot measures to apportion their districts fairly; some states rejected such measures repeatedly.

There was one exception, and it proved the rule. Only the state of Washington, one of two western states with majority urban populations, passed an initiative creating equitable apportionments. It did so twice. In 1930, 57 percent of the residents of Washington lived in urban areas, and in that year the state reapportioned using the initiative. Those district lines drifted out of alignment with population over time. In 1956, the electorate corrected the problem and, again, passed an equitable apportionment plan. Washington's state legislature, however, amended the 1957 initiative, producing significant deviations in district populations. The proponents of the initiative challenged the legislature's unilateral rewriting of an initiative, but the Washington Supreme Court upheld the legislature's power to amend ballot measures. Even when it succeeded, the ballot could be undone by the legislature.

Worse still, the rural majorities in the initiative states had the votes to prevent the erosion of their own power. Through the initiative, the rural majorities could alter their states' constitutions to cement their political position long into the future. That is exactly what they did.

Like their counterparts in the other regions of the country, rural legislators and voters in the West saw the rising tide of their states' cities and the political threat it posed. Urbanization in the West lagged behind that in the East and Midwest, but it was just as predictable. Los Angeles, Phoenix, Seattle, Denver, Las Vegas, Oklahoma City, and Salt Lake City are twentieth-century cities. Their populations expanded very rapidly between 1900 and 1960. Los Angeles was already the largest city in the state in 1900, having 14 percent of the state's population. But by 1930, the city tripled in population and contained over one-third of all people living in California. Arizona's cities had less than one-third of the state's population in 1920, but the urban areas, driven mainly by the growth of Phoenix, contained 62 percent of the population of Arizona in 1960.

Five states considered ballot measures that proposed representation of places in lieu of representation of people. All five passed. In 1932, the people of Arizona and Colorado approved of measures that increased the representation of smaller counties at the expense of Phoenix and Denver. In 1952, Michigan wrote its legislative districts into the constitution via the initiative. Those boundaries could only be changed by a constitutional amendment, and they supplanted the requirement that the state legislature periodically draw new districts so as to ensure equal representation of people. Arkansas made the same decision in 1956. The most extreme initiated changes occurred in California. In 1926, the voters of California put forward an initiative, Proposition 28, that struck the state constitution's requirement of equal representation of people in the state senate and replaced it with a rule that no county could have more than one seat in the forty-member senate. As a result, the millions of voters in Los Angeles and San Francisco elected the same number of senators as the few thousand people in Alpine, Sierra, and Mono counties. In all five cases, the electorates of the state chose to skew representation toward less populous counties, at the expense of the cities.

Voters were not duped. They voted their self-interest. Repeatedly, the large cities in the states voted overwhelmingly for equal population representation and against measures that called for minimum county representation or one county, one vote. In Michigan and Arkansas, Detroit and Little Rock stood against the remainder of their states. In Colorado and Arizona, Denver and Phoenix overwhelmingly voted against county representation, while every other county returned large majorities for it. People did not hold tight to an abstract principle of political equality when they considered apportionment measures; rather, they voted their interests. The cities lost for the simple reason that the voters who stood to gain from malapportionment outnumbered those who would lose power.

California stands as a puzzling exception. The large majority of the state lived in cities and their surrounding metropolitan areas by 1920. In fact, 62 percent of the population lived in the three most populous counties—Los Angeles, San Francisco, and Alameda. Proposition 28 would give each of these counties a single senate seat, cutting their representation as much as tenfold. California's three most populous counties could determine their own fate. Not only did the electorate approve Proposition 28 in 1926, but the Californians refused to undo it through initiatives in 1928, 1948, 1960, and 1962. Why couldn't California's urban majority hold on to its political power?

The California state constitution of 1879 stipulated that there be forty Senate and eighty Assembly seats and that the legislature draw the districts "as nearly equal in population as may be," with every decennial census. From 1880 to 1911, the legislatures did their duty. Following the 1910 census, the three most populous counties had just under half of the population and were assigned 19 of 40 senate seats: Los Angeles received 8; San Francisco, 7; and Alameda, 4. The other fifty-five counties shared the remaining 21 senate seats; each either held exactly 1 senate seat or were part of a senate seat. The 1920 census would tip the balance decidedly to the urban areas. The new count showed that these three counties contained 62 percent of the state and deserved 25 senate seats, a solid majority. Complicating matters further, almost all of the population growth had occurred in Los Angeles. Attempts to draw new district boundaries following the 1920 census repeatedly ended in stalemate. Every session of the legislature took up the matter, but the urban legislators simply did not have the votes to push through an apportionment in line with the new census. The legislatures serving from 1921 to 1927 reflected the 1911 apportionment, under which rural counties held a majority of the seats. In 1926, the legislature decided to refer the matter to the voters. The Republican leadership in the assembly crafted Proposition 20. This referendum would allow a commission to apportion the state if the legislature failed to pass a plan. By narrow margins, the assembly and senate decided to refer Proposition 20 to the public, but those dissenting prompted business groups to place an alternative measure on the ballot, Proposition 28.

Propositions 20 and 28 were opposites. Proposition 20, referred by the legislature, would keep the constitutional guarantee of equal representation of population in both chambers, and it would use the threat of a commission to force the legislature to complete its task. Proposition 28 emerged through the initiative process, from the people. That proposal left unchanged districting for the Assembly, but would make the Senate represent counties rather than people. The similarity to the U.S. Congress prompted its proponents to label Proposition 28 "the federal plan."

The big-city newspapers pounded the drum in opposition to Proposition 28. William Randolph Hearst's San Francisco papers ran daily editorials against the "federal plan." And, in those days, the papers did not demurely tuck the editorials inside the back page of the front section. These were on the front page. During the final week of the campaign, Hearst ran daily editorials against the propositions and printed sample ballots in the papers showing readers to vote NO on 28. The *Los Angeles Times* showed more restraint but was equally strong in its editorial opposition to Proposition 28. The paper remained neutral toward the legislature's proposed commission.

The votes on Propositions 20 and 28 revealed the complex politics that created and sustained unequal representation in the United States. Proposition 20 won just 40 percent of the vote statewide and received the support of only 60 percent of those in Los Angeles, the only county where the legislature's referendum won a majority. The defeat of Proposition 20 could be read as contentment with the existing districting process. It was not. At the same time that they turned down the proposed commission, a majority of the Californians voted for the federal plan. It is tempting to consider this an accident of history or a profoundly irrational act on the part of many voters. The state's politics, however, were as fractured as its geography.

The 1926 election returns expose several cross-cutting cleavages in the state that led to the malapportionment of the state senate. The first divided rural and urban areas. Already by the 1920s, California's three major cities had strong economies rooted in industry, manufacturing, and banking. The rest of the state, including the state capital, Sacramento, had an agricultural economy. The cities and their surrounding areas voted heavily Republican up through the 1930s, while the rest of the state leaned Democratic. The second schism cut regional lines. California politics have long cleaved between north and south, and Southern California begins at the Kern County line. Third, the state's two great cities were bitter rivals. Although they voted firmly Republican, Los Angeles and San Francisco competed against each other for control over the state's vast resources, including water rights, control of public lands, and state money for public works. Finally, as in the nation as a whole, the California parties divided deeply over a handful of very salient issues. Democrats in the Central Valley strongly favored Prohibition, but the immigrant-oriented Democratic organizations strongly opposed it. Within the Republican Party, Progressives in Los Angeles County, whose favored candidate had won the Republican nomination for governor that year, differed sharply with the laissez-faire Republicans in San Francisco, who often found themselves aligned with the Democrats in the state legislature. The divisions within the state, then, were not just city versus farm. They were perhaps even more deeply city versus city.

The balance of political power had tipped in 1920, not only in the favor of the cities according to the 1920 census, but decidedly in the direction of Los Angeles. The census showed that Los Angeles would gain disproportionately more than the Bay Area. And the population trend cast an ominous cloud over San Francisco's political future. The county had dominated state politics since its emergence as a financial and shipping center during the Gold Rush. But it had clearly lost its position. Los Angeles grew from 14 percent of the state's population in 1900 to 34 percent in 1920. It would hit 40 percent of the state's population in 1930. Los Angeles was ascendant.

At the 1926 general election, Los Angeles County returned an overwhelming majority against Proposition 28, but its votes did not carry the day. It was the only county to oppose the measure. Three out of every five voters in San Francisco and Alameda voted yes on Proposition 28. It was a last-ditch effort to stunt the growing political power of Los Angeles and the possible formation of a Southern California political bloc within the Republican Party and the state as a whole. To stop Los Angeles, San Francisco and Alameda voted to give away their own political power.

For San Francisco and Alameda, this was a pyrrhic victory. The cost to these counties in terms of state funds, as Chapter 9 demonstrates, would be dramatic, but the political future looked even bleaker than the path they chose.

The adoption of one county, one vote in California bears a poignant lesson. Neither the voters nor the legislatures could solve the apportionment problem. Legislators would follow their self-interest. They would act to hold on to their political power, even if that meant refusing to reapportion. Direct democracy would prove to be a weak instrument of control, even a flawed one. Voters faced the same unfortunate incentives as their legislators. Competition among cities meant that the great urban majority could not find common ground. Distrust of cities made reapportionment a political albatross for politicians who pushed it. Nearly everywhere, the urban interests met defeat. There seemed to be no way that democracy, either directly or working through representative government, could ensure political equality. As society changed and populations shifted, those with power would do all they could to keep it.

Justice Felix Frankfurter's faith in the political process to solve the problem of malapportionment was wholly misplaced. Neither the legislature nor the people could be relied on to ensure equal representation. They had too many other interests at heart, and inequality served those ends much better than grand principles such as fairness, equity, and even self-rule.

4

Winners and Losers

Malapportionment affected every sort of community—city, suburb, town, and farm; every social group; every socioeconomic class; every political party. It distorted the value of the votes people cast and tipped the balances of political power across the United States. Who won and who lost as a result of unequal representation in the American states? Who was the uncounted majority?

Unlike the redistricting battles in legislatures today, debates over apportionment in most states were not typically charged with partisan and racial politics. In some states, unequal representation magnified disparities in the political voice of racial groups and social classes, but in most regions of the country it cut across race and class. In some regions, the Democrats were advantaged; in other states, the Republicans. In some states, unequal representation carried overtly partisan overtones; in other states, neither party gained an upper hand. Tennessee is a case in point. There, white Democrats sued other white Democrats.

Malapportionment held subtly different consequences from state to state and region to region for political parties, racial groups, and social classes. But throughout the United States, unequal representation reflected one fundamental driving factor; rural political power. Where cities became the centers of wealth and industry, those interests found themselves much less powerful than their resources would suggest. Where smaller counties disproportionately reflected one side of the partisan divide, that party benefited. Where political lines had changed little in generations, representation reflected generations-old political divisions. Unequal representation in the United States maintained rural power, with all of the political implications that carried.

URBAN, SUBURBAN, AND RURAL AMERICA

Malapportionment stemmed from and magnified one fundamental division in American politics: the cleavage between urban and rural America. By 1960, the vast majority of people in the United States lived in metropolitan areas, but the sparsely populated rural counties elected the lion's share of state legislators in the country. As the figures cited in chapters 2 and 3 reveal, rural counties received excessive representation at the expense of large metropolitan counties. Political inequities mapped almost directly into the urban-rural division in the United States. The minority parties in some states suffered as well from malapportionment, but the consequences were slight and localized compared to the effects on cities and suburbs. Party, race, and income—factors that drive political debate over districting today—played only a secondary role, and then only to the extent that they mapped into the fault lines dividing urban, rural, and suburban America.

Population provides a simple classification of urban and rural counties. The Bureau of the Census groups the counties in the United States into four categories. Highly urbanized counties have populations above 500,000 people. These highly urbanized counties contain large cities, such as New York, Chicago, Los Angeles, Philadelphia, and Detroit, and many mid-sized cities, such as Providence, Rhode Island. Counties with between 100,000 and 500,000 people fall into the urban category as well, though they have somewhat less dense populations or lie on the fringe of large cities. These counties include midsized cities, such as Little Rock, Arkansas, and Peoria, Illinois, and also suburban areas, such as Stamford, Connecticut, and the largely rural Dutchess County, New York, whose largest city, Poughkeepsie, has a population of almost 30,000. Counties having 50,000 to 100,000 people typically contain small cities and large towns, such as Dubuque, Iowa, as well as the surrounding rural areas; a few of these counties were suburban by 1960. Counties with fewer than 50,000 people are classified as rural. They have very few people per square mile and high agricultural or mining employment. Almost all counties with fewer than 50,000 people in 1960 had less than 90 people per square mile. By contrast, counties with more than 100,000 people averaged 1,000 people per square mile in 1960. Although this classification can be refined further, it captures the broad differences between rural and metropolitan areas.

Comparison of urban and rural counties reveals the severity of the discrepancies in representation. Approximately 2,500 counties—two-thirds of all counties—had populations lower than 50,000 people in 1960. Only 23 percent of the U.S. population lived in these counties, yet these counties elected 52 percent of seats to lower houses in the states and 56 percent of seats to upper houses. And the 12 percent of the population living in counties with fewer than 25,000 people elected more than 35 percent of lower house seats and 38 percent of upper house seats.

The more urbanized the community, the less representation it had. Forty percent of Americans lived in the 63 highly urbanized counties in the United States. Another 26 percent of the population lived in 240 counties with populations ranging from 100,000 and 500,000 people. All told, two-thirds of the population lived in 300 of the roughly 3,200 counties. In other words, less than 10 percent of all counties had two-thirds of the population. Unfortunately, because counties served as the basis for districts and because population concentrates in just a few counties, the urban majority was a political minority. Urban counties elected only one-third of the legislative seats—31 percent of their states' upper houses and 36 percent of their states' lower houses.

Rural counties dominated state legislatures. Approximately 2,500 counties had populations lower than 50,000 people in 1960. Only 23 percent of the U.S. population lived in these counties, yet these counties elected 52 percent of seats to lower houses in the states and 56 percent of seats to upper houses. And the 12 percent of the population living in counties with fewer than 25,000 people elected more than 35 percent of lower house seats and 38 percent of upper house seats.

County population predicted representation extremely well in most states. Of all the social, political, and demographic indicators, population was by far the strongest predictor of malapportionment: the more population a county had, the less representation it received.

Correlations between counties' populations and their relative share of legislative seats show just how strong this schism ran. A correlation of −1 indicates that each additional percentage of population a county had meant that it lost a percentage in representation. Correlations above .7 or below −.7 reflect a very strong degree of association. In twenty states, the division among city, suburb, town, and farm perfectly or almost perfectly determined political representation in at least one chamber.[1] In another sixteen states, the correlation between population and representation was exceedingly strong, ranging from −.7 to −.9. Nine states had correlations between −.5 and −.7. Only four states—Indiana, Tennessee, Texas, and Virginia—had correlations between county population and county share of representation in the range of −.2 to −.5. All four states apportioned seats unequally, but a handful of rural counties suffered along with the urban areas, breaking the otherwise strong negative association between population and representation. In every other state, the contours of political

---

1. The correlation is between the logarithm of the county's share of the state's population and the logarithm of the county's share of representation.

representation followed county populations, with the map of representation descending rapidly as it approached the cities.

But this was not only a matter of city versus farm. The other major segment of the electorate adversely affected by malapportionment lay just beyond city limits. Suburban America blossomed in the two decades following World War II, and legislative representation of these areas lagged far behind their populations. Their political difficulties stemmed from their size and their proximity to cities.

The populations of suburban counties and the suburban areas of urban counties rivaled the populations of many cities and dwarfed the rural counties by 1960. Suburbs sprang from farm lands in the 1940s and 1950s as young urban populations sought safer communities and more space. The size of the suburban population over the decades leading up to the reapportionment cases is difficult to gauge because the Census Bureau did not separate the core city population from the suburban population in its measure of the population of metropolitan areas until 1970. But by the 1970 Census, fully half of the people living in metropolitan areas resided in the suburbs.[2]

As a result of their postwar growth, the towns that neighbored major cities suffered politically. State legislatures' refusal to reapportion between 1940 and 1960 affected the suburbs even more than the cities. The least-well-represented areas in most states were not the cities but their suburban ring. In Maryland, Baltimore City was reasonably well represented by 1960, but the counties of Baltimore and Prince George's had the least representation in the state. In Michigan, Macomb, and Oakland counties, suburban Detroit, had the least representation; in New York, it was Suffolk and Nassau, containing the Long Island suburbs; in Illinois, it was Lake and DuPage, just north and west of Chicago; in Missouri, it was Saint Louis County, which like Baltimore County is independent from its city; in Pennsylvania, it was Bucks County, the well-heeled suburbs of Philadelphia. Rural politicians held the posts that suburban voters stood to gain.

Suburban representation was also squeezed by the cities. Almost all urban counties contain suburban areas as well as large cities. At-large elections, widely used to represent urban counties, relegated the suburban voters to permanent minority status within their own districts. The city vote and city political organizations dominated the at-large elections.

2. Historical and 2000 population data from U.S. Bureau of the Census, 1990 Census Tabulations, *Population and Housing Unit Counts, August 23, 1993*. Data on suburbs from the SOCDS (State of the Cities Data Systems) database, distributed by U.S. Department of Housing and Urban Development, are accessible at socds.huduser.org/index.html and from *Statistical Abstract of the United States, 2001*, U.S. Census Bureau, Appendix II, 892.

Such was the situation in Memphis. The city of Memphis accounted for approximately two-thirds of Shelby County's population. The county elected its eight seats in the lower house at-large: voters could choose up to eight candidates, and the top eight vote-getters won the seats. In every election in the 1930s, 1940s, and 1950s, Shelby County's representatives invariably had Memphis addresses. The courts forced the states to abandon at-large elections because of such vote dilution. Immediately, the suburban areas found representation in the state legislature. In the 1970s, one-third of Shelby County's representatives came from suburban communities.

The clear winners from legislatures' refusals to reapportion were rural counties and towns. Journalists mockingly described state legislatures as "prisoners of their past," "oxcart governments," and havens of "horse and buggy politics."[3] H. L. Mencken summed up the national situation in his reflections on Maryland: "The yokels hang on because old apportionments give them unfair advantages. The vote of a malarious peasant on the lower Eastern Shore counts as much as the votes of twelve Baltimoreans. But that can't last. It is not only unjust and undemocratic; it's absurd."[4]

However absurd, rural interests left their imprint on the political leadership and organization of the states. The rosters of house Speakers and other legislative leaders came disproportionately from rural counties, and these leaders often commanded a disciplined rural bloc. In Tennessee, for example, a succession of powerful rural legislators—I. D. Beasely, James Bomar, and Jim Cummings—controlled the House of Representatives. The Crump political machine, if it was to get anything in the state legislature, had to bargain with the rural bloc. Soon after reapportionment, the Tennessee house elected a pro-labor, urban speaker.[5]

The structure of committees—the places where legislatures do their work—also served rural interests. The formulation of, jurisdictions of, and composition of state legislative committees followed the interests of the rural majorities in the state legislatures. Minnesota offers a particularly telling example of how rural overrepresentation led to the organization of the legislature in line with rural interests. Before reapportionment and the resulting legislative reorganization, the Minnesota legislature had not one but four agricultural committees—one

---

3. William V. Shannon, "Massachusetts: Prisoner of the Past," and Richard L. Maher, "Ohio: Oxcart Government," in *Our Sovereign State*, ed. Robert S. Allen (New York: Vanguard Press, 1949); Kenneth C. Sears, "Horse and Buggy Politics," *Chicago Sunday Times*, April 30, 1939.

4. Quoted in Howard D. Hamilton, ed., *Legislative Apportionment: Key to Power* (New York: Harper & Row, 1964), 97.

5. That would not last long, as the state was still majority rural and the county faction within the Democratic Party reasserted itself during the mid-1970s.

for grains, one for livestock, one for dairy, and one for agriculture. These were consolidated into a single committee in the late 1960s, after representation was brought in line with the overall needs of the state.

Rural blocs flexed their power most strongly in taxation and spending. Florida provides one of the most striking cases of rural power.

By any measure, Florida ranked among the least representative legislatures. District populations were highly unequal in both its lower and upper chambers up until 1966; just 15 percent of the population could elect majorities in the state house and senate. The rural counties exploited their political advantage fully. From the 1920s through the 1960s, a rural faction, nicknamed "the Pork Chop Gang" by one newspaper editor for their shrewd control of pork barrel spending, ran every aspect of the Florida legislature. The Pork Choppers consisted of representatives from thirty or so rural counties throughout the state. They selected every speaker and every committee chair, and they determined committee assignments. To prevent infighting, the rural faction instituted a system of rotation through the positions of power within the legislature. Legislators would rotate through the dozen or so positions of power. A member might serve as speaker one term, then chair of the Ways and Means Committee, then chair of Public Works, then majority whip, and so forth. In this way, positions of power, and the spoils they brought, were spread evenly among the rural faction. The cities made their own situation worse. Unlike the rural areas, Miami, Palm Beach, Tallahassee, and Tampa Bay viewed one another as rivals; this allowed the Pork Choppers to play off the urban politicians against each other, undercutting efforts to assert an urban policy agenda in the state. The Pork Choppers repeatedly upset the formation of an urban faction in its nascency by offering an occasional position of value to a small number of urban legislators.[6]

The success of rural factions from Florida to Minnesota rested mainly on the nature of political districts in the United States. Rural legislators had a common interest in maintaining an old way of life, one based on an agrarian economy and rural social ties, and a common threat—urban and suburban expansion. Rural populations had been in decline for almost a century, from the end of the Civil War, yet malapportionment allowed them to hold on to power.

The result was that the organization and operation of state legislatures across the country remained oriented toward the interests of rural areas, long

6. William C. Havard and Loren P. Beth, *The Politics of Misrepresentation: Rural-Urban Conflict in the Florida Legislature* (Baton Rouge: Louisiana State University Press, 1962). Florida, although an extreme case, reflected a broader pattern throughout the United States. Case studies of Kansas, Iowa, Minnesota, Mississippi, Michigan, Oklahoma, Utah, Georgia, and the New England states tell nearly the same story as Florida. See Robert S. Allen, ed., *Our Sovereign State* (New York: Vanguard Press, 1949).

after rural populations had shrunk to a small minority in most states. Robert Burns wrote in his influential blueprint for reform of state government that unequal representation had created a "serious handicap under which state legislatures had labored for years":

> For decades, state legislatures had been dominated by rural interests which constituted a diminishing minority of their population. In form and structure, state legislatures were geared to the paces and problems of an earlier, simpler America, not to the increasingly urgent and intricate needs of an urban, technology-oriented society.[7]

DEMOCRAT VERSUS REPUBLICAN

The political geography of the American states, in turn, distorted the electoral strength of the political parties, and often tipped the balance of control in the legislatures.

On its face, the political geography of 1961 appeared stacked against the Democrats. After all, urban areas generally tend to vote much more Democratic than rural areas. Dating well into the nineteenth century, urban political machines provided one of the core elements of the Democratic vote throughout the United States. Maps of county voting patterns today reflect the continued heavy urban orientation of the Democratic Party. As cities like Detroit, New York, and Chicago grew and their legislative delegations did not, their voters lost representation relative to other parts of the states, and those cities voted strongly Democratic. Public opinion data from the late 1950s and early 1960s also indicated that the typical urban resident voted Democratic 60 percent of the time in presidential elections from 1956 through 1964, while the typical rural resident voted Democratic 45 percent of the time.[8] Underrepresentation of the urban counties, then, ought to have reduced the political power of the Democratic Party in the states. State legislatures, as one pair of observers put it, were "constitutionally Republican."[9]

But the story of political winners and losers in the era of malapportionment is not so simple.

7. Robert Burns and Citizens Council of State Government, *The Sometime Governments: A Critical Study of the 50 American Legislatures* (New York: Bantam Books, 1971), 3.

8. Figures compiled by the authors from the American National Election Studies (www.electionstudies.org), THE 1948–2004 ANES CUMULATIVE DATA FILE [dataset], Stanford University and the University of Michigan [producers and distributors], 2005.

9. Gus Tyler and David I.Wells, "New York: 'Constitutionally Republican,'" in *The Politics of Reapportionment*, ed. Malcolm Jewell (New York: Atherton Press, 1962), 221–48.

Soon after the Court handed down the reapportionment cases, scholars began to examine in earnest the partisan consequences of malapportionment. These earlier researchers immediately encountered a surprising and puzzling finding: there was no systematic relationship between the counties' Democratic share of the vote and their relative representation in the state legislatures, nor did the extent of malapportionment in a state portend an increase in the Democratic share of seats won. Rather, the pattern of partisan gains and losses varied across the states. Some states' districting maps indeed contained large biases that advantaged the Republicans, but in other states the apportionment evidently benefited the Democrats, and in still others inequities in representation gave neither party the upper hand. Nationwide, the correlation between a county's share of the Democratic vote in presidential elections and its share of representation in the legislature was trivial for both the upper and lower houses, and partisan biases averaged to approximately 0 across the country. Neither distortion of votes nor partisan bias gave either party a clear edge nationwide.[10]

This nonfinding was deeply troubling. How could such large discrepancies in representation have no political consequence? A closer look at the variation in party voting and its relationship to malapportionment reveals the answer. Inequities in district populations magnified the Democratic vote in the South and the Republican vote in the North.

To calculate the extent of the distortion requires that we reconstruct the vote itself. State legislative election returns are not immediately helpful because a large number of seats had no competition and the lack of competition was a consequence of malapportionment. Political scientists instead use the Democrats' share of the two-party vote in statewide or national offices, such as governor and U.S. senator, to gauge the support for the Democratic Party over the Republican Party in each county. (Equivalently, one may use the Republican share of the two-party vote, as that equals 1 minus the Democrats' share.) The average Democratic share of the two-party vote in a county in each year is called the Normal Democratic Vote, or just the Democratic Vote. We computed the Democratic Vote for every county in the United States, and in New England every town, from 1948 to 1962 using election returns for president, governor, and U.S. senator. Legislators and consultants who draw districting maps today begin by making a similar calculation for each precinct; they proceed to construct districts out of the many building blocs. Our aim is to assess the overall distortion of the normal or expected

---

10. Robert Erikson conducted one of the earliest and most comprehensive studies of the partisan effects of malapportionment. He focused on the non-South and measured partisan bias along the lines discussed below. Robert Erikson, "The Partisan Impact of State Legislative Reapportionment," *Midwest Journal of Political Science* 15 (February 1971): 57–71.

vote due to inequities in district populations that existed before 1962, when politicians could protect their political fortunes and the interests of their constituencies without the convolutions that mark modern districts, by doing nothing.

The distortion in the vote equals the difference between the Normal Vote in the average legislative district and the Normal Vote in the state as a whole. This is, again, comparing what is with what ought to be. That is, we are comparing two methods of voting. One system corresponds to what ought to be and assigns all people an equal vote: the expected partisan division of the vote is the division of the Normal Vote statewide. A second system reflects the malapportionment of the time: each person in a county has the same vote, but the weight of the votes varies from county to county. In some counties, the votes count two, three, or even ten times what they do in other counties. The Relative Representation Index discussed in chapter 3 measures exactly the weight that each voter in every county receives under malapportionment. The difference between the first (equal weight) system and the second (unequal) system for each county equals the distortion of the votes in each county due to malapportionment, and the statewide average of that difference captures the overall distortion of the vote.

This distortion is calculated quite simply as the difference between the average vote for the Democrats statewide and the average Democratic vote under the existing unequal population districts.[11] A positive difference means that Democratic voters were overrepresented in the given chamber, and a negative difference means that Democratic voters were underrepresented. For most states, the analysis occurs at the county level. For the New England states and Delaware, where there are few counties and town-level data is available, we use town-level data.[12]

The extent and patterns of distortion of the vote are clearly evident with the aid of two maps. Figure 4.1 displays states where malapportionment inflated the vote of Democrats at the expense of Republicans; Figure 4.2, the states where malapportionment inflated the vote of Republicans. The darkest shade in each map highlights the states with the strongest bias toward the specific party; the lighter shade identifies states with weak or modest biases. We left unshaded those states where malapportionment either inflated the votes of the

11. We multiply these differences by 2 since any overrepresentation of one party's voters automatically implies an equal degree of underrepresentation of the other party. If the difference is k percentage points and if the population-weighted *Normal Democratic Vote* is x percent, then the seat-weighted *Normal Democratic Vote* is $x + k$ percent and the seat-weighted *Normal Republican Vote* is $x - k$ percent, giving the Democratic voters an advantage of $2k$ percentage points relative to Republican voters. This holds in a world where all voters adhere to one of the two parties, which is approximately true in all U.S. states.

12. New Jersey had county-based representation. See Alan Shank, *New Jersey Reapportionment Politics: Strategies and Tactics in the Legislative Process* (Rutherford, NJ: Farleigh Dickinson University Press, 1969).

FIGURE 4.1. *States with Democratic bias, 1940s–1950s*

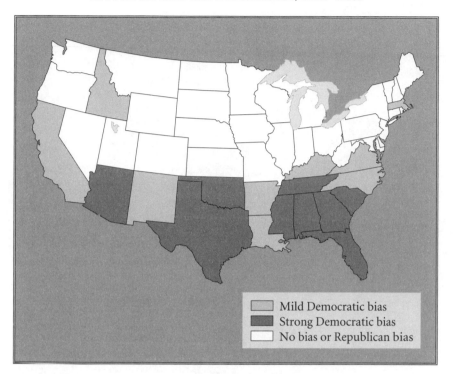

Mild Democratic bias
Strong Democratic bias
No bias or Republican bias

other party or had no substantial effect.[13] States with no partisan distortion due to malapportionment include Oregon, the Dakotas, Wisconsin, West Virginia, Delaware, and Maryland. With the exception of those states with no bias, the maps are two sides of the same coin.

The maps display a striking regional pattern. Malapportionment magnified the vote of the Democrats in every southern state, and in most cases the bias was large. The largest inflation of the Democratic vote occurred in the Florida and Georgia state senates, where district lines magnified the Democratic vote by 14 and 12 percentage points, respectively. By contrast, nearly every state in the Northeast and Midwest exhibited a pro-Republican slant, with the strongest distortions occurring in New England. District lines magnified the Republican vote share by 13 percentage points in the Connecticut lower house, 11 points in the Rhode Island senate, and 16 points in the Vermont lower house. The exceptions were those states with no bias and Massachusetts. Massachusetts, birthplace of the Gerry-Mander, is the one of the few states where malapportionment had

13. Strong distortion corresponds to 4 or more percentage points; weak distortion, 1 to 4 percentage points; no distortion, less than 1 point.

FIGURE 4.2. *States with Republican bias, 1940s–1950s*

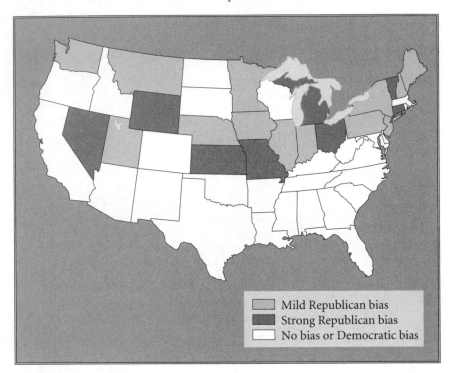

Mild Republican bias
Strong Republican bias
No bias or Democratic bias

failed to take root; perhaps it was unnecessary. The western United States showed a highly mixed picture, with Arizona having a strong Democratic bias and Nevada and Wyoming strong Republican biases; malapportionment produced moderate inflation of Republican votes in California, Idaho, and New Mexico and moderate inflation of Democratic votes in Montana, Utah, and Washington.

These distortions in the vote in the 1940s and 1950s were of a sufficiently large magnitude that they determined which party controlled the state legislatures. Most legislative elections operated under districting plans that slanted heavily toward one of the parties. Three-quarters of all state legislative elections were conducted under districting systems where the partisan bias exceeded 5 percentage points. Only one in four elections occurred in states where biases could be considered small.

Distortions in the two-party vote created by malapportionment frequently decided control of the legislature. Table 4.1 displays how vote distortion and election outcomes determined the frequency with which Democrats or Republicans won a majority of seats in the legislature. The rows of the table divide elections into those that the Republicans clearly won (when the Democrats won less than 45 percent of the vote statewide), those that the Democrats clearly won (Demo-

TABLE 4.1 *Vote distortion, election outcomes, and control of state legislatures, 1942–1962*

Statewide election result	Direction of vote distortion in districting plan		
	Pro-Republican	Weak or no bias	Pro-Democratic
Republican win	113 Rep majority	13 Rep majority	no cases
(Dem% < 45)	0 Dem majority	0 Dem majority	
Even division	171 Rep majority	46 Rep majority	5 Rep majority
(45 < Dem% < 55)	42 Dem majority	54 Dem majority	54 Dem majority
Democratic win	17 Rep majority	0 Rep majority	0 Rep majority
(Dem% > 55)	20 Dem majority	50 Dem majority	96 Dem majority

Source: Compiled by authors.

crats won more than 55 percent of the vote statewide), and those where the parties divided the electoral outcome evenly (Democratic vote between 45 and 55 percent). The columns divide the states into those where districting plans exhibited strong Republican biases, strong Democratic biases, or weak or no partisan bias. Each cell of the table shows the number of times the Republicans won a majority of seats and the number of times the Democrats won a majority of seats for a given statewide election result and given direction of partisan bias.

Most states during this era had very competitive elections, where the two-party division of the vote was within 5 percentage points of 50–50. In states where the elections were within 5 points of 50–50 and there was a pro-Republican bias of 5 percentage points or more, Republicans won a majority of seats approximately 80 percent of the time. In similarly competitive states where there was a pro-Democratic bias, Democrats won a majority of the seats 92 percent of the time. And in close elections in states that had no clear biases, Democrats and Republicans won majorities about equally often. Partisan biases, then, strongly determined the outcomes in close elections, which accounted for over half of all instances.

The distortion of the vote caused by districting plans also insulated the parties from electoral insurgencies. In thirty-seven instances, a party won more than 55 percent of the vote statewide, but the districts were substantially biased against that party. The party that won the vote in these cases captured a majority of seats slightly more than half the time (54 percent). However, the rest of the time, the skew in the districting system prevented the winning party from capturing a majority of seats.

Partisan bias due to malapportionment, widespread throughout the country, tipped the balances of power in two out of every five legislative elections outside the South in the era immediately before *Baker v. Carr*. All told, there were 709 legislative elections for which we could estimate the bias. In just 163 legislative elections, the biases were small and the outcomes determined solely by who won the most votes. In 267 instances, the party favored by the bias in the districting plan also won a majority of the vote. In the remaining 279 cases, either the elections were very close and biases determined the outcome, or one party won a majority of votes but lost a majority of seats.

But which party benefited? Looking across the entire nation, neither party, on average, gained an advantage.

Therein lies the puzzle. One expects that Republicans ought to have gained from the partisan bases attributable to malapportionment. The typical rural voter nationwide identified as and voted Republican, and the typical urban voter identified as and voted Democratic. Overrepresentation of the rural vote in state legislatures should have further magnified the Republican political advantages in state and federal elections.

That distortion worked its way through the entire political system. The state legislatures are, so to speak, the farm team of American politics. The state legislatures are the foundation of the political hierarchy. They provide the talent pool from which the parties recruit candidates for higher offices; most U.S. House members pass through the state legislatures; secretaries of state, attorneys general, and U.S. senators cut their political teeth in the state legislatures. Before the mid-1960s, the most available talent came from rural areas, and some states had very few urban and suburban state legislators to even recruit candidates for higher office. But malapportionment did not generate a national political advantage for Republicans among the states or in the nation as a whole.

The tint of a solution to the puzzle lies in the maps showing the distortion of the party vote (Figures 4.1 and 4.2).

There is no small irony in these maps. They look exactly opposite to the political geography of American politics today. Red and Blue America, made famous by the *New York Times* columnist David Brooks and other current political writers, runs Republican in the South and Mountain West and Democrat in the North and Pacific states. Before 1960, the states aligned Republican above the Mason-Dixon Line and Democratic below it. Reapportionment was a shock to this political system. It contributed to the erosion of the old order and began the slow evolution of a new one.

The relationship between the American political map of 1960 and that of 2000 is no accident. Malapportionment preserved old political stock. It magnified the state legislative and U.S. House vote of the rock-ribbed rural

Republicans of New England and the Midwest. It insulated rural Democrats throughout the South and in parts of the West. Malapportionment had kept in place political divisions among the American states that existed in the final decades of the nineteenth century. By the 1960s, state politics reflected increasingly outdated partisan alignments, down to the level of counties, cities, and towns.

Those alignments had three distinct effects on the translation of votes into legislative representation, but the forces in the South ran in completely opposite directions to the forces at work in the Northeast and Midwest.

First, malapportionment hurt the Republican suburbs as well as the Democratic cities. As we discussed earlier, malapportionment devalued the votes of those in cities and in suburbs. While central city residents tended to vote Democratic, suburban residents tended to vote Republican. According to the American National Election Studies (ANES) surveys, 57 percent of those in cities voted for the Democratic presidential candidate from 1952 to 1964, compared with 45 percent of those in suburban areas and 47 percent of those in rural areas. Underrepresentation of the metropolitan counties diluted the strength of urban Democrats; it also lessened the voting power of their more Republican neighbors.

Second, not all cities are cut from the same political cloth. Most cities, especially those in the Northeast and Midwest, vote strongly Democratic. The highest levels of Democratic voting in any region came from the northeastern and midwestern cities in the 1950s and early 1960s, where Democratic presidential candidates won on average 60 percent of the vote. But many cities at this time, especially in the western United States, were Republican strongholds, including Phoenix and Tuscon, Arizona; Long Beach, Los Angeles, and Oakland, California; Grand Rapids and Lansing, Michigan; Wilmington, Delaware; Cincinnati and Columbus, Ohio; and Tampa–St. Petersburg, Florida. Again, the ANES surveys reveal the regional variation in city voting patterns. From 1952 to 1964, 59 percent of urban residents in the Midwest and Northeast and 55 percent of urban residents in the South reported voting for Democratic candidates, but urban residents in the West gave 53 percent of their votes to Republicans and just 47 percent to Democrats.

Third, and most perhaps most important, the rural areas in the South voted completely opposite to the rural areas in the Midwest and Northeast. Rural voters in the Northeast and Midwest were the staunchest Republicans. Only 38 percent of rural voters in these regions voted Democratic in the 1950s and 1960s. Rural voters in the South were among the most loyal to the Democrats: 55 percent of them chose the Democrats in presidential elections in the 1950s and 1960s.

The urban-rural cleavage varied across the nation. In the Northeast and Midwest, that division pitted Democrats against Republicans. According to the results of the ANES surveys, 58 percent of urban voters in the Northeast voted Democratic from 1952 to 1964, but 45 percent of suburban and only 35 percent of rural voters in the Northeast voted Democratic. In the Midwest, a similar pattern held, with 59 percent of urban voters and just 42 percent of rural voters choosing Democrats. The urban-rural political schism in the South and West certainly existed at a cultural level, but it was not partisan. Fifty-seven percent of rural voters in the South chose Democrats for president between 1952 and 1964, while 55 percent of urban southerners voted Democratic. Southern Republicans concentrated in the suburbs. In the West, 54 percent of rural voters chose the Democrats for president over the decade before reapportionment, while just 47 percent of urban voters in this region voted Democratic. The foundations of the solid Democratic South and West were laid in the rural counties of these regions.[14]

Malapportionment, then, did have strong partisan orientation, but its effects were completely opposite in the southern and northern states. In the Northeast and Midwest, underrepresentation of metropolitan areas diluted the Democratic urban vote and magnified the voice of the overwhelmingly Republican rural areas. As a result, Republicans gained everywhere in the Northeast and Midwest from unequal district populations. Their gains were tempered only by the degree of underrepresentation of the suburban communities, whose partisan orientations lay somewhere between those of the rural and urban voters.

Quite a different picture emerges in the South and West. In these regions, the rural areas voted most strongly Democratic in national and state elections. The suburbs and the cities, especially in the West, supported the Republican Party. As a result, malapportionment inflated the vote of Democrats in the South and of Republicans in the North and helped preserve a long-standing party alignment that dated back to the end of the nineteenth century.

Reapportionment would turn the geographic alignment of American politics on its head. Districting practices before *Baker* allowed these state political alignments to survive for decades, even centuries, and often at odds with the

14. Further evidence of the regional variation in the relationship between malapportionment and party comes from county-level correlations of representation and presidential vote. The correlations between percentage vote for the Democratic presidential candidate and representation were .28 in Alabama, .21 in Arkansas, .61 in Florida, .53 in Georgia, .65 in Louisiana, .33 in Mississippi, .13 in North Carolina, .35 in South Carolina, .59 in Tennessee, .40 in Texas, and .18 in Virginia. In many northern states, equally strong but opposite relationships between partisanship and representation held. The correlation between Democratic vote and representation was highly negative: −.41 in New York, −.6 in Connecticut, −.44 in Maine, −.49 in New Hampshire, −.37 in New Jersey and Ohio, and −.32 in Pennsylvania.

national political alignment. The Court's reapportionment decisions would eventually force the states to align themselves according to a common set of political schisms. They would break the last vestiges of the political alignment and hierarchies of the nineteenth century, which lived on in the district boundaries found in long-established constitutions and state laws.

SOCIAL INEQUALITIES

Inequalities in representation reached a breaking point at the same time that American society grappled with other great social problems, especially those of race and poverty. The struggle for racial equality in the United States escalated into open protest and violence during the late 1950s and early 1960s, culminating in court orders to integrate schools and other public places, deployment of national guards to enforce those decrees, and sweeping civil rights legislation in the mid-1960s. The federal and state governments also undertook bold new projects to combat poverty in the United States. On January 8, 1964, Lyndon Johnson in his first State of the Union address declared a War on Poverty. That initiative led to the creation antipoverty programs, ranging from income assistance to housing developments to public health and, ultimately, Medicare.

Equal opportunity and fairness served as the cornerstones of this new American ethos, and equal voting rights became an essential means to achieve a just society.[15] A fair political system, it was thought, would eliminate the barriers to representation that squelched the voices of the powerless. Social theorists and reformers saw the same forces working against lower-income Americans. Political and social theorists of the time, such as C. Wright Mills, Michael Lind, and Robert Dahl, documented how social resources, such as income, education, and standing in the community, translate into political influence. Democratic politics reflect and magnify social inequalities. Higher-income people have the resources to control the political system at all levels of government in the United States and use their political influence to expand further their wealth and social power. A simple Golden Rule elegantly expresses this radical and populist critique of American politics: those who have the gold make the rules. The aphorism retains its currency today, equally embraced by populists on the right and radicals on the left.

---

15. On the Great Society ethos, see Samuel Beer, "The Public Philosophy," in *The New American Political System*, ed. Anthony King, (Washington, DC: American Enterprise Institute, 1979). On the political ethos in the United States generally and its relation to equal opportunity and fairness, see Herbert McCloskey and John Zaller, *The American Political Ethos* (Cambridge, MA: Harvard University Press, 1983).

Racial politics in the 1950s and 1960s provided a compelling example of this notion of political power. Systematic exclusion of blacks from the political process and discrimination in the economic arena sustained high levels of poverty in the black community. Racial gerrymandering cases beginning in 1960 documented instances of the discriminatory use of legislative districting and malapportionment. Court rulings followed by the Voting Rights Act sought to eliminate the practices that muted the political voice of the black community.

Political and social equality do not, however, always walk hand in hand. Legislative districting is a case in point. The great debate over malapportionment concerned the deep schism between urban and rural politics in America and the resulting partisan alignment of the country. That debate most assuredly was not about race; it was not about social class; and in many ways, the effort to end political inequality ran completely counter to the political impulses of the time to tackle the problems of social and economic inequality.

One would expect the socially powerful to have considerable influence over districting and use it as an instrument to further their power; after all, if the wealthy can buy the legislature, they ought to also stack the rules in a way that would have increased further their political pull. That is the essence of the radical critique of politics—that wealth, class, and other social inequities translate immediately into political power. Malapportionment would seem to be an easy case for the radical critique. Indeed, radicals were highly critical of the *Baker* decision and the liberalism it embodied. But the radical critique does not work at all in the case of representation, and a closer look at patterns of malapportionment reveals why.

The social characteristics of over- and underrepresented counties shows a surprising set of relationships. Table 4.2 presents the correlations between a county's relative representation in the upper and lower chambers of the legislature

TABLE 4.2 *Correlations of relative representation with income, poverty, and race for upper and lower chambers, 1960*

	Non-Southern states		Southern states	
	Upper chamber	Lower chamber	Upper chamber	Lower chamber
Per capita income	−.49	−.63	−.64	−.67
Percentage in poverty	.52	.60	.63	.64
Percentage black	−.14	−.15	.14	.16

Note: Correlations are population weighted.

and its average income, its poverty rate, and its percentage black.[16] Correlations between −.2 and .2 are considered weak. Both the strength and the direction of the association between representation and social categories are instructive about how unequal representation magnified and muted social inequalities.

Malapportionment ran counter to the canonical view of political power in America. Unequal district populations increased the political representation of poorer counties and undervalued the power of wealthier communities. Counties with higher income were more likely to be underrepresented than counties with lower income, and the correlations are very strong, ranging from −.5 in the upper chambers outside the South to −.67 in the lower chambers inside the South. Counties with income in the highest 25 percent of the population had one-third less representation than they deserved. Counties with income in the lowest quartile had 75 percent more representation than they deserved. Poverty rates tell the same story. Counties with higher rates of poverty were more likely to be overrepresented than counties with less poverty. The wealthier counties and populations, not the poorer communities, suffered from malapportionment.[17]

Underrepresentation of wealthier areas, of course, did not rise out of attempts to combat poverty. It was an artifact of the geography and demography of the

16. The data are weighted by population, so the correlations represent the association between whether an individual is represented and the characteristics of the county he or she lives in.

17. An alternative way to portray the relationship between social indicators and representation is to divide the indicators into categories—in this case, quartiles of the distribution of income relative to the state, poverty relative to the state, and percentage black relative to the state. The average value of the Relative Representation Index indicates the representation in the upper and lower chambers among those counties in each quartile of the relevant variable.

	Relative representation	
Poverty rate	Lower chamber	Upper chamber
Lowest 4th	.76	.70
Third	1.07	1.10
Second	1.37	1.45
Highest 4th	1.74	1.90
Income		
Lowest 4th	1.74	1.75
Third	1.37	1.49
Second	1.08	1.14
Highest 4th	.74	.67
Percentage black		
No blacks	1.38	1.45
< 50% of state average	1.13	1.22
50% to state average	.99	.95
Above state average	.89	.81

American population. Cities and their surrounding suburbs contain the large majority of people in the United States; they are also centers of great wealth and industry. Cities have much higher economic growth, which is why so many people live there. Metropolitan areas certainly have their social ills and pockets of intense poverty, but rural areas, especially in 1960, suffer from much more intense levels of poverty. Envy, distrust of modernity, and the desire to hold on to political power, rather than a sense of social justice, led legislatures to permit the growing disparities in legislative district populations.

Race and apportionment tell a different story, but with a similar lesson. Racial reapportionment and districting presents one of the central and most difficult issues in election law to this day. Malapportionment did not, however, contribute to the systematic disenfranchisement of blacks and Hispanics.

If unequal district populations were a tool of political exclusion, one would expect that counties with larger minority populations would have less representation. In the Northeast, Midwest, and West, inequalities in district populations correlated negatively but not strongly with the racial composition of counties. The last row of Table 4.2 presents correlations between race and representation, and outside the South the correlations lie in the neighborhood of −.15, a modest relationship. This fact reflected entirely the concentration of blacks in northern and midwestern cities.[18] No rural counties outside the South had sizable black populations.

Curiously, inside the South, counties with higher percentages black had more representation in state legislatures than counties with smaller black populations. The correlations are weak, only .14 and .16 for the upper and lower chambers, respectively, but positive nonetheless.[19] Considering the pervasive discrimination against blacks through other electoral procedures, such as poll taxes and literacy tests, the positive association between percentage black and representation surprised us. Racial representation was an acute problem in the American South. Blacks constituted 25 percent of the population in the American South in 1960 but had no representatives in the state legislatures. Why, then, is there a positive relationship, albeit weak, between race and representation in the South?

Unlike the rest of the United States, southern blacks were distributed fairly evenly between urban and rural counties. As elsewhere, southern cities such as New Orleans and Atlanta had sizable African American populations. Southern

18. When one controls for income and population, the partial correlation between county percentage black and relative representation approaches 0.
19. V. O. Key noted the similarly weak and uneven correlations. See V. O. Key, *Southern Politics* (New York: Vintage, 1949), 542–54.

cities fared no better than their counterparts in the Northeast, Midwest, and West. Malapportionment effectively kept the cities out of power in the southern legislatures, as well as the political agendas of unions, progressive reformers, and southern liberals who wanted to undo the web of laws that maintained discriminatory practices throughout southern society.

Parts of the South also had large rural black populations. The rich black soil in the stretch of country from northern Lousiana through northern Georgia and into South Carolina and southern North Carolina gave rise to an unfortunate nickname for this fertile crescent—the Black Belt. Here lay the heart of the plantation economy of the Old South. The Black Belt contained considerable black populations; these counties also held a disproportionate share of seats in southern state legislatures.

But African Americans had very little political influence within the Black Belt counties. Jim Crow laws kept blacks away from the polls in large numbers, allowing white voters control of politics in the Black Belt counties. Poll taxes, literacy tests, and other election procedures combined with outright intimidation worked to lower black voting rates to less than 10 percent of the black adult populations in most southern states. According to the Census Bureau, only 20 percent of southern blacks were registered to vote in 1960, compared with 60 percent of southern whites. As a consequence, whites cast a majority of votes throughout the South, even in the most overwhelmingly black counties. The excess representation of Black Belt counties, then, did not empower blacks. Rather, it magnified the political strength of rural whites at the expense of rural blacks and the urban counties.[20]

THE FAILURE OF STATE GOVERNMENT

The consequences of malapportionment went beyond the zero-sum politics of rich versus poor and black versus white. In a much broader sense, everyone lost. Unequal representation in the states limited the capacity of government to deal with social problems and many other basic issues of governance. State legislatures did not represent their populations well, and as a result, neither the public within the states nor the national government viewed state government as true agents of the people.

20. A simple, realistic example illustrates the point. Consider a county 80 percent of whose population were blacks; only 5 percent of all southern counties were at least 80 percent black. In such a county, the electorate was majority white. Approximately 10 percent of the blacks voted but 50 percent of the whites voted, so 55 percent of voters in such a county were white.

Voters had little faith in state government. Their legislatures were highly un-representative of their states as a whole and could not be trusted to pass laws that would reflect the preferences of the general public. Bitter conflicts between the governors, who represented the entire state, and the state legislatures were common and often resulted in stalemates over new policy initiatives.[21] Even when the electorate passed initiatives directing the legislature to take action, the legislatures often ignored such instructions.[22] In this climate, it made little sense to have a powerful, professional state legislature. Most state constitutions provided for only part-time, amateur legislatures, whose members received low pay and had little staff assistance. Over the course of a century, the state legislatures evolved from the wellsprings of American government into political backwaters. Agitation to professionalize the state legislatures went hand in hand with reapportionment.[23]

The federal government also lacked confidence in the state legislatures. It would not entrust funds to the states or responsibility for the administration of programs. Both parties at the national level grappled with the increasing dysfunction of state governments.

During the 1952 presidential campaign, candidate Dwight Eisenhower attacked the growth of government in Washington and promised to return discretion, power, and money to the states. Once elected, President Eisenhower directed the Commission on Intergovernmental Relations to map out a plan of action to implement his agenda of dismantling the New Deal welfare state. The president appointed Meyer Kestenbaum, a prominent businessman, to direct the study; after two years of study and over fifteen volumes of reports, the Kestenbaum Commission cautioned against Eisenhower's proposal. "The effectiveness of state government was impaired," the Commission concluded, "by unduly limited and poorly representative state governments."[24] Devolution of power to the states, the Kestenbaum Commission concluded, required a more effective state government. The idea would eventually be reborn as Ronald Reagan's New Federalism; but before Eisenhower's proposed devolution of power could work, state government would have to change.

---

21. Havard and Beth, *Politics of Misrepresentation*, offer an excellent study of this problem in Florida, but case studies of the politics of the New England states and New York and Michigan revealed similar problems. See Duane Lockard, *New England State Politics* (Princeton, NJ: Princeton University Press, 1959); Karl A. Lamb, William J. Pierce, and John P. White, *Apportionment and Representative Institutions: The Michigan Experience* (Washington, DC: Institute for Social Science Research, 1963); and Frank J. Munger and Ralph A. Straetz, *New York Politics* (New York: New York University Press, 1960).

22. See Havard and Beth, *Politics of Misrepresentation*.

23. Belle Zeller, *American State Legislatures*, Report of the American Political Science Association (Washington, DC: APSA, 1954); John Burns and Citizens' Conference on State Legislatures, *The Sometime Government* (New York: Bantam Books, 1971).

24. Meyer Kestenbaum, "To Strengthen Our Federal System," *State Government* 28 (August 1955): 73.

The Kestenbaum Commission traced the root of the problem to several causes—chief among them, the severe inequities in representation. "In a majority of states," the report observed, "city dwellers outnumber the citizens of rural areas. Yet in most states the rural voters are overwhelmingly in control of one legislative house, and overweighted if not dominant in the other."[25] If the federal government were to redirect funds and authority to the states, the state legislatures would skew public spending toward communities not on the basis of need or fairness, but on the basis of power. The rural factions that dominated the state legislatures would surely redirect funds disproportionately to their constituents. Large majorities of the populations, then, would not get resources or programs simply because they lacked sufficient representation in the states. As a result, the federal government in the 1950s committed many fewer resources to social programs than it may have otherwise.

Democratic leaders began to awaken to this problem as well. A young Senator John F. Kennedy took up the cause of the cities as he began to lay the groundwork for his own bid for the presidency. In "The Shame of the States," in an influential opinion piece published in the *New York Times Magazine* in May 1958, Kennedy descried the host of ills that had befallen the cities: crime, pollution, congestion, inadequate education, poverty, and insufficient housing. The cities are the great economic engines of the states, Kennedy argued; their health and problems affect us all. Businesses, families, and individuals in the cities "contribute the lion's share of Federal and state taxes, but an equitable share is rarely returned to them." As a result, municipal leaders lacked the resources and support from the state and federal governments to adequately address the failures in essential services. "[T]he root of the problem is that the urban majority is political a minority and the rural minority dominates the polls. . . . The failure of our governments to respond to the problems of the cities reflects this basic political discrimination."[26]

The state governments, both the Eisenhower and Kennedy administrations agreed, are essential partners of the federal and local governments in addressing critical social problems and providing essential public goods. The states were much closer to the problems and could deal much more effectively with them. The federal government was simply too removed but was increasingly dragged in to deal with very local problems. Yet the state legislatures lacked the political will to address problems facing the cities because the legislatures primarily represented rural interests and were organized to address rural problems. Federalism inched steadily toward the crisis that Eisenhower and, later,

25. Quoted in Gus Tyler, "The Majority Don't Count," *The New Republic* (August 1955): 14.
26. John F. Kennedy, "The Shame of the States," *New York Times Magazine*, May 18, 1958, p. 12.

Kennedy faced. Without the state governments as partners, the national and local governments could not address effectively the problems of inadequate education and crime, health care and poverty, congestion and pollution that ailed the American cities in mid-century.

Democrat and Republican, liberal and conservative—all felt acutely the crisis of government to which malapportionment contributed. By 1970, however, a resurgence of state legislatures had begun. Many commentators saw reapportionment as the first step toward the modernization of the state legislatures and state governments. With equal representation came new optimism that the states could address the problems of governance and resolve the mounting urban crisis.[27] Whether that faith was justified would ultimately have to await the test of history. Reapportionment at least brought the possibility of the revitalization of state government that Eisenhower sought by aligning the state legislatures with the preferences of their states' electorate.

The states themselves were incapable of bringing about this renewal, as they were incapable of resolving the apportionment conundrum. It would take bold action by the federal courts to bring the American state legislatures back in line with the public.

27. See, for example, John Burns and Citizens' Conference on State Legislatures, *Sometime Governments*, chap. 1.

The Warren Court, October 1961. Front row l–r: William O. Douglas, Hugo L. Black, Earl Warren, Felix Frankfurter, Tom C. Clark; Back row l–r: Charles E. Whittaker, John Marshall Harlan II, William J. Brennan Jr., Potter Stewart. Source: Photograph by Harris & Ewing, The Collection of the Supreme Court of the United States.

PART II

The Least Dangerous Branch

5

Judicial Restraint

Demand for fair representation intensified with the continued growth of urban and suburban communities, but the political system seemed incapable of righting itself. State legislatures resisted reapportionment; executives could not force the issue; and majorities of the states' voters, fearing domination by the largest cities, chose to have unequal legislative representation. One possible corrective to malapportionment remained—the courts.

As if the deus ex machina in a great drama, the Supreme Court entered in 1962 and cleared the way for the states to achieve political equality. The Justices asserted their authority to intervene in such cases in *Baker v. Carr*. Two years later, they declared a broad and absolute right to equal representation. Equal protection under the law was not a right limited to particular groups or to some circumstances. If that idea meant anything at all, it meant that all people had the right to have their voices counted equally: one person, one vote.

Within five years, every state had complied with the philosophy expressed by the Court. While some additional marginal adjustments were to occur, by 1967 every state had adopted state legislative and U.S. House districts with nearly equal populations. But even this transition was not without struggle. The U.S. Supreme and state courts struck down laws, suspended elections, drew new maps, and, in the end, forced the state legislatures to abide by a strict standard of equal district populations. Paradoxically, the most undemocratic institution of the government was necessary to make the democratic institutions function properly. "Guardian Democracy," Ward Elliott called it.[1]

Baker v. Carr and *Reynolds v. Sims* today stand as the expressions of self-evident rights, of truth revealed. But at the time, the constitutional guarantees of an equal weight, an equal say, in what the government decided and, especially, the courts' authority in protecting that right were highly contested.

The authority of the judiciary in ensuring equal representation is unquestioned today, but the courts' entry into legislative districting was far from easy or automatic. The experience of the judiciary in this area prior to the 1960s had not been terribly successful. Legislatures often simply ignored rulings from the state courts, a pattern that threatened the broader authority of the judiciary. The U.S. Supreme Court approached the subject with extreme caution, and for much of the twentieth century it simply declined such cases. Indeed, before *Baker v. Carr*, the reigning legal doctrine was that the courts had no jurisdiction over a subject so fundamental to the operation of the legislative branch of government.[2]

THE "POLITICAL THICKET"

The nature of the courts' initial forays into legislative districting ranged from timidity to confusion to colossal failure. Late in the late nineteenth century, suits brought in Illinois, Indiana, Kentucky, Massachusetts, Michigan, New York, and Wisconsin sought to strike down district plans because boundaries crossed county lines, a sure sign of gerrymandering, or because districts had highly unequal populations.[3] Each case contained a substantial political risk for the judiciary. These suits pitted the courts against the legislature, and sometimes also against the people. However, if a court were to strike down the legislature's apportionment, it faced the prospect of losing a political struggle that could undermine its effectiveness as a check in the political system.

The state courts were variously ignored or, realizing the political risks to their own credibility, refused to get involved. If the court overturned an existing apportionment statute, the law would revert to a more outdated set of

1. Ward E. Y. Elliott, *The Rise of Guardian Democracy* (Cambridge, MA: Harvard University Press, 1974).
2. We are deeply grateful to our colleagues Sam Issacharoff and Dan Lowenstein, our guides through the field of election law. This section of the book delves into the politics on the courts. For more on the legal issues involved see Samuel Issacharoff, Pamela Karlan, Richard Pildes, and Daniel Lowenstein, *Election Law*, Carolina Press, and Stephen Ansolabehere and Samuel Issacharoff, "The Story of *Baker v. Carr*," *Constitutional Stories*, Michael Dorf ed. Foundation Press: NY, 2004.
3. V. O. Key, "Procedures in State Legislative Apportionment," *American Political Science Review* 26 (December 1932): 1050–58.

districts. In considering the 1892 gerrymander of its state, the New York court of appeals explained the dilemma all courts faced: "If the act of 1892 is void, the act of 1879 is also plainly void, and no election of the assembly should be tolerated under it. They might relegate the people to the act of 1866. . . . This would be a travesty on the law and upon all ideas of equality, propriety, and justice."[4] Courts in other states, including Kentucky, Indiana, and Michigan, took the other path and voided laws with the unfortunate consequence that even more unequitable districting lines from past plans were revived. In Wisconsin, the state supreme court found that the legislature had indeed gerrymandered the district map and created unequal representation. But, the court ruled, it had no jurisdiction, as the legislature had the authority to set its own rules. State courts seemed incapable of solving the apportionment problem.

There was one exception: Massachusetts. Repeated lawsuits in 1916 brought the Massachusetts state legislature to comply with that state's constitutional requirement of equal representation in both the upper and lower chambers of the legislature. It is unclear why the courts succeeded in Massachusetts. Perhaps the existing political alignment or culture favored an equitable solution; perhaps the judges, by repeatedly declaring the districts illegal, just wore the legislature down. Until the 1960s, it stood as the one ray of hope that the courts could solve this problem. Elsewhere, though, the courts either refused to hear apportionment cases or, when they did get involved, made matters worse.

As the twentieth century wore on, the scope of the apportionment fight widened. The federal courts entered the political fray in the wake of the struggle over the 1920 U.S. House apportionment. After eight years of wrangling, Congress finally resolved the matter with the 1929 Federal Apportionment Act. Citizens in Kentucky, Minnesota, Mississippi, Missouri, and Virginia promptly challenged their state legislatures' implementation of the act. These cases, however, propagated even more ambiguity. The only solution the lower courts could fashion was to elect all legislators at-large in the absence of a valid districting plan. The Supreme Court variously imposed at-large elections in some states but vacated that method in others. The Justices set down the absence of a valid statute as the basis for judicial intervention, but they construed that narrowly.

Minnesota's situation was perhaps the most bizarre. Minnesota lost one U.S. House seat as a result of the 1929 law. The state legislature had passed a new districting plan, but the governor vetoed it and the legislature did not override the veto or pass a new plan. As a result, Minnesota stood to elect more legislators than it was apportioned. Minnesota Secretary of State Holm ruled that the 1911 Apportionment Act no longer held and that the 1931 legislative districting

4. *People v. Rice*, 31 N. E. 921 (1892).

plan, even though vetoed by the governor, was valid. This was, Holm reasoned, a political matter, not a legal one, and the body politic acted through the legislature. The state supreme court agreed. In *Smiley v. Holm*, the U.S. Supreme Court overturned the state court. The legislative process had played out to its end and reached no new districting plan. Because Minnesota had lost a seat, its existing districting plan was completely inappropriate for its new apportionment. "Unless and until new districts are created," Chief Justice Hughes wrote, "all Representatives allotted to the state must be elected by the state at large."[5]

Elsewhere that year, federal and state courts voided districting laws, leaving the states without congressional districts for the upcoming general elections. The federal district courts in Kentucky and Mississippi struck down the states' districting statutes because of gross inequities in district populations.[6] The state supreme courts in Missouri and Virginia similarly found their state districting plans in violation of state laws requiring equal populations.[7] Lacking a valid districting plan with just months to go before the 1932 election, the courts required all candidates for Congress to run at-large. Urgent appeals were filed with the U.S. Supreme Court, which agreed to hear the Mississippi and Missouri cases. As in Minnesota, the governor of Missouri had vetoed that state's new districting plan. Relying on its decision in *Smiley v. Holm*, the U.S. Supreme Court ordered that Missouri elect its congressmen and congresswomen at-large. Mississippi, the Court reasoned in *Wood v. Broom*, presented another matter. The legislature had passed a statute, and the governor signed it. The state courts were the ones to declare it unconstitutional. Here the U.S. Supreme Court ruled there was a valid legislative process, so it let stand the Mississippi act.

Throughout, the Supreme Court artfully dodged the question of equality. It overturned some of the state and federal court decisions that found inequities problematic, but it did so on the narrowest of grounds—whether a state law had been passed. The line between the Justices' treatment of the situation in Mississippi and the situation in Missouri was fine indeed. In one instance, they required at-large elections when they found apportionment plans to be no longer legal or valid. In the other instance, the Supreme Court voided the use of at-large elections in situations where the states had passed districting plans even though the plans violated state laws or constitutions. The Justices merely said that when the political process fails to produce a plan consistent with the apportionment, the state must elect its house contingent at-large. The Court avoided the tricky questions of whether the law violated equal protection.

5. *Smiley v. Holm*, 285 U.S. 355, 374-375 (1932).
6. Kentucky—*Hume v. Mahan*, 1 F. Supp. 142; Mississippi—*Broom v. Wood*, 1 F. Supp. 134.
7. Missouri—*State ex rel. Carroll v. Becker*, 45 S. W. (2) 533; Virginia—*Brown v. Saunders*, 166 SE.

The courts found themselves mired in politics whenever they took up districting cases. Each case immediately challenged the courts' authority, and the available remedies, such as at-large elections or reverting to prior districting plans, only worsened representation. Only in Massachusetts were the courts able to force the legislature to create appropriate districts, and that occurred only after repeated rulings and the threat of suspending elections.

A separate line of cases also pulled the judiciary increasingly into the political arena. Those cases involved the abrogation of voting rights of African Americans in the southern states following the end of Reconstruction. Southern state legislatures and party organizations had created a variety of legal barriers to black political participation and representation, including poll taxes, literacy tests, and the white primary. In the 1920s and 1930s, the courts intervened to protect the voting rights of individual African Americans in particular circumstances. Such cases did not declare entire laws unconstitutional, but they did establish a standard of judicial intervention in electoral politics for the protection of African American voting rights in the enforcement of the fourteenth and fifteenth Amendments—two of three amendments guaranteeing the political and civil rights of African Americans following the Civil War.

The most stunning legal blow to the southern political establishment came in 1944. The case *Smith v. Allwright* challenged the exclusion of African Americans from the Democratic primary in Texas.[8] Not only did the Court side with the plaintiff, granting $5,000 damages for violation of his voting rights, but it issued a declaratory judgment striking down the use of the white primary in any state as a violation of the Fifteenth Amendment. Here at last the Supreme Court declared a state law in violation of constitutional guarantees of equal voting rights. It seemed a small leap from the rights of one group of citizens to the rights of all citizens to have equal representation. In 1946, the Court at last had to address that matter directly.

COLEGROVE V. GREEN

Political deadlock in Illinois prevented the state from drawing new U.S. House district lines following the decennial census in 1920, 1930, and again in 1940. Urban population growth meant that the cities and their surrounding areas deserved greater representation. In fact, Illinois had the most unequal district populations among all states in the U.S. House in 1940. Chicago bore the brunt of malapportionment in Illinois. Chicago's 2nd, 3rd, and 6th U.S. House districts

8. *Smith v. Allwright*, 321 U.S. 649 (1944).

had approximately 600,000 people each in 1940, and the 7th district contained almost 1,000,000 people. The district representing East St. Louis had 360,000 people. Elsewhere in the state, district populations ranged from 110,000 to 300,000.[9]

Efforts to redistrict the state repeatedly ended in failure. The very same urban population growth that had overrun the state's U.S. House districts produced unequal state representation in the state assembly. The "downstaters" held the bulk of the assembly, and they had the power to block any apportionment plan for the federal or state elections that would weaken their representation. From 1910 to 1946, they did just that.

The Illinois state legislature was not without its critics. One such voice rose from Kenneth C. Sears, a professor at the University of Chicago law school. Sears had written extensively on election laws, and in a *Chicago Sunday Times* feature article he lambasted the Illinois state legislature's "Horse and Buggy Politics."[10] Sears described a legislature dominated by rural interests that had little understanding of the urban engine driving state economic growth: the rural interest taxed the cities heavily and passed laws that stunted Chicago's progress. Sears pushed a new progressive reform: ending the "rotten borough politics" of state legislatures.

Sears lived on the south side in a district with 625,000 people that was the home of progressive reformers such as Harold Ickes and Charles Merriam. He teamed up with Kenneth W. Colegrove, a professor in the Northwestern University political science department, who lived in a district on the north side of the city that had 914,000 people, and with Peter Chamales, an attorney in the city. Marshall Field, the department store and publishing magnate, underwrote the case, and they retained Urban A. Lavery, a prominent Chicago lawyer, to craft the case. It was an unlikely team with an unlikely lead. Colegrove had few professional dealings with state government, and his professional expertise was in the area of Japan and international conflict. He was an internationalist and a cold warrior. He was no liberal reformer.

On January 8, 1946, the team sued Governor Dwight H. Green, State Auditor Edward J. Barrett, and Arthur C. Lueder in federal district court. As members of the Primary Certifying Board, Green, Barrett, and Lueder had responsibility for determining which candidates were to run for which seats. Lavery and his colleagues asked the court to hold the 1901 law unconstitutional and to enjoin state officials from applying the law in the April 1946 primary elections.

9. Urban Lavery, "Complaint for Declaratory Judgment and Injunctive Relief," *Kenneth W. Colegrove et al v. Dwight H. Green et al.*, 46 C 46, District Court of the United States for the Northeastern District of Illinois, Eastern Division, January 8, 1946, Exhibit A.
10. Kenneth C. Sears, "Horse and Buggy Politics," *Chicago Sunday Times*, April 30, 1939.

The remedy proposed was familiar: hold all U.S. House elections in Illinois at-large in the 1946 primary and general elections, as the courts had required of Minnesota and Missouri in 1932.

The argument set out a wholly new path. Urban Lavery's suit put the issue of equality under the law squarely before the courts. The complaint and supporting brief brilliantly set out four main points: Illinois districts violate Article 1 of the Constitution, which stipulates that the House represents population; they violate successive Acts of Congress, which state that "Congressional districts in each state shall contain 'as nearly as practicable, an equal number of inhabitants' "; they violate the constitution of Illinois and the Northwest Ordinance of 1787, which provides for equal representation; and, most important, they violate the equal voting rights of citizens, which are protected under the fourteenth Amendment to the Constitution. Throughout the seventy-four-page brief, Lavery focuses unwaveringly on the inequalities within Illinois and the philosophical and legal basis of equal representation in the United States.

For all of the brilliance in the argument, the case had some glaring legal weaknesses. Unlike circumstances in the Minnesota and Missouri cases in 1932, Illinois had not lost a seat in the federal reapportionment. Although the state legislature and governor had failed repeatedly to forge an agreement on a new district map, Illinois voters would not have elected more House members under the 1901 state law than the federal apportionment allotted. There was an easy out for the courts, and one sketched by Chief Justice Hughes in his opinions in *Smiley* and *Wood*. The courts only needed to intervene when the existing districting law would have elected too many or too few House members. That was not the case in the suit Lavery and his colleagues brought.

The remedy proposed—at-large elections—heightened the political issue. Willard Shelton, writing in the *Chicago Sun* two weeks after Urban Lavery filed *Colegrove v. Green*, praised the "ingenious" argument and concluded that if the case succeeded "the citizens of Illinois will have the horse laugh on their politicians. Two things might happen. Governor Green conceivably might call a special session of the Assembly to revise the laws and pass a new—and equitable—districting statute. Far more likely is that all Illinois congressmen this year would be elected at large. . . . Each voter would cast a ballot for 25 candidates, and the 25 with the highest number of votes over the whole state would win."[11] According to the 1940 Census, over half of the population of the state lived not just in urban areas, but in one urban county—Cook County—and almost half of all state residents lived in the City of Chicago. The people of

11. Willard Shelton, " 'Rotten Borough' Suit an Ingenious Blow at Old Evil," *Chicago Sun*, January 17, 1946.

Chicago could elect the entire House delegation under at-large elections, and at that time Chicago was strongly controlled by an urban political machine.

Finally, time was short. Urban Lavery filed the suit on January 8; the primary elections were to be held in just four months and the general elections in ten months.

The federal district court dealt with the case promptly. Citing the standard set forth in *Wood v. Broom*, a three-judge panel concluded that a valid districting law was on the books. That governed the election.

On expedited appeal, the case was argued before the Supreme Court on March 7 and 8, 1946. The Supreme Court, however, did not decide the case until June, after the primary elections had passed. While the plaintiffs sought a decision that would apply to the primary elections, the delay provided a ray of hope. Whatever the Justices decided, this would not be a simple application of earlier rulings.

Why the delay?

The spring of 1946 was an odd time for the Supreme Court. Only seven Justices were in residence. Justice Robert Jackson was on leave to the war crime trials at Nuremburg. Chief Justice Harlan Stone had passed away at the beginning of the year, and the term of the new Chief Justice, Frederick Vinson, had not yet begun.

The Court was also deeply divided. Long-standing norms of universalism had broken down. Up until 1937, dissenting opinions were rare, issued in less than one in ten cases; but from 1937 to 1942, minority opinions were penned in nearly one in four cases. And starting in the 1942 term, dissent became the norm. From that term on, in at least half of all decisions the Justices in disagreement with the majority have issued written opinions expressing their own reasoning about the cases, a pattern that continues today.[12] Ironically, this divided Court emerged among Justices that President Franklin Delano Roosevelt appointed. Following his defeat on the Court-packing plan, Roosevelt appointed in a four-year span seven Justices: Hugo Black, Stanley Reed, Felix Frankfurter, William O. Douglas, Robert Jackson, Frank Murphy, and Wiley Rutledge—almost the entire Court.[13] But that was no guarantee of agreement, and, indeed, a deep rift emerged almost immediately on the bench that Roosevelt appointed.

The sharpest split among the Justices was between Hugo Black and Felix Frankfurter. Along with William O. Douglas and Frank Murphy, Black

---

12. Lee Epstein, Jeffrey A. Segal, Harold J. Spaeth, and Thomas G. Walker, *The Supreme Court Compendium: Data, Decisions, and Developments.*, 2nd ed. (Washington, DC: CQ Press, 1996), 195.
13. FDR also appointed James F. Byrnes to the Court in 1941, but he resigned in 1942.

anchored the liberal end of the Court. They pushed their colleagues to become more active and involved in questions such as reapportionment and race relations, where the courts had traditionally stayed out, and favored expansion of the civil rights of individuals. Frankfurter was a traditionalist on such matters. He saw threats to the authority of the Supreme Court were it to become embroiled in political conflicts. He advocated restraint. And along with Reed and Jackson, Frankfurter generally favored more conservative positions on political issues involved. Frankfurter and Black disagreed in their voting more than any other two Justices in this era. Increasingly over their time on the Court, the division between them defined the ideological poles of the Court. Black's liberal progressive agenda pushed the Court to intervene especially in areas of civil rights; Frankfurter saw the limitations of the judiciary and the need to conserve its power.

Both sides seized on *Colegrove*. The case offered an opportunity for the liberals to expand their theory of political rights. The traditionalists, led by Frankfurter, saw the chance to lay down a principle that would keep courts out of this highly political issue and would thus conserve the judiciary's authority within the constitutional system of checks and balances. The two Justices issued opinions that pulled the Court in opposite directions.

Felix Frankfurter, in his opinion on *Colegrove v. Green*, set forth the theory of judicial restraint in the clearest possible terms. In spite of the unfairness of the Illinois apportionment, Frankfurter believed that the Court had no role to play in solving the problem. "The petitioners ask of this Court," Frankfurter wrote, "what is beyond its competence to grant."

First, he rightly saw the limited ability of the judiciary to fashion a remedy. Courts are not administrative agencies: they lack the technical ability and political wherewithal to craft suitable lines. "[N]o court could affirmatively remap the Illinois districts so as to bring them into conformity with the standards of fairness for a representative system. At best we could only declare the existing electoral system invalid. The result would be to leave Illinois undistricted."[14]

Second, Frankfurter repudiated the solution sought by the plaintiffs and applied by the Supreme Court in the past: at-large elections offered a far worse solution. Districts protect the minority against tyranny by the majority. Here Frankfurter relied on Chancellor Kent, America's leading legal theorist and jurist of the nineteenth century and a strong advocate of minimum county representation during New York's Constitutional Convention of 1821.

14. *Colegrove v. Green*, 328 U.S. 549, 553 (1946).

Quoting Kent's *Commentaries on American Law* directly, Frankfurter wrote as follows:

> This requirement [of legislative districts] was recommended by the wisdom and justice of giving, as far as possible, to the local subdivisions of the people of each state, a due influence in the choice of representatives, so as not to leave the aggregate minority of the people in a state, though approaching perhaps to a majority, to be wholly overpowered by the combined action of the numerical majority, without any voice whatever in the national councils.[15]

Third, Frankfurter saw this as a fundamentally political action, and the courts have a responsibility to stay out of politics. They did not involve "recovery for damage because of the discriminatory exclusion of the plaintiffs from rights enjoyed by other citizens. . . . In effect this is an appeal to reconstruct the electoral process of Illinois." Such an action by the Court, Frankfurter foretold, raised the spectre of noncompliance. The U.S. House has the right to seat its own members. That body might, he speculated, simply ignore the results of an election conducted under the Court's order. This was just one of many possible political reactions to a ruling that held for Colegrove and his colleagues. Such responses would bring the courts into "immediate and active relations with parties" and legislative politics, the determination of which "this Court has traditionally held aloof."

Finally, Frankfurter saw Court intervention in legislative districting as fundamentally destructive of a core constitutional idea—the separation of legislative and judicial branches. "To sustain this action would cut very deep into the very being of Congress," Frankfurter concluded.[16]

> This is one of those demands on judicial power which cannot be met by verbal fencing about 'jurisdiction.' It must be resolved by considerations on the basis of which this Court, from time to time, has refused to intervene in controversies. It has refused to do so because due regard for the effective working of our Government revealed this issue to be of a peculiarly political nature and therefore not meet for judicial determination.[17]

15. Chancellor Kent, *Commentaries on American Law,* 12th ed. (1873): 230–31, n. (c). Quoted by Frankfurter in *Colegrove,* 328 U.S. 549, 553.
16. *Colegrove,* 328 U.S. at 556 (Opinion of Frankfurter, J.).
17. 328 U.S. 549, 552.

"Courts," Frankfurter famously concluded, "ought not to enter this political thicket."[18]

This dictum was to become the governing principle in legislative districting and other electoral cases—at least for the next sixteen years. Frankfurter's doctrine, though, presented a strong departure from a string of decisions made by the courts. Justice Hughes's opinions in *Smiley* and *Wood* drew a very practical distinction between circumstances when the courts could resolve an unresolved issue because state law conflicted with the federal apportionment and when the courts did not have to act because a valid law existed. In other situations, such as enforcement of the provisions of the fifteenth Amendment in the American South, the federal courts could invalidate a state's election laws. All of this amounted to "verbal fencing about 'jurisdiction.'" The details of Frankfurter's opinion, especially in the assertion of the special status of electoral districts, contradicted existing practice in a large number of states and past Supreme Court decisions. The "political thicket" doctrine called for the courts to pull back significantly from such political questions.

Hugo Black and his colleagues set forth an even more radical view. Black inferred a broad political right that no prior opinion had asserted. In an opinion that presaged the philosophy that would emerge under the Warren Court in the 1950s and 1960s, Black read into the equal protection clause of the Fourteenth Amendment a far-ranging political guarantee of equality.

> While the Constitution contains no express provision requiring that Congressional election districts established by the states must contain approximately equal populations, the Constitutionally guaranteed right to vote and the right to have one's vote counted clearly imply the policy that state election systems, no matter what their form, should be designed to give approximately equal weight to each vote cast. To some extent this implication of Article One is expressly stated by Section 2 of the Fourteenth Amendment which provides that 'Representatives shall be apportioned among the several States according to their respective numbers. . . .' The purpose of this requirement is obvious: It is to make the votes of the citizens of the several States equally effective in the selection of members of Congress. It was intended to make illegal a nationwide 'rotten borough' system as between the States. The policy behind it is broader than that. It prohibits as well Congressional 'rotten boroughs' within the States, such as the ones here involved. The policy is that which is laid down by all the Constitutional provisions regulating the election

18. *Id.* at 556.

of members of the House of Representatives, including Article One which guarantees the right to vote and to have that vote effectively counted: All groups, classes, and individuals shall to the extent that it is practically feasible be given equal representation in the House of Representatives, which, in conjunction with the Senate, writes the laws affecting the life, liberty, and property of all the people.[19]

As for the theory that the courts had no jurisdiction, Black argued that the U.S. Supreme Court had already ventured into this issue. They had established their authority to do so in the white primary cases and the House apportionment cases in 1932. The plaintiffs from Illinois, like African Americans in the South, had no clear way to achieve equal representation in the aftermath of every decennial census. The state had been unable to craft a new apportionment law in almost forty years. Only the courts could offer relief.

Frankfurter and Black expressed two views on the proper role of the judiciary that could not have been more different. Frankfurter relied on the principle of judicial restraint and the notion that the courts had no jurisdiction on political questions. The proper functioning of a system of separation of powers demanded that. For him, though, the issue was as much a matter of practicality as principle. Involvement in a matter so fundamental to the operation of the Congress and the livelihood of its members would surely pit the judiciary against the legislature—a battle the courts would likely lose. Black embraced the notion that the judiciary must protect the individual's rights from the government. And fundamental individual rights implied in the Constitution impelled the courts to act.

The Justices divided evenly. Justices Reed and Burton sided with Frankfurter. Justices Murphy and Douglas sided with Black. That left one pivotal vote—Justice Wiley Rutledge.

Rutledge was to have it both ways. He concurred in the result, but not the principle. Were it not for the ruling in *Smiley v. Holm*, he wrote, he would be inclined to think the courts did not have jurisdiction over "so delicate a matter." But Chief Justice Hughes's opinion in *Smiley*, on which the Court was unanimous, clearly established the authority of the judiciary in legislative apportionment and the ability of the courts to fashion solutions.

However, Rutledge argued, the courts could not grant equity in Colegrove's case as a practical matter. With the primary past and a few months remaining before the general election, the political process could not create new district boundaries in time for the election. Throwing out the existing districts with

19. 328 U.S. 549, 570–71 (Opinion of Black, H.).

just a few months remaining before the general election would create chaos. At-large elections, the solution proposed by the plaintiffs, would be worse than the existing unequal districts, as they would give excessive power to one-half of the state and no power to the rest. The City of Chicago might end up with all of the seats or no representation—a cure surely worse than the disease. No legal solution was possible in such a short time frame.

Rutledge's decision stunned his liberal colleagues. Rutledge anchored the liberal wing of the New Deal Court along with Justices Black, Douglas, and Murphy. His apparent split with them handed Frankfurter a victory that could damage all manner of progressive and liberal political reforms, as it allowed Frankfurter to express in bold terms his ideology of judicial restraint.

Justice Rutledge's concern with the practicalities of the case weighed against Colegrove and his colleagues. Perhaps more than any other Justice at the time, Rutledge was mindful of how decisions were to be implemented. If the Court reversed the district court, the state legislature would have to draw new districts, a feat it had not accomplished in thirty-five years, and the courts would likely have to hear challenges to those suits. With less than five months until Election Day, there really was little time to hammer out a solution, short of imposing at-large elections, and Rutledge saw the problems with that solution. Rutledge was also quite sensitive to the issues federalism presented. The states carry the responsibility for the conduct of elections; that responsibility should be respected to the greatest extent possible by the institutions of national government in order to ensure a properly functioning federal system.[20]

But practical considerations were not decisive; they were a convenient out. Justice Rutledge's brief opinion on this matter at once establishes the rights of the courts to intervene in such matters but states that intervention in this particular case is not appropriate. Two years later, Rutledge would reiterate even more forcefully his opinion in *Colegrove*.[21] The opinion seemed like a catch-22. The Supreme Court can—indeed, should—intervene, but we should not intervene in these cases. Why the ambivalence?

Rutledge saw that *Colegrove* raised a profound political difficulty for the liberals. Although the liberals may have had a majority of votes of those present in 1946, they did not have a majority of votes on the Court.[22] Rutledge realized that siding with Black would prompt Frankfurter to delay the case until Vinson took his position as the new Chief Justice and Jackson returned from Nuremburg.

20. One biographer asserts that practical considerations were Rutledge's primary concern. See Fowler V. Harper, *Justice Rutledge and the Bright Constellation*. (Indianapolis: Bobbs-Merrill, 1965), chap. 9. That argument is hard to square with Rutledge's reiteration of his opinion in *MacDougall*.

21. *MacDougall v. Green*, 335 U.S. 281 (1948).

22. The situation was unchanged in 1948 when the Court took up *MacDougall*.

Vinson and Jackson would surely support Frankfurter, creating a five-Justice majority in support of Frankfurter's opinion. The "political thicket" doctrine would then have the status of a precedent that would bind future courts. The liberals' only hope was to cut their losses and gamble that at same time in the future the Supreme Court would change directions. Had the four liberals on the Court in 1946 forced Illinois to elect its congressmen at large, their action would have likely been reversed when the Court was at full membership. Through his concurrence, Rutledge gave Frankfurter a temporary victory on the immediate matter of whether the courts would intervene in the Illinois U.S. House election of 1946. However, Rutledge's oddly ambivalent opinion meant that Frankfurter's political thicket doctrine did not, and in the end would not, have the authority of a precedent.[23]

Wiley Rutledge did not see the final success of his feint. He and Justice Murphy died suddenly in 1949, and with their passing only Black and Douglas remained of the liberal bloc. Felix Frankfurter's political philosophy would dominate the Court for the next decade, but Rutledge's decision would ultimately prove to be the crack that destroyed the foundation of rural power in the United States. It left enough of an opening through which the Tennessee lawyers, Archibald Cox, and William Brennan could push through. *Baker v. Carr* was the end-game of Justice Rutledge's wily political maneuver.

But for the time being, the decision offered little relief in Illinois. The two lawyers—Urban Lavery and Peter Chamales—and the two professors—Kenneth Colegrove and Kenneth Sears—had failed.

COLEGROVE'S WAKE

Kenneth Colegrove, Kenneth Sears, Peter Chamales, and Urban Lavery came together with a common interest. They bore the cost of a legal effort that would have benefited large numbers in the Chicago area. Groups such as this rarely survive long. The team that brought *Colegrove v. Green* was no exception.

Other interests and activities soon pulled the principals away from their common cause. Later in 1946, Colegrove stirred up another legal challenge—this time, to the states' legislative districts. Lavery's response to his appeal was not encouraging. Having lost their first case, the path forward became less clear and less likely to end in success. Communications between the two continued into early 1947, but Lavery's interest in a subsequent case never piqued. Colegrove, Chamales, and Sears, though, did follow through with the suit. The

23. Irving Bryant, "Mr. Justice Rutledge—The Man," *Iowa Law Review* (1950), 563–64.

courts, however, set aside their challenge to the constitutionality of the Illinois state legislative reapportionment. Citing *Colegrove v. Green*, the district court decided that it lacked jurisdiction, and the Supreme Court dismissed the appeal "for want of a substantial federal question."[24] After that, Colegrove's efforts on legislative districting dissipated and he turned his attention back to scholarly affairs, especially his interest in international relations in Asia and the rising specter of communism. Sears also pulled back from political activism on reapportionment, but he continued his academic interest in the subject, publishing, six years later, *Methods of Reapportionment*, a guide to equitable apportionment among the states.

Curiously enough, their case had the desired effect. Despite its failure, Colegrove's lawsuit spurred Illinois to draw new House districts. It put reapportionment squarely on the political agenda and created a political opening in Illinois where none had existed previously.

The initiative came not from the vanquished but from the victors. Governor Dwight Green took up the issue of apportionment of the U.S. House and the state legislature in his Biennial Message to the state legislature. On January 8, 1947, exactly one year after Urban Lavery filed suit against Governor Dwight Green, the governor called on the legislature to reform the districting process for the state's U.S. House seats and General Assembly. "In bringing this matter to your attention now, I urge you to find a real solution that may end this very unsatisfactory situation."[25] Governor Green expressed the shame the state had experienced by virtue of a lawsuit such as Colegrove's reaching the U.S. Supreme Court and laid the blame squarely on the state legislature for its failure to act since 1910. "While that Court refused to invalidate the present obsolete districts," the governor cajoled, "it called attention to the gross inequity which exists, and suggested that the matter might be properly considered by Congress itself."[26]

Within the year, the General Assembly of Illinois had created new U.S. House districts with approximately equal populations.

Beyond the particulars of that case, however, the Supreme Court's decision in *Colegrove v. Green* was read as the end of judicial intervention in legislative districting and representation. In Illinois, Colegrove's own attempt to challenge the state legislative apportionment foundered as the courts decided that they lacked jurisdiction. In Pennsylvania, a three-panel judge recognized the sever-

24. *Colegrove v. Barrett*, 330 U.S. 804 (1947).

25. "Biennial Message of Governor Dwight H. Green of Illinois Delivered before a Joint Session of the 65th General Assembly of Illinois at Springfield" (January 8, 1947), 16. Dwight H. Green, Speeches, 1946–1947, Illinois State Library, Springfield.

26. Ibid.

ity of the political inequalities stemming from the underrepresentation of Philadelphia County, but, citing Frankfurter's doctrine and the decision in *Colegrove v. Green*, they dismissed the suit for lack of jurisdiction.[27] With no more than a single sentence, the U.S. Supreme Court stated its agreement with the lower court.[28] In Oklahoma, the federal district court dismissed for want of jurisdiction a challenge to the constitutionality of that state's apportionment, which dated to statehood. The U.S. Supreme Court affirmed without dissent or comment.[29] State and federal courts took the plaintiffs' defeat in *Colegrove v. Green* as affirmation of Frankfurter's doctrine.

Usually, the courts dismissed such cases with little more than a comment that they "lacked jurisdiction" or they saw "no substantial federal question." But in two cases the liberals decided to fight.

In 1948, Chicago was once again the scene of the controversy. The very same district court that heard *Colegrove* was called on to judge the validity of the state law determining the number of signatures required to qualify for the ballot. State law required that any candidate for statewide office must receive two hundred signatures in each of fifty counties in order to be listed on the ballot, even though half of the state's residents live in one county. The Progressive Party failed to muster enough signatures in the downstate counties and, having failed to qualify by this standard, sued the state elections board, the governor, the attorney general, and the county election officers. The case was *MacDougall v. Green*. Once again, Governor Dwight Green found himself defender of political inequities and principles with which he personally disagreed.

The courts' decisions relied almost exclusively on Frankfurter's opinion in *Colegrove v. Green*. The district court dismissed the case for want of jurisdiction. The Supreme Court used the case to consolidate its new-found policy in electoral matters: "It would be strange indeed, and doctrinaire, for this court, applying such broad constitutional concepts as due process and equal protection, to deny a state proper diffusion of political initiative as between its thinly populated counties and those having concentrated masses. . . . The Constitution—a practical instrument of government—makes no such demands on states."[30]

The position of the minority on the Court solidified as well. Wiley Rutledge offered a concurring opinion in *MacDougall v. Green*, underscoring his judgment two years earlier that the courts could not offer a remedy. Indeed, in *MacDougall* the situation was even more dire—the election was only one week away.

27. *Remmey v. Smith*, 102 F. Supp. 708 (D. C. E. D. Pa).
28. 342 U.S. 916.
29. *Radford v. Gary*, 145 F. Supp. 541 (D. C. W. D. Okla); 352 U.S. 991.
30. *MacDougall v. Green*, 335 U.S. 281, 284 (1948).

Hugo Black, William Douglas, and Frank Murphy once again asserted their interpretation that the Fourteenth Amendment ensured equal political rights. "The theme of the constitution," Justice Black wrote, "is equality among citizens in the exercise of their political rights. The notion that one group can be granted greater voting strength than another is hostile to our standards for popular government."[31]

Two years later, Frankfurter's political thicket doctrine collided with the principles espoused in the white primary cases. *South v. Peters* challenged Georgia's county-unit rule. In primary elections for governor, U.S. senator, and other statewide offices, candidates vied for the unit-votes of each county. The largest counties had six votes each; the next thirty largest counties had four unit-votes; the remaining counties had two votes each. If the candidate won a plurality within a county, he or she received that county's vote. The result was to dilute the power of the Atlanta area—Fulton and DeKalb counties—and create inequities in which some voters in some counties counted hundred times more than voters in other counties.

The county-unit system had fueled racial tensions in Georgia following World War II. Herman Talmadge played the race card in the 1946 gubernatorial primary in order to appeal to conservative white Democrats, especially in rural counties. Talmadge lost the statewide vote to an insurgent candidate backed by unions and veterans groups, but he won a majority of counties and the unit-vote. Following Herman Talmadge's sudden death, Eugene Talmadge maneuvered the legislature to appoint him to replace his father. With the 1950 gubernatorial election approaching, unions, veterans groups, black leaders, and other activists pushed for elimination of the unit-rule as a violation of equal voting rights. The unit-rule was also one more battlement to breach in the assault on the tangle of election laws that sustained the southern political system. But unlike the white primary laws, the unit-rule affected all residents of a county, regardless of their race.

Justice William O. Douglas observed in his dissent to *South v. Peters* the obvious conflict between the Court's decisions in this instance and the white primary cases. "I suppose," he began, "that if a State reduced the vote of Negroes, Catholics, or Jews so that each got only one-tenth of a vote we would strike down that law." Georgia's unit-rule increased the weight of a rural vote many times over and devalued the vote of urban voters. The white primary cases ensured the equal voting rights of particular groups of voters—African Americans. *South v. Peters* asked for the extension of those rights to all persons. "I can see no way to save that classification under the Equal Protection Clause,"

31. 335 U.S. 281, 290 (1948).

Douglas concluded. "The creation by law of favored groups of citizens and the grant to them of preferred political rights is the worst of all discriminations under a democratic system of government."[32]

The Supreme Court, in a per curiam decision, dismissed the appeal with one sentence. Citing its decisions in *Wood*, *Colegrove*, and *MacDougall*, the opinion of the Court stated in matter-of-fact words: "Federal courts consistently refuse to exercise their equity powers in cases posing political issues arising from a state's geographical distribution of electoral strength among its political subdivisions."[33] The political thicket had become common wisdom; Frankfurter's philosophy had prevailed.

Colegrove allowed the courts to keep legislative politics at arm's length, but the decision had two critical weaknesses.

One fault was purely legal. Courts applied the doctrine expressed in Frankfuter's opinion widely during the 1940s and 1950s. The U.S. Supreme Court dismissed at least seven cases on appeal with little more than a comment during this time; federal and state courts set aside countless more challenges to legislative apportionments. But Frankfurter's opinion in *Colegrove* did not technically have the standing of a precedent. In order for an opinion to have the status of a precedent, a majority of a court must have approved the decision. This is the doctrine of *stare decisis*. There was, however, no decision to let stand. The Court had split three to three to one in the spring of 1946. Only three of the seven Justices serving at the time signed on to Frankfurter's opinion. In fact, four Justices—Black, Douglas, Murphy, and Rutledge—actually asserted that the courts did have jurisdiction.

Over the course of the decade or so after the *Colegrove* decision, the traditionalists on the Court certainly had their opportunities to establish a precedent. The liberal wing of the Court waned in the late 1940s. Justices Murphy and Rutledge died within months of each other in 1949, and President Truman chose two moderates to replace them, Tom C. Clark of Texas and Sherman Minton of Indiana. Shortly after Clark and Minton arrived, the Supreme Court decided the Georgia unit-rule case, *South v. Peters*. The new Justices sided with Frankfurter. Justices Black and Douglas were now a minority of two on questions concerning intervention in legislative districting. Frankfurter now had the votes he needed to make the "political thicket" doctrine a precedent, a standard that would bind other courts and the Supreme Court well into the future. Curiously, though, he never wrote such an opinion. The Justices merely asserted in *South v. Peters* and subsequent cases that because of *Colegrove* they

---

32. *South v. Peters*, 339 U.S. 276, 289 (1950).
33. 339 U.S. 276, 277.

lacked jurisdiction. The rationale and forceful argumentation expressed originally in Frankfurter's *Colegrove* decision resurfaced only when it was too late, in the minority opinion in *Baker v. Carr*.

Felix Frankfurter was a masterful jurist. It is striking that he did not cement the political-thicket doctrine in stare decisis. Perhaps this was just an oversight, or perhaps he had a false sense of the security of his position, or perhaps it was intentional. Given the emotional battle that the Justices waged over *Baker v. Carr*, Frankfurter's failure to establish in the late 1940s and early 1950s a ruling that would bind future courts appears in retrospect to be an immense strategic blunder. It left the opening Wiley Rutledge had hoped for.

The second weakness with the political-thicket doctrine was political. For all the Justices' desires to stay out of politics, Frankfurter's doctrine forced the Court to take sides in a deeply political matter. On one level, the political thicket argument allowed the Court to stay out of the issues involved in specific apportionment battles and thus to keep its political reputation intact. On a deeper level, however, the principle forced the Court to take sides. By deciding not to get involved, the Court effectively handed political power to those already in control in state legislatures.

By the early 1950s, the Court took Frankfurter's doctrine of the political thicket as given. Citing lack of jurisdiction, the Supreme Court turned back a dozen suits challenging legislative apportionments; the state and lower federal courts dismissed countless more. Yet the frequency of such suits did not abate.

Frankfurter's doctrine simply did not solve the underlying problem. Rural counties held tight to their legislative seats in the decades after World War II even as their populations continued their relative decline.[34] But political inequalities and pressure for some form of relief intensified as the population of urban and suburban communities continued to grow. Indeed, continued growth of metropolitan populations put pressure on cities and urban counties to provide more infrastructure, but counties lacked the fiscal capacity and mayors increasingly turned to the states for assistance. Legislatures became increasingly unrepresentative at a time when there were increasing demands for state governments to build roads, support public education, and expand public health and welfare systems.

During the 1940s and 1950s, the issue itself changed as its scope expanded to encompass the suburbs. In many states, the areas with the least representation were not the cities themselves but the communities just beyond the cities' limits: the suburbs. One could no longer argue that malapportionment served the societal interest of limiting the power of urban political machines or served to balance rural interests against an urban political bloc.

---

34. *Statistical Abstract of the United States, 1972*, U.S. Census Bureau, p. 17, table 17.

Political pressures to change the districting process in the states intensified. The National Municipal League, the National Association of Governors, the National Association of Mayors, the League of Women Voters, the American Federation of Labor, and other organizations interested in stronger urban legislative representation sought to change state legislative apportionment through the ballot, legislation, and legal action.[35] The legal and academic community became increasingly critical of the political thicket doctrine too, and editorials and scholarly articles increasingly called for judicial intervention.[36] Occasionally, these efforts yielded a significant state court cases, but the state courts, citing Frankfurter's opinion in *Colegrove,* chose to stay out of the legislative process.[37]

The courts, though, were not the true obstacles to equal population representation. Three political obstacles proved nearly insurmountable during the 1950s. First, most states required constitutional revision. In 1962, thirty-five state constitutions contained provisions that inevitably produced unequal district populations.[38]

Second, in many states, the electorate supported malapportionment. Between the *Colegrove* and *Baker* decisions, at least ten states voted on measures that sought to change the apportionment of legislative seats or to force the legislature to abide by existing requirements.[39] In all but Washington State, initiatives to make representation based on population in both chambers failed. Initiatives in Arkansas and Michigan put new, permanent boundaries in place in the 1950s, locking in place inequities in district populations. Indeed, it was the initiative process that gave California its "federal plan," the most inequitable representation in the entire country.[40]

Third, state legislatures continued to block efforts to draw new districts, even when it was their constitutional duty to do so. Twelve state legislatures in 1962 had significant malapportionment because they had failed or refused to comply with constitutional requirements of equal district populations at each

---

35. Ward E. Y. Elliott, *The Rise of Guardian Democracy.* (Cambridge, MA: Harvard University Press, 1974), 13–16.
36. See, for example Anthony Lewis, "Legislative Apportionment and the Federal Courts, "*Harvard Law Review* 71, no. 6. (April, 1958): 1057–98
37. See Justice Harlan's dissent in *Reynolds v. Sims*, 377 U.S. 533, 589–625.
38. Gordon Baker, *State Consitutions: Reapportionment.* (New York: National Municipal League, 1960), 1–26, 63–70; Robert McKay, *Reapportionment: The Law and Politics of Equal Representation.* (New York: Twentieth Century Fund, 1965), 459–71.
39. These are Arkansas, California, Colorado, Florida, Illinois, Michigan, Missouri, Oregon, Texas, Washington. Compiled by the authors.
40. Stephen Ansolabehere, James M. Snyder Jr., and Jonathan Woon, "Why the People of California Voted to Disenfranchise Themselves" (paper presented at the Annual Meeting of the American Political Science Association, Atlanta, GA, September 1999).

decennial census.[41] In 1956, the voters of Washington state approved through the initiative a new state legislative district map that would have created equal population representation. The state legislature promptly amended the initiative to keep the boundaries substantially the same as before the initiative.[42]

The courts were not the obstacles, then; they were the last resort. That fact was inescapable.

A BREECH IN TENNESSEE

The Tennessee legislature's refusal to reapportion in fifty years was symptomatic of broader sociological factors that affected all states and specific political factors at work in the state. As in many other states, the rapid growth of Tennessee's urban population at the end of the nineteenth century prompted those in power to keep their positions by not reapportioning.[43] Tennessee, however, was somewhat unusual in that a majority of its population lived in smaller towns and rural areas rather than in cities. More peculiar still, it was a coalition of urban and rural areas within the state legislature that blocked repeated attempts to reapportion the state legislature, as was called for in the state's constitution.

Paradoxically, state politics in Tennessee were dominated not just by a rural faction, but by a powerful urban machine that was led by a single individual. From 1932 to 1954, Edward Hull Crump controlled the sizable Memphis vote through political control of city and county jobs and by managing the African American vote. He was then able to leverage that vote into the controlling share within the statewide Democratic primaries.[44] Within the legislature, Crump forged an alliance with eastern Tennessee Republicans and rural Democrats to block his rivals within the legislature from the other cities—Chattanooga, Knoxville, and, especially, Nashville. East Tennessee Republicans gained safe U.S. House seats in exchange for their support of this arrangement, and rural Democrats were given disproportionate power within the state legislature.

41. Alabama, Indiana, Kansas, Kentucky, Michigan, Minnesota, Nebraska, Oklahoma, Tennessee, Washington, Wisconsin, and Wyoming were noted by Robert McKay, *Reapportionment: The Law and Politics of Representation* (New York: Twentieth Century Fund, 1965), 460–75, for their failures to reapportion in line with state constitutional requirements. Minnesota had slight reapportionment in 1959 under court order, but not enough to create districts with equal populations.
42. McKay, *Reapportionment*, 444.
43. The problem appeared much earlier in England. See Charles Seymour, *Electoral Reform in England and Wales: The Development of the Parliamentary Franchise, 1832–1885.* (New Haven: Yale University Press, 1915).
44. V. O. Key, *Southern Politics* (New York: Vintage, 1949), chap. 4.

Even though it was underrepresented, Memphis in this way was able to broker the power within the legislature.

Shortly after World War II, the Memphis machine suffered twin setbacks in statewide elections, setting the stage for the legal challenge to malapportionment. In 1948, Estes Kefauver defeated U.S. Senator Tom Stewart; then, four years later, Albert Gore Sr. defeated U.S. Senator K. D. McKellar. Although Kefauver and Gore by no means controlled the state's politics, they served as prominent critics of the state's Democratic establishment. While the Crump organization still brokered power within the state, it now had prominent rivals who held a different vision of civil and political rights. More than that, Kefauver and Gore were the inspiration for a new generation of reformers. That generational change accelerated, along with the disintegration of the political alignments within the state, when Boss Crump died in October 1954.

Reapportionment politics took a decided turn that year as well. In the fall of 1954, Haynes and Mayne Miller, brothers and partners in their own law firm in Johnson, Tennessee, decided to raise a legal challenge to the state's legislative apportionment. Mayne Miller had recently returned home from Nashville, where he had been employed as a lobbyist at the state legislature. Mayne had his sights set on a run for the U.S. House, but as a Democrat in eastern Tennessee he found the path effectively blocked by Republican dominance of eastern Tennessee House elections.[45] At his brother's suggestion, Haynes Miller had set upon the reapportionment of the state legislature as a new "project" for their law practice, and, with Ella V. Ross, the dean of women at East Tennessee State University, they formed an organization to bring suit against the state.[46]

Mayne Miller brought on board Tom Osborn, a personal friend and trial lawyer in Nashville, to partner with them on the case. Osborn's presence in the case brought strong ties to the city of Nashville, as well as a talented lawyer. Miller and Osborn had met in law school in the summer of 1948, when they became fast friends. Osborn was a gifted orator and a rising star among trial lawyers in Nashville.[47] After two years as assistant U.S. attorney, Osborn joined the firm of Armisted, Waller, Davis, and Lansden, which was closely tied to Senator McKellar and where Osborn developed a professional tie to the state's political establishment. His next position, though, would transform him.

45. Gene Graham, *One Man, One Vote: Baker v. Carr and the American Levellers* (Boston: Atlantic, Little Brown, 1972), 42.
46. Ibid, 44.
47. Harris Gilbert, interview by Stephen Ansolabehere, April 29, 2002.

Osborn left Armisted, Waller, Davis, and Lansden to become an attorney for the city of Nashville in 1953 and its new mayor, Ben West.

Osborn brought to his partnership with the Miller brothers and Ross a hard-nosed understanding of the effects of malapportionment, an understanding that shaped not only the present challenge but the subsequent effort on *Baker v. Carr*. Speaking to Gene Graham, who wrote the definitive history of the *Baker* case, Osborn recounted:

> Now, I knew of the existence of the problem prior to that [his service as city attorney], but I did not personally have any genuine interest until I had been exposed firsthand to the way in which the legislature divided the tax money. I realized there was inequitable apportionment but it meant nothing. As a matter of fact, prior to going to City Hall, if anything I approved it. I was more or less *status quo*. And it was not until I went over to City Hall and actually saw the abuse to which city dwellers were being subjected, moneywise, that I changed my feelings about it.[48]

With Osborn's ties to Nashville, the group now spanned eastern and central Tennessee. The organization fell short of a truly statewide effort. Memphis was notably absent. Ella Ross and the Millers cultivated support from one of the state's most prominent political leaders, Memphis Congressman and mayor Walter Chandler. They invited Chandler to bring the suit forward in February 1955. Chandler courteously declined the honor.[49]

Shortly before the Millers began their crusade, another member of the new generation in Tennessee politics began his career and was to join the push for reapportionment, but this time in the legislature. Maclin Paschall Davis Jr., a young attorney from a prominent legal family in Nashville, ran for one of six seats for state representative from Davidson County. Winning the Democratic primary at that time was tantamount to winning the election, and out of forty-six candidates on the Democratic Party ballot in August 1954, Maclin Davis came in sixth.

As a freshman legislator in January 1955, Maclin Davis received a lot of advice from his colleagues, especially the leaders of his party, that he "should be careful not to rock any boats" and above all "should be loyal to the Democratic Party."[50] But the freshman from Nashville was driven by more than the instinct to "go

---

48. Quoted in Graham, *One Man, One Vote*, 48–49.
49. Ibid., 51–53.
50. Maclin Davis, Personal communication with one of the authors, October 20, 2001, p. 3.

along." Davidson County deserved nine seats in the state house of representatives, not six, and the county deserved three seats in the state senate, not two:

> In spite of all of that advice, I knew it was my duty to represent the people of Davidson County and to do what I could to obtain for them the equal representation in the Legislature that they were guaranteed by the Constitution. Therefore, I devised a plan that I thought would result in increasing the representation of the under-represented counties and eventually result in the equal representation in the Legislature guaranteed by the Constitution. My plan was to introduce a bill to reapportion the House of Representatives by increasing the representation in the most under-represented counties by approximately one-third of the increase that would have given them equal representation and to apportion the House seats among the 99 new House districts in such as way that, if the Representatives from districts that would gain representation and the Representatives that would not be affected, would all vote for my reapportionment bill, the bill would receive affirmative votes of approximately 60% of the members of the House and Senate.[51]

Maclin Davis's confidence in the political self-interest of the affected areas proved misplaced. Not only did the proposed reapportionment fail, but the entire Shelby County delegation, the county that stood to gain the most, fell in line with the entrenched rural legislative leadership. By March 1955, the legislative process for reapportioning the state legislature once again ended without bringing the districts in line with the state's constitution.

Although his bill had died in the legislature, Davis found that his efforts had new life in the courts. Tom Osborn, Maclin Davis's friend from their years together at Armisted, Waller, Davis, and Lansden, invited Davis to join the legal challenge to the state's reapportionment. The death of Davis's bill proved a very important legal point—the state legislature refused to abide by the state constitution. Given this fact, it was important to act against the current legislature, but by March 1955 time was running out on the legislative session.

Unable to entice Walter Chandler to join the suit, the Millers chose Gates Kidd, an automobile dealer from Washington County and chair of their organization's finance committee, to lead the list of plaintiffs.[52] They struck out widely against the state establishment. They sued the state attorney general, George F. McCanless, the secretary of state, three members of the state elec-

---

51. Ibid., p. 4.
52. Graham, *One Man, One Vote*, 53–54.

tions board, thirty-seven members of the Republican state Primary Election Commission, thirty-six members of the Democratic state Primary Election Commission, and county election commissioners in Washington, Carter, and Davidson counties. On March 10, 1955, the Millers filed *Kidd v. McCanless* in Davidson County chancery court.[53]

The case seemed star-crossed from the beginning. It became unnecessarily complicated. One of the defendants from the list of Republican primary committee members, Hobart Atkins, persuaded his party to sue Governor Frank G. Clement and the state legislature in a cross-action.[54] This added a clearly partisan dimension to the suit, as well as putting the state legislature on both sides of the case. Atkins's action drew in the governor and the leadership of the state house and senate. The plaintiffs were no longer involved in a legal action against the attorney general and the legislature. Their fight had expanded to the entire state political establishment.[55]

To make matters worse, their legal strategy evidently backfired. The plaintiffs had chosen Davidson County chancery court as a venue on the belief that veteran chancellor Thomas A. Shriver Sr. might be a receptive judge. Three months before the case was to be heard, Shriver was elevated to the Tennessee Court of Appeals. Governor Frank Clement chose his replacement, thirty-three-year-old Thomas Wardlaw Steele. This looked like a particularly bad turn of events. Not only had Governor Clement selected Steele after the case was filed, but Steele had served as a loyal member of the Tennessee House of Representatives in 1949 and 1950, representing a district that encompassed two agricultural counties, Tipton and Lauderdale.[56]

Arguments before the court followed a familiar turn. The plaintiffs documented the extent of inequalities in the state. They argued that these inequities violated the state constitution, which provided for equal representation of population in the upper and lower chambers. The 1901 Apportionment Act, as Maclin Davis's briefs to the chancery court documented, violated this provision when the act was passed, and through the legislature's inaction the discrepancy from population representation had only worsened.[57] The state

53. Ibid, p. 57.; Maclin Davis, personal communication with author, October 20, 2001.
54. Graham, *One Man, One Vote*, 57–58; Maclin Davis, personal communication with author, October 20, 2001, p. 5.
55. Although Hobart Atkins's cross-filing complicated matters considerably, he would prove an invaluable part of the legal team that championed the cause of equal population representation in *Kidd* and, later, *Baker*.
56. Graham, *One Man, One Vote*, 60.
57. "Cross-Defendants' Memorandum Brief in Opposition to Demurrers," *Kidd v. McCanless*, Chancery Court for Davidson County, Tennessee, No. 75993, October 28, 1955; "Cross-Defendants' Supplemental Brief in Opposition to Demurrers," *Kidd v. McCanless*, Chancery Court for Davidson County, Tennessee, No. 75993, October 28, 1955.

attorney general echoed the state and federal courts: this was a political matter, and the courts lacked jurisdiction. A line of cases within the Tennessee state courts maintained that the courts have no jurisdiction to entertain actions against the other branches of government. Moreover, the attorney general argued, the U.S. Supreme Court had ruled in *Colegrove* that the courts cannot rule an apportionment act unconstitutional.

Chancellor Steele weighed the legal and political matters before him carefully. Tennessee's constitution stated explicitly that the legislative districts have equal populations, but no court had ever resolved what that meant or whether the state courts had the authority to weigh in on that matter. Beneath those questions lay a political minefield. If there was ever a situation in which an apportionment case would put the courts at odds with the other branches of government and the political establishment, this was it. Because of Hobart Atkins's cross-filing, the case pulled in the powerful party leaders I. D. Beasely and Jim Cummings, and further implicated Governor Clement.

Maclin Davis recalled years later that no one in Steele's courtroom on the day *Kidd* was argued could tell which way the chancellor would decide the case. Steele would later divulge that there were no legal and political ambiguities in his mind but one. The complaint clearly exposed the legislature's violation of the state constitution, and that persuaded him of the need to intervene—the establishment be damned. The only question was whether he could do so. He sequestered himself as he dissected the line of decisions at the federal and state levels that bore on the matter and thought through the implications for Kidd's suit.

Chancellor Steele shocked the Tennessee political establishment. In a tightly reasoned fifty-three-page opinion, he challenged the existing apportionment. He separated, as much as possible, the issues at hand from their political ramifications. "The Court's only concern is, has been, and must be to judge—whether or not any rights of the complaining parties have been, are, or may, in the future, be denied them or impaired by the defendants in the situation of which they complain."[58] Viewed from that perspective, he concluded that the 1901 act in fact violated the state's constitution and the rights of the plaintiffs "to equal suffrage in free and equal elections guaranteed them by the Constitution of Tennessee, and the equal protection of the laws guaranteed them by both the Constitution of Tennessee and the Fourteenth Amendment to the Constitution of the United States."[59] By extension, the sitting state legislature

58. "Chancellor's Opinion," *Kidd v. McCanless*, Chancery Court of Nashville, Tennessee, November 21, 1955, p. 2.
59. Ibid, p. 6.

was not a constitutionally elected body. Steele declared that any future elections held under the existing apportionment would be "without any legal authority whatever."[60] This was not Frankfurter's principle of restraint. Rather, Steele gave voice to the ideals expressed by Black, Murphy, and Douglas.

As for the difficult question of jurisdiction, Steele's decision was nothing short of revolutionary. He systematically applied the string of Tennessee cases on separation of powers that the attorney general had relied on to argue that the state courts lacked jurisdiction. Steele agreed with the attorney general that Hobart Atkins's suit against the governor and against the party leaders in the legislature violated existing state laws and legal decisions, but he felt that these cases did not apply to Maclin Davis's action against the attorney general and the legislature. Moreoever, Steele agreed with Davis's interpretation that the constitution did not rest the sole authority over districting with the legislature, but instead left open the possibility of executive and judicial involvement. This careful analysis of state law clearly left the courts room for action on the state legislature's apportionment. This led him to the federal cases, most notably *Colegrove*.

Steele challenged the very doctrine of judicial restraint. He discovered the weakness in the *Colegrove* decision, the trap that Rutledge had laid. "An examination of the decision in *Colegrove v. Green*, supra," the Chancellor wrote, "discloses that a majority of the court did not approve and sanction the above-quoted doctrine."[61] Rather, Steele noted that Rutledge, although agreeing with Justices Frankfurter, Reed, and Burton that the Court could not grant Colegrove's request, had in fact sided with Justices Black, Douglas, and Murphy on the general question of jurisdiction. Steele turned the *Colegrove* decision on its head. The vote for jurisdiction, he concluded, was four in favor of jurisdiction and three against.

Eroding Frankfurter's doctrine further, Steele cited a long list of state cases from across the country in which state courts had entertained suits on apportionment. In Pennsylvania, Indiana, Illinois, Kentucky, Kansas, Massachusetts, Michigan, New Jersey, Oklahoma, Colorado, and Missouri, the state courts had repeatedly weighed in on questions of state legislative districting. In the states' legal traditions, Steele saw the true statement of the role of the courts in the separation of powers. The legislature is not the sole expression of the popular will, he claimed. "The courts in interpreting and passing upon the validity of laws, and the acts of public officers under their authority, represent the sovereign will of the people just as much as does the Legislature which enacts the law in the first instance. The jurisdiction of the Court to thus act is one of

60. Graham, *One Man, One Vote*, 73–75; Maclin Davis, personal communication with author, October 20, 2001, p. 6.
61. "Chancellor's Opinion," *Kidd v. McCanless*, Chancery Court of Nashville, Tennessee, November 21, 1955, p. 20.

the settled principles of our State Jurisprudence. . . . [I]t is a sound principle which serves as a guaranty of the design and spirit of our institutions."[62]

Steele concluded his assessment of the question of jurisdiction by baldly contradicting Frankfurter's opinion in *Colegrove*: "That this is a novel matter for the courts of our State cannot be disputed. But in this Court's opinion, its jurisdiction of the controversy could be sustained on the general principles of reason and the fact that justice must be done. In addition, however, the Court has clear case authority as precedent for its decision."[63]

And with that, in Nashville's chancery, came the first breach of Frankfurter's doctrine.

The victory was short-lived. Upon appeal, the Tennessee Supreme Court reversed the chancellor's ruling, holding that the court did not have jurisdiction over legislative apportionment. Citing Frankfurter's opinion in *Colegrove*, the Tennessee Supreme Court toed the established line of thought.[64] In the months that followed, the plaintiffs, their lawyers, and other supporters of the legal action considered filing a federal lawsuit, but here the team split. As strong states' rights advocates, Mayne Miller and Maclin Davis further objected to an end run around the state supreme court on principle. Tom Osborn and Hobart Atkins pushed on. They appealed *Kidd v. McCanless* to the U.S. Supreme Court, only to have their writ of certiorari denied.[65]

Despite their failure, the Tennessee legal team differed from the group that brought *Colegrove*. Even though Colegrove himself tried to push the reform movement forward, the reason for doing so quickly vanished. The state legislature with cajoling by Governor Green at last passed a U.S. House districting map that had approximately equal populations. Kenneth Colegrove and his colleagues had succeeded in their immediate political goals. No such political relief was available to the Tennesseans.

But the Tennesseans had a more important asset—a legal victory and a revolutionary legal argument. Chancellor Steele's opinion had exposed the fundamental weakness in the political thicket doctrine: Rutledge, Murphy, Black, and Douglas had cast more votes for jurisdiction than Frankfurter, Reed, and Burton had cast against. The idea was too powerful to let pass. Hobart Atkins and Tom Osborn were soon to set out on a second assault on the state legislative apportionment. The expertise that the Millers assembled and Chancellor Steele's 53-page ruling provided the core for a nearly identical, but ultimately successful, legal challenge two years later: *Baker v. Carr*.

62. Ibid., 22.
63. Ibid., 23.
64. *Kidd v. McCanless*, 292 S.W.2d 40 (Tenn. 1956).
65. *Kidd v. McCanless*, 352 U.S. 920 (1956), *cert. denied.*

6

Into the Thicket

Kidd v. McCanless was ahead of its time. Two years ahead, to be precise. The U.S. Supreme Court decided not to hear the case in the spring of 1956, but even at that moment the High Court was on the cusp of dramatic changes, both in personnel and in philosophy.

In 1953, President Eisenhower made the first of his five Supreme Court appointments—Chief Justice Earl Warren. Under Earl Warren's leadership, the liberals on the Court gained new life. Warren had been a popular Republican governor in the State of California and was often mentioned as a possible GOP presidential candidate. Once on the Court, Warren allied himself closely with Hugo Black and William O. Douglas, especially on questions of civil and political rights. Warren also guided the Court to take on the state political and social institutions, especially the complex of laws and practices that created racial segregation in the American South. In 1954, a unanimous Supreme Court in *Brown v. Board of Education* reversed the long-standing precedent that "separate, but equal" facilities offered equal protection and ordered the states to desegregate "with all deliberate speed." This was the beginning, according to legal scholars, of the Warren Court—a fifteen-year period in which the U.S. Supreme Court radically expanded civil and political rights and the authority of the courts as a check on legislative and executive power in America.

Dwight Eisenhower eschewed political conflict, but his hand-picked Chief Justice had a nose for it, beginning with *Brown v. Board of Education*. Desegregation dragged Eisenhower into tense and at times violent confrontations with southern political leaders. Southern communities refused to desegregate their

schools, their public transit systems, their government offices, their restaurants—
virtually everything. The President even had to mobilize the National Guard
just to force desegregation of schools. School desegregation, though, was just
the beginning of the tumultuous years of the Warren Court. On matters ranging
from the rights of the accused to the treatment of the poor to pornography and
free speech to the separation of church and state, the Supreme Court under Earl
Warren's leadership established a liberal conception of the rights of individuals
against society and government. "Impeach Earl Warren" read billboards around
the country protesting the Court's intervention in a wide range of matters from
race to religion. Eisenhower would later describe his appointment of Earl Warren as the single largest mistake of his administration.

A close second was his appointment of William J. Brennan Jr. Eisenhower
picked Brennan to replace Justice Sherman Minton on the Court in 1956. Like
Warren, Brennan was by all accounts a good Republican and a moderate. Republican governors in New Jersey has appointed Brennan to the superior court
and then to the New Jersey State Supreme Court, where he shone as a jurist.
Once on the U.S. Supreme Court, though, Brennan proved a strong ally of Earl
Warren. Every Monday, first thing in the morning, Brennan and Warren met
privately in Warren's chambers to discuss the issues before the Court. What
transpired in those private meetings is unknown, but the coordination between the two Justices produced one of the closest relationships in the modern
history of the Court. As one of Brennan's clerks described it, "in their voting
records, there wasn't a crack of sunlight between Brennan and the Chief."[1]

It takes four votes among the Justices to grant a writ of certiorari, a request
to have the Supreme Court hear a case. Brennan's ascension to the Court alongside Warren, Black, and Douglas meant that on questions of political rights
those four votes were now in place. The liberals on the Court did not yet have a
majority; they had to rely on one of the other Eisenhower or Truman
appointees—especially Potter Stewart, Charles Whittaker, or Tom Clark. But
with the appointment of William Brennan, the liberals could at least bring matters before the Court. In a private memo to Brennan in 1962, Roy Schotland,
one of the Justice's two clerks, wrote, "Since the end of the 1957 term, it had
been fairly clear that soon the Court was going to take a legislative apportionment case and test the vitality of *Colegrove v. Green*."[2] That challenge would
come from the same state, and indeed from nearly the same set of plaintiffs, as
the case for which the Court had just denied certiorari.

1. Roy Schotland, interview by Stephen Ansolabehere, September 9, 2004.
2. Memorandum from Roy Schotland to William J. Brennan, from Roy A. Schotland, *Notes*, in Opinions of
William Brennan Jr.—October term 1961, in the personal files of Stephen Ansolabehere.

THE ORIGINS OF *BAKER*

Given the political history of Tennessee, it is significant that *Baker v. Carr* originated not in Nashville or eastern Tennessee, but in Memphis. In the two years following Boss Crump's death, the political organization and alliances that he had constructed unraveled completely, and without them Shelby County's political influence within the state declined. I. D. Beasely, from rural Sevier County in central Tennessee, consolidated power within the Tennessee House of Representatives with a strongly disciplined rural Democratic bloc vote and by playing the cities off one another. Beasely, as much as any other politician, took Crump's place as the state's power broker. Memphis now found itself in the same political position as its rival, Nashville, and that meant that Memphis also found that it now received nowhere near its fair share of state funds and jobs.

David Harsh, the chairman of the Shelby County Commission, saw the political bind that the county had put itself in. By blocking past attempts at reapportionment, such as Maclin Davis's bill, Shelby County guaranteed that it got less from the state than it deserved, and by 1957 Harsh and his colleagues in Memphis were eyeing the same path that Mayne Miller had taken—a legal challenge to the state's 1901 apportionment act. The opportunity came the following year when Frankfurter's opinion in *Colegrove* suffered its first setback in a federal court.

Minnesota had grown into the same political conundrum as Tennessee. The state had not changed the boundaries of its House and Senate districts since 1921. Even in a heavily agricultural state like Minnesota, the farm population had fallen sharply, while the population of the state's largest cities had ballooned with the postwar migration.[3] Shipping and mining companies took root in Duluth to exploit the state's mineral-rich Iron Range. Heavy manufacturing had moved to the south side of St. Paul and North Minneapolis. And old-line industries and companies such as Pillsbury and General Mills flourished throughout the mid-century. The House and Senate districts that represented these industrial areas grew rapidly in population, but the rural-dominated state legislature refused to increase the number of city seats, especially where there were large numbers of union workers.

Legislative districts in St. Paul and Minneapolis often had five to ten times as many people as districts in neighboring counties did. A credible run for a legislative seat in an urban area was a costly and difficult task. Dan Magraw, an auto mechanic at Ford Motor Company in St. Paul and a union employee, had

---

3. According to the U.S. Census, 34 percent of Minnesota's population lived on farms on 1920. That fell to 23 percent by 1950.

the ambition to represent the 42nd House District of St. Paul. After an unsuccessful bid to represent the sprawling district, Dan Magraw and his friend Frank Farrell brought suit against the State of Minnesota and Secretary of State Donovan to reapportion the state legislature.

Magraw v. Donovan attacked the political question directly with a mix of legal arguments based on the Fourteenth Amendment and an analysis of the demographics of the state legislature developed by two political scientists. On July 10, 1958, a federal panel of the district court ruled that the courts did have jurisdiction over the apportionment of the Minnesota state legislature "because of the federal constitutional issue asserted."[4] They did not impose at-large elections or a particular districting plan, but instead struck down the existing districts and required the legislature to create new boundaries. How the courts would resolve the situation in Minnesota was a wide-open matter.

David Harsh had followed the Minnesota case closely. He saw in it the prospect for relief for Memphis. Since *Brown v. Board of Education,* the Court had embraced a broader interpretation of the Fourteenth Amendment than that expressed in *Colegrove,* and the Minnesota decision had reopened the apportionment question. *Kidd v. McCanless* was just two years past, but the time seemed ripe to challenge the state's apportionment.

The most telling indicator of the change in the state's politics was the change of heart of one of Memphis's leading citizens: Congressman and former mayor Walter Chandler. Three years earlier, Chandler had spoken for Memphis and declined Ella Ross's appeal to join her, Mayne Miller, Tom Osborn, and Maclin Davis's suit. When Harsh initiated legal action late in 1958, he retained Chandler to represent the county, and in May 1959 it was Walter Chandler who filed *Baker v. Carr.*

While the facts of *Baker* were not appreciably different from those of *Kidd,* the legal strategy was. From the beginning, the goal was to win a federal appeal. Walter Chandler realized that any state decision would produce a conflict with existing legal rulings. Any ruling either would contradict the Tennessee Supreme Court's 1956 decision in *Kidd v. McCanless* or would conflict with the Minnesota Federal District Court's 1958 decision in *Magraw v. Donovan.* Such contradictory rulings would virtually guarantee a ruling by the federal appeals courts, perhaps even the U.S. Supreme Court.[5]

In terms of the details of the case, Chandler turned to the general strategy that the Millers and Ella Ross had used in bringing *Kidd*: build a statewide, nonpartisan coalition. Indeed, Chandler decided to construct the *Baker* case around the same group that brought *Kidd.* He invited the Millers, Maclin

4. *Magraw v. Donovan,* 163 F. Supp. 184, 177 F. Supp. 803.
5. Harris Gilbert, interview by Stephen Ansolabehere, April 29, 2002.

Davis, Tom Osborn, and Hobart Atkins to join the case. Osborn and Atkins jumped at the opportunity. They set out to build the constitutional case around the framework that Chancellor Thomas Steele had laid out in his opinion.

They had to establish, first, that the state legislature refused to craft districts in compliance with the state constitution. Chandler persuaded the Shelby delegation in the state legislature to introduce an apportionment bill strikingly similar to that of Maclin Davis in 1955 and again in 1957. That bill and another apportionment bill were defeated in the state senate in 1959; the house never bothered to take them up.[6]

Walter Chandler also brought in legal expertise for making the appeal. He retained a noted lawyer, Charles Rhyne, to aid in the construction of the case and to take over the case once it reached the federal level. The choice of Rhyne had a political dimension. Rhyne was a close friend of Lee Rankin, Eisenhower's solicitor general. Rhyne's ties to the administration, it was hoped, would improve the chances that the U.S. attorney general would side with the plaintiffs.

The legal team took a page from the Minnesota case, too. Magraw and Farrell enlisted two political science professors from North Dakota State University to provide statistical and historical data regarding the discrepancies in district populations. Osborn enlisted the City of Nashville. Mayor Ben West had assigned the city auditor and a young attorney, Harris Gilbert, to compile a report on the discrepancies in district populations in the state.[7] The audit went much further and documented the corresponding discrepancies in the distribution of state money to county and local governments, especially for schools and highways. Gilbert also assembled an analysis by the state historian showing a pattern of discrimination and speeches by James Cummings showing the intention to discriminate against urban areas.[8] Finally, West provided one other resource lacking in *Kidd*: money. At his request, the City Council authorized $25,000 for the legal defense, enough to defray most of the costs of the challenge. With this commitment, Chattanooga and Knoxville joined the case as well.

The case proceeded quickly. In December 1959, the U.S. district court unsurprisingly held for the defendants in *Baker v. Carr*. The district court ruled that although the state legislature failed to comply with the constitution, the courts do not have jurisdiction over such political matters. An appeal to the U.S. Supreme Court was now set. In November 1960, the U.S. Supreme Court voted to grant certiorari. Justices Hugo Black, William O. Douglas, and

6. Gene Graham, *One Man, One Vote: Baker v. Carr and the American Levellers* (Boston: Atlantic, Little Brown, 1972), 136.
7. Gilbert, interview.
8. Ibid.

William Brennan, as well as Chief Justice Earl Warren, voted to place the case on the Court's docket. The conflict between the Minnesota federal district court decision in *Magraw v. Donovan* and the Tennessee Supreme Court in *Baker v. Carr* raised a federal issue.

The legal strategy in setting up the case fell into place in 1959; but just as the case gelled, the plaintiffs immediately faced three political setbacks.

First, the Minnesota state legislature agreed to draw new district boundaries that would accommodate in part the ruling in *Magraw v. Donovan*. Thus the conflict between the Minnesota and Tennessee courts became less pressing. In addition, the fact that the Minnesota legislature was willing to reapportion appeared to underscore Frankfurter's contention that these matters could be addressed in the legislatures.[9]

Second, the morass of school integration cases following on *Brown v. Board of Education* buttressed Frankfurter's view that the courts were ill equipped to deal with social problems. School integration throughout the country required extensive intervention and management by the courts. It was not a political thicket, but a thicket nonetheless. Chandler's team realized that for their case to be successful they would have to show that equal representation of population could be interpreted and enforced easily, and with a minimum of court oversight.[10]

Third, Richard Nixon lost the presidential election in 1960. By the time their case reached the Supreme Court, the Republicans would no longer hold the Solicitor General's office. Thus Charles Rhyne's ties to the solicitor general were of no value. Further, it was unclear how the new Kennedy administration would view the case, but the prospects looked dim, considering that *Baker* was widely viewed as a matter of states' rights and was, thus, opposed in principle by many within the Democratic Party. Through the winter of 1960, the team scrambled to find an inroad to the new administration.

It was at this point that Tom Osborn called his friends John Jay Hooker and John Seigenthaler in the new administration to arrange a visit to Washington, D.C., to meet the new attorney general. On February 3, 1961, Tom Osborn, Harris Gilbert, and John Jay Hooker crashed the offices of the Solicitor General. Their meeting with Archibald Cox happened more by accident than design. Hooker had gotten them an appointment with Attorney General Robert F. Kennedy, but Kennedy was detained in other meetings. While killing some time, Hooker took them by the Solicitor General's office to see John Seigenthaler. Seigenthaler, who had reached prominence as a reporter for the *Nashville Tennesseean* covering Senator McLellan's investigations of unions

9. Ibid.
10. Ibid.

and organized crime in Tennessee, had known Hooker from Nashville, but the two had become particularly close while working together on the Kennedy campaign. Organized crime was a particular concern of Robert F. Kennedy, and Siegenthaler was an ideal person to work with the attorney general's right-hand man, Solicitor General Archibald Cox.[11]

As Harris Gilbert later recalled, "Cox really amazed us. He denied that he had any prior knowledge of our case, but he started immediately with questions that cut right to the core of the matter." The meeting went on late into the afternoon as Cox plumbed many of the angles of the case with Osborn and Gilbert. By the time the meeting ended, Bobby Kennedy had already gone home. They would have to wait to hear whether the administration would support them with an amicus brief, and they would never have the opportunity to put their case before the Attorney General. But after their meeting with Archibald Cox, Tom Osborn and Harris Gilbert were satisfied that they had a full hearing.[12]

Cox did want the administration to take the case. He shared the plaintiffs' vision of the political rights embodied in the Fourteenth Amendment, and he understood where the President's preferences lay. After all, as a U.S. senator, John F. Kennedy labeled malapportionment and its attendant consequences "the shame of the states." When they finally did have a chance to meet two weeks later about the apportionment case, Robert Kennedy let his solicitor general use his own judgment.

Cox offered more than just an amicus brief in support of the case. The young solicitor general decided to use the privilege of his office and argue the complaint before the Court. This would be the first case the administration presented to the Court. The personal stakes for Cox were greater still. He would have to mount a challenge to one of the most important legal doctrines developed by Felix Frankfurter, his teacher and mentor from Harvard Law School.

GETTING ON THE DOCKET

Baker v. Carr at last reached the U.S. Supreme Court in the fall of 1960. The Justices decided to hold the case pending their decision in *Gomillion v. Lightfoot*, which involved racial gerrymander of the political boundaries of the city of Tuskegee, Alabama. The Court ruled unanimously in that case that the drawing of political boundaries to dilute the votes of black citizens violated those voters' constitutional rights. None other than Justice Frankfurter wrote

11. John Seigenthaler, interview by Stephen Ansolabehere, April 30, 2002.
12. Gilbert, interview.

the opinion, and he went to great lengths to distinguish this case from political districting in general, as this case involved the voting rights of blacks as guaranteed in the Fifteenth Amendment to the Constitution. A week after the Court handed down its unanimous decision overturning the lower court in the Tuskegee case, it turned to *Baker*.

Simply getting on the Court's docket, though, proved difficult. Every Friday, the nine Justices of the Warren Court met in conference to discuss the cases before it and to choose which of the many appeals they would hear. On November 21, 1960, the conference considered whether to note probable jurisdiction on the Tennessee apportionment case.[13]

The Tennesseans' suit appeared dead at that first meeting on the case. History weighed against them. A memo from one of Justice Tom Clark's clerks in the 1960 term summarized the situation: "in *Kidd v. McCanless* . . . this Court has once already refused to review a dismissal (by the Tennessee Supreme Court) of a suit brought upon the same grounds. I suggest you Affirm [the lower court decision]."[14] That, evidently, was reason enough. A majority of the Court chose not to hear the complaint at all. Five Justices—Tom Clark, Felix Frankfurter, John Marshall Harlan, Potter Stewart, and Charles Whittaker—voted against bringing the case forth. Four Justices—Hugo Black, William Brennan, William Douglas, and Earl Warren—voted to note probable jurisdiction and to hear oral arguments.

Fortunately for Osborn and his colleagues, the Supreme Court's rules allow for some leeway. In order to protect minority rights, probable jurisdiction or a writ of certiorari requires support from a minimum of four Justices (the Rule of Four), not a majority. Were it not for the Rule of Four, the Tennesseans' suit would have ended at that first conference and the lower court's decision would have stood.

The 5 to 4 vote against hearing the case, though, sent a strong signal about the likely outcome. Once a person has taken a stand among his or her peers, it becomes especially hard to change from that position. Felix Frankfurter had the votes to hold the line on his opinion in *Colegrove*. Richard S. Arnold, one of Justice Brennan's two law clerks for the 1960 term, wrote in his diary that day, "Probable juris[diction] noted in *Baker v. Carr*, No. 103. . . . Four votes to note: the Chief, HLB, WOD, and the boss. They want to overrule *Colegrove*. The boss doubts they will have the votes. So do I."[15] Oral argument was set for April

---

13. A more common way that cases reach the Court is through a grant of a writ of certiorari. Probable jurisdiction involves a direct appeal to the Court owing to the presence of substantial constitutional questions.
14. Memorandum from "MTM" dated 7/26/60, Thomas C. Clark Papers, University of Texas.
15. Quoted in Anthony Lewis, "In Memoriam, William J. Brennan, Jr.," *Harvard Law Review* 111 (November 1997): 29. The Chief is Chief Justice Earl Warren, HLB is Black, WOD is Douglas, and the boss, as his clerks affectionately called him, is Brennan.

19, 1961. The plaintiffs, and the liberal Justices on the Court, had five months
to figure out how to win over the critical fifth vote.

For all of the political difficulties the Tennessee lawyers faced, theirs was the
ideal case. Taken narrowly, *Baker v. Carr* presented only one question for the
Court: does the judiciary have the authority to decide cases involving apportionment of the legislature?

A three-judge panel of the federal district court had not reached its decision
on the basis of the merits of the case. The three-judge panel did address the
substance of the claims, and it agreed with the complaint. Tennessee's state
constitution clearly required that the state house and senate districts have populations as equal as practically possible without dividing county lines. The existing legislative districts did not comply with those requirements. The
legislative districting map lacked a rational basis. The state legislature had
failed in its duty for sixty years. The lower court steered clear of the question of
how inequities should be remedied.

Rather, the district court, citing the Tennessee Supreme Court's decision in
Kidd v. McCanless and Felix Frankfurter's opinion in *Colegrove v. Green*, concluded that courts lack jurisdiction over legislative districting. They chose to
stay out of the matter for that reason alone.

Other apportionment cases coming up through the appellate and state
courts—from New York, Minnesota, Michigan, Oklahoma, Indiana, and New
Jersey—presented compound legal issues and arose in more complicated political circumstances. One such case reached the U.S. Supreme Court just a few
months after *Baker*, in the spring of 1961.

August Scholle, the leader of the Michigan State Federation of Labor, seven
years after failing to pass an initiative requiring equal population districts, decided to sue the state to force the issue. Detroit and its surrounding cities and
towns received many fewer seats in the state senate than they would have received under an equal population apportionment. The Detroit area, heart of
the automotive industry, also has a very high density of union workers, and
underrepresentation of Michigan's cities muted labor's clout in the state legislature and diluted the Democratic vote. Scholle sought to restrain the secretary
of state, James Hare, from conducting elections using the existing districts because, Scholle's case argued, they violated the Fourteenth Amendment requirement of equal protection.

The first complication in Scholle's case involved the politics of the state. Unlike Tennessee, the people of Michigan also had alternative avenues through
which they could enact laws and constitutional amendments, most notably the
ballot. In fact, a majority of voters in the state of Michigan had approved the
state's existing apportionment in the 1952 general election. That plan provided

for representation of people in the lower chamber and of geographic areas in the upper chamber. Also on the ballot that year was an initiative sponsored by the Michigan Federation of Labor to require equal population votes in both chambers. That proposal failed to gain a majority of the votes in the 1952 election.[16] August Scholle's suit challenged a popularly approved law.

Scholle's case also faced a trio of legal difficulties. First, no court had ever interpreted the Fourteenth Amendment to require equal population districts. The Michigan Supreme Court, in its ruling for Hare, concluded that nothing in the Fourteenth Amendment's equal protection clause "prohibits a State from establishing senate electoral districts by geographic areas drawn generally along county lines which result in substantial inequality of voter representation favoring thinly populated areas as opposed to populous ones."[17] Second, unlike Tennessee, the Michigan legislature was in compliance with its own constitution, as amended in 1952. Third, the Michigan case coupled the question of jurisdiction and the question of remedy. The Michigan court concluded not only that there was no violation of equal protection, but that even if there were the courts could offer no remedy. Courts can merely decide the constitutionality and legality of legislative actions; they cannot craft new laws, and they cannot leave the state without a way to choose its legislature.

The U.S. Supreme Court, were it to deal directly with the issues in *Scholle v. Hare*, would have had to grapple with the standards for representation, as well as the question of jurisdiction. Even among the liberals on the Warren Court in 1962, there was no clear agreement about the implications of equal protection for a state's legislative apportionment practices. What did equality require? Could factors other than population come into play, such as income or administrative and political boundaries? Must equality apply to both chambers? Should the courts become involved if there were other avenues through which reapportionment could occur and those other avenues had been used successfully? Consensus existed on none of these questions.

Archibald Cox saw each of these difficulties with the Michigan case. In the spring and summer of 1961, August Scholle's attorney, Theodore Sachs, corresponded with the Solicitor General, hoping to gain the government's support of the Michigan case. Archibald Cox refused. "Your case does seem much more difficult than the Tennessee case," Cox wrote to Sachs in September 1961, "and we thought it necessary to acknowledge that the claim that the Fourteenth Amendment was violated by malapportionment by only one House of a

16. The "balanced senate apportionment," as it was referred to, received 1,269,807 votes for and 975,518 votes against. The vote in the Detroit area was overwhelmingly against, but the remainder of the state even more strongly favored the plan.
17. *Scholle v. Hare*, 360 Mich. 91, 104 N. W. 2d 110 (1960).

bicameral legislature was much harder to maintain than where the malapportionment affects both Houses. . . . [T]he main point was to persuade the Supreme Court that such issues are justiciable and canvassing the differences in degree among the several possible situations appeared to be an essential part of the argument." Years later, Sachs wrote critically of the Solicitor General's unwillingness to take on Scholle's case and his approach in the Tennessee case. "I thought that Professor Cox took an unnecessarily cautious—and counterproductive—position."[18]

Had the Michigan case reached the U.S. Supreme Court first, a very different history likely would have unfolded. Potter Stewart, the pivotal vote in *Baker v. Carr*, expressed in conference his support for the electoral arrangements in Michigan. For him, such "balanced legislative" representation did not violate the guarantee of equal protection, and he saw no guarantee of exact equality as argued by Scholle and his attorney, Theodore Sachs. He would not have re-versed the decision of the Michigan Supreme Court.

The circumstances in Tennessee differed considerably from those in Michigan. The state constitution required equal population representation; the state legislature had failed to comply with that rule for over half a century; tremendous inequalities in legislative district populations had arisen; and there was no other recourse but the courts. Even still, the liberals lacked the votes.

BEFORE THE COURT

Archibald Cox saw the problems the case faced as clearly as anyone else involved. The Solicitor General knew the politics of the Court extremely well. He had argued numerous cases before the Court, he had served as a clerk, and he had close relations with some of its members, especially Justice Frankfurter. He understood the force of the 5-to-4 vote against probable jurisdiction, and that getting a fifth vote for that position would be extremely difficult, perhaps impossible.

Potter Stewart and Charles Evans Whittaker looked like the only conceivable converts, and the chances of getting either seemed remote. Tom Clark had already weighed in on this matter when he sided with majority in *South v. Peters*. Felix Frankfurter would surely stand his ground, as would John Marshall Harlan, an Eisenhower appointee who was closely allied with Frankfurter. Charles Whittaker was the wild card. His concurring opinion in *Gomillion v. Lightfoot*—decided on

18. Theodore Sachs, "*Scholle v. Hare*—The Beginnings of 'One Person–One Vote,'" *Wayne Law Review* 33, no. 5 (1987): 1617.

November 14, 1960, just one week before the jurisdiction vote on *Baker*—asserted a broad right to "the same vote" based on the Fourteenth Amendment. But Whittaker almost always followed Frankfurter's lead. Potter Stewart was difficult to read. He had not participated in legislative apportionment cases, except for *Gomillion v. Lightfoot.* In the Tuskegee case, he had embraced the liberal position and sided with the Court in protecting black voting rights. But Justice Stewart's judicial philosophy was also profoundly conservative: he held a deep commitment to precedent. It was unclear how he would read the string of opinions from *Wood v. Broom* to *Colegrove* to *Kidd.*

Walter Chandler's legal team and the solicitor general both saw Stewart as their best hope, but they took different approaches in trying to win the Justice over. The Tennessee lawyers followed the script laid out by Chancellor Thomas Wardlaw Steele in *Kidd.* They emphasized the extent to which the Tennessee apportionment violated the voting rights of the eleven plaintiffs and focused on the facts of the case. On the question of jurisdiction, they argued, the Court repeatedly ruled on such matters, even in *Colegrove.* Archibald Cox offered a much more nuanced argument. The government asked not for a remedy or even a judgment about whether the plaintiffs' voting rights had been violated. Rather, the Court need only to clarify that judicial remedy was possible under appropriate circumstances. This was the smallest possible movement in the law. Even that point would be difficult to win.

Oral arguments began on April 19, 1960. They exceeded three hours and the better parts of two days, an unusually long hearing for the Supreme Court.

Charles Rhyne rose first to present the plaintiffs' arguments. The stately Virginian began succinctly and forcefully: "This is an individual voting rights case brought by eleven qualified voters in the state of Tennessee. In their complaint, they allege that . . . their voting rights have been diluted and debased to the point of nullification. A United States District Court, a three judge court, dismissed their complaint on the grounds that it had no power to protect their voting rights on the basis of the Fourteenth Amendment. We contend that decision was in error."[19]

Rhyne then offered the first of four broad arguments: the facts of the case showed gross violation of voting rights in the state and violation of the state's constitution. Rhyne cited various figures demonstrating the inequalities in representation in the state. Twenty votes in Shelby County carried the same weight as one vote in each of several rural counties. Thirty-seven percent of the people in the state elect twenty of thirty-three senators. Forty percent of the

19. Audio recordings of the oral arguments before the Court are available through Oyez, www.oyez.org. Specifically, consult The Oyez Project, *Baker v. Carr,* 369 U.S. 186 (1962), www.oyez.org/cases/1960-1969/1960/1960_6/.

people elect sixty-three of ninety-nine House members. One-third of the people control two-thirds of the legislators.

Eleven minutes into the presentation came the first question from the bench. Potter Stewart sought clarification of how the state apportionment law actually treated counties. Did each county receive at least one seat? Could counties be divided? Justice Whittaker pushed further on the representation of counties, leading up to the question of remedy: "You don't contend, I would suppose, then that there has to be exact equality?" "No, no," replied Rhyne, "we don't insist on exact mathematical equality but as near as may be as practical." John Marshall Harlan weighed in: "Didn't the three-judge panel conclude that there was nothing the courts could do about it?" "Yes. Yes. That is true."

Rhyne moved on to a second broad theme: all avenues of state relief are closed. It is impossible to get "those who have usurped this power to ever let it loose." He distributed to the justices a brief on the distribution of the state's education and highway funds prepared by Harris Gilbert, an attorney for the city of Nashville. The brief detailed the state legislature's per capita expenditures on public education and on the gasoline tax for highways and their relationship to representation. The underrepresented counties received much more per person from these funds. Gilbert prepared his brief to show that the individual plaintiffs had suffered harm as a result of malapportionment. Rhyne gave the facts and figures a slightly different spin. They demonstrated that a majority in the legislature had no interest in overturning the existing apportionment act. Potter Stewart tried to turn the numbers on their head: "Would the urban areas dominate the legislature under a new plan?" Rhyne hemmed and hawed. The discussion that ensued again returned to the difficult and sensitive question of what remedy the courts should endorse and whether the legislature had the ultimate say in these matters. Chief Justice Warren changed the subject with a strikingly hostile question that challenged the public financing data: "Are these expenditures tied to representation, or are other factors involved?" Rhyne replied: "Other factors are involved. . . . But we're not asking for any money back. We're just showing how they have favored themselves."

The attorney for the plaintiffs continued through the interruptions. The state legislature had repeatedly voted down bills to reapportion itself. There is no initiative and referendum in the state, and any constitutional amendment must first go through the state legislature. Justice Frankfurter continued to cast doubts on Rhyne's line of argumentation: "How does congressional apportionment work in the state? Does the state legislature do that adequately and fairly?" Rhyne passed the question to Walter Chandler, who had represented Memphis in the U.S. House of Representatives. Chandler interjected that there is no problem with congressional apportionment in the state; the legislature does manage to create nearly equal U.S. House districts.

Rhyne picked up a third line of argument: the federal courts have jurisdiction. He first focused on the interpretation of the Fourteenth Amendment, the powers vested in the judiciary under the Voting Rights Acts of 1957 and 1959, and the decisions of the Court itself. The Supreme Court, in *Smiley v. Holm*, *Wood v. Broom*, and other congressional apportionment cases, repeatedly asserted its jurisdiction over apportionment. It did not always side with the plaintiffs, but it did hear their appeals and make decisions on the merits of the cases.

One-half hour into his presentation, Rhyne at last confronted *Colegrove v. Green*. He characterized it as a frequently "misunderstood decision." There were audible stirrings among the Justices.

In *Colegrove*, Rhyne pointed out, four of the seven Justices present had voted that the Court had jurisdiction. Justice Rutledge had voted with Justices Black, Douglas, and Murphy that the Supreme Court could rule on questions of legislative apportionment. Rutledge broke with his liberal brethren on whether they could grant equity—the election was simply too soon for the Illinois legislature to act, and holding an election at-large would have been worse than keeping the existing districts. Rhyne went on to distinguish *Wood v. Broom*, the Michigan U.S. House case in which the Court refused to impose a solution, as that involved a federal law, not a state constitution.

Frankfurter stung back: "Are you saying that Congress can create second-class voting rights? Wouldn't that be unconstitutional?" Rhyne retreated: "I'm not agreeing with your opinion, I'm only distinguishing it from this case. In so far as *Colegrove* is concerned, I'm just saying it voted 4-3 for jurisdiction."

Finally, Rhyne presented his fourth line of argument: many remedies are available to the state and the courts. He listed the steps that the courts and the legislatures might take to secure a remedy. Supporting his case that the legislature would act, Rhyne cited New Jersey and Minnesota, where the courts required legislative action and the legislatures complied. Frankfurter kept up his assault: "You might want to cite Illinois [which had reapportioned after failing to secure the Court's support]." "They haven't done too well," Rhyne shot back. "They've done as well as these other states you've listed," Frankfurter replied. Illinois's experience was telling for Frankfurter's position. After *Colegrove*, Governor Green successfully pressured the state legislature to reapportion not only the U.S. House districts at stake in that suit but the state legislative districts as well. A state could reapportion itself more equitably without judicial intervention and oversight. The question of remedy, though, was essential to Rhyne's case. He had to show that many plausible actions were available to the courts; the state legislatures and courts could choose their own solutions. He forged ahead, listing various scenarios under which a remedy would be worked out. Justice Harlan began picking apart the wisdom of several of the suggestions. Charles Whittaker, as if to tip his sympathy for the plaintiffs, interrupted: "One need simply say that there is time enough" for the legislature to find a solution if that situation arises. Hugo Black testily stepped in: "Why do we have to consider these things at all?"

After forty-five minutes of back-and-forth with the Justices, Charles Rhyne summarized the case and granted the rest of his time to the solicitor general. The Justices' questions showed the intensity of Frankfurter's and Harlan's opposition and raised some fundamental problems with the Tennesseans' case, but there was also the encouraging possibility that Whittaker might side with the plaintiffs.[20]

Archibald Cox—tall, gaunt, professorial—began: "The United States appears in this case as amicus curiae partly because it involves the constitutional right of a large number of citizens both in Tennessee and elsewhere but also because it raises issues that lie very close to the heart of our system of government. It involves not only the integrity of the electoral process but also, of course, a difficult and delicate question concerning the proper role of the judiciary in securing voters' fair representation in their state legislatures."

Cox then laid out three arguments that he would make. First, this case involves "an alleged depravation" of the right under the Fourteenth Amendment "to be free from arbitrary discrimination in the exercise of the franchise, which is sufficiently personal as to give the victims of the discrimination standing to sue." Second, malapportionment "presents a justiciable controversy in the sense that courts can hear, decide matter, and grant equity under suitable circumstances, and it may not grant equity if the circumstances are such that that is not possible." Third, "at this stage of case, there is at least enough likelihood that the case below, sitting as a court of equity, could find some administrable form of relief."

At that moment, just three minutes into the solicitor general's presentation, Potter Stewart interrupted.

Stewart: "That's interesting. As I heard it, none of your three points had to do with the basic substance of this case, whether or not this is a violation of the Fourteenth Amendment."

Cox: "I think that is involved to this extent: the court below had jurisdiction if the complaint states a claim under the Fourteenth Amendment, whether the complaint is well founded or not. . . . We think that the point is involved at

20. Gilbert, interview.

least to the extent that we should show that this isn't a futile, silly claim. It does not seem necessary or indeed not even appropriate for the Court to rule now whether there has or has not been a violation of the Fourteenth Amendment. If it decides there is a substantial claim, then there was jurisdiction and there ought to be a ruling by the lower court."

Stewart seemed won over: "Well, that's right. Then there would have to be implicitly a ruling that the allegations of this complaint allege a violation of the Fourteenth Amendment." Cox paused to dwell on this point. It lay at the heart of his argument: "they allege a violation but [do] not [seek] a determination of what they allege is a violation." Quoting Oliver Wendell Holmes, Cox continued: "If you state a claim of federal rights, even if it is not well founded, the court has jurisdiction, at least where the claim isn't patently frivolous."

"Mr. Solicitor," Chief Justice Warren interjected, "if we should take your view, need we do more than hold that the complaint states a cause of action and that the District Court must exercise it [jurisdiction]?"

"All that you need hold," Cox replied, "is that the case is within the jurisdiction of the federal courts and that courts below need to adjudicate the claim."

This was a stunningly brilliant argument. Cox had reasoned that the argument of Walter Chandler's team went too far to capture Stewart's or Whittaker's votes. If the Court ruled that the state legislature had violated the voting rights of the plaintiffs, it would also have to declare Tennessee's 1901 Apportionment Act unconstitutional, just as Charles Rhyne had suggested. The Justices could not, however, leave Tennessee without a method for electing its legislature. They would have to deal immediately with finding a solution, a remedy. Black, Brennan, Douglas, and Warren were prepared to go that far, but not any of the other Justices.

The Solicitor General's argument advanced the law by an incremental step, calculated to win over at least one of the two pivotal Justices. Seeing that *Colegrove* had not in fact set a precedent, Stewart, in particular, might be willing to follow a more restrained approach—declare that the judiciary had the right to hear such cases, do not make any judgments about this particular case except to note that it involves a federal issue, and send the case back to the lower court. The district court, in this instance, had agreed with the facts of the case but felt restrained from acting.

Cox's line of reasoning also appealed to a baser political instinct. He asked merely that the Court not give away its authority over apportionment, not give away some of its own political power. "A denial of jurisdiction over the subject matter would exclude all apportionment cases from judicial consideration as a category without regard for the seriousness of the constitutional wrong, without regard for the ability of the Court to grant relief, and indeed without regard for many other matters." Indeed, ruling against jurisdiction would amount to overturning decisions in which jurisdiction had been granted, including *Colegrove*. "On the other hand, if you have jurisdiction over the subject matter and follow the lines of Mr. Rutledge's analysis, then you may examine the merits and judge whether courts can usefully act and provide flexible treatment according to necessities of particular cases."

The task of defending the existing apportionment laws fell to Tennessee's assistant attorney Jack Wilson. The state's case rested on familiar arguments. First, this was a matter of state law, not a federal concern: "The ultimate effect of plaintiffs' position is to put the courts on a primrose path of state-federal relations." Second, the courts lacked jurisdiction, as the U.S. Supreme Court itself indicated in letting stand the Tennessee State Supreme Court's ruling in *Kidd v. McCanless*. "What was the effect," the state's attorney asked, "of this Court's dismissal of the appeal [in *Kidd*]? . . . The exact same issues are involved. The same statutes are involved. If there is a federal question now, there was one then." Third, the plaintiffs lack standing because the complaint does not assert a private wrong. There was no personal harm felt; their only "interest is in a republican form of government." Finally, even if the courts had jurisdiction, no judicial remedy was possible. Jack Wilson underscored the problem with the case set forth by Charles Rhyne. "The ultimate result," he emphasized, "of finding the apportionment act unconstitutional by reason of the lapse of time would deprive us of a present legislature and of a means of electing a new one."

The argument of the state, though, left matters in an age-old political conundrum. Calling forth the history of representative government, from the time of King James I of England, through the U.S. Constitution, to the Tennessee state constitution of 1870, the state's attorneys argued that only the legislature has the right to determine its own members. The sovereignty of the people is embodied in the legislature. "Any question that arises in connection with an election must be decided by the legislature itself."

That, Charles Rhyne echoed in rebuttal, was the nub of the problem. No remedy was possible in Tennessee because any change in the apportionment act must be approved by the very legislature elected under it.

After two days of argument and intense questioning, the oral proceedings drew to a close on April 20, 1961. Conference was the following day.

Justice Frankfurter dominated the deliberations. He walked gingerly about the conference room, quoting judicial opinions and legal treatises. He offered the real defense of the Tennessee Apportionment Act and of *Colegrove*, a defense that lasted several hours. It was pure genius.

For all that, the Justices' votes were predictable.

Justice Douglas took notes on the conference.[21]

> WARREN: I agree with the case as presented by [the solicitor general of] the United States, and I reverse [the federal district court] on that argument.
>
> BLACK: I reverse. My dissent in *Colegrove versus Green* covers this.
>
> FRANKFURTER: Unless we affirm [the district court's decision], we will get into great difficulty and this Court will rue the results. I think that the solicitor general was irresponsible in stating that there is a permissible remedy. . . . The costs will be very serious.
>
> DOUGLAS: I reverse.
>
> CLARK: The precedents are against us. . . . Equality is not a basic principle in American political voting.
>
> HARLAN: I agree wholly with Felix's views. I think the solicitor general was reckless in his desire to inject the judiciary into this field. . . . This Court is not competent to solve this type of problem. I affirm.
>
> BRENNAN: The purpose of the Fourteenth Amendment was to give equality. . . . I do not believe that the remedies are insoluble—I have worked it out with a judicial remedy. I reverse.
>
> WHITTAKER: If we wrote on a clean slate, I would say that petitioners have standing to sue and that they are being denied equal protection of the laws. . . . Precedents, however, say that this is a "political" issue. I am reluctant to overrule those cases. So I would affirm, but I would do so only on an equity ground.[22]

Four to four. The case rested entirely in Potter Stewart's hands. "I am not at rest on this issue," Stewart began.

"I have trouble seeing that disproportionate voting is a violation of equal protection. A state can divide up its jurisdiction into unequal political units. I would uphold the Michigan system that is here in another case [*Scholle v. Hare*] we are holding. Tennessee is different, because it has a law that requires equality, and that state's failure to apply it may raise an equal protection point. I have sufficient doubt that I pass."

Archibald Cox's understanding of the positions of the Justices proved right. There was not a majority to hold that the Fourteenth Amendment required equality in district populations, as the Tennessee attorneys argued. But there

21. Justice William O. Douglas Papers, Library of Congress.
22. Del Dickson, ed., *The Supreme Court in Conference (1940–1985): The Private Discussions behind Nearly 300 Supreme Court Decisions* (New York: Oxford University Press, 2001), 845–47.

might still be a majority in favor of judicial intervention in this area. Charles Rhyne, echoing Chancellor Steele, had raised a critical doubt about the meaning of *Colegrove*. The Solicitor General's arguments were perhaps too new and too unsettled in Justice Stewart's mind. Just one day after the argument, he had not yet resolved the fine legal distinctions drawn and the practical implications of asserting jurisdiction.

The Justices took up the issue again a week later. At the conference on April 28, Justice Douglas immediately directed the deliberations to Potter Stewart. "This case was passed for him," groused Douglas. "I think that this is as important a case as our school desegregation cases," Stewart announced. "Under our precedents, we can go either way. It will establish a big precedent if we go in and let the federal courts supervise these affairs. I would suggest putting the case down for rehearing." The other Justices assented.

Baker v. Carr was set for a second hearing on October 9, 1961. It is rare for a case to be argued twice before the Supreme Court, but this was an exceptional case. For the Justices, it meant postponing until a new term and a new set of law clerks. For the plaintiffs, the delay brought the next election six months closer. There was now the risk that the justices might defer judgment for the very practical reason that the election was too soon to grant their request.

ROUND TWO

Pressure on Justice Stewart came immediately from both sides. Each side in the case put forth its best arguments, often in unusually long memos and letters that went into many more directions and much greater depth on the substance of the law than the briefs filed by the plaintiffs and defendants. The oral arguments were really just the beginning of extensive deliberations among the Justices.

The exchanges among the Justices are most revealing about the politics within the Court. The personal papers of the Justices contain many notes and memos passed among themselves concerning points of law and concerns about the consequences of the case. And that paper trail is truly the tip of a much larger set of in-person conversations and other communications that occurred among the Justices. What we have been able to recover of these discussions shows that the politics of the Court was not the politics of vote trading and arm twisting, but of true deliberation.

Felix Frankfurter wasted no time. On May 1, the Monday after the decision to rehear the case, Frankfurter wrote to Stewart emphasizing the need for judicial restraint to avoid judicial abuses. "[W]hile the matter is fresh in my mind,"

Frankfurter wrote in a lengthy letter to his younger colleague, "let me say a word about the hypothetical extreme case that you put, of an apportionment restricting voting to men six feet high. . . . I think the legitimate fear of an abusive extension of a doctrine was well answered long ago by Harlan I [John Marshall Harlan's grandfather], when the Court found unreviewable authority in the Secretary of War to grant or deny applications for constructions of navigable streams . . . [T]he widest scope for dealing with arbitrary abuses, the correction of which does not open the door to more and greater difficulties than the difficulties to be remedied."[23]

Communications among the Justices on points of law continued into the fall and intensified as the date of the rehearing and the fourth conference on the case approached. By early October, reapportionment was becoming a daily topic of discussion, and it became clear that not only Stewart but also Whittaker could cast the deciding vote. On October 6, 1961, just three days before the reargument, Felix Frankfurter wrote to Justice Whittaker. "Dear Charlie," he began, "Unashamedly I bother you some more on *Baker v. Carr*. Unless I misunderstood what you said yesterday, what gives you concern is this: . . .'Tennessee is stuck with its policy.'"[24] Frankfurter, appealing to Whittaker's sense of federal relations, argued that the case raised a purely state matter. The Tennessee Supreme Court, not the U.S. Supreme Court, was the arbiter and interpreter of the Tennessee constitution. That court had in its power the ability to solve this problem in 1955, when it took up *Kidd v. McCanless*, but it left in place the existing apportionment act.

Meanwhile, Archibald Cox and proponents of reapportionment took their case to the public. Professors Paul T. David and Ralph Eisenberg of the University of Virginia issued a press release of "the first nation wide analysis" of the devaluation of the urban and suburban vote.[25] The release was timed for maximum impact, even though the study was not yet published. David wrote to Archibald Cox on October 5, 1961: "The University decided to go ahead with a press release on our voting study. . . . It has gone out to the wire services and to about 300 newspapers for use next Sunday, October 8. . . . We hope this will prove to be a useful contribution to public discussion at this time. I expect to be in Washington on Monday and hope to be in Court when the reargument begins on the Tennessee case."[26] It is unclear if the David and Eisenberg study

23. Felix Frankfurter to Potter Stewart, 1 May 1961, John Marshall Harlan Papers, Princeton University.
24. Felix Frankfurter to Charlie Whittaker, 6 October 1961, Felix Frankfurter Papers, Harvard University.
25. Press release by Paul T. David and Ralph Eisenberg, 5 October 1961, William J. Brennan Jr. Papers, Library of Congress, Box I.
26. Paul T. David to Archibald Cox, 5 October 1961, of William J. Brennan Jr. Papers, Library of Congress, Box I.

and the press it received affected the Justices at all. However, the press release primed the newspapers for the decision, prompting editorials and cartoons on both sides.

Reargument felt like an anticlimax. The same cast presented the cases. One addition to the official list of lawyers, though, was Z. Thomas Osborn Jr.—Tommy Osborn, the lawyer who had held the case together since the Millers conceived it in 1954. Archibald Cox granted Osborn the five-minute rebuttal period. He would wait patiently for two hours for his moment before the Court.

The attorneys—Rhyne, Cox, and Wilson—went over familiar ground, and the arguments they offered deviated little from their presentations in April. The solicitor general closed by quoting Justice Jackson: "A court which is governed by a sense of self-restraint does not thereby become paralyzed. It simply conserves its strength to strike more telling blows in the cause of working democracy." That occasion, Mr. Cox ended, had arrived.

The questioning by the Justices was familiar, if more pointed. Assistant Attorney General Wilson spoke first. Douglas and Black raised the questions that highlighted violations of voting rights and the unacceptability of two sorts of voting rights, one federal and one for the states. Then it was the plaintiffs' turn. Throughout Rhyne's and Cox's arguments, Frankfurter and Harlan seized on matters of jurisdiction and precedent, to appeal to Stewart, and whether this was in fact a federal question, to appeal to Whittaker. Chief Justice Warren sought to find a middle ground in which the states would have considerable flexibility.

At last, Tommy Osborn stood. He began in a gentle Tennessee drawl, summing up the inequities rooted in the Tennessee legislative districts and the long struggle for relief. He quickly wound up, though, into a fiery oration, the sort reserved for summation in the trial courts of Nashville. He was, as Harris Gilbert recalled later, on a roll. The Tennessee constitution required equality, and that, Osborn pounded, is what they sought.

Frankfurter interrupted. He had them. In Osborn's own words, the question of jurisdiction and remedy were inextricably linked. The courts would be dragged into a prolonged struggle with legislatures throughout the land to impose a rule that it had not yet formulated.

"You're telling us today that thirty-three percent of the Tennessee electorate elects sixty-six and two-thirds of the legislature, and we should agree with your position that some way or another—with a magic wand probably—there will be some remedy worked out. So the Court will agree to some alleviation. And next year forty percent will be electing sixty percent of the legislature. You'll be right back up here complaining about that, won't you?"

"Yessir," replied Osborn smartly, "for a fee." The courtroom burst into laughter.

Osborn's rebuttal and the second hearing drew to a close. Little new was added to either case, though the lines were more sharply drawn.

The following day, the private debate among the Justices resumed. The fourth conference to deal with *Baker v. Carr* was just four days away. On October 10, 1961, Felix Frankfurter took the unusual step of distributing to his brethren a sixty-five-page memorandum warning of the dire consequences that would follow were they to accept jurisdiction over legislative districting cases. That document served as the foundation for his opinion on the case. "Deeply believing, as I do, that the function of the Court Conference is to disclose and exchange views to the fullest relevant extent regarding the issues of a case," Frankfurter wrote in a cover letter, "I find it necessary to state in comprehensive detail the problems involved in this case, the disposition of which has such far-reaching implications for the well-being of the Court."[27]

Justice Harlan appealed to Potter Stewart and Charles Whittaker personally. Harlan, ever the gentleman, did not want to overstep the bounds of propriety and was reluctant to push his colleagues hard on the case. After discussing the matter with Frankfurter, though, both felt he should try. At issue was a basic principle of judicial restraint under which the Court had operated for the better part of two centuries. Frankfurter and Harlan saw it eroding rapidly, not just on this issue but on a range of questions before the Court. On October 11, two days before the Court Conference, Harlan wrote a three-page letter to Stewart and Whittaker. He delved not into matters of law but into the delicate and potentially destructive political situation into which the Solicitor General's position would place the Court. *Baker v. Carr,* as Harlan saw it, threatened the very legitimacy of the Court.

> Dear Charlie and Potter:
>
> Unless I am much mistaken, past events in this case plainly indicate that your votes will be determinative of its outcome.
>
> While I have no idea as to how the issue now lies in your minds, believing, as I do, that from the standpoint of the future of the Court this case involves implications whose importance is unmatched by those of any other case coming here in my time (and by those in few other in the history of the Court, not excluding the Desegregation cases), I would like to put to you those implications as I see them, possibly somewhat differently than they have been put before. They have, I believe become obscured in our debates up to now.

27. Memorandum, 10 October 1961, Felix Frankfurter Papers, Harvard University.

I need hardly argue to you that the independence of the Court, and its aloofness from political vicissitudes, have always been the mainspring of its stability and vitality. Those attributes have been assured not alone by the constitutional and statutory safeguards which surround the Court, but also to a large extent, I believe, by the wise restraint which, by and large, has characterized the Court's handling of emotionally-charged popular causes. I believe that what we are being asked to do in this case threatens the preservation of these attributes. . . .

This letter calls for no answer, but I do bespeak for it your earnest consideration. I apologize for the length of this. It reflects a deep concern which I felt I ought to share with you.

Sincerely, JMH[28]

That was Wednesday. On Thursday, Justice Brennan circulated his own Memorandum to the Conference. This was not a draft of an opinion or a consideration of the political problems to come, but data—raw facts—showing the extent of the inequalities in Tennessee. "Enclosed is a chart," Brennan wrote to his colleagues, "prepared from the Record to depict the variances in county representation among counties of the same relative population. . . . This chart was prepared by my clerk, Roy Schotland, after a thorough analysis of the exhibits in this case. I find them personally very helpful in seeing the precise picture in Tennessee. . . . I should think that at the very least the data show a picture which Tennessee should be required to justify if it is to avoid the conclusion that the 1901 Act applied to today's facts, is simple caprice. W. J. B."[29] That chart and Brennan's concluding words weighed heavily on at least one of his colleagues. The conference was the next day.

The conference on October 13, 1961, drew a briefer but more pointed discussion than in April. The Chief Justice suggested that the Court adhere to the political compromise laid out by Archibald Cox: "There is a violation of equal protection shown here. . . . All that we need to do here is to say that this shows an arbitrary and capricious practice. The Court has jurisdiction. I would reverse solely on jurisdiction."[30]

Justice Frankfurter stuck to his guns, but he lacked the ebullience he had had in the spring. We already decided to stay out of this case in *Kidd*, he reasoned. This case is no different. "Asserting jurisdiction in this case is fraught with such consequences that to me are so dangerous to our whole system that I

28. JMH to Charlie Whittaker and Potter Stewart, 11 October 1961, John Marshall Harlan Papers, Princeton University.
29. Memorandum from W.J.B., 12 October 1961, William J. Brennan Jr. Papers, Library of Congress, Box I.
30. Notes, William O. Douglas Papers, Library of Congress.

would stay out." Frankfurter, perhaps believing that the time for extensive deliberation had passed, decided to let Justice Harlan carry the load.

Hugo Black took on *Colegrove* directly. "Felix's memo in this case," Black spoke up, "is a good brief for a weak cause. *Colegrove v. Green* is a weak reed on which to hang any notion of an established rule. That opinion was only agreed to by Frankfurter, Reed, and Burton." As to the merits, the issue for Black was the irrationality of the Tennessee law. "Does this act bear so unequally and arbitrarily as to deny equal protection? I think that it does, and I reverse."

Justice Harlan, sensing the shift in the Court, pled for judicial restraint with intense emotion.[31] "My earlier views have been reinforced by reargument." For Harlan, *Baker* would embroil the Court unnecessarily in a constitutional struggle. This was not a federal matter; it dealt with the state's right to choose the means by which it formed its own government. This was not an equal protection claim, as it had to do with the balance between urban and rural areas, not individuals' voting rights. And most of all, this was not a judicial matter; it concerned the sovereignty of the legislature and the long-established right of the legislature to determine its own membership. Judicial intervention in legislative districting would drag the judiciary into the politics of the legislature, political conflicts that would cost the judiciary its independence and legitimacy: "I would plead for the protection of this Court against getting into these political contests."

Justice Black responded that Justice Harlan was right about the results that would ensue; at least in the South, this case threatened whites' control over political power. But the question here was whether there was a violation of equal protection, and whether the courts had the power to intervene. On both matters, the answer was yes.

Douglas underscored Black's argument, taking on Frankfurter's memo directly. "The difficulties of the judiciary doing nothing about [the voting rights violations in Tennessee], great as they are, can't deter us from doing our job."

Clark, then, joined in and threw his support to Frankfurter: "The petitioners failed to show that they had exhausted other avenues to relief. . . . Even if there was jurisdiction I would not exercise it."

Justice Brennan, however, drew a clear line between Tennessee and other situations. Whatever might be true elsewhere, the apportionment in Tennessee defied rational explanation, and this clearly violated voting rights without basis in any theory of representation, even the notion that one should balance rural and urban interests. "This is an equal protection problem presented here. Here there is a capricious and arbitrary denial of equal protection." Brennan echoed

31. Schotland, interview.

the Chief. "I would assert jurisdiction, but not direct a specific decree." As to the past history of the Tennessee case, Brennan concluded: "I don't think *Kidd* should be taken too seriously. We passed over quite a few Sunday Law cases before the last term, when we took the cases and decided them. I would reverse for a hearing on the merits of the complaint."

That left Whittaker and Stewart.

Whittaker spoke first and expressed his deep ambivalence. "I affirmed last term but was very shaky on it. I have written two memos diametrically opposed to each other—one for asserting jurisdiction and one for affirmance. I now affirm. . . . The federal court has jurisdiction to entertain this type of claim, but there is no right to enforce."

Once again, the decision came down to Stewart's vote. He spoke at length. The question of jurisdiction, Stewart felt, was settled: "The district court had jurisdiction. This is not a so-called political question . . . the determination of which the Constitution has precluded from the courts and placed in another branch of government." Frankfurter and Harlan strenuously disagreed with Stewart's assertion, but he read the Fourteenth Amendment differently.

As Stewart saw matters, jurisdiction was the least of the Court's concerns in this case. For him, all turned on the burden of proof. Stewart objected to the argument put forward by Rhyne and by his colleagues Black and Douglas that there had clearly been discrimination. "On the merits there is an assumption than equal protection requires the legislature to apportion votes so that there is no discrimination. Our entire history presumes the contrary, and on that history I follow Frankfurter's memo." Equal protection, in Stewart's assessment, would permit a wide range of apportionment plans, including districts with very unequal populations. "I couldn't say that equal protection requires representation approximately commensurate with voting strength. States could give towns only one vote, whatever their size. States could allocate voting rights by taxes paid, education, and so forth." Stewart would have allowed all such rules to stand. The state, he felt, does not have to justify every deviation for exact population equality or even what procedure it chooses. Rather, "the greatest burden of proof [of a violation of equal protection] is on the plaintiffs to show an arbitrary and capricious system."

"Conceivably," Stewart continued, "there can be a denial of equal protection in an apportionment case." That was the force of his hypothetical questioning concerning tall people, and Frankfurter's concern with that point. If discrimination occurred on the basis of some arbitrary criterion, such as against tall people or red-haired people, then the Court would have little difficulty judging that a violation of equal protection. Was there such a capricious action in Tennessee? "The giving of greater weight of votes to rural blocs is O.K.," Justice

Stewart concluded. That has some rational basis. But Tennessee was different. The state's apportionment map lacked any clear justification, and the plaintiffs had shown sufficient evidence that there was a potential violation of federal voting rights. "On the merits I agree more or less with Bill Brennan."

It was decided. Stewart had cautiously joined Black, Brennan, Douglas, and Warren. The courts could enter the political thicket.

Less clear, though, was exactly what was decided. There remained the difficult task of writing an opinion that captured the opinion of the majority, and the risk that Stewart might write a separate opinion, as Rutledge had in *Colegrove*, that might prove the undoing of the fragile coalition.

7

A Fragile Coalition

Chief Justice Earl Warren wanted to write the majority opinion in *Baker v. Carr* himself. The case had the makings of a landmark decision. It addressed questions fundamental to American democracy—the rights of citizenship and the delicate position of the courts in securing those rights. It involved a significant reversal in the approach that the Court had taken to apportionment cases, at least since the *Colegrove* decision. And it had immediate implications for Warren's Court. Up until this decision, the conservatives on the Court had managed to build working majorities to block the liberals at most turns. Stewart's assent in *Baker* was the beginning of a profound swing in the Court.[1]

But the Court Conference on October 13, 1961, as well as discussions with Hugo Black and William Douglas, gave Warren pause. Stewart was with the majority, but just barely. The liberal Justices could ill afford a decision in this hard-won case weakened by a badly split Court. Such a decision could create more problems in the future. More distressing still, it remained unclear exactly what the Justices had decided. They had agreed that courts could intervene in districting cases, but had they also agreed on remedies? How far could the liberals push toward political equality?

Hugo Black and William Douglas met with the Chief privately about the assignment of the opinion. Neither they nor the Chief Justice should write the opinion, they counseled. Each of them saw this case as a straightforward

---

1. Lucas A. Powe Jr., *The Warren Court and American Politics* (Cambridge, MA: Belknap, 2002), dates the beginning of "the Second Warren Court," a period of unprecedented judicial decisions, to the 1961 term. Most of the cases associated with the Warren Court come on the heels of *Baker*.

violation of the voting rights of the plaintiffs as guaranteed by the Four-teenth Amendment. Stewart would never go along with that line of reason-ing. Were one of the liberals to write the opinion, a divided Court would surely result.

What about assigning the case to Justice Stewart himself? He had cast the deciding vote. Allowing him to write the opinion would surely secure the ma-jority. Black and Douglas objected. In a 1963 interview, Justice Douglas re-counted the situation to Walter Murphy: "Stewart's views, put into an opinion, would probably reflect a very narrow aspect of the problem and perhaps cast a shadow, by innuendo and whatnot, on the merits, making the reversal merely a technical victory, and that the end result would be the same as in the past, namely, that courts should not be of any effective relief."[2]

Worse still, the division between Stewart and Douglas threatened the very coalition. If Stewart did write the opinion, Douglas might not join the opinion and write on his own, likely along the lines of his opinion in *South v. Peters*. Douglas's interpretation of the Fourteenth Amendment would surely give Stewart pause, and he might swing back toward Frankfurter and Harlan.[3]

Douglas recommended that the Chief Justice assign the case to William Brennan. Stewart stated in conference that he was in agreement with Bill Bren-nan on the merits. In Douglas's own assessment, Brennan's position lay some-where between his own and Stewart's. And Brennan had a gift for finding common ground and striking compromises.

From the Chief's perspective, the choice could not be better. Brennan and Warren were close, extremely close. They met privately every Friday before conference, and their voting records over their many years together on the Court show few differences.

On the second Monday after the conference vote, Warren went to see Bren-nan early in the morning and assigned the majority opinion in *Baker v. Carr* to him. Later that day, Brennan sent Douglas a brief note of thanks. "Bill—The Chief told me this morning he's giving me #6, *Baker v. Carr*, and that your view expressed to him yesterday had decided him. Thanks so much. He was going to give it to Potter but I urged him to talk first with you."[4]

It was a great honor—and a monumental task.

---

2. "Transcriptions of Conversations between Justice William O. Douglas and Professor Walter F. Murphy," 1981, cassette 7b, Seeley M. Mudd Manuscript Library, Princeton University Library, infoshare1.princeton .edu/libraries/firestone/rbsc/finding_aids/douglas/douglas7b.html.

3. Douglas's interview with Walter Murphy suggests that this would have been the case; Roy Schotland's in-ternal memo to Brennan also states that this would have been a likely outcome had Stewart assigned the opinion.

4. Memorandum, William J. Brennan Jr. Papers, Library of Congress, Box I.

COMPROMISE

Brennan's draft of his opinion came along slowly. He struggled to find a rationale for action that he felt would at once satisfy Potter Stewart and transcend the
immediate circumstances of the Tennessee case. The case just was not becoming clear to the Justice. To make matters worse, there was nothing to react to
but Frankfurter's sixty-five-page memo. None of the other Justices had written
down their opinions.

In early December, Brennan experienced the first of many "black nights," as
his clerk Roy Schotland termed them. Brennan's lack of progress weighed
heavily on him. No opinion would be ready to circulate to the other Justices for
some time, and the election year was just around the corner. Roy Schotland,
who frequently drove home with Brennan, wrote in his journal that Brennan
was losing sleep and becoming dispirited because of *Baker*. It was unclear
whether an opinion could be crafted that would satisfy Potter Stewart and produce a coherent, general, and lasting legal decision. The great case seemed to be
going nowhere.[5]

January, however, brought a renewal to Brennan's vigor, and by the middle
of the month he had completed a first draft of the majority opinion. He
wished to proceed carefully, though, so as not to upset others in their coalition
and not to tip his hand to Frankfurter. Brennan sent Justice Stewart a copy of
Print #1 of the majority opinion for comment. The theory behind the majority opinion was simple. They would go as far as the Solicitor General suggested. Only three issues needed to be decided in this case. First, the district
court has jurisdiction in this matter. Second, the plaintiffs in the case have the
standing to sue. Third, the allegation of a denial of equal protection under the
law presents a "justiciable constitutional cause of action." *Colegrove* was not
binding as this was not a "political question," and earlier decisions had established the courts' jurisdiction over legislative apportionment. After establishing that courts could hear such cases, the Supreme Court would send the case
back to the district court in Tennessee for a hearing of the case on its merits.
Such a hearing would determine whether the existing apportionment law satisfied the Tennessee constitution's requirement of representation of population. The Justices need not determine what the remedy ought to be or what
equal protection meant as a general rule. Deciding that apportionment was
not a "political question" and that the courts could hear such cases would be
victory enough.

5. Roy Schotland, *Notes*, in opinions of William Brennan Jr.—October term 1961, William J. Brennan Jr.
Papers, Library of Congress. Roy Schotland, personal communication with author, April 29, 2004.

Potter Stewart phoned to express his satisfaction with the report and to say that he had a number of minor changes. He was, however, willing to go no further.

Brennan incorporated these changes, and during the last week of January he circulated the memorandum to the other Justices in the majority—Black, Douglas, and Warren. In his cover to the memorandum, Brennan explained that "contrary to his tentative reaction at conference, Potter now agrees with me that we should not pass on any issues except the three actually requiring decision at this time. . . . I should say further that, after much thought, I believe that the full discussion of the 'political question,' and its bearing on apportionment suits, is required if we are effectively and finally to dispel the fog of another day produced by Felix's opinion in *Colegrove v. Green*."[6] Brennan had succeeded in writing an opinion that kept Stewart with the majority but that thoroughly defeated Frankfuter's political thicket doctrine.

Justice Black phoned Brennan at home. He was delighted with the opinion and surprised that Stewart was in the fold, considering how far Brennan went in asserting the power of the courts to intervene in legislative districting under the Fourteenth Amendment. The Chief Justice was also thrilled with Brennan's draft.

Justice Douglas, however, thought differently. He was upset by the treatment of the "political question." He wanted an opinion that vindicated his own dissent in the Georgia unit-vote case, *South v. Peters*. Brennan and his clerks worked diligently throughout the remainder of the week to satisfy Douglas. At last, print #4 was ready for circulation. It differed little in substance from #1. Justice Douglas agreed to join the majority opinion, but he had also decided to write a concurring opinion of his own.

Print #4 of Brennan's opinion was sent to all nine Justices on January 27. That day, Frankfurter popped into Justice Clark's chambers and declared, "they've done it just as I expected." The majority opinion, if it survived the ensuing deliberations, gutted Frankfurter's political thicket doctrine.

A COURT IN CRISIS

On February 1, Brennan and Warren left for a ten-day judicial conference. They returned to a crisis.

In their absence, Frankfurter circulated his dissent again, noting that Justices Clark and Harlan had joined it. Little had been heard from Whittaker and

---

6. Memorandum from W. J. B. to The Chief Justice, Mr. Justice Black, and Mr. Justice Douglas, 27 January 1962, William J. Brennan Jr. Papers, Library of Congress.

Stewart, but the pressure was clearly on. Frankfurter and Harlan lobbied their junior colleagues hard—to keep Whittaker in line and to try to break Stewart free. On February 8, Justice Harlan had sent Potter Stewart a *New York Times* editorial reproving the political maneuvers and partisan politics in the apportionment of the U.S. House. The editorial, Harlan wrote to Stewart, describes "exactly the sort of thing that should give us pause, and more pause." Harlan went on to describe his own ideas for a dissent, and he implored Stewart to keep an open mind. "Feeling as I do about the shortsightedness and unwisdom of what is proposed to us, I hope you will not think it presumptuous of me to ask you to weigh (if your mind is still open) what I am writing (which will not be long), before casting what will be the decisive, and if I may say so, fateful vote in this case."[7] Stewart shot Harlan a message back: "Needless to say, I appreciate your note. I shall look forward with interest to reading what you write, and shall try to bring an open mind to it, although as of now I find myself in agreement with Bill Brennan's opinion."[8] The coalition seemed to have come together at last.

Unfortunately, Justice Douglas could not leave well enough alone. Without telling Warren and Brennan, Douglas wrote a concurring opinion that well beyond the compromise and sent it to the other brethren. Douglas believed the Court would settle the case the following Monday. Based on their conversations in late January, Brennan had thought that Douglas would limit himself to the question of jurisdiction, but Douglas had taken on the merits of the case. His draft concurrence stated in no uncertain terms that Tennessee had discriminated and violated the Fourteenth Amendment right to equal protection. Tennessee's legislature, he went on, must represent population equally. He would overturn the lower court not on the narrow question of jurisdiction, but on the merits.

William Douglas's draft threatened to blow apart the delicate coalition that Brennan had cultivated and to undermine the entire case. On getting Douglas's draft, Schotland wrote in his notes, Potter Stewart "evidently hit the ceiling or came damn near. . . . [H]e'd set his teeth and was really determined to go forward in just that posture, without pause."[9] Justice Stewart penned a civil note to Brennan explaining the situation: "Dear Bill, In view of the concurring opinion which Bill Douglas has written I feel obligated to file a separate concurrence in this case."[10] He enclosed a one-and-a-half-page memo sketching his opinion. It

7. John Marshall Harlan to Potter Stewart, 8 February 1962, John Marshall Harlan Papers, Seeley M. Mudd Library, Princeton University.

8. Memorandum from P. S. to Mr. Justice Harlan, 8 February 1962, John Marshall Harlan Papers, Seeley M. Mudd Library, Princeton University.

9. Schotland, *Notes*.

10. Justice Stewart to William Brennan, 13 February 1962, William J. Brennan Jr. Papers, Library of Congress.

was now February 13. Just two weeks after the release of the majority opinion, that opinion was in serious jeopardy.

With Stewart and Douglas at odds, the coalition was crumbling. The two Justices had recently crossed swords over other decisions, and Stewart was in no mood to compromise with Douglas. Worse still, Douglas had given his own spin on the majority opinion. Douglas viewed Brennan's opinion as a vindication of his dissent in *South v. Peters* and as tacitly embracing his theory that the Fourteenth Amendment asserted a broad right to equal representation. Stewart viewed this as a grossly inaccurate characterization of what the majority opinion stated. He could not disagree more with such an interpretation of the meaning of the majority opinion.

The whole theory behind the decision was that the majority spoke with a single voice in support of the simple claim that the courts have jurisdiction generally in matters of apportionment under the Fourteenth Amendment. If the majority split, Brennan's opinion would have the same standing as Frankfurter's in *Colegrove*, perhaps less. Other courts had taken *Colegrove* as a standard. Without a clear majority in support of justiciability, *Baker* would only apply to this specific circumstance.

Without Stewart clearly in agreement, would the opinion have any teeth? That depended critically on what Stewart wrote. Justice Brennan and his clerks decided to stay in close communication with Justice Stewart. Shortly after the Douglas opinion went around, Brennan and Stewart spoke on the phone. They both agreed, according to Schotland's notes, that "they were damned if they knew what certain sentences of WOD's meant. They also agreed that they were damned if the majority opinion said what WOD represented it as saying. The Justice pointed out that the concurrence wholly departed from what he'd expected."[11] Stewart promised not to circulate his concurring opinion to the entire Court without first sending it to him and Warren. This, at least, allowed Brennan to make any changes in the majority opinion to appease Stewart; it might even give Brennan leverage over Douglas, possibly forcing him to temper his concurrence or withdraw it altogether. But most troubling to Justice Brennan was the memo that Harlan had written to Stewart. Potter Stewart told William Brennan in that critical phone conversation that Harlan had written him asking him "to please please not commit himself until he'd read" Harlan's dissent. The communiqué raised the possibility that Brennan might lose his majority altogether. How close was Stewart to bolting?

Justice Harlan circulated his dissenting opinion on February 13. He argued that Tennessee had followed its legislative process and had chosen not to reap-

11. Schotland, *Notes.*

portion. He argued that *Colegrove* stood as a precedent tying the hands of the current Court. And he presented in great detail the problem that the Court would face in finding a solution. Justice Stewart sent word to Brennan. Upon receiving Harlan's opinion, he had decided to write, and to write on the merits of the case. "At this point I plunged for the bottom," Roy Schotland wrote in his diary; "the whole conception of our opinion . . . was out the window."[12]

Justice Stewart circulated his concurring opinion on February 15. Brennan's clerks, anxious that the opinion might include some new bombshell, read aloud the Stewart piece in their office. This was a cause for celebration. Stewart's concurrence stated succinctly that the Court had decided that the district court has jurisdiction, that the appellants have standing, and that this challenge does not present a "political issue." Stewart's decision further found that the Tennessee apportionment was utterly arbitrary and lacked rationality. He noted, however, that the majority opinion did not decide what courts should do or what exactly the Tennessee constitution said regarding legislative apportionment. Stewart had neither wholly reversed himself, nor, it seemed, had he weakened the theory behind the majority. Only small changes in the opinions remained, and these could be hammered out. Brennan proceeded to serve as intermediary between Douglas and Stewart, negotiating changes in each of their opinions so as to satisfy the other. Although Douglas intended to go ahead with his opinion, he accommodated a long list of changes recommended by Stewart, and Stewart incorporated three changes in his opinion that Brennan had conveyed to him. Stewart and Douglas were appeased.

The majority had held.

At the time, that was not obvious. Brennan "could only see black in it all," according to Roy Schotland. Schotland himself wondered whether Stewart's opinion would "prove to be the first dangerous crack, as I think it will not be, or the sign that it's settled."[13]

For all of the problems Brennan had in holding the majority together, Felix Frankfurter faced an even more difficult task. He was far from a majority. Only Tom Clark and John Marshall Harlan had agreed to sign on to his dissent at the end of January. Despite repeated entreaties to join Frankfurter, Clark, and Harlan, Stewart showed every sign of sticking with the majority. And where was Whittaker? At the second conference, back in October 1961, Justice Whittaker had stated his agreement with the general principle espoused in the majority opinion, were it not for *Colegrove*. Throughout the struggle in January and into early February 1962, Whittaker had not yet committed to Frankfurter's opinion.

12. Ibid.
13. Ibid.

That mystery was solved in mid-February. The same day Potter Stewart's concurrence came down, Justice Frankfurter circulated a revised memorandum that included Justice Whittaker in dissent. Evidently, with deep ambivalence and after considerable pressure, Whittaker agreed to join Frankfurter.

Complicating matters further, Justice Clark chose to write a separate dissent. The people of Tennessee, he felt, had options other than the courts available to them. Indeed, the U.S. Congress, not the courts, had the authority and responsibility to solve this problem. On February 3, 1962, Clark wrote to Frankfurter: "Your dissent is unanswerable except by ukase. As you suggested by telephone, I will prepare something on the failure to exhaust other remedies." Justice Clark was to leave for vacation to Florida for much of the month of February; the break would give him the time to craft a dissent, away from the pressures of the Court. "I hope my delay," Clark signed off in his note to Frankfurter, "will not too long deprive [Tennessee] of a constitutional form of government, i.e., control by the 'city slickers.' "[14]

Clark's absence only added to the anxiety about the case. The liberals wanted to record the decision quickly, now that Stewart was on board. On March 2, 1962, Justice Douglas sent a memo to his brethren imploring them to reach a decision. Each day they inched closer to Election Day and risked making a decision too late to allow for a practical remedy.

Then came the most surprising turn in the case. Justice Clark returned from vacation and announced to Justice Frankfurter that he had completely reversed directions. On March 7, 1962, Clark wrote to his colleague:

> Dear Felix,
>
> Preparatory to writing my dissent in this case, along the line you suggested of pointing out the avenues that were open for the voters of Tennessee to bring about reapportionment despite its Assembly, I have carefully checked into the record. I am sorry to say that I cannot find any practical course that the people could take in bringing this about except through the Federal courts.
>
> Having come to this conclusion I decided I would reconsider the whole case, and I am sorry to say that I shall have to ask you to permit me to withdraw from your dissent. I regret this, but in view of the fact that the voters of Tennessee have no other recourse I have concluded that this case is controlled by *MacDougall*. . . . My best always, T.C.C.[15]

14. Tom Clark to Felix Frankfurter, 3 February 1962, Tom C. Clark Papers, University of Texas.
15. T.C.C. to Felix Frankfurter, 7 March 1962, Tom C. Clark Papers, University of Texas.

Tom Clark had indeed struggled with this decision. The Justice had taken on his vacation the voluminous briefs and appendices prepared for the case, including Harris Gilbert's memorandum on the disparities in county representation and public expenditures and Roy Schotland's table on county and district populations. His vacation must not have been a relaxing one. Over the three-week span, he wrote three different drafts of his opinion. The first begins, "Mr. Justice Clark, dissenting." He distinguishes this case from *Colegrove* and others that dealt with congressional districting. He goes on to explore his main line of argument about various legislative actions that Tennessee could take and the prospect for congressional intervention. Justice Clark's first draft ends, however, with a curious critique of the majority opinion. It gives the people no remedy. "No standards are laid down for the guidance of the District Court. . . . I do not agree with this disposition. The record is entirely sufficient for decision now once the Court hurdles the technical difficulties. I would decide it now holding that the present apportionment violates the equal protection clause of the Fourteenth Amendment." That line of reasoning completely undid all that he had argued earlier.

Clark's second draft begins, "Mr. Justice Clark, concurring in part and dissenting in part." The thrust of this new opinion is that the Court does have the authority to be involved and that there is a substantial violation of equal protection in Tennessee. But he would go much further than the majority. He would decide on the merits. The plaintiffs had shown adequate evidence of discrimination. The Supreme Court, he felt, should record that and fashion relief immediately, rather than force the Tennessee lawyers to go back to the district court.

A third and final draft became Justice Clark's concurrence. Gone were the grounds for dissent. He expressed his agreement with the majority and his willingness to assert a right under the Fourteenth Amendment. In a now famous passage, he identified what was at once the problem in Tennessee and a minimal standard for a solution:

> [T]he apportionment picture in Tennessee is a topsy-turvical of gigantic proportions. . . . [C]omparing the voting strength of counties of like population as well as contrasting that of the smaller with the larger counties—it leaves but one conclusion, namely that Tennessee's apportionment is a crazy quilt without rational basis."[16]

"A crazy quilt." The phrase captured the essence of the apportionment problem in Tennessee, indeed in the nation. There was simply no way to justify what

16. Concurrence of Tom Clark on *Baker v. Carr*, 369 U.S. 186, 254 (1962).

had happened in Tennessee and so many other states and, without the courts, no clear way out.

Tom Clark's about-face dramatically altered the meaning of the decision, without changing a word of the majority opinion. His addition solidified the coalition Brennan had struggled to assemble and maintain for the better part of a year. Brennan, Warren, Douglas, Black, Stewart, and now Clark were a majority of six. Whatever Potter Stewart wrote, William Brennan's opinion would undoubtedly speak with the voice of the majority. The decision would certainly apply beyond the circumstances of the Tennessee apportionment. The size of this majority signaled the complete defeat of Frankfurter's political thicket doctrine.

The Court was now on a new path forward. A majority of the Court could and would go even farther to the left of the majority opinion in *Baker*. Tom Clark expressed a wider view of the responsibilities of the federal courts on this matter. Potter Stewart's view was no longer pivotal. Even without Stewart, a majority of the Justices supported a more expansive role for the courts and a wider application of equal protection in the next apportionment case, and there soon would be others.

Tom Clark's new position on apportionment raised an intriguing immediate possibility. Perhaps Brennan should revise the majority opinion in *Baker* to incorporate Clark's views. William Brennan proposed such a revision to Potter Stewart. The new opinion would have gone beyond the questions of whether the courts could hear legislative apportionment cases and whether the Tennessee lawyers had the right to sue. He wanted to embrace Clark's argument that the Tennessee apportionment plan lacked rationality, thereby establishing a minimal standard. Stewart evidently balked. Brennan wrote to his brethren on March 10 that Stewart had gone as far as he would go. There was no further room for negotiation: "The changes represent the maximum to which Potter will subscribe. . . . Potter felt that if [more substantial changes] were made it would be necessary for him to dissent from that much of the revised opinion."[17]

Brennan backed down and decided to stick with the decision he had already crafted. It would be better to have a larger majority, if even on a narrower question. The future of the liberal position on apportionment now looked very bright. He had won the day.

A revision this late in the process might also backfire. It could upset the coalition and delay a decision. The entire theory of the case up to this point was

17. Memorandum from W. J. B. to The Chief Justice, Mr. Justice Black, and Mr. Justice Douglas, 10 March 1962, William J. Brennan Papers, Library of Congress.

to assert the power of the Court to decide such cases, thereby overturning *Colegrove*. Clark's desire to fashion a remedy would take the Court into a new realm. The majority opinion would have to consider what the remedy should be. The Justices' deliberations, even among the liberals, had not yet resolved that weighty question. It would be best to leave closed Pandora's box. The decision would adhere exactly to the principles that Brennan had set out—the judges could decide apportionment cases under the Fourteenth Amendment.

The last weeks of March brought a final blow to Frankfurter's position. Justice Whittaker, under great stress from the Court's cases and his responsibilities on the circuit court, had fallen ill. He took leave from the Court just a week shy of the *Baker* decision and, in the end, did not participate.The Justices met one more time in conference on *Baker v. Carr*. Frankfurter and Harlan were alone in their dissents. The final vote was 6 to 2. *Baker v. Carr* was decided at last.

On Monday, March 26, the Court announced its decision to the public. Frankfurter arrived in Court in exceptionally good spirits, but Harlan's demeanor was dark and brooding. Brennan was nervous; he was to present the most important case of his career on the Court. One observer that blustery March Monday was young David Broder, then a reporter for the *Washington Star*. "Justice Brennan peered out over a tense and crowded Supreme Court chamber and began reading the majority opinion," Broder wrote a year after the decision. "When he finished it was clear the Court had opened a new chapter in American legal and political history."[18]

The text of that chapter was yet to be written.

---

18. David S. Broder and Dana Pullen, "Reapportionment Leaves Wave of Legal Moves," *Washington Sunday Star*, March 24, 1963, p. B-3.

8

One Person, One Vote

The majority opinion in *Baker v. Carr* asserted a new judicial power. Until that Monday in March 1962, the legislatures ruled supreme. They acted as the sole authority in apportionment and districting. Until that day, the courts held back, but now they could reign in the legislatures. *Baker* did not, however, clarify how the judges should exercise their new power and what those constraints were.

"What has actually happened," Walter Lippmann wrote in his weekly column in the *New York Herald-Tribune* on April 2, 1962, "is that the six Justices of the Court have opened a little the one door of federal judicial relief. They have opened it only a crack at the moment, but there is no doubt that the two dissenting Justices are fully justified in warning the country that if the door is opened wide, the courts may become dangerously involved in state politics all over the union." The Court's new power, Felix Frankfurter warned, will be "destructive depending on the wisdom and restraint with which it is exercised."

Walter Lippmann was one of a chorus of political commentators and legal scholars who wanted to put the genie back in the bottle. Some, such as Philip C. Neal, dean of the University of Chicago Law School, saw that no legal remedy was possible. A large number of legal scholars proposed their own solutions to the issue. Others argued with Frankfurter that apportionment was still fundamentally a political problem and ought to be addressed in the political arena. "We must not do again," Walter Lippmann warned, "what was done after the 1954 decision in the school segregation case. We must not leave the application of the new rule to haphazard local lawsuits." He called for political leadership from the president and the Democratic and Republican leaders in Congress to chart a strategy for reapportioning state legislatures. The burden should be on the politicians, not the judges.

The politicians, however, would prove Lippmann and others still wishing for a political solution naïve. Legislatures did not act without the Court's leadership. *Baker* itself prodded a dozen states to attempt some form of reapportionment, but even those efforts produced marginal and symbolic changes in district maps. Most of the states hoped to ride out the storm without having to draw new boundaries. The U.S. Congress offered no solutions to the apportionment question. If anything, the national legislature tried to block any change. Congress was not to exert the leadership that political commentators hoped for.

The responsibility for charting a new course, then, lay not with the politicians. The burden fell by default on the judges.

A NEW COURT

Baker signaled the end of what historians of the Supreme Court term the First Warren Court and the beginning of the Second. A deep ideological cleavage among the justices divided the First Warren Court, which spanned the first nine years of his tenure. The schism hamstrung even the greatest decisions issued during this period, most notably *Brown v. Board of Education*. Warren insisted on a unanimous decision in *Brown* and won over the last two holdouts on that momentous case through the insertion of the phrase "with all deliberate speed." The compromised language had the regrettable consequence of allowing local politicians to slow the implementation of the decision. Every decision from 1953 to 1962 seemed to follow the same pattern of division and compromise.

The Second Warren Court came with a dramatic turn to the left following Charles Whittaker's departure. The new liberal majority issued a string of decisions establishing civil liberties and rights and wide-ranging judicial powers. The *Baker* decision came just on the cusp of this political transition on the bench.

Charles Whittaker was not one of the leading personalities on the Court, nor was he considered a powerful jurist or legal theorist. But he was a reliable vote on the conservative end of the bench. In a Court split between the four liberals (Black, Brennan, Douglas, and Warren) and the four conservatives (Clark, Frankfurter, Harlan, and Whittaker), a departure on either end could have upset the balance. Whittaker's withdrawal and Tom Clark's epiphany swung the Court sharply to the left.

Then, on April 26, 1962, Felix Frankfurter suffered a debilitating stroke. He was the intellectual and political powerhouse of the Court's conservatives. The stroke left him hospitalized well into the summer. He would consult with John Marshall Harlan frequently and often sent his brethren articles and notes, but he never returned to the Court. Over the summer he retired, and three years later he died.

President John F. Kennedy picked Deputy Attorney General Byron White, the number two man in the Department of Justice, to replace Whittaker. Kennedy named Arthur Goldberg, his secretary of labor and a labor lawyer, to take Frankfurter's seat at the bench. Both appointments moved the Court dramatically to the left, especially on questions of civil rights, civil liberties, and economic regulation. Over the course of his career on the Court, White proved notoriously difficult to pin down ideologically, but he was certainly more liberal than Whittaker. Goldberg represented a more definite move to the left. He issued his most well-known opinion in *Griswold v. Connecticut,* asserting a broad right to privacy.[1] In his voting, he aligned closely with Douglas, Black, Warren, and Brennan.

Byron White and Arthur Goldberg cemented the liberal coalition that dominated the Second Warren Court. Over the next six years, the Court would issue far-reaching decisions that affected nearly every aspect of civil and criminal law in the United States. The period 1962–1968 was the heyday of the Warren Court.

Frankfurter's and Whittaker's departures clearly altered the direction that the Court took on apportionment, as well as many other matters. Byron White and Arthur Goldberg voted invariably with William Brennan as the Court cut through dozens of apportionment decisions over the next five years. There were now five sure votes for the liberal position on apportionment. Had Frankfurter and Whittaker remained on the Court just two more years, the political struggle that led to the *Baker* decision would have continued. The dozens of cases that the Court decided would have certainly come out differently.

As for Tom Clark and Potter Stewart, they swapped places. From 1963 through 1965, when the Court did most of its work on the apportionment question, Potter Stewart voted with John Marshall Harlan against nearly every liberal majority. Tom Clark truly did have a change of heart and voted with liberals more often than not, though he sometimes sided with Harlan. Clark often allowed exceptions to general rulings and favored a more nuanced approach that would have given lower courts and states more flexibility. Had Frankfurter

---

1. *Griswold v. Connecticut,* 381 U.S. 479 (1965).

and Whittaker remained, Clark would have been the pivotal Justice, and Clark's approach to the apportionment question closely resembled the approach that the Court took to the segregation cases. He wanted to proceed incrementally, on a case-by-case basis, allowing circumstances such as the presence of an initiative or special cases such as the "little federal plan."

Potter Stewart's eventual alignment with John Marshall Harlan reveals just how close the Court was in 1962 to following an entirely different path. Stewart might have just as easily sided with Frankfurter and closed the courts to legislative districting cases for good. In the October 1963 term, the Court heard *WMCA v. Lomenzo*, a case challenging the New York state legislative apportionment and one quite similar in its facts to the Tennessee suit. Facing a return of the *Baker* decision, Potter Stewart this time voted the other way. As with *Baker*, he opposed granting a writ of certiorari (hearing the case to begin with), but in the final vote he sided with Harlan, as he would on most of the cases raised over the next two years. He now saw where the Court was heading and became a staunch adherent to the position staked out by Harlan and Frankfurter.[2] Had he foreseen this turn of events, Potter Stewart surely would have sided with the conservatives in that first conference on *Baker* in April 1961. And if Frankfurter had garnered five votes at that meeting, the decision would have established the political thicket doctrine espoused in *Colegrove* as a true precedent.

Instead, the new Court that assembled in the fall of 1962 gave Warren and Brennan six liberal votes and considerable leeway in charting a new course. With the additions of Goldberg and White, Potter Stewart and even Tom Clark no longer held the pivotal votes. Brennan and Warren had a ready voting bloc in William O. Douglas, Hugo Black, Arthur Goldberg, and Byron White. Tom Clark would prove loyal to the reapportionment cause as well; his change of heart was sincere and lasting. Warren and Brennan no longer needed to negotiate their way to resolution of the apportionment cases. With the political stalemate on the Court broken, the painful negotiations and delays that marked the Tennessee case from 1960 to 1962 were over. The liberal majority could now act quickly and decisively.

Still, defining the Court's new role required prudence and self-restraint. By the fall of 1962, it had already received a dozen appeals challenging state and federal apportionments; that number grew to seventy-five complaints by 1963. The Court looked to be headed down a similar path to the one it followed in

2. The opinion would not come down until June 1964. For an excellent history of this case, see Calvin B. T. Lee, *One Man, One Vote: WMCA and the Struggle for Equal Representation* (New York: Charles Scribner and Sons, 1967).

desegregation. Many local complaints and cases could lead to many different and confusing rules, and they could place the local courts in the impossible role of serving as administrative agencies forced to implement state and federal rulings, just as they did with school desegregation.

At the time that they had decided *Baker*, the Justices held two other apportionment cases. One challenged the apportionment of New York's state senate; the other contested the Michigan apportionment plan. Neither case was as clear as the situation in Tennessee. Both New York and Michigan had reapportioned within the past decade. In Michigan, the people could pass constitutional amendments and laws through the initiative, and in fact the public had approved the plan that August Scholle sought to invalidate. Fortunately, in both instances, the lower courts merely ruled that they lacked jurisdiction, as they interpreted *Colegrove* to mean. They had not heard or judged the facts of the cases. The U.S. Supreme Court quickly dispensed with both cases. Citing their ruling in *Baker v. Carr*, the Justices sent these cases back to the lower courts for hearings on the merits. Both cases would return for a judgment on the merits the next term. The New York and Michigan cases presented complications that would have given both Potter Stewart and Tom Clark pause had *Baker* not already been decided. In the case of Michigan, the state had the initiative, and the public had even passed the existing apportionment plan via the ballot. That surely would have persuaded Clark to stick with Frankfurter and likely would have swayed Stewart. In New York, the state legislature was not out of compliance with its own constitution, as it was in Tennessee, because the malapportionment was written into the constitution. Both cases required overturning parts of state constitutions and begged the question of a remedy. Tennessee was much easier, as the only course of action the Court needed to take involved sending the case back to the state courts for a trial. The timing of the cases was a stroke of good fortune, one of the few that the Tennessee case seems to have enjoyed. Had the Michigan or New York cases arrived before the Tennessee case, it seems likely that Frankfurter would have prevailed.

A handful of other cases were already on their way through the lower courts in March 1962. Indiana's state legislature had failed again to reapportion in 1961. The state supreme court held the legislative elections unconstitutional, creating a constitutional crisis in that state. New Jersey's state supreme court had asserted jurisdiction over the state's apportionment; that dispute was under appeal as well. State courts were already beginning to cast off the U.S. Supreme Court's bridle. Then *Baker* struck.

Within days of the ruling in favor of Charles Baker, individual voters filed lawsuits challenging the electoral districts in Georgia, Alabama, Delaware, Maryland, Florida, Hawaii, and Mississippi. Barely a month after the decision, the *New York Times* reported apportionment suits in at least twenty-two states. The ruling, while it may have opened the door to federal judicial relief just a crack, had in fact opened the courts at all levels to hear such cases. The two dozen cases heard by the lower courts in 1962 would invariably lead to appeals to the U.S. Supreme Court.

The onslaught of cases called out for a systematic, methodical approach to the problem. The Justices needed to establish clear standards that could guide lower courts and state legislatures. On this question, the liberals disagreed.

William Douglas argued that the Justices should embrace a strict egalitarian standard, as he and Justice Black espoused in *South v. Peters*. The Chief Justice wanted to preserve exceptions in a large number of cases. Warren defended the "federal" system, which allowed representation of population in one chamber and of geography in the other.

William Brennan saw the matter more clearly than anyone else on the Court. *Brown v. Board of Education* carried an important lesson. Proceeding incrementally would result in a painful and confused process, and one that might ultimately fail. Addressing the apportionment problem required a single absolute standard. The Court's standard had to ensure equality and had to be easily and unambiguously applied. Equally important, it must be rooted in constitutional principles and fundamental rights. There was, Brennan understood even in the spring of 1962, just one such standard: equality.

However, until the Justices could fashion such a standard, they should hold off on making any rulings. During the 1963 term, the Justices imposed something of a moratorium on apportionment cases. They would not decide the cases until they could agree on a rational approach to the problem as a whole.[3]

There was one very important exception—Georgia's primary election law.

Just days after the *Baker* decision, James Sanders, a resident of Atlanta, decided to challenge the county-unit rule. Under the Niell Primary Act of 1917, every county received a fixed number of votes, and whichever candidate won a plurality in the county won those unit-votes. The problem was that unit-votes were not proportionate to population, and Fulton and DeKalb counties had many fewer unit-votes than their populations warranted. Sanders sued both the chairman of the state Democratic Party, James H. Gray, on the grounds that the Democratic primary was tantamount to the general election, and the secretary of state, the chief election officer in Georgia.

On the same day that the district court heard Sanders's case, the Georgia state legislature passed a bill that altered the county-unit system. The amended

---

3. Memorandum for the Conference from Hugo L. Black, 31 January 1964, William J. Brennan Jr. Papers, Library of Congress.

Neill Act increased the number of unit-votes for the larger counties and required that candidates in the first round of the election win a majority of votes as well as a majority of county unit-votes. The district court held that it had jurisdiction and that there is a right to having one's vote count the same as someone else's, but its decision applied to the old law, not the amended Act.

James Sanders appealed the decision to the U.S. Supreme Court on May 11, just five weeks after the *Baker* decision. The case sped to the Court. In conference on June 18, 1962, the seven Justices then serving (Goldberg had not yet arrived and Frankfurter had not yet stepped down) voted unanimously to hear Sanders's suit. The Justices heard the case on January 17, 1963, and they reached a decision the following Monday. Seven Justices sided with James Sanders; only Harlan dissented.

The case was somewhat unusual. It did not concern the state legislatures or even the U.S. House. Instead, it attacked the nominating procedures for statewide offices. But the case allowed the Court to revisit and overturn an earlier Supreme Court decision. *Gray v. Sanders* was exactly the situation considered in *South v. Peters*. William Douglas had written the dissent in that case, only to be stymied by Frankfurter. *Gray v. Sanders* gave the Court the opportunity to revisit its decision in *South v. Peters* in light of *Baker*. For William O. Douglas, the decision was a long-awaited victory.

The Chief Justice gave Justice Douglas the duty of writing the opinion of the Court. For most of the seven-page opinion, Douglas focused on the particular questions raised in the case. He argued that *Baker* established the Court's jurisdiction in this matter, that the Fourteenth Amendment protected the voting rights of all citizens, and that the U.S. Constitution did not sanction the unequal weighting of votes, except in the compromise that created the union among the many states. Writing with a new majority, Douglas could state more forcefully exactly what *Baker* meant.

> The conception of political equality from the Declaration of Independence to Lincoln's Gettysburg Address to the Fifteenth, Seventeenth, and Nineteenth amendments can only mean one thing—one person, one vote.[4]

CLEARING THE THICKET

"One person, one vote." Justice Douglas's elegant words expressed a self-evident truth. The phrase captured a new concept that Americans immediately

---

4. 372 U.S. 368, 381.

embraced as an essential part of their political ethos.[5] Professor Robert Mc-Closkey of Harvard Law School, although sympathizing with the judicial restraint espoused by Felix Frankfurter and John Marshall Harlan, concluded that *Baker* and subsequent decisions had tapped a "latent consensus," a common belief in the fundamental value of political equality.[6]

But what did it mean?

Among legal scholars, theorists, and judges, the decision sparked a heated debate about what the Court should do next. The search was on for a legal standard, a set of rules derived from laws and precedents that would guide what courts would do and when they would do it. Who can sue and when, and what did they need to show? How could states defend their practices? What exactly did one person, one vote mean? Were there exceptions or conditions when the rule did not apply? These were the practical questions that awaited a more expansive decision—or, more likely, a series of decisions.

The Court was widely attacked for the very presumption that an acceptable standard could be found. Many commentaries expressed the commonsense notion that without first enunciating possible standards, judicial intervention made no sense. No standard may even exist. Felix Frankfurter most clearly enunciated this view in his dissent to *Baker*. After Frankfurter's departure, John Marshall Harlan continued to pound this drum in his repeated dissents to the apportionment cases.

Legal scholarship published the very same year as the *Baker* decision only underscored Frankfurter's misgivings. Dean Phil C. Neal of the University of Chicago Law School wrote the most extensive critique of the *Baker* decision. He made an exhaustive survey of the proposed remedies and the legal standards on which they could be based. "The courts," he concluded, "have simply assumed that, having entered the field of reapportionment, they have unlimited authority to bring about reformation of the State legislatures." This was not "a great example of the rule of law in our society,"[7] but of "the role of fiat in the exercise of judicial power."[8] This was politics in search of law.

More pointed attacks, from both the right and the left, faulted the courts for what they had already done. Professor Alexander Bickel of Yale Law School

5. In his travels in the early 1970s, Richard Reeves reports that political equality was one of three pillars of the American political ethos of the day. Richard Reeves, *American Journey* (New York: Simon & Schuster, 1982). See also Herbert McCloskey and John Zaller, *The American Political Ethos*, (Cambridge, MA: Harvard University Press, 1986).

6. Robert G. McCloskey, "The Supreme Court, 1961 Term," *Harvard Law Review* 76 (1962): 54, 59.

7. Quoted in Nicholas Katzenbach, "Some Reflections on *Baker v. Carr*," *Vanderbilt Law Review* 15 (1962), 829, 836.

8. Phil C. Neal, "*Baker v. Carr*: Politics in Search of Law," *Supreme Court Review* (1962): 252–327.

warned in November 1962 that *any* standard would be dangerous.[9] Eventually, the Court would have to let an apportionment stand; it would have to say this is what we will allow, and not that. The very act of creating a standard would legitimate inequalities. A standard-setting opinion would necessarily have to call some perfectly acceptable arrangements unconstitutional. In so doing, the Supreme Court would unintentionally make some political institutions second class. This eventual outcome, Bickel ominously concluded, was the same sort of mistake that the Court had made in *Plessy v. Ferguson.*

A radical critique came as well. Professor Alfred DeGrazia argued that the Court had placed one standard of political equality above others. Equally valid notions of equality consider social outcomes, not just population. Urban and suburban areas had much higher incomes and wealth than rural America. Equal population apportionment would, on average, benefit wealthier areas and voters at the expense of the poor. Existing state legislative apportionments served as a counterweight to economic inequalities in American society, and reapportionment would only magnify existing social and economic inequities.

Most commentary on the *Baker* decision focused not on whether the Court had erred but instead on the next steps forward. What standard should the Court set?

In the months following the ruling, a tremendous range of ideas poured forth. They ranged from the very incremental steps to quite far-reaching reforms. At one extreme were those who argued that state law should determine the solutions; the courts should merely determine when a state legislature fails to comply with the state constitution. At the other extreme were those who put forth wholly new concepts of representation. The editors of the *Yale Law Journal* proposed one such idea—the Court should maximize legislative responsiveness to constituencies.[10] Population amounted to just one of many factors, including economic interests, social groups, and political identities. Relatively little of this academic speculation, however, led to a clear standard. *Baker* and *Gray* had closed the door on reverting to state law; state laws were part of the problem. As for the more creative proposals, it was unclear how they could be implemented. Besides, the Justices had already taken the first tentative moves toward a solution.

The Court had started down not one but two paths. The real question was which it would ultimately follow.

The most obvious approach was to insist on equal results, equal outcomes. That could only mean mathematical equality of district population. Justice

9. Alexander Bickel, "The Durability of *Colegrove v. Green,*" *Yale Law Journal.* 72, no. 1 (November 1962): 39–45.
10. "*Baker v. Carr* and Legislative Apportionments: A Problem of Standards," *Yale Law Journal* 72, no. 5 (April, 1963): 968–1040.

Douglas's opinion in *Gray v. Sanders* stated this in no uncertain terms: the Fourteenth Amendment meant one person, one vote. How these apportionments scheme came about and whether there was a rationale mattered not. Professor Katzenbach, among many others, took this to be the true meaning of the majority opinion in *Baker*. Proponents of mathematical equality argued that the Court silently assumed equality as the ultimate answer to the apportionment question.

Tom Clark's concurring opinion pointed to another way out, what Professor Robert McCloskey later called the "procedural standard." The U.S. Supreme Court could not declare mathematical equality as the law of the land. One could not read that in the U.S. Constitution and its amendments or from legal precedents. Rather, equal protection protected people against invidious discrimination and arbitrary treatment. Judges could decide whether a plan was rational and was created from a legitimate political process, nothing more. The key test for an apportionment was whether the apportionment derived, ultimately, from the consent of the governed and followed some discernable principle. The people of Tennessee had not consented to the existing apportionment act because the legislature had not passed an apportionment act since 1901, and the state offered no means for public expression of consent because it did not allow the initiative. The districting plan itself was irrational, a "crazy quilt." Clark's crazy quilt established a minimum criterion that any plan had to pass. Such a standard would allow states to have unequal districts so long as the majority in the state assented.

Clark had further argued in his concurring opinion that even where there was invidious discrimination, the courts need not require mathematical equality. Rather, they could require the creation of additional at-large seats or award seats to the counties that experienced the most egregious discrimination so as to break the stranglehold of those controlling the legislature and to permit passage of a constitutional apportionment plan.

Justice Brennan saw that mathematical equality offered the only true way to produce anything resembling equality. That was the simple, commonsense meaning of one person, one vote. And it was doable. Many states had achieved nearly equal populations in their U.S. House districts, and a few states had achieved this standard in at least one chamber of their state house. Brennan saw that a procedural approach, on the other hand, simply would not work. One could not reasonably strike down legislative districts that had a modest degree of inequality that evolved gradually and at the same time allow highly unequal district populations elsewhere because the state had a rationale for a districting plan that the citizenry approved through the initiative.

Brennan also understood fully that the courts could create a tangle of contradictory legal rulings if they followed the usual judicial process. Cases come to the Court willy-nilly, one at a time. They do not arrive in an order that lends to a natural progression of questions that the Court must address. Sequence would matter. A majority on one narrow issue could lead the Court down a path that led to inconsistent rulings and criterions. Without a general strategy, the courts could easily render a series of decisions that made it impossible to achieve even the most basic, general principle of political equality.

As cases began to arrive on appeal during the summer and fall of 1962, the possibility of contradictory rulings became painful clear. The most difficult issue would be the "federal analogy"—requiring equality in one chamber but allowing inequality in the other. A majority of the Justices likely would have allowed states to follow the federal model. Warren certainly leaned that way, as did Stewart and Clark. White or Goldberg might also side with the Chief. Harlan surely would have gone along with this group, given the alternative of equality in all chambers. Under the guise of equal protection, then, the Court might approve farcically large inequalities in district populations, as existed in California's state senate and Connecticut's assembly. If the Court first ruled on the federal analogy, it would preclude a later ruling for mathematical equality. If, however, the Court first declared that equal protection meant mathematical equality of population, then the federal analogy would surely fail as a justification for malapportionment.

By the time the Justices decided the Georgia unit-vote case in January 1963, they had already received a dozen appeals raising a wide range of issues. What does equality mean? How should the states apportion under this new order? What circumstances and countervailing considerations should be considered in judging apportionment plans?

Ten key cases cut to the core issues distinguishing the two possible standards—results versus procedure.

Two cases brought apportionment of the U.S. House before the Court. *Wesberry v. Sanders*, filed in October 1962, attacked the population inequalities in Georgia's congressional districting system. *Wright v. Rockefeller* challenged New York's house districting plan. The Court combined these cases under the title *Wesberry v. Sanders*, though the New York case raised issues of racial districting. *Gray* and *Wesberry* revisited two older cases, *South v. Peters* and *Colegrove*.

Cases from six states concerned state legislative apportionment. On March 29, 1962, just three days after *Baker*, a district court in Alabama filed an injunction against holding state legislative elections under the existing districting plans, which dated from 1962. Three suits emerged to challenge the districting plan that the state legislature passed over the summer of 1962. *Reynolds v. Sims* and *Vann v. Baggett* were both filed in October 1962, and *McConnell v. Baggett* was filed in November 1962. The Court grouped these together in a single case, *Reynolds v. Sims*; it would become the centerpiece of the apportionment rulings. At the same time, cases from New York, Maryland, and Virginia reached the Court. *WMCA v. Lomenzo* attacked the New York apportionment, especially the "ratio formula" used to apportion seats in the state's senate. *Maryland Committee v. Tawes* challenged the apportionment of the state senate in the Maryland constitution, which grossly underrepresented the Baltimore suburbs. Shortly thereafter, in February 1963, the Court received *Davis v. Mann*, a suit against Virginia's apportionment. Virginia raised the tricky issue of how large a deviation the Court would tolerate. The state was among the best apportioned in the country, but the lower court ruled that there was no rationale behind the deviations that did exist.[11]

Two additional cases, which arrived in the summer of 1963, challenged the idea that social compacts and popular consent justified malapportionment. *Roman v. Sinnock* attacked Delaware's long-established apportionment rules. The state's three counties had created the state in 1776, and county representation in the state reflected that original compact. *Lucas v. Colorado Legislature* presented perhaps the most difficult case. The people of the state had approved the apportionment plan through the initiative, and the resulting apportionment plan resulted in only modest inequities. Lucas's suit argued that even popular rule could not justify political inequality.

The Solicitor General joined all seven cases as amicus curiae. Once again, the Solicitor General would prove an essential ally to those seeking relief.

The immediate problem for the Court, though, was how to deal with the very large number of cases and how to prevent contradictory decisions. Appeals from a dozen other states arrived, and many more were winding their way through the state and federal courts. The apportionment cases presented a bewildering array of circumstances and issues. It was unclear where to begin.

William Brennan and Earl Warren decided on a strategy. The Court should address all of these cases, and the many issues they raised, at one time. They should hold all of these suits and map out a general solution. If ever there was an instance of the Court making policy, this was it.

The Chief Justice chose to handle the ten key cases before the Court as a single package. The Justices discussed the entire set in conference on one day, June 10, 1963.[12] Unlike the *Baker* case, there was little question about whether to accept these cases. In every instance, the vote to "note probable jurisdiction" or

---

11. In addition, two suits from Hawaii were combined with other cases.
12. The Delaware and Colorado appeals had not yet arrived; jurisdiction was noted a month later, and they were scheduled for hearing along with the others.

to grant a writ of certiorari was unanimous. The Justices heard arguments on the apportionment cases over a three-day period, from November 12 to November 14, 1963. And on November 26, 1963, Earl Warren assigned himself the task of writing the opinion of the Court in every one of the state legislative apportionment cases. The Justices held off on making decisions on any one until they had agreed on a strategy that would encompass all of the cases. Again, the clock was ticking. The 1964 elections were coming up in just a year; the Justices would have to resolve the question of standards by spring, summer at the latest.

Chief Justice Warren and Justice Brennan worked closely together throughout their time together on the Court. That relationship proved essential in the apportionment cases.

William Brennan assigned his clerks the task of preparing a brief that would address the entire apportionment question. Over the winter of 1962 and spring of 1963, his clerks assembled the mounting commentary and legal argumentation on apportionment. The summer of 1963 brought a new class of law clerks to the Court. Brennan handed over the volumes of law review articles, lower court rulings, and legal documents to one of his new clerks, Stephen Barnett. Barnett immediately began to map out the newly formed landscape, and by the beginning of November 1963 he had written what became the Justices' guide.

We discovered Barnett's brief in Justice William Brennan's papers four decades after it was written. It was no longer in one piece. Brennan had divided it into pieces corresponding to each case. What is striking about the fate of Barnett's work is that even though Brennan did not write any of the other key apportionment decisions, the brief clearly shaped all of the cases. Justice Douglas penned *Gray*. Justice Black wrote *Wesberry v. Sanders,* the congressional case. And Chief Justice Warren tackled at once the state legislative apportionment cases in Alabama, Colorado, Delaware, Maryland, New York, and Virginia. The majority opinions in all of these cases followed the clerk's logic and, at times, language quite closely—a testament both to how closely the liberals worked on these cases and to the importance of clerks' work.

"Standards for Reapportionment," Stephen Barnett's 350-page brief, accomplished three vital tasks for the Justices. First, it examined every significant standard proposed in legal scholarship, political science, popular commentaries, and judicial opinions in light of *Baker, Gray,* and other precedents. Second, the brief tested the apportionment standards in each of the pending cases. Third, the brief sought to discover a workable solution.

Barnett found acceptable only one standard, that proposed by the Solicitor General. During his argument in the Alabama case, *Reynolds v. Sims,* Archibald Cox laid out a detailed legal interpretation of the Fourteenth Amendment and its implications for legislative apportionment. The Solicitor General attempted to establish a comprehensive interpretation of the equal protection clause that subsumed Clark's crazy quilt as well as the prohibition on discrimination on the basis of race. Unlike much of the scholarly writing, the Solicitor General's standard clearly stated the how the courts would proceed.

Cox began with what seemed like a procedural approach. The Fourteenth Amendment, he conjectured, provides a guarantee against unreasonable discrimination. It does not insist on mathematical equality of legislative district populations. In this respect, Frankfurter, Neal, and others are correct.

Equality does, however, play a central role in the Cox's formulation. Equality serves a natural benchmark. It is the norm against which gross deviations in legislative district populations must be measured and justified. Plaintiffs need only provide evidence of unequal district populations to establish the grounds for a legal challenge to a legislative apportionment plan. States may defend their plans if they can show that inequalities are "justified by an apportionment policy that is rational and legitimate and adequate to support them."[13] A policy is rational if it is based on a clear criterion or rule, such as providing less populous counties with more seats or poorer counties more seats than wealthier ones. Such countervailing principles must be weighed against equal population. A policy is legitimate if the public consented to be governed and if that policy does not create invidious or arbitrary discrimination. A policy is adequate if it does not "prevail over the interest in population equality."

The Solicitor General's approach did not involve an overly broad interpretation of existing precedents and interpretations. It provided clear guidelines as to how state and federal courts could proceed. It offered flexibility in addressing different apportionment rules. Barnett was particularly keen on salvaging the "federal analogy," and this approach had enough "play in the joints" to do so.

The bulk of "Standards of Apportionment"—two hundred pages or so—applies the Solicitor General's approach to cases before the Court from five different states: Alabama, Delaware, Maryland, New York, and Virginia. The concluding note to the brief sums up the situation succinctly: "I am somewhat more satisfied with the general standard proposed than with its application to the five cases." Alabama, Delaware, and Maryland clearly violated equal protection. Alabama, like Tennessee, had created a crazy quilt. Its apportionment law had not changed in sixty years, and population drift, not a clear, rational policy,

13. Stephen Barnett brief "Standards for Reapportionment," 1963, William J. Brennan Jr. Papers, Library of Congress.

accounted for the gross disparities in district populations. Maryland and Delaware had passed apportionment laws, but the inequities were not clearly based on a legitimate standard other than the protection of the old order.

Virginia and New York, however, created a problem. These cases pulled the Court in opposite directions. Virginia ranked among the least malapportioned states in the nation, but the federal court had thrown out the districting plan because it viewed the population deviations as invidious discrimination. New York had considerably more inequality than Virginia, especially in the state senate, and a history of gerrymandering and malapportionment. The lower court in New York, however, held that the state had followed a rational approach to apportionment. The legislature regularly reapportioned to adjust for population, and the state constitution's formula for senate apportionment did not create invidious discrimination. "I find it difficult," Barnett reflected, "to regard the irrational discrimination in Virginia as worse than the calculated one in New York."

The Solicitor General's standard, then, did not go far enough. It could be used to validate highly inequitable systems and, at the same time, strike down relatively fair districting plans. The Court stood at a fork; this would be the last important choice it faced in figuring out the standards for apportionment. It could content itself with eliminating extreme abuses. Such an approach would be beyond criticism and would not impair the Court's stature in the states or the country as a whole, but it would lead to uneven results, as in New York and Virginia. The only way to save the federal model, the brief concluded, was to mix "into the formula a liberal dose of 'lower court discretion.'" That, however, is precisely what got the Court into trouble in the segregation cases.

Alternatively, the Court could insist on a relatively high degree of equality. It could go even farther than the Solicitor General argued and insist on equal population districts in all chambers of all legislatures regardless of circumstances. That would result in more consistency across states and in lower court decisions. It would lead the courts deeper into this issue and would disrupt state politics and governments across the nation. The reaction, Barnett predicted, would be no worse than the reaction to *Baker v. Carr* itself. Paradoxically, the more extreme approach would be easier to implement. It would be easier for courts to interpret and apply, and the political reaction would be no worse than what they already encountered. Politics pointed toward taking the more extreme approach, and that is the route they would take.

At the last conference before Thanksgiving in 1963, the Justices decided to overturn the apportionment laws in all ten cases they held. The Court would need to speak with one voice, and that voice would be the Chief Justice's. Over the next three months, the Chief Justice set about to craft the opinions that would steer the Court out of the mathematical quagmire that Felix Frankfurter foretold, and out of the political thicket.

The first of the Court's new apportionment decisions addressed representation in the U.S. House. The principal case, *Wesberry v. Sanders*, challenged population inequalities in Georgia's U.S. House districts. James Wesberry and a group of Fulton County residents protesting Georgia's House apportionment sued the governor of Georgia, Carl Sanders. This was the question raised in *Colegrove*. Like Chicago, Atlanta was the dominant city in the state, and its house districts had two to five times the population as districts elsewhere in the state. The Tennessee case made vulnerable house district maps throughout the United States that had grossly different populations, and the Atlanta group took up the charge. *Wesberry v. Sanders* provided an ideal opportunity to exorcise *Colegrove* directly and completely.

Warren decided to separate the U.S. House cases from the others and to decide them first thing in the new year. This was possible because, as Barnett argued in "Standards for Reapportionment," the House apportionment question could be decided on a separate basis. It was also politically expedient. Hugo Black wrote to his colleagues: "The Chief Justice tells me he will wait about writing the State apportionment cases until after other arguments on that question are heard in March. Under these circumstances, I think it highly desirable that the congressional cases come down without further delay."

The Chief Justice assigned the case to Hugo Black, one of two remaining dissenters from *Colegrove*. The first case announced in the new year was *Wesberry*. Justice Black based the decision on section 2 of Article I of the Constitution, which states that the representatives be chosen "by the People of the several States." That phrase, he wrote in the majority opinion, means that "one man's vote in a congressional election is to be worth as much as another's."[14] This was exactly the argument laid out in "Standards of Reapportionment." Black pointedly avoided any mention of a general standard of equal political representation that might apply beyond the U.S. House. Indeed, he noted in footnote 10 of the decision that the majority's opinion did not address the question of whether the apportionment violated the equal protection rights of the plaintiffs. Rather, Justice Stewart joined John Marshall Harlan in his dissent. The conservatives feared that Black's opinion put the Court in a most dangerous position and risked a constitutional crisis. Justice Black had in effect declared illegal every House election in which populations were not as equal as practically possible. The Supreme Court had cast "grave doubt" on the constitutionality of the U.S. House of Representatives itself. The reapportionment revolution was now in full swing.

14. *Wesberry v. Sanders.* 376 U.S. 1, 8 (1964).

By early March 1964, Chief Justice Warren was ready with his opinions in the state legislative apportionment cases. He would go much farther toward mathematical equality than even he originally intended. The difficulty reconciling the New York and Virginia apportionment cases revealed to him that even the flexibility permitted in the Solicitor General's standard allowed too much leeway. Barnett's brief was a long thought-experiment in the apportionment process under Cox's flexible standard, and it did not lead to a satisfactory approach. The Court faced a stark choice. It could permit a considerable degree of political inequality and strike down only the extreme cases, or it could force the potentially painful but consistent result of mathematical equality. Warren chose the latter path.

Reynolds v. Sims served as the flagship of the reapportionment rulings. *Reynolds* was in many ways a perfect starting point. Alabama's apportionment closely resembled Tennessee's. The state had not reapportioned since the beginning of the century. There was no initiative process offering voters a direct way to revise legislative district boundaries. Considerable malapportionment had grown by accretion in both houses of its state legislature. The state legislature had made some effort at reapportionment following the *Baker* decision, but gross inequities remained. Alabama's new apportionment law shrank the ratio of the most populous district and the least populous district from 41-to-1 to 16-to-1 by increasing the number of seats in Montgomery, Mobile, and Jefferson. The district court struck down that apportionment plan. It evaluated the plan using the procedural approach proposed in Justice Clark's concurring opinion in *Baker* and concluded that the new apportionment plan still lacked rationality.

Warren circulated his first draft of the opinion on March 16, 1964; in it, he took on not just the question of equality but the difficult problem of the "federal analogy." The Chief Justice's opinion applied the reasoning of the Solicitor General. There were four key questions. First, was there a violation of the norm of equal population? Yes. District populations in both chambers under the new plan deviated excessively from equality. Second, was the discrimination harmful and invidious? Again, Warren concluded it was. Third, was there a rationale? Warren agreed with the district court's assessment that the new apportionment plan lacked a clear rationale. In its defense of the apportionment before the Supreme Court, the state had offered another rationale: the federal analogy. Inequalities in one chamber balanced out the inequalities in the other chamber. This defense put the federal model front and center. Fourth, was the rationale legitimate? Warren's opinion left no doubt on this matter. The federal analogy does not justify malapportionment. The division of the legislature into two chambers serves the public interest, not the representation of particular interests or areas. It enhances deliberation and makes it difficult for factions to control the legislative process. Bicameralism accommodates representation of states in Congress, but that is not its primary purpose, and it cannot justify malapportionment. The state must apportion both chambers "substantially on the basis of population," and it had to act promptly. Warren shied away from phrases such as "all deliberate speed"; he gave them a specific time frame and stated the consequences. Alabama had to pass an equitable plan in time for the 1966 election, or state and federal courts would take appropriate actions, including ordering at-large election of the entire state legislature.

Six Justices immediately signed on. John Marshall Harlan continued his opposition to the Court's intrusion in this matter. Tom Clark was uneasy about the opinion, as was Potter Stewart. Clark immediately sent the Chief a note expressing his reservations. The opinion went too far. The Justices did not need to rule on the federal analogy. The Court need only declare that there was "invidious discrimination in both chambers."[15] Both Clark and Stewart agreed that the state's apportionment discriminated against those who were underrepresented, but they would not agree to the sweeping argument of the majority. There was, however, no need to bargain. A majority of six agreed with the Chief. On March 18, the Chief Justice circulated what would be the final version of the majority opinion in *Reynolds*.

Two years after it had entered what Felix Frankfurter called the "mathematical quagmire," the Supreme Court had arrived at a solution. William Brennan had guided the Justices to a simple standard that one person, one vote allowed no exceptions; the Court would push a draconian solution: mathematical equality.

The Court's announcement of its decision in the Alabama case would wait for the completion of all of the state apportionment cases. With *Reynolds* as a precedent, the Maryland, Colorado, Delaware, New York, and Virginia cases fell immediately into line. They raised exactly the same issues, with only slight variations in the extent of inequality and the rationale behind the original apportionment. The Chief's reasoning in the Alabama cases applied immediately to the other five states. The delay came from the large number of other appeals that the Court had received just since January. In the spring of 1964, the Justices heard a dozen new apportionment cases as well, and the Chief Justice decided to hold off on an announcement of the *Reynolds* decision until all of the apportionment cases could be addressed. Finally, at the end of the term, the Court was ready.

On Monday, June 15, 1964, the Court cut a wide swath through the apportionment field. The Justices first read *Reynolds*, then *Maryland Committee v.*

15. Tom Clark to Earl Warren, n.d., Tom Clark Papers, University of Texas.

Tawes. WMCA v. Simon, Mann v. Davis, Roman v. Sinnock, and *Lucas v. Colorado* followed. In one day, the Court had established a new standard for apportionment. The states had to create legislative districts with equal populations. No exceptions were allowed. The federal analogy was dead. Only the U.S. Senate escaped the axe, and then only because of its special status granted by the Constitution.

One week later, the Court announced nine more apportionment decisions. No region was untouched. The Justices struck down apportionments in Connecticut, Florida, Idaho, Illinois, Iowa, Michigan, Ohio, Oklahoma, and Washington. In just two weeks, the Justices had declared unconstitutional the apportionments in seventeen states. Come October, even more state legislative apportionments would fall. The Court's opinions made clear that every state legislature would have to redraw districts and rewrite its apportionment laws in line with the new doctrine of one person, one vote.

COUNTERREVOLT

"At first it was total disbelief—total, total disbelief—that anybody'd be so stupid as to interfere with the state constitution. . . . Then the bulk of the people in the legislature said, 'Well, we'll just ignore it for a few years. After all, what can they make us do?' "

That, according to Stephen Teale, was the immediate reaction to *Reynolds* in the California state senate. But when Teale, then a state senator from Calaveras County, went to the Democratic National Convention in Atlantic City that summer, he realized that the *Reynolds* decision was no passing storm. In Atlantic City, he met colleagues from across the country, from other state legislatures and from Congress, who faced the same choice—to fight the Court or to obey it.[16] Among the California state senators, opposition to the *Reynolds* decision was unanimous, and as Teale traveled across country through the summer of 1964, he found that common ground with state legislators throughout the nation. "Everybody was talking about passing a federal constitutional amendment or simply ignore Chief Justice Warren and tell him to go to Hell."[17] For his part, though, Teale realized they were "going to have to do it."[18] But change would not come without a fight.

16. James H. Rowland, "Interviews with Stephen P. Teale," in *One Man–One Vote and Senate Reapportionment, 1964–1966*, Governmental History Documentation Project (Berkeley: University of California, Regional Oral History Office, Bankroft Library, 1979), 15.

17. Ibid, 16.

18. Ibid.

Congress immediately struck back at the Court. Members in both the U.S. House and Senate quickly introduced bills to undo the reapportionment decisions. State legislatures across the country began to organize similar efforts to resist. The counterrevolt would ultimately fail because the Court had so completely changed the political landscape. Nothing short of an amendment to the U.S. Constitution could overturn *Baker*, *Reynolds*, and their brethren. The reactionaries simply could not muster the required super-majority of votes.

The effort in the U.S. House attempted to deny the federal courts jurisdiction over state legislative apportionment. In July 1964, barely a month after *Reynolds*, Representative William Tuck (D-VA) introduced a House bill, HR 11296, that declared that neither the Supreme Court nor the federal district courts have the right to review any "petition or complaint seeking to apportion or reapportion any legislature of any state." The bill was assigned to the House Judiciary Committee, where Chairman Emanuel Cellar (D-NY) signaled his opposition to the bill following a brief round of hearings. Not willing to let the movement die, the southern Democrats and Republicans in the Rules Committee took the highly unusual action of forcing the Judiciary Committee to release the bill for consideration by the entire House.[19] Opponents attacked Tuck's bill as clearly unconstitutional; moreover, many states had already begun their reapportionments. Nonetheless, the Tuck bill passed the House on August 15, 1964. A large majority of Republicans and southern Democrats sided with each other against a bloc of northeastern, midwestern, and western Democrats. Just two months after *Reynolds*, Congress was primed to challenge the Court.

The Senate, meanwhile, set out on a different line of attack—allow reapportionment, but protect the "federal plan." Unlike their House counterparts, the counterrevolutionaries in the Senate understood that they would have to amend the U.S. Constitution. On August 4, 1964, Senator Everett Dirksen (R-IL) introduced a constitutional amendment that would allow inequalities in one chamber of a legislature so long as the state provided equal representation in the other chamber. He also proposed a four-year stay in the implementation of any court orders for reapportionment. The delay, he hoped, would buy time to revise the Constitution. His measure also would have overturned parts of the *Reynolds* decision and declared acceptable states with "federal plans." Senate majority leader Mike Mansfield (D-MT) joined Dirksen's cause.

Senate liberals dug in and began a two-month-long filibuster of the Dirksen Amendment. On September 10, Dirksen and Mansfield organized a vote to end

19. The Rules Committee vote was 10 "yea," 4 "nay," and 1 "present." The "yea" votes were almost all from southern Democrats and Republicans (five Democrats, from AL, AR, MS, VA, and CA, plus all five Republicans on the committee). The "nay" votes were from northeastern or midwestern Democrats (MO, NY, IN, MA).

the filibuster, but it failed miserably, losing on a vote of 30 in favor of ending debate to 63 against. The liberals continued to block the amendment. Two weeks later, Mike Mansfield proposed a compromise—a resolution stating the "sense of the Congress" that the Court had gone too far. Mansfield hoped to end the "gross incompetence and demeaning futility" on display in the Senate. Eugene McCarthy (D-MN) and Jacob Javits (R-NY) signed on; the filibuster ended, and the Mansfield compromise passed easily, 44 to 38. Dirksen saw the compromise as a "toothless cop-out" and voted against the measure. Immediately after the impasse ended, South Carolina senator Strom Thurmond, who had declared himself a "Goldwater Republican" just days earlier, introduced the Tuck bill to the Senate. The Senate overwhelmingly rejected it, 21 to 56. The House effort to deny federal courts' jurisdiction had failed. Dirksen continued to push for his constitutional amendment, but the Mansfield compromise had deflated much of the anger over his bill, and as the fall recess approached on October 3, the Senators were anxious to finish other business and return home.[20]

The 1964 presidential campaign election was now in full swing. Barry Goldwater openly criticized the Warren Court's apportionment decisions in a speech before the American Political Science Association on September 11, 1964. The Republican Party promised in its national platform "support of a constitutional amendment, as well as legislation, enabling states having bicameral legislatures to apportion one house on bases of their choosing, including factors other than population."[21] President Lyndon Johnson chose not to take sides on the issue. Why rock the boat on the way to one of the largest landslide victories in American history in the 1964 election?

That fall, a second campaign began. The American Farm Bureau Federation and the Chamber of Commerce joined forces to organize a call from the grassroots for a national constitutional convention on the apportionment question. Their aim was to call a convention for the express purpose of approving Everett Dirksen's amendment. Article V of the Constitution—the same article that guarantees the equal representation of states in the Senate—provides that two-thirds of the states (thirty-four states) would have to approve petitions for a convention, and never in U.S. history had that succeeded. By early 1965, twenty states had already officially approved the call. "The campaign for the Dirksen amendment has been the No. 1 issue since January," reported a spokesperson for the Farm Bureau in July 1965. "In the long run, the reapportionment issue

20. "Court Reapportionment Decree Challenged," in *CQ Almanac 1964* (Washington, DC: CQ Press, 1965), 386–97.
21. Ibid. 396.

is more important to the farm people than any one year's farm bill. This fight will have effects for many years to come."[22]

The Court had clearly changed the game. No simple law would overturn *Baker* and *Reynolds*. State legislatures could not allow the old order to continue simply through inaction. Equal representation stood on the Fourteenth Amendment; Congress and the states needed to approve a constitutional amendment to reverse course. The Court's opponents were now forced to take unusual measures.

Senator Dirksen and Representative Tuck regrouped for a last charge. When the new Congress convened in January 1965, they chose to focus the House and Senate efforts on the Dirksen Amendment. Representative Tuck introduced the Dirksen Amendment into the House on January 5. The following day, Senator Dirksen reintroduced the Dirksen Amendement in the Senate. Members of Congress introduced a total of twelve bills and resolutions concerning reapportionment in January, but the legislative debate would revolve around the Senate's efforts to reverse *Reynolds* and salvage the "federal plan."

As the debate wore on from January into early spring, lobbying on both sides of the issue intensified. Most of the debate concentrated in the Senate Judiciary Committee, which held extensive hearings throughout April and May 1965. Every major agricultural group, led by the Farm Bureau, lined up in support of Dirksen, and the major business groups, including the Chamber, the National Association of Manufacturers, and the National Association of Real Estate Boards, joined their effort. They also found a surprising ally in the American Bar Association. Every national labor union except the Teamsters lined up in opposition. They were joined by the major civil rights organizations and the National Council of Mayors, which had agitated for equal representation since the 1940s.[23]

The Dirksen Amendment at last came to a final vote on August 4. Northern Democrats voted almost unanimously against the bill; northern Republicans and southern Democrats voted for it. It won: 59 yeas against 39 nays. A very strong majority had at last sided with the Dirksen Amendment, but this was not enough. The counterrevolt fell 7 votes short of the two-thirds required to amend the Constitution. Senator Dirksen would try again in 1966 but come nowhere near as close. The counterrevolution in Congress had failed, foiled by the very rules protecting "minority rights" against tyranny of the majority.[24]

---

22. "State Apportionment Plan Loses in Senate," in *CQ Almanac 1965* (Washington, DC: CQ Press, 1966), 523.

23. Ibid., 527. Thirty-two unions, rights organizations, and municipal groups testified in opposition to Senate Joint Resolution 2 during hearings in March, April, and May; seventeen farm and business groups testified in its support.

24. Ironically, the very next vote was on the Voting Rights Act, and it passed overwhelmingly.

Meanwhile, the drive for a constitutional convention continued apace. Local arms of the national Farm Bureau and Chamber of Commerce joined the drive, as did the National Farmers Union, local affiliates of the Grange, and the National Association of Manufacturers. By the end of the year, the House Judiciary Committee had received twenty valid calls for a constitutional convention from state legislatures in Alabama, Arizona, Arkansas, Florida, Idaho, Kansas, Kentucky, Louisiana, Maryland, Minnesota, Mississippi, Missouri, Montana, Nevada, North Carolina, Oklahoma, South Carolina, South Dakota, Texas, and Virginia. The Chamber of Commerce reported convention calls from seven other states: Georgia, New Hampshire, New Mexico, Tennessee, Utah, Washington, and Wyoming.[25]

The farmers' campaign, however, would get no closer. It was already too late. The reality of the situation had sunk in for most legislators. They had to draw new boundaries and do so immediately. Delay would only raise the personal political risks. If the legislators did not come up with new lines by the next election, then they faced the prospect that the courts would take over legislative elections and hold elections at-large. Incumbent legislators were not willing to wait and see if a constitutional amendment, either through Congress or a convention, would succeed. As the state legislatures convened throughout 1965, nearly every one began the process of drawing new district boundaries.

The Farm Bureau and the Chamber made a last push to organized state legislators to lobby one another. It backfired. Don Allen, an assemblyman from Los Angeles, recounted the failed efforts of California state legislators to persuade other state legislators to pass the Dirksen Amendement.

> Jerry Waldie, who was an assemblyman and a floor leader, told me that he had gone to Massachusetts. . . . And they told him to get his ass out of their state. That's just exactly what he told me. . . . We'll run our business. We don't need any help from you Californians. And he got the same thing in New Hampshire. And when these guys came back, they were defeated, because none of the Eastern people wanted any part to do with them. See what I mean? It broke them up. The California legislators touring other states who were turned down on the Dirksen amendments decided it was time to get down to business and proceed to carry out the Court's edict.[26]

The judges had outpoliticked the politicians. They had entered Frankfurter's thicket, and they leveled it.

---

25. "State Appointment Plan Loses in Senate," 523.

26. James H. Rowland, "Interviews with Don A. Allen," in *One Man–One Vote and Senate Reapportionment, 1964–1966*, Governmental History Documentation Project (Berkeley: University of California, Regional Oral History Office, Bancroft Library, 1979), 39–40.

PART III

Politics Remade

Apportionment of Seats in the House of Representatives—1951*

(95 Tennessee Counties)

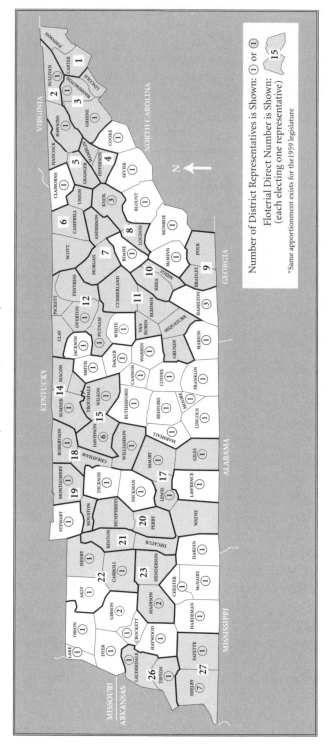

Number of District Representatives is Shown: ① or ①

Floterial Direct Number is Shown: 15
(each electing one representative)

*Same apportionment exists for the 1959 legislature

The change in representation in Tennessee: Maps from the City of Nashville's brief in Baker

Number and Distribution of Direct Representatives According to Tennessee's Constitutional Formula and Based on the 1960 Voting Population According to the 1960 U.S. Census

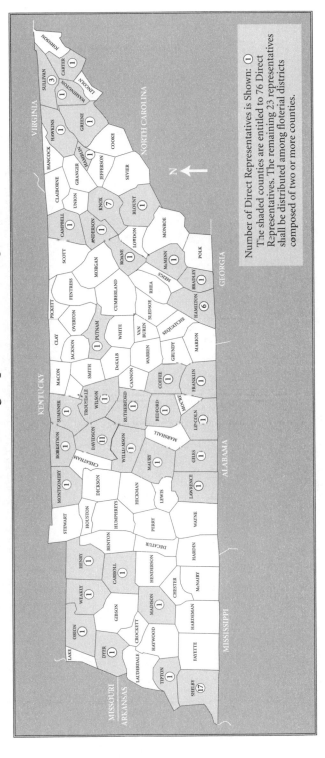

Number of Direct Representatives is Shown: ①
The shaded counties are entitled to 76 Direct
R-presentatives. The remaining 23 representatives
shall be distributed among floterial districts
composed of two or more counties.

9

Equal Votes, Equal Money

The Court's decisions in *Baker v. Carr* and then *Reynolds v. Simms* set off a cataclysmic shift in American politics. Rural areas had maintained their numbers in the legislatures over the decades despite dwindling shares of the states' populations. *Baker* asserted the power of the courts to review legislative districting in order to ensure equal protection; *Reynolds* imposed a solution.

The magnitude and scope of the changes were staggering. One person, one vote affected nearly every legislative district in every state legislature. In 1964, the Court set out a rule of thumb for an acceptable degree of population inequality. The judges would allow deviations from strict population equality of about plus or minus 10 percent. Over time, some state and federal courts have adopted even stronger rules, and in one instance they have required exact population equality.[1] Even still, only one in seven districts met the 10 percent rule in 1964. According to the population figures produced by the 1960 Census, only 1,148 out of 7,881 state legislative districts had populations within 10 percent of equality; one-third of the districts (2,485) contained excessively large populations, and well over half of all state legislative districts (4,248) were too small. Districts outside the acceptable range of equality would have to be changed significantly in order to comply with the new standards, and bringing the legislatures into line with the law would ultimately require changing every legislative boundary in the country.

Remarkably, all states eradicated gross disparities in legislative district populations within five years. The American states began the 1960s as the most

1. *Larios v. Cox*, 300 F. Supp. 2d 1320 (2004).

unequal representative bodies in the world, and they finished the decade adhering to one of the strictest standards of equal representation. By the beginning of the 1970s, equal representation of population had become a new fact of political life. A fresh cohort of politicians, who represented newly created urban and suburban constituencies, rose to power. These new politicians would remake the legislatures and political parties in their states as they pushed the interests of their constituents, just as the rural politicians they replaced had done.

Reapportionment unraveled rural majorities in the state legislatures across the country. Legislators from rural areas constituted a majority of at least one chamber in 43 of the 50 states in the early 1960s. New boundaries immediately eliminated rural majorities in 17 of these 43 states. California, Florida, Michigan, Ohio, Pennsylvania, and Texas all had rural majorities in at least one chamber that were undone by redistricting. By 1982, rural majorities remained in only a handful of states. City politicians did not supplant the farmers. Just five states saw the cities gain outright majorities of legislative seats between 1965 and 1970. More commonly, state legislatures reflected a new reality of American society: the population spread fairly evenly across urban, rural, and suburban communities. So, too, would the new state legislatures.

The era of rural dominance of state legislatures had ended abruptly. A new era of political equality had begun. The reverberations would be felt nationwide, as nearly every state legislature had extremely unequal representation and nearly every county stood to lose or gain political voice.

Our own fascination with the reapportionment cases developed long after the legal and political questions were settled. This dramatic realignment of votes is for political scientists what an earthquake is for geologists. Most of what we see lies only on the surface and reflects the gradual shifts that occur naturally over time. Typically, it is hard to detect the fundamental forces at work. Upheavals lay bare the raw structure and reveal how the thing itself operates.

Such is the case with the reapportionment of American legislatures in the 1960s. The sudden, surprising shift in representation exposes the simple mechanics of democratic politics. It allows us to see in clear relief the political and social consequences of political equality and inequality. Reapportionment, then, speaks directly to the most profound questions about democratic representation: What is the value of the vote? In a society where political power is unequally held, who gets what? And what is the consequence of making equal what was once not?

Pluralists and radical writers, such as Robert Dahl[2] and Alfred deGrazia,[3]

---

2. Robert Dahl, *Who Governs?* (New Haven: Yale University Press, 1961).
3. Alfred de Grazia, *Apportionment and Representative Government* (New York: Praeger, 1963).

argue that those with greater wealth or concentrated interests will dominate the poor and diffuse interests. Rural legislators, whose constituencies were poorer and less geographically concentrated than their urban counterparts, expressed exactly that fear. Left to its own devices, the urban majority, it was argued, would tyrannize the minority. That is not, however, what happened.

The aftermath of *Baker v. Carr* points to a much simpler view of political power. In a democratic society, political power is directly proportionate to votes. Power is the ability to join with others, to form coalitions, in support of a particular set of proposals for how the government should use its resources. Those who have more power win, and they win more often. For political scientists, money is the yardstick of power. While political power shapes all manner of public decisions, money unambiguously reflects the power that different segments of society and the polity have in the public arena. All seek to win a slice of the public weal, and as big a slice as possible. Money can be distributed and redistributed among the winners and losers, among those who have more power and those who have less. The division of public expenditures reveals the value of the vote.[4]

VOTES AND POWER

The Tennessee suit was not just a matter of principle or abstract rights. It was about who got what from the legislature. It was about the most basic substance of politics. It was about money; it was about power. And Nashville lacked both.

The Nashville attorneys certainly argued that their case raised a fundamental constitutional right—the right to equal protection under the laws as guaranteed by the Fourteenth Amendment to the Constitution. But that was not the motivation. The deeper motivation was self-interest. Their county did not have sufficient representation in the state house of representatives and senate, and as a consequence their country did not receive its fair share of money for roads from the gasoline tax fund or for public education from the general fund. Harris Gilbert, the city's attorney, prepared a detailed brief for the Court showing the populations and seats of each county and also the amount of money each county received from these two funds. The brief became integral to the case; it showed the harm done. Shelby, Davidson, Hamilton, and Knox counties combined contained 42 percent of the state's population. These four counties, however, elected

---

4. This chapter draws on research with our colleague Alan Gerber at Yale University. See Stephen Ansolabehere, Alan Gerber, and James M. Snyder Jr., "Equal Votes, Equal Money," *American Political Science Review* 96, no. 4 (2002): 767–77.

only 22 percent of the state legislative seats and received only 29 percent of the money that the state distributed to the counties for education and roads. The relief they sought was real and substantial.

Recognition of that problem raised a deeper question. What is a fair allocation of votes? Justice Brennan reasoned that legislative seats must be allocated strictly on the basis of population. His argument was a legal one that relied on the principles of equality and fairness. A fair political process and fair political institutions would lead to equitable outcomes, Brennan wrote. In an electoral system in which legislators represent areas, those ideas required that every area have representation commensurate with its share of the state's population. That would certainly have increased the representation of the cities, but would it have resulted equitable outcomes for all areas of the state?

Votes are the stock in trade of democratic politics, but they are not the ends in themselves. They are merely property rights—the opportunity to influence government decisions. They are potential power, not actual power. How votes are translated into political outcomes and results depends on the nature of politics inside the legislatures.

The battle over state legislative apportionment pitted against each other two very different views of representation and political power.

Defenders of the old order saw politics as the competition among blocs of interests—urban against rural, city against farm, rich against poor. In that struggle, urban politicians held a natural advantage. Large, concentrated, and wealthy interests always seem to dominate small and diffuse interests. Rural counties and interests were dispersed widely within states. Any project that benefited one area of a state, such as a road or a bridge, would have little benefit to a rural county in another part of the state. Metropolitan counties, on the other hand, had a common interest around which they could readily coalesce and form a voting bloc. Any project within a metropolitan county benefited all in that county. With minimal effort, it was argued, the urban interests would create a formidable voting bloc.

Cities were also centers of political and economic organizations in the states. Urban political machines could deliver the vote on Election Day and elect a loyal slate to the state legislature. In Memphis, Boss Crump's political organization relied on a coalition of city employees, blacks, and city Democrats. The city elected eight legislators at-large, and the vote nearly always followed a straight ticket. The Crump slate won two-thirds of the vote against all opposition. Inside the legislature, any politician, rural or urban, had a strong incentive to court the Memphis bloc in order to build a winning coalition behind an appropriations bill or particular project. In Tennessee, even though the speaker of the house almost always came from a rural county, the Memphis machine was pivotal in deciding which rural politician would rise to power. Even in a state that was majority rural, as in Tennessee, the urban bloc apparently held power well beyond its mere voting strength. Tennessee was no different from other states in this regard, and fear of urban machines or of large metropolitan interests shaped apportionment debates in nearly every state. Malapportionment was a simple means of ensuring that urban areas did not form blocs to dominate state legislatures. Unequal representation, it was argued, allowed rural areas to defend themselves against large and powerful urban interests.

The attack on malapportionment expressed a very different view of politics. The basic premises were the same. To win approval for a particular project or spending bill, legislators would have to build coalitions with others. Votes were the assets that legislators had to trade in forming such coalitions. However, political blocs, if they could form, would be unstable. Every legislator, urban or rural, was the agent of a particular constituency and its advocate. Individual legislators, then, were not motivated by projects that would benefit an entire city or all rural areas; they wanted projects that would benefit their own voters. City legislators would compete with and undercut one another, just as they would compete with rural legislators.

Equal representation, the argument went, would make for equitable outcomes. Every constituency would have an equal chance to be in a particular coalition on a specific piece of legislation, and coalitions would vary from bill to bill or project to project. Across many legislative actions, all districts would have as much influence. Urban legislators would be just as likely to coalesce with rural legislators as with other urban legislators. Equal representation would make for a level playing field in politics and would result in a fair distribution of public spending.

Political and legal theorists weighed in on the question as well. Academic debates over the logic of coalition formation yielded a flurry of articles and books on the nature of political power and new ways to measure influence and power.[5] One legal scholar dubbed these the "new math of effective representation."[6] Perhaps the most famous work in this vein was John F. Banzhaf's examination of weighted voting and his resulting index of voting power.[7] According to this line of reasoning, voting power derived from the number of coalitions in which a legislator or

5. See L. S. Shapley and Martin Shubik, "A Method for Evaluating the Distribution of Power in a Committee System," *American Political Science Review* 48, no. 3 (September 1954): 787—92; William H. Riker, *The Theory of Political Coalitions* (New Haven: Yale University Press, 1962); and Samuel Krislov, "The Power Index, Reapportionment, and the Principle of One Man, One Vote," *Modern Uses of Logic in Law* (June 1965): 37–44.

6. Robert G. Dixon, *Democratic Representation* (New York: Oxford University Press, 1968), 537.

7. John F. Banzhaf III, "Multimember Electoral Districts—Do They Violate the 'One Man, One Vote' Principle?" *Yale Law Journal* 75 (1966): 1309.

bloc of legislators cast the deciding vote on a bill. This theoretical analysis provided the link between the number of legislators the citizens voted for and their influence in the legislative process. Banzhaf's and others' writings revealed that various schemes of districting, such as multimember districts and weighted voting in the legislature, could produce dramatic inequalities. The thinking of political theorists at the time, then, reduced to just this: single-member districts with equal populations would ensure citizens had equal influence on legislative outcomes. All else could easily produce substantial inequities in power.[8]

The proof of who actually holds power lay in outcomes. The more powerful a constituency or interest is, the more influence it will have on decisions about what the government does. In this regard, the distribution of public funds to pay for education, roads, and other goods provides the cleanest expression of the power of the vote and the value of representation. Everyone wants a cut of public money. Every constituency would like the state or federal government rather than the local government to pay for new roads, schools, or hospitals in the area. Elected officials, seeking to stay in office, will use their influence to gain as much as they can for their constituents, and the more seats per person elected by an area, the more weight that area will have in legislative decisions.

The division of the public dollar expresses the political power of different constituencies and interests. The question, then, is how do votes translate into power? Two very different pictures emerged of what was to happen when the courts ordered equal district populations. If the levelers were right, then before the courts' interventions the amount of money a county received from the state should have mirrored that county's share of state legislative seats. On the other hand, if fears of urban power were justified, then reapportionment should have given urban counties a disproportionate share of state funds.

THE MEASURE OF POWER

For political scientists, reapportionment offers a rare natural experiment for studying political power in a democratic society. The realignment of American state politics that the Court initiated speaks directly to the most basic questions about democratic politics: What is the nature of political power in democratic government? How does representation shape what government does, and who wins, and who loses? What is the value of the vote?

In normal times, it is hard to discern the value of representation. Legislative decisions reflect the balance among many competing interests and constituents.

8. See Dixon, *Democratic Representation*, 537–43.

They reflect the hierarchies, norms, and organization within the legislature, including those of party and seniority. They reflect deals from the past and expectations about the future. The distribution of seats across geography surely matters, but it is hard to untangle the importance of representation from the many other factors that shape legislation. Today, with equality holding in every legislative chamber except the U.S. Senate, it is impossible to gauge the effect of inequality. The imposition of equal population representation, however, disrupted the equilibrium of the old order, and that shock to the political system allows us to see in clear relief the value of our votes.

Suppose, for the sake of argument, that we could do a pure experiment. We would determine the number of state legislative seats that each county would elect. In particular, in our hypothetical experiment, we would assign one county one seat, and another county of similar size two seats, and another county three seats, and so on. Some counties we would use as control groups, assigning them the level of representation that they deserve; to other counties we would give excessive amounts of representation; and to still others we would give very little representation. We would then allow the legislature to authorize and appropriate funds; next we would, observe how much money each county received in state revenues. We might further choose a different distribution of legislative seats and then observe how the distribution of funds changes in response. Of course, political scientists cannot, and should not, engage in such political engineering. The courts, however, did.

Court-ordered redistricting was not a pure experiment, but close. With few exceptions, the distribution of seats in state legislature was determined not by the current legislature but by political institutions that had existed for decades, even centuries. The Court's decisions in *Baker* and *Reynolds* forced the states to change the distribution of state legislative seats—a distribution that the states would not themselves have adopted. The Court's decision in 1962 was also unexpected. State legislatures did not have time to adjust their political behavior to appease urban interests in their respective states or to raid the treasury in advance of the coming change. And, perhaps most important, the treatment—the change in the distribution of votes—occurred on a very large scale, affecting nearly every sort of community in the United States. A basic principle of experimentation is to compare treatments with very different levels in order to see the effects of the experiment most clearly. That was certainly the case with malapportionment. Reapportionment, then, approximated well the ideal circumstances for observing how the distribution of voting power in a society affects the product of representative government.

What are the treatments, and what are the outcomes?

The treatments in this natural experiment are the shares of state legislative seats apportioned to each county or town within a state. In chapter 2, we presented one measure of the representation that each area within a state had: the Relative Representation Index (RRI). This index captures the treatment of the natural experiment exactly.

To recount briefly, the Relative Representation Index is the share of state legislative seats that a county holds relative to its share of state population. It measures what *is* against what *ought to be*. Prior to *Baker,* each county was allotted a share of the state's legislative seats by the state district laws. That distribution was the *is* of representation. Under equal representation, each county *ought* to have received a share of legislative seats equal to its share of the state population. Dividing the share of seats by the share of state population—that is, comparing what is to what ought to be—is mathematically equivalent to the calculation David and Eisenberg made. Thus a county that has a Relative Representation Index value equal to 1 has representation equal to the ratio one would expect under a rule of one person, one vote. Values less than 1 reflect underrepresentation, and values over 1 indicate overrepresentation.[9]

The Relative Representation of the counties changed dramatically from 1962 to 1972. Malapportionment before 1962 gave the populations of the counties widely disparate representation. Some counties had several hundred times as much weight in the legislature as they would receive with an equal population apportionment, while other countries deserved to have ten times as many seats. By 1970, the state legislatures had equalized the populations of all districts. The percentage difference between the most populous district and the least typically equaled no more than 3 percent. This dramatic change in representation is measured as the difference between the Relative Representation a country had after reapportionment and the Relative Representation the country had in 1962. Since district populations were nearly equal after 1970, the change in representation is approximately 1 minus the RRI of 1962.[10]

Measuring money requires some care. Ideally, one would like to know how much money all local governments within every state legislative district received from the state government as well as the number of people represented by each district. The lowest level of government at which there are comprehensive data on public finances and representation are the counties. Fortunately, the counties provide a fairly accurate mapping of the distribution of money and votes.

9. When a county is split across more than one district, the RRI is the weighted average of the representation of the various parts of the county. For example, suppose that one-third of a county is in district A and there are 10,000 people for every seat in A, and that two-thirds of a county are in district B and that there are 20,000 people for every seat in B. The number of representatives per person in this county, then, is (2/3) (1/20,000) + (1/3) (1/10,000).

10. See Council of State Governments, ed., *The Book of the States*, vol. 18 (1970/1971) (Lexington, KY: Council of State Governments, 1971), for information on the maximum deviations in district populations.

Before *Baker*, representation was divided primarily among the counties. The exceptions lay in New England, where towns served as the basis for representation. Throughout the country, state legislative districts coincided with counties and did not cross county lines. Most state legislative districts were the counties themselves—or, in New England, the towns. Metropolitan counties commonly had multiple seats per county, and many metropolitan counties with multiple seats conveniently elected their legislators at-large. Other metropolitan counties were divided into more complicated districts. These boundaries never crossed the county lines. The districting of metropolitan counties (including Wayne County, Michigan; Los Angeles County, California; Cook County, Illinois; and New York, New York) does make it difficult to measure the exact populations of every district. Where district population data are not available, we are forced to aggregate to the county level. Public finances are also not reported at the state legislative district level, making it impossible to measure how much money every district in the United States received.

Counties are also the basic administrative units of public finance in the states. They handle transfers of funds from the states to the local administrative units. Most important, the counties report state transfers to all local governments within the county in the U.S. Census of Governments. This provides a comparable measure among all of the counties of the amount of money received by each local government through the state legislative process. The congruence between (1) counties as a basic unit of administration of public finances, and (2) counties as a unit of representation means that this level of aggregation is the natural level at which to study the effects of representation on who gets what from state government.

There are over 3,100 counties in the United States. This is both a blessing and a curse. The blessing is that the very large number of administrative units allows us to measure quite precisely the consequences of unequal representation and the effects of equalization. The curse is in the data collection. Few scholars have ventured into these county-level data. Those who did study this issue before us aggregated the information they had to the state level and then correlated measures of the degree of political inequality in each of the fifty states to the variability of state expenditures across counties. That level of aggregation, however, does not establish which counties got what. In order to determine who got what, we compiled data on representation and public finances of all 3,000-plus counties.[11]

We seek to explain the *distribution* of public money by the states to their counties. Spending bills present the ideal situation in which coalition politics

11. Our analysis omits much of New England. Both representation and public finance followed town lines, rather than counties, for most of the region.

should arise. Every legislator champions his or her own constituency's interests; and to get that education project, highway, or hospital funded, legislators must find others with whom to trade votes. Such coalition formation is quite fluid. From spending bill to spending bill, different groupings of legislators will form—and strange coalitions can form indeed. Urban legislators seeking public transit money can find common ground with rural legislators seeking a highway extension. And no single bill will capture the extent of logrolling on spending bills that occurs. Rather, one must look at the distribution of all money across all counties or districts to gauge who got what.[12]

The Census of Governments reports total transfers from the state and the federal government to all local governments in a county. The Census of Governments has been conducted every five years since in 1957. We are interested in the changes that occur from before the imposition of one person, one vote to the decade following. The years 1957 and 1962 provide a picture of expenditures before *Baker*. Battles over redistricting occurred mainly from 1965 through 1972. By the mid-1970s, legislative politics were well in line with the new electoral districts. Transfers to counties in 1977 and 1982, thus, measure the distribution of revenues to counties once the rule of one person, one vote is in place. To smooth over year-to-year variations in expenditures, we average the 1957 and 1962 revenue reports and the 1977 and 1982 reports. Analysis of each year separately shows the same pattern as the pairs of years combined.

Transfers encompass all funds that states distribute to counties and local governments within the counties either through appropriations for specific projects or through programmatic appropriations, such as formulaic spending for highways. These funds span a large class of programs, including highways and roads, health and welfare, and education. Were transfers a single line item, they would be the largest category of state spending and of local revenue. In 1960, state governments spent a total of approximately $31 billion; of this amount, $12 billion comprised transfers to local governments for specific projects or as part of formulaic expenditures. Fully 40 percent of all money spent by the states went to local governments directly, making transfers an ideal way to see the effects of representation on influence on the distribution of government resources.[13]

---

12. Bickers and Stein have conducted excellent studies of federal expenditures. See Kenneth N. Bickers and Robert M. Stein, "The Congressional Pork Barrel in a Republican Era," *Journal of Politics* 62, no. 4 (November 2000): 1070–86; and Kenneth N. Bickers and Robert M. Stein, "The Electoral Dynamics of the Federal Pork Barrel," *American Journal of Political Science* 40, no. 4 (November 1996): 1300–26.

13. The average state transfer to counties equaled $71 per person in 1962 and $131 in 1977 (all figures in 1967 dollars). New Hampshire had the lowest average transfers per capita to counties in 1962 ($13) and in 1977 ($52). Colorado had the highest average transfer per capita to counties in 1962 ($140), and New York had the highest average transfer per capita to counties in 1977 ($258).

Public finances and state transfers to local governments vary considerably across states and over time. In order to compare across states, we calculate the amount of money per person transferred to each county relative to the average amount transferred to all counties in a given state. We compute the total transferred to each county divided by the county's population, and then we divide this by the average per capita amount transferred to counties in the state. This is equivalent to the county's share of total state revenues transferred to all counties per capita. This measure parallels the Relative Representation Index.[14] To gauge political power, one may simply assess how the change in the distribution of votes translated into the distribution of money.

VOTES AND MONEY

The simple theory of democratic power suggests that the distribution of public finances should have tracked quite closely the distribution of voting strength of the towns and counties. The effect of political representation on the distribution of public expenditures exhibits this in two ways. First, the political inequality that existed before the mid-1960s should have produced highly unequal divisions of the public dollar. Second, equalization of representation from the 1960s to the 1970s should have led to equalization of the distribution of money. In addition, we must confirm that other important forces, such as the War on Poverty, did not drive the equalization that we observe.

To demonstrate these two conjectures at work, we begin by examining a single state—Florida. Florida routinely ranked among the states with the most unequal representation. Although some states had a single chamber with larger inequities (such as the California senate and the Connecticut house), the combined Relative Representation Indices of Florida's upper and lower chambers exhibited the largest disparities in the country. Dade County, which consists almost entirely of the city of Miami, should have elected seven times as many members of the state assembly and six times as many members to the state senate as it did. Broward, Duvall, Hillsborough, and Pinellas counties each had one-third the representation they deserved. And these were the most populous counties. At the other end of the spectrum lie counties such as Lafayette and Gilchrist, with a hundred times the representation per capita as Miami. The five most populous counties contained just over half the state's population but elected only 13 percent of the lower chamber and 15 percent of the upper chamber. The forty-two least populous counties elected a majority of the

14. We exclude Alaska and Hawaii because they joined the Union in 1959.

FIGURE 9.1. *Relationship between money and votes in Florida, 1960*

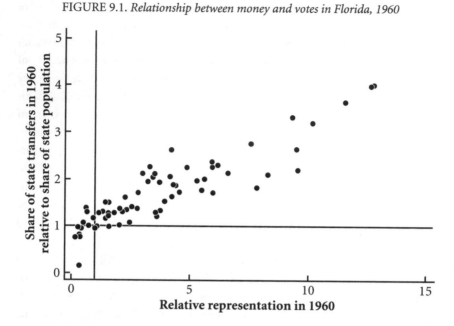

Florida house and senate, even though they contained just 12 percent of the state's population. These rural Florida counties had seventeen times the representation as the five most urban counties in the state.

First, did the unequal distribution of votes correlate directly with an unequal distribution of money? The contrast between the five most underrepresented and the forty-two most overrepresented counties reveals a clear relationship between representation and shares of state revenue in Florida. The five most populous and most underrepresented counties received $35 per person from the state for schools, highways, health care, and other local government functions. The forty-two most overrepresented and least populous counties received $105 per person in state transfers to local governments.

An even closer correlation between money and votes arises when we consider the finer gradations of the distributions of money and votes. Figure 9.1 displays the association between a county's share of state transfers relative to state population and its relative representation in the upper and lower chambers. Horizontal and vertical lines at 1 denote the level of equal disbursements of funds according to population and equal division of seats according to population.

Florida exhibits a very strong relationship between a county's share of representation and its share of state revenues. The correlation between money and votes exceeds .9, and the relationship displayed in the figure can be well summarized by a straight line. The analysis reveals that a county with double the amount of representation as another county received 40 percent more money from the state.[15]

The high payoff to the smaller Florida counties also made them highly dependent on state transfers as a source of revenue. Approximately one-quarter of all local government revenues came from the state in 1962, and the dependency was especially strong among the rural counties. Only 16 percent of local government revenues in Dade, Broward, Duvall, Hillsborough, and Pinellas came from the state. By contrast, almost half of all local government revenues for the forty-two most overrepresented counties in Florida came from the state. It is important to note that this pattern contradicts those who defended malapportionment, as the urban areas clearly could not form a bloc to protect their interests. Individually and collectively, they received much less than they deserved from the state. When reapportionment hit, it hit the rural communities hard. They would be faced with cutting local government expenditures or raising local taxes.

Second, did the equalization of representation in the state reduce, or even eliminate, the inequities in state transfers? To measure the effect of reapportionment, we consider changes in a county's share of state transfers to local governments from 1962 to 1982, well after the reapportionment and reformation of the legislatures, and how the change in revenue corresponded with changes in representation. Each county's representation was equal within a few percentage points by 1972, so the change in relative representation equals 1 minus the RRI in 1960.

Equalization of revenue was driven, in turn, by the equalization of representation. The relationship between the change in revenue and the change in representation was such that it almost entirely leveled what had existed earlier. The relationship between change in shares of revenue and change in shares of representation mirrors the relationship between representation and transfers before reapportionment. Counties whose representation doubled (grew by 100 percent) from 1960 to 1970 saw their share of state revenues grow by 34 percent from 1960 to 1980; likewise, those counties whose representation was halved witnessed their share of state resources fall by 34 percent.[16] This

15. The regression line summarizing the linear relationship in Figure 9.1 is as has a slope of .22 ($SE=.01$) and an intercept of .88 ($SE=.06$). The R^2 is .82. The variance of the dependent variable is .58, and the MSE is .11. To measure the percentage differences, transform Shares of Revenue and Shares of Representation into logarithms. The regression of log Revenue on log Representation has a slope of .40 ($SE=.03$) and an intercept of .07 ($SE=.05$). The R^2 is .69, and the variance of the dependent variable and MSE are .24 and .08, respectively. In both regressions, there are 67 observations.

16. A regression of percentage change in shares of revenue on percentage change in relative representation has a slope of .34 ($SE=.08$) and an intercept of −.08 ($SE=.08$). The R^2 is .20, and the variance of the dependent variable and MSE are .59 and .48, respectively. A regression of the linear change in Shares of Revenues on change in Shares of Representation has a slope of .15 ($SE=.01$) and an intercept of −.12 ($SE=.06$). The R^2 equals .64, and the variance of the dependent variable and MSE are .36 and .13, respectively. There are 67 observations in each regression.

FIGURE 9.2. *Money and votes in 1960*

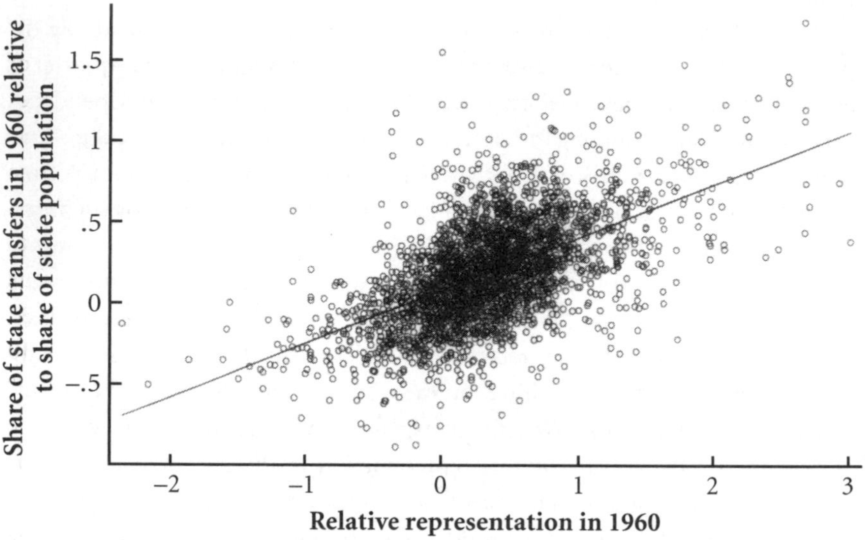

redistribution was almost enough to offset the unequal relationship between money and votes that existed before reapportionment.

The attack on malapportionment charged not only that political inequality produced inequities in public policies, but that equalization would correct these. In fact, the inequalities across counties fell sharply. The total amount of variation in the distribution of spending across counties was almost four times larger in 1962 than it was in 1982.[17] Moreover, the malapportionment that existed before 1964 no longer had any relation to the distribution of funds in 1982.

Florida demonstrates nicely the general pattern that adhered across all states. Looking nationwide, a strong positive relationship holds between money and votes. As in the previous discussion, let's consider each of the questions in turn.

First, was there a strong relationship between county representation and revenue received from the state in 1960, when representation was highly unequal? The overall pattern, though not as crisp, runs parallel to that in Florida. Figure 9.2 displays the relationship between shares of revenue that local governments in each county received from the state governments and the Relative Representation Index for all counties in the United States.

We change the scale in this figure to the percentage deviation of representa-

---

17. Specifically, the variance of shares of intergovernmental transfers was .57 in 1962 and .15 in 1982.

tion and of revenue from equality. The value of 0 corresponds to exact equality; a value of, say, 1 means that the country has 100 percent more representation or more money than it would receive under an exactly equal apportionment of legislative seats or of revenue. Nationwide, the distribution of shares of revenues and of shares of legislative seats is highly skewed, and percentage deviations correct that skew.[18] To correct for this skew, we change the scale of Relative Representation and Relative Shares of Revenue into the percentage deviations from equality.[19]

Immediately before the Court imposed one person, one vote on the state legislatures, there was a strong positive relationship between legislative seats per person apportioned to counties and state revenues per person transferred to counties. Nationwide, representation accounted for approximately 40 percent of the variation in the distribution of public expenditures in 1960.[20] The best-fitting line to these data has a slope of .33 and an intercept of .07. The interpretation is that a county with 100 percent more representation than another county receives 33 percent more money.

To understand what that means, consider two counties. One has twice as much representation as its population merits, and the other has half as much.[21] The relationship between money and votes implies that the overrepresented county received a 53 percent higher share of state funds than the underrepresented county. In addition, the positive value of the intercept reveals that even those counties with representation proportional to their populations received shares of transfers from the state in excess of their shares of the population. Specifically, the intercept of .07 implies that a county with Relative Representation equal to what it ought to receive (i.e., a value of the Relative Representation Index equal to 1) received about 7 percent more money per capita than its share of the population would warrant. The positive intercept means that counties that received exactly as many seats as their population size warranted in 1960 received

18. Another way to state this is that the RRI scale is asymmetric. A value of .5 in Relative Representation is comparable to a value of 2 in the following sense. If a county had half as much representation as it deserved, then doubling its seat share would bring what it actually had into alignment with what it ought to have had. Likewise, a county with double the representation of what it ought to have had can be brought into alignment with what it ought to have by halving the number of seats.

19. Specifically, we use a logarithmic transformation. The natural logarithm is such that $\ln(1/x) = -\ln(x)$. Hence, the natural logarithmic transformation makes the RRI and Relative Shares of Revenue measures symmetric: $\ln(1/2) = -.69$ and $\ln(2) = .69$; $\ln(1/3) = -1.09$ and $\ln(3) = 1.09$; $\ln(1/7) = -1.95$ and $\ln(7) = 1.95$; and $\ln(1/20) = -2.99$ and $\ln(20) = 2.99$.

20. This is calculated from a regression that holds constant the state. The coefficient on RRI is .33, and the beta weight is .56. The R^2 from this regression is .41.

21. The difference in these counties' Relative Representation is 1.3 in the logarithmic scale, which implies a difference in relative shares of state spending of .43 in the logarithmic scale.

somewhat more money from the state than equality would dictate. Most people lived in a very small number of grossly underrepresented but wealthier urban counties. The devaluation of the urban vote benefited all of the other countries, as they spread the urban wealth around. Thus even those not grossly overrepresented enjoyed spoils from the system of malapportionment.

A second, and even stronger, conjecture about the nature of political power holds that equal votes would lead to equal money. The simple theory of democracy embraced in the notion of one person, one vote implies that if all constituencies have equal voice in the legislature, then, on average, each will have equal political power and each will receive an equal share of public funds.

The alternative view expressed by those defending malapportionment held that the reapportionment of state legislatures would shift power wholly to the urban areas. Overrepresented areas certainly appear to have benefited from their malapportionment, but increasing urban representation may have created a large urban bloc and swung political power dramatically to the opposite pole. The result, rural voters feared, would be urban domination of legislatures and the complete exclusion of those outside of metropolitan areas. The numbers certainly looked daunting. Chicago itself had almost half of the population of the state of Illinois. New York, Seattle, Minneapolis–St. Paul, Atlanta, and Detroit had at least 40 percent of the populations of their states. By 1960, nearly every state had a majority of its population living in several metropolitan areas.

During the late 1960s and through the 1970s, legislative politics had time to adjust state budgets to accommodate the new political reality. As a result, the distribution of public expenditures in 1980 looked markedly different than it did just two decades earlier. The aggregate level of inequality in expenditures shrank over the course of the 1970s. By 1982, the spread in the distribution of state transfers to local governments was roughly half of what it had been in 1962.[22] Exact equality did not hold because government programs still sought to meet various demands, including alleviating poverty and maintaining basic government services. Nevertheless, the 1970s saw a tremendous equalization in public expenditures across counties.

---

22. The average and standard deviations of the distribution of counties' shares of state transfers bear this out clearly. Equality predicts a mean relative per capita transfer near 1 with a variance near 0. The average relative per capita expenditures in 1957 and 1962 equals 1.25, and the variance around this average is .17. The average relative per capita expenditure in 1977 and 1982 equals 1.06, and the variance is .09. In other words, state transfers to the typical county exceeded an equal division of funds by 25 percent in 1960, and that excess in the typical district shrank to just 6 percent by 1980.

FIGURE 9.3. *Money in 1980 versus votes in 1960*

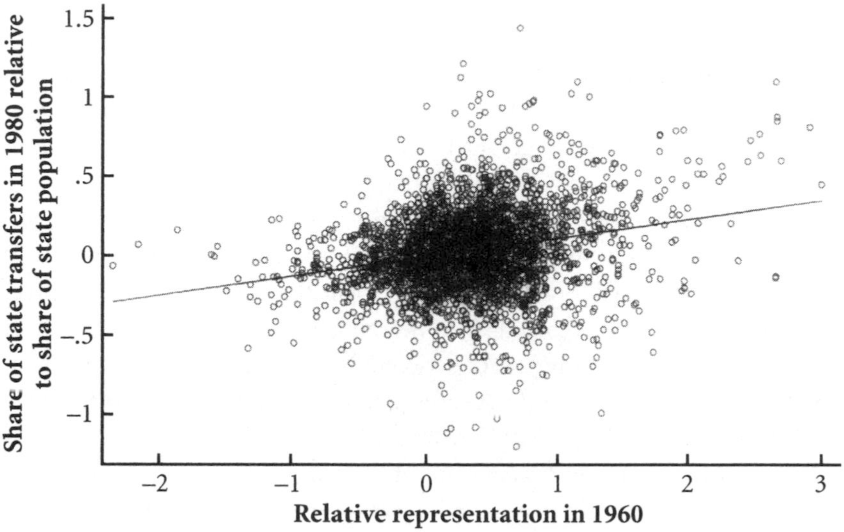

Within a decade, reapportionment had razed the inequalities in political power that had accumulated over the course of the preceding fifty years. By 1980, whatever advantage a county received from excessively high representation in its state legislature was nearly completely wiped out. Figure 9.3 graphs the relationship between a county's representation (votes) in 1960 and the amount of money it received in 1980. The relationship, in contrast to that in 1960 (see Fig. 9.2), is quite flat. The intercept is not statistically different from 0, and the slope is approximately .1. The slope remains above 0 because the rural faction still dominated in a handful of states. In most states, reapportionment completely leveled past political arrangements, and there was a complete or nearly complete correction in the distribution of public spending. In several states, we observed a substantial but not complete correction by 1980.

Nationwide, the equalization of public expenditures from 1960 to 1980 occurred in direct response to the equalization of representation. The comparison of Figures 9.2 and 9.3 strongly suggests that this was the case; but to convince ourselves, we examined more closely how the change in a county's representation from 1960 to 1980 translated into changes in that county's relative share of state revenues. Changes in revenue over this period equal the difference between (1) shares of state transfers to counties, and (2) the state averages in 1980 and in 1960. Positive values mean that the county's share of state revenue relative to what it received in 1960 rose; no change would mean that the county kept pace with the growth in state spending; negative values mean that the county fell behind what it received in 1960. The change in representation can be measured as the difference between the Relative Representation Indices in 1980 and 1960. Between 1964 and 1968, nearly every state adjusted its state legislative districts to comply with the Court's edicts. Reapportionment again in 1971 reduced population differences to less than 3 percent in nearly every state. Consequently, by 1980, every county had Relative Representation of 1—in other words, equality. The change in representation, then, is the deviation of the RRI in 1960 from 1. To correct for the asymmetry in these measures, we translate both measures to logarithms before computing the change from 1960 to 1980. Because all of the variables are measured in logarithms, the differences between the two periods can be thought of as percentage changes in the variables. In essence, then, we take the difference between the values in Figure 9.2 and Figure 9.3 for each county, and we estimate how much of the change in revenues can be accounted for as the change within representation.

The change in the distribution of revenues from 1960 to 1980 almost completely undid the inequalities produced by representation before 1960. The relationship between the percentage change in representation between 1960 and 1980 and the percentage change in revenues has a slope of .21 and an intercept of .08. Doubling a county's relative share of representation from .5 to 1 raised its share of state revenues by roughly 20 percent over the course of the two decades from 1960 to 1980, and shrinking a county's representation toward equality lowered the share of revenues it received. Moreover, the shrinking is toward equality. The changes in the distribution (slope of .21) nearly completely offset the original inequality in the distribution due to malapportionment (slope of .33). The changes did not lead to an excess of revenues going to urban areas. Equalizing representation, then, leveled the distribution of state revenues.

Representation, of course, is not the only factor driving the distribution of public funds. It is possible that the changes we have documented reflect not the change in representation but other changes in American society during this era. Several very powerful social forces in the 1960s also pushed for equality and redistribution in American society. Two stand out—the civil rights movement and the Great Society. President Lyndon Johnson's administration oversaw the creation and implementation of major government initiatives to alleviate poverty throughout the United States, and for the black community in particular. Great Society programs such as Medicaid created partnerships between the federal and state governments in the Johnson administration's War on Poverty. The Civil Rights Act and Voting Rights Act and activism of the civil rights movement forced states to remove racial barriers to basic government and social services and to address long-standing problems of poverty in the black community. The great shift that we have observed may have been caused not by the equalization of political representation but by the national effort to achieve social equality. If the civil rights movement and the War on Poverty account for the changes from 1960 to 1980, then the patterns we observe should be accounted for by indicators of the racial composition of the counties and income and poverty levels within the counties.

A further advantage of the counties is that the U.S. Census reports many social indicators at the county level; such data are not reported for small towns. Using the U.S. Census data, we constructed measures for the percentage black, the median household income, and the percentage living in poverty for each county in the nation. In addition, the single largest component of state transfers goes to schools. States pay for construction, basic education, and services, such as school lunch. To capture this important component of the demand for state funds, we use Census data to measure the school-age population of each county.

The strong relationships shown in Figure 9.2 and Figure 9.3 remain even after holding constant race, income and poverty, and school-age population. A full statistical analysis is provided elsewhere.[23] Race, poverty, income, and other demographics matter, but their inclusion does not alter the implications of our analysis. The estimated effects of representation on shares of revenue are unchanged when we control for the demographic features of the counties. Doubling a county's representation raises its share of per capita expenditures by 20 percent.

Moreover, the consequence of equalizing representation, holding constant race, poverty, income, and age, was to virtually flatten the distribution of public expenditures across counties. Consider two counties with similar racial, economic, and social profiles, but suppose one county had four times as much representation as it deserved in 1960 and the other had just one-quarter the representation it deserved. In 1960, the overrepresented county received approximately 40 percent more money from the state than it deserved, while the underrepresented county received approximately 25 percent less money from the state than it deserved. By 1980, the disparities between such similar counties were nearly completely eliminated: the previously overrepresented county received only 6 percent more than it deserved, and the previously underrepresented county received only 9 percent less than it deserved. This is not to say that race, poverty, and other factors do not matter. They do. Rather, representation was the driving force behind the equalization of public spending across areas. Equal votes led to equal money.

Race, poverty, and especially school-age population also shaped the distribution of state funds. Analysis of the Census data reveals that social indicators had statistically noticeable effects on the distribution of state money. The

23. See Ansolabehere, Gerber, and Snyder, "Equal Votes, Equal Money."

importance of schools in state public funding grew considerably from the 1960s to the 1980s. A county that had double the state average enrollment received 8 percent more money than the average county in 1960. A county that had double the state average enrollment, other things being equal, received 37 percent more money than the average county in 1980. Poverty was an important driver throughout. A county with roughly twice the state's poverty rate, other things being equal, received approximately 30 percent more money than the average county in 1960 and approximately 20 percent more money than the average county in 1980. And on race there was a significant reversal. A county that was 25 percent black received 6 percent less money from the state in 1960 than a county with no black population. By 1980, a county that was 25 percent black, other things being equal, received approximately 2 percent more money from the state than a county with no black population.

But these other factors cannot account for the tremendous equalization of state funds across counties that occurred from 1960 to 1980. The story is slightly different for poverty than for race and age. Poverty cannot explain the observed equalization for two reasons. First, the distribution of poverty across counties changed very little from 1960 to 1980. Approximately 50 percent of counties had poverty rates that were between .78 and 1.22 times more than the state average in 1960 compared with .81 and 1.17 times the state average in 1980. That difference pales in comparison with the change in representation. Second, poverty had a weaker effect in explaining the distribution of public expenditures in 1980 than it did in 1960, suggesting that the War on Poverty had not radically altered the spending priorities of the American states.

Race and age actually worked against greater equalization of spending across counties. As people sorted into different types of communities, especially suburban areas, the variability in percentage of black and of school-age populations across counties actually rose from 1960 to 1980. Changes in the distribution of race and age across counties, then, predict larger differences across counties, rather than equalization. States certainly responded to these different social needs created by poverty, race, and school-age populations, but such needs did not pull in the direction of equalization of public expenditures across areas.

Among the three great social forces of the 1960s and 1970s—reapportionment, civil rights, and the War on Poverty—only reapportionment could possibly explain the great equalization of public spending that occurred from 1960 to 1980. After controlling for the race, age, income, and poverty rates of the counties, we find that representation continues to have a strong effect on the division of public expenditures. The effects of equalizing voting power and representation cut across other social factors affecting the demand for public expenditures. Even in the face of the tremendous social changes wrought by civil rights and government efforts to fight poverty, it was the equalization of representation that led to the equalization of public spending.

What of the argument that the large urban areas would form powerful voting blocs and dominate the relatively weak and fractured rural interests of states? This was the great fear expressed by those defending the old order, and, if true, it implied that the states, especially those with large cities, would overcompensate and overcorrect. After reapportionment, the distribution of funds should have decidedly favored the largest counties, where it was thought legislative blocs would emerge. The shift should have been strongest in the most urbanized states and those states with single dominant cities, such as Illinois, New York, Georgia, and Missouri.

Such was not the case. In fact, in 1980 the distribution of funds continued to slightly favor more rural areas, if there was any correlation with population at all. The states where the distribution of funds tended to favor the largest counties in 1980 were Kansas and Wyoming, and the effects were on the order of 10 percent. A county with twice the average county population received approximately 10 percent more money. In the states with megacities, such as Illinois and New York and California, the distribution of funds did not tilt in the urban favor. Rather, the correlations between population and money were typically 0 or slightly negative by 1980. The urban blocs simply did not form. As a result, in nearly every state, legislative bargaining appears to fit the pattern of bargaining among many equals, resulting in a roughly equal per capita division of the public weal.

With the hindsight of history, it is clear that the Tennessee lawyers were right. The seemingly simple and naïve theory of democracy that they put forward, and that Court ultimately embraced, held true. Votes translated directly into political power. Separation of powers, especially through the governor's veto and ability to propose budgets, may have muted the effects of malapportionment, but they did not counterbalance the inequities in political power that unequal representation would produce. Nor was it the case that the large, wealthy urban areas would form political blocs that would dominate the legislative process, as the defenders of malapportionment argued. Rather, the American experience with reapportionment has proved a fundamental rule of democratic politics. Equal representation leads to equal political power.

REAPPORTIONMENT AND REDISTRIBUTION

Reapportionment altered the most fundamental aspect of democratic politics— the representation that individuals have in the legislature. The resulting shift in the distribution of spending immediately reveals the value of the vote; it also had very practical consequences for the states and counties. State transfers account for approximately one-third to two-fifths of local government revenues, and with these funds local governments invest in the basic infrastructure of the nation. They build roads and schools; they provide public health through hospitals and waste treatment; they ensure public safety through police and fire protection; they educate the next generation. Reapportionment fundamentally altered the ability of local governments—especially the overrepresented, less populous counties—to provide such basic services.

One way to gauge the long-term consequences of the *Baker* decision is to consider a counterfactual scenario. What if Joseph Carr and the State of Tennessee had won? Had the Court not imposed one person, one vote, what would the distribution of state revenues have looked like in 1980?

Had the State of Tennessee prevailed, the malapportionment that existed in 1960 would have remained. For their part, the state legislatures had no incentive to change district boundaries. Most of them had refused to do so for the better part of the twentieth century, and any attempt to make district populations more equal would have threatened large numbers of sitting legislatures. Further complicating matters, constitutional amendments were required to make any appreciable alterations in most state legislative districting schemes. Political inertia and rational self-interest, it appears, would have kept the 1960 state legislative boundaries. Malapportionment would have continued throughout the 1970s and 1980s. Indeed, it would have worsened as population continued to shift from rural counties to metropolitan areas.

Keeping the 1960 boundaries in place would have distorted further the distribution of public funds. There is a peculiar asymmetry in this redistribution: it hurt rural counties more than it may have helped the metropolitan areas. The distributions of votes and money are quite lopsided owing to the differences in county populations. About three-quarters of all counties had more voting power before *Baker* than they did afterward, though the overrepresented counties had just 29 percent of the nation's population. Counties in the bottom 25 percent of the distribution of representation had 71 percent of the nation's population. A relatively small percentage of the population (29 percent) held the balance of power in many states, and they had the most to lose.

Using the analysis of the relationship between money and votes, we can calculate how individual counties gained and lost with reapportionment. In the most underrepresented counties, the lowest 5 percent in terms of right to vote, equal votes increased state revenues by $88 per person per year. In the most overrepresented counties, the rule of one person, one vote reduced state revenues by $268 per person per year.

The cumulative effect on the distribution of funds was substantial. Elsewhere, we estimate that reapportionment led to a shift of approximately $7 billion annually of state transfers to local governments from counties that had previously been overrepresented to counties that had previously been underrepresented. Had malapportionment continued, the overrepresented areas would have received about $7 billion more from the state than they received, and the underrepresented areas would have received that amount less each year through the 1970s and 1980s. Reapportionment, then, resulted in a massive redistribution of public finances. It cut approximately 25 percent of the revenues that overrepresented counties raised from all sources—state transfers, federal transfers, property taxes, and other taxes and fees.[24]

This restructuring of public finances had a ripple effect for local economies. Over the long run, the gains that came with greater political power translated into higher growth rates within counties that were previously underrepresented. Holding constant the level of per capita income in 1970, we find that those counties whose representation grew witnessed relatively faster economic growth from 1970 to 1980. This result arises upon considering a standard macroeconomic model of growth. The rate of income growth declines with the initial level of income: richer areas have slower percentage growth than poorer areas. Against this baseline, one can judge whether the political gains and the resulting changes in state economic policies that came from reapportionment further magnified county income growth. Reapportionment had a noticeable effect on income growth above and beyond what one would normally expect given income levels in 1970, just as malapportionment ended. Consider two counties with comparable incomes, but one has half as much representation as it deserves and the other has twice as much as it deserves. The analysis of growth patterns predicts that on average the first county grew 3.3 percent more than the second county over the entire decade from 1970 to 1980, or about three-tenths of 1 percent more annually during this period.[25]

Economic gains and losses resulting from reapportionment were especially pronounced in the poorer counties. State transfers per capita amounted to a much larger share of income and local government resources for smaller and poorer counties than in richer urban and suburban counties. As a result, the economic consequences of reapportionment should have been most pronounced among the poorer counties in the United States, and in fact they were. Restricting attention just to counties with income less than their state's average, we find that

24. Ibid.

25. The regression is as follows: Change in Log Median County Income = $-.024$ log RRI $-.207$ log Median Income 1970 + 1.845. The R^2 equals .36. The predicted effect of the hypothetical example is $-.024*(\ln(.5)-\ln(2)) = .033$.

the effect of reapportionment on the growth rate was nearly 40 percent larger than the analysis for the nation as a whole.[26] Consider again two hypothetical counties with comparable incomes, but one has half the representation it deserves while the other has twice as much representation as it deserves. Now, however, both counties have incomes below the state average. The first county grew 4.8 percent more than the second county over the course of the 1970s.

Reapportionment, then, had a ripple effect on the state economies. It led to a substantial shift in political power, resulting in a shift in state spending and related policies. Over the long run, not only did counties that gained political power receive more money from the state, but they witnessed more rapid growth than comparable counties.[27] By the same token, those that lost representation slowed relative to their counterparts. The value of the vote, then, is seen not only in terms of who gets what out of government, but also in terms of broader benefits that government spending might bestow.

THE LEGACY OF THE U.S. SENATE

The Court's rulings left unchanged one legislative institution central to the American system of government: the U.S. Senate. Article V of the U.S. Constitution sets forth the procedures for amending the Constitution through acts of Congress and the states, with two provisos. First, the states and Congress cannot alter the ban on the importation of slaves after 1808. Second, "no State, without its Consent, can be deprived of its equal Suffrage in the Senate."[28] That protection was necessary to get the smaller states to agree to give up the power they held under the Articles of Confederation, in which every state had one vote in the Congress.

The legacy of equal representation of states in the U.S. Senate is increasingly unequal representation of population in the national government. The megastates—California, Texas, Florida, New York, Illinois, Pennsylvania, Ohio, and Michigan—have as much representation in the Senate as small-population states

26. Among the poorer counties, the regression predicting county income growth is: Change in Log Median County Income $= -.035$ log RRI $-.302$ log Median Income 1970 $+ 2.662$. The P^2 equals .46. The predicted effect of the hypothetical example is $-.024^*(\ln(.5)-\ln(2)) = .033$.

27. We do not view these analyses as definitive of the general economic benefits or costs of government expenditures for the society as a whole. A very extensive literature in economics has debated the economic stimulation and drag that government spending and taxation exert. Rather, our analyses pertain to the narrower question of whether reapportionment might have accelerated growth.

28. Article V reads as follows:

> The Congress, whenever two thirds of both Houses shall deem it necessary, shall propose Amendments to this Constitution, or, on the Application of the Legislatures of two thirds of the several States, shall call a Convention for proposing Amendments, which, in either Case, shall be valid to all Intents and Purposes, as Part of this Constitution, when ratified by the

such as Wyoming, North Dakota, Vermont, and Alaska. The House of Representatives reduces the differences in representation, and the discrepancies are not as bad as the worst of state legislatures before 1962, but they are substantial nonetheless. Wyoming, for instance, has 4 times as many seats per person in Congress as California; Vermont has 3.4 times as many seats per person in Congress as Texas; North Dakota has 3 times as many seats per person as New York. Ignoring the representation attained in the House, the inequalities of representation within the Senate itself are stunning. A person in Wyoming has 70 times as much representation in the U.S. Senate as a person in California; a person in Vermont has 40 times representation in the Senate as a person in Texas; a person in North Dakota has 32 times the representation in the Senate as a person in New York.

Such discrepancy from political equality has not escaped the scrutiny of scholars. For their part, empirically oriented social scientists have examined the disparities in public finances related to Senate representation along the lines of our analysis of the states. A team of researchers at the University of Southern California measured the difference in federal spending per capita between overrepresented and underrepresented states in the U.S. Congress. They found that from 1972 to 1990, the period when states were equalizing expenditures across areas, the disparities among the states were considerable. On average, overrepresented states received $576 per capita in federal transfers, net of taxes, and underrepresented states lost a net of $70 per capita.[29] The asymmetry owes, of course, to the much larger number of people in the underrepresented states among whom taxes and expenditures are spread. Of course, such studies cannot also see the effects of equalization of political power, because such equalization has not occurred. But the relationship between legislative representation in the U.S. Congress and the division of public funds among the states is a strong one.[30]

Reflecting on these and other empirical research reports and on the American experience, Robert Dahl, one of America's preeminent political scientists, argues that the U.S. Senate is one of the primary obstacles to political equality

---

Legislatures of three fourths of the several States, or by Conventions in three fourths thereof, as the one or the other Mode of Ratification may be proposed by the Congress; Provided that no Amendment which may be made prior to the Year One thousand eight hundred and eight shall in any Manner affect the first and fourth Clauses in the Ninth Section of the first Article; and that no State, without its Consent, shall be deprived of its equal Suffrage in the Senate.

29. Cary M. Atlas, Thomas W. Gilligan, Robert J. Hendershott, and Mark A. Zupan, "Slicing the Federal Government Net Spending Pie: Who Wins, Who Loses, and Why," *American Economic Review* 85, no. 3 (June 1995): 624–29.

30. Similar research by Frances Lee has confirmed the findings of Atlas, Gilligan, Hendershott, and Zupan and has explored the detailed ways that coalitions form in the Senate. See Frances Lee, "Representation and Public Policy: The Consequences of Senate Apportionment of Geographic Funds," *Journal of Politics* 60, no. 1 (February 1998): 34–62.

in the United States.[31] Among the world's legislatures, the U.S. Senate creates perhaps the most unequal representation, and that inequality, Dahl continues, translates directly into inequities in political power that run counter to fundamental principles of fairness and liberty. The tensions between the doctrines of fairness and equality and the institution of the U.S. Senate are deep and will continue to grow. Dahl concludes his treatise with a call for action and reform. We are not so optimistic, given how firmly the Senate is rooted in the Constitution, but reform is also not our mission.

Rather, we see in the U.S. Senate the exception that proves the rule. The *Baker* and *Reynolds* rulings could not affect the Senate. The continued inequality of representation in the U.S. Senate serves as an important confirmation of the lessons from the reapportionment revolution. It might be the case that the changed distribution of funds that we observe reflects a rage for equality, and not the change in political representation within state legislatures. If that were the case, then we should have seen an equalization in the distribution of federal funds to states. That is not what happened. Equal representation in the state legislatures had evened the distribution of state money across locales, but unequal representation of states in the Senate continues to produce a highly unequal division of federal expenditures across states.

The main lesson of the reapportionment revolution, then, is just this: a fair and equal electoral process leads to equitable outcomes—one person, one vote, one value. Regardless of other social objectives operating in the society, equalization of political representation drove a more equal division of public spending within the states.

As for our understanding of political power, the reapportionment revolution points very strongly to the simplest and most naïve theory of political power: political power is directly proportionate to a constituency's voting strength. The institutions of the legislature, the check of the governor, and the organization of the parties all complicate public decision making; but over the long run, in a democratic society it is the electoral process that drives political outcomes. Those constituencies with more representation win more often, and when political representation is equalized, so, too, is the power of the different segments of society.

---

31. Robert A. Dahl, *How Democratic Is the American Constitution?* (New Haven: Yale University Press, 2003).

10

Left Shift

Money offers one expression of the power of the vote. The balance between competing ideologies provides a second.

Legislative politics determine not just who gets what but which ideas about the public good will prevail. Such questions concern the size and power of government, the levels of spending and taxation, the amount and content of government regulation. To use the language of political science, these are ideological or spatial issues. In any policy domain, such as the level of spending or taxation or the extent of regulation, the legislature faces a continuum of choices. For simplicity, political scientists discuss these choices in ideological terms—left, center, and right; liberal, moderate, and conservative. Every politician holds a belief about what policy is best; in bargaining over specific bills, every politician wants the final bill to be as close as possible to his or her own most preferred outcomes. Moderates want centrist policies, conservatives want to move policy to the right, and liberals want to move the laws to the left. Everyone on one side of a question would benefit if it were decided their way and would lose if policies were to shift in the other direction.

Most observers and advocates expected the reapportionment revolution to shift public policy dramatically to the left. The reasons seemed obvious. Voters in metropolitan areas on the whole held more liberal views than rural voters and supported a wide range of legislative initiatives, such as unionization laws and minimum wages, mass transit, regulation of pollution and workplace safety, restructuring of state taxes, and increased spending on education, welfare, and health care. The rural-dominated legislatures took a decidedly conservative legislative approach to such questions. Reapportionment looked to change the ideological balance in the legislatures and give the urban agenda a major boost. One person, one vote would sweep aside large numbers of rural seats and replace them with urban ones. Equal representation of people, it appeared, would make the legislature more liberal and more in line with urban interests. The new metropolitan majority would finally implement its progressive program.

But herein lies a puzzle. Reapportionment appeared to leave little imprint on the orientation of the public policies and public laws that the states passed, a conclusion that left the critics of the Warren Court to gloat. Immediately after the reapportionment decisions settled down, academic researchers trained their lenses on the question of whether public laws shifted to the left. The experience of the states immediately stymied political science researchers. States with high levels of malapportionment did not spend less than other states overall, nor did they have lower public expenditures on education, health, and welfare programs central to the liberal agenda.[1] Studies examining changes in state expenditures in the years immediately after redistricting occasionally found statistically significant differences, but the results were largely mixed.[2] Badly malapportioned states did not exhibit systematically larger increases in total spending or social spending after reapportionment.

The overall thrust of this initial wave of research led to the conclusion that court-ordered equalization of legislative district populations had little if any

1. See Herbert Jacob, "The Consequences of Malapportionment: A Note of Caution," *Social Forces* 43 (1964): 256–61; Thomas R. Dye, "Malapportionment and Public Policy in the States," *Journal of Politics* 27, no. 3 (August, 1965): 586–601; Thomas R. Dye, *Politics, Economics, and the Public* (Chicago: Rand, McNally, 1966); Richard I. Hofferbert, "The Relation between Public Policy and Some Structural and Environmental Variables in the American States," *American Political Science Review* 60, no. 1 (March, 1966): 73–82; David Brady and Douglas Edmonds, "One Man, One Vote—So What?" *Trans-Action* 4 (1967): 41–46; Allan G. Pulsipher and James L. Weatherby, "Malapportionment, Party Competition, and the Functional Distribution of Government Expenditures," *American Political Science Review* 62, no. 4 (December, 1968): 1207–19; Brian R. Fry and Richard F. Winters, "The Politics of Redistribution," *American Political Science Review* 64, no. 2 (June, 1970): 508–22; Robert S. Erikson, "The Partisan Impact of State Legislative Reapportionment," *Midwest Journal of Political Science* 15, no. 1 (February, 1971): 57–71; and Robert S. Erikson, "Reapportionment and Policy: A Further Look at Some Intervening Variables," *Annals of the New York Academy of Science* 219 (1973): 280–90. Pulsipher and Weatherby ("Malapportionment, 1219) conclude: "it is possible to accept the hypothesis that malapportionment tends to depress and party competition tends to elevate some of the more important categories of state and local government expenditure." Their results do not support this conclusion, however, at least with respect to malapportionment. The estimated effect of malapportionment is statistically insignificant at the .05 level in 10 out of 12 cases, and one of the 2 significant coefficients is positive rather than negative (Table 5, p. 1216).

2. See H. George Frederickson and Yong Hyo Cho, "Legislative Reapportionment and Fiscal Policy in the American States," *Western Political Quarterly* 27 (1970): 5–37; and Roger A. Hanson and Robert E. Crew Jr. "The Policy Impact of Reapportionment," *Law and Society Review* 8 (1973): 69–93.

effect on public policies. Even scholars who found some evidence of policy effects admitted that the effects were uneven and more often than not statistically no different from 0.[3] "Political scientists," Herbert Jacob and Michael Lipsky summed up, "have substantially discredited two highly regarded precepts of American political life—that malapportionment and low levels of party competition are substantially related to the level of outputs."[4]

Forty years after *Baker v. Carr*, that assessment remains the received wisdom among legal scholars and political scientists. Gerald Rosenberg concludes in *The Hollow Hope* that "an overall reading seems to be that any effects that can be traced to reapportionment are small. . . . Legislatures were reapportioned, but the reformers' liberal agenda did not then automatically come to pass."[5] The noted Harvard law professor Alexander Bickel offered the most pointed critique. "Chief Justice Warren is quite wrong," Bickel wrote in 1971. "His court's apportionment decisions are no significant achievement. They gave us no new birth of majoritarianism, any more than they changed the substantive course of American politics."[6]

Bickel's words offered a poignant critique of the Warren Court, but they amount to an indictment of the American view of representative democracy generally. Both in common conversation and in hard-nosed political analyses, Americans characterize electoral politics as a battle among left, right, and center. Swings in election outcomes toward the middle or to either side are thought to change the course of government policy.[7] Reapportionment supposedly produced a large change in the weight of one group over another, shifting the center of gravity in legislative elections toward the urban left. Curiously, that appears to have had no effect on public policy.

For political science, this is a very provocative and theoretically significant claim. One of the central theoretical predictions of modern political science

3. Yong Hyo Cho and H. George Frederickson, "Apportionment and Legislative Responsiveness to Policy Preferences in the American States," *Annals of the New York Academy of Sciences* 219, no. 1 (November, 1973): 267.

4. In a similar vein, Erikson writes: "no researcher has been able to show that any amount of tinkering with potential control variables allows state apportionment scores to amount for an appreciable share of the variance in any state policy." See Erikson, "Reapportionment and Policy," 280.

5. Gerald Rosenberg, *The Hollow Hope* (Chicago: University of Chicago Press, 1993), 297–98.

6. Alexander Bickel, "The Supreme Court and Reapportionment," in *Reapportionment in the 1970s*, (Berkeley: University of California Press, 1971), 58. An exception is William E. Bicker, ed. Nelson Polsby "The Effects of Malapportionment in the States—A Mistrial," in Reapportment in the 1970s, ed. Nelson Polsby (Berkeley: University of California Press, 1971), 151–201, who argues that these studies were plagued with methodological and conceptual problems, including measurement error, studying the wrong dependent variables, and using measures of malapportionment that did not accurately capture the extent to which apportionment distorted the relative strength of urban and rural interests.

7. James A. Stimson, *Tides of Consent: How Public Opinion Shapes American Politics* (New York: Cambridge University Press, 2004).

holds that ideological politics will tend to produce laws that are close to the preferences of the median voter in the legislature. If a proposed bill is too far to the right, the median legislator can introduce amendments or hold out for a substitute bill; because all legislators to the left of the median would prefer to have the rightist measure lose, they will support the median legislator. The same logic applies when a proposal is too far to the left, but in this case legislators to the right of the median will find common ground with the centrists. The push and pull of legislative negotiations will, thus, lead ultimately to legislation that is close to the preferences of the median legislator. State politics before the mid-1960s certainly seemed to reflect the rural bias of state politics.

Decades of overrepresentation of rural areas pulled state laws disproportionately in the direction of rural interests and ideologies. State laws reflected the accumulation of many years of rural rule.[8] As populations increasingly drifted to urban areas, the median voter in the legislature drifted further from the median voter in the population. State legislatures repeatedly thwarted efforts to pass elements of the urban policy agenda. The conflicts often manifest themselves in open political battles between governors and legislatures. Since governors compete statewide, they placed more weight on metropolitan interests; the malapportioned legislature did not. Reapportionment ought to have made the typical constituency a more liberal one, changing the median legislator to one who favored more spending, more redistribution, and more government regulation, pulling public policy in that direction. Or so the theory predicts.

This line of political thought evidently rests on a very shaky foundation. The pivotal voter in the old order leaned toward the right, pulled in that direction by the inflation of the value of the rural vote. After reapportionment, the median voter in the state electorates should have snapped to the left, and public policy should have followed. Evidently, the electoral connection had long since broken.

A variety of possible explanations have been suggested. There is the radical critique that powerful economic interests determine the laws and that elections, indeed, matter little.[9] There is the public interest view that the legislature tries to do what it thinks is best, and thus laws do not follow the electorate closely. There is the institutionalist view that rural areas maintained their

---

8. Case studies are numerous. See, for example, Robert S. Allen, *Our Sovereign State* (New York: Vanguard, 1949); and Malcom Jewell, *The State Legislature: Politics and Practice* (New York: Random House, 1962).
9. The great twentieth-century sociologist C. Wright Mills captured this view forcefully in *The Power Elite* (New York: Oxford University Press, 1956). Alfred deGrazia took the same perspective in his analysis of the reapportionment cases in *Apportionment and Representative Government* (New York: Praeger, 1962).

power because they kept control of positions of leadership and seniority in the legislatures.[10] There is the pessimistic view, which has great currency in political science, that voters do not know enough about the laws to really have an effect on public policy.[11] All of these arguments cut to the foundational assumption of democratic representation. For one reason or another, votes do not matter.

Another line of responses argued that the districting process remained flawed in ways that the courts could not fix. Gerrymandering supplanted malapportionment.[12] The conservative legislators who controlled the redistricting process could draw district lines that pack the liberal parts of metro areas into a few districts and combine other liberals in districts with rural and suburban conservatives—districts that are 40 percent liberal and 60 percent conservative and will typically elect a conservative and "waste" large blocs of liberal votes. While this argument might be relevant for a few states or legislative chambers—example, the New York senate—it seems unlikely to account for the overall pattern. The courts in the mid-1960s and 1970s tended to be liberal and therefore likely to favor liberal Democrats.[13] Gerrymanders that strongly favored Republicans or conservatives were therefore more likely to have a difficult time in the post-Baker courts.

Perhaps the most compelling explanation recognized the variation within the metropolitan counties. The "urban vote" was not a majority in most states, nor was it the only underrepresented voice. Suburban voters were also severely underrepresented, and these voters generally held conservative views. In many cases, suburbanites were even more conservative than rural voters, so the effect of reapportionment was to add weight to voters to the right of the median as well as to the left, and the effect of increasing the weight of suburban conservatives may have roughly cancelled out the increased power of

10. Alvin D. Sokolow, "After Reapportionment: Numbers or Policies," *Western Political Quarterly* 19, no. 3, supp. (September, 1966): 21, discusses this for California; and Howard A. Scarrow, "The Impact of Reapportionment on Party Representation in the State of New York," *Policy Studies Journal* 9 (1980/81):937–46, discusses this for New York. William Grigsby Cornelius, John Anderson, and American Assembly, *Southern State Legislatures in American Politics* (Atlanta: Emory University School of Law, 1968), shows this for Georgia. For example, in 1967–1968, the eight largest counties in Georgia, which accounted for 41 percent of the population, controlled only 27 percent of all committee chairs in the state senate and only 8 percent of all committee chairs in the state house.

11. See Warren Miller and Donald Stokes, "Constituency Influence in Congress," *American Political Science Review* 57, no. 1 (March 1963): 45–56.

12. See, example, Bickel, "The Supreme Court and Reapportionment," 69–70, who argues: "The one person, one vote, rule, I have suggested, gave us no new birth of majoritianism. . . . That is so because, even assuming the existence of a stable popular majority, any districted legislature is as likely to misrepresent as to register it. . . . The device for ensuring this result is called gerrymandering."

13. See Gary Cox and Jonathan Katz, *Elbridge Gerry's Salamander* (New York: Cambridge University Press, 2002).

urban liberals.[14] While devaluation of the suburban vote is surely part of the story, it cannot be all of it, as the driving force was the enormous overrepresentation of rural America.

Each of these explanations assumes that state policy did not shift. We show that it did, but most past commentary and research misunderstood where it should have happened and where it should not have and how big it ought to have been. As our analysis in chapter 4 suggests, malapportionment had quite different effects on party competition across the regions of the country. Voters' policy preferences followed similar contours. Markedly different schisms between urban and rural areas held in the South and West than the stereotypical picture emerging out of the Northeast and Midwest. In the Northeast and Midwest, overrepresentation of rural areas magnified Republicans' votes greatly and pulled public policy to the right. In the South and West, both rural and urban voters were more moderate ideologically, and little shift in policy should have been expected. Suburban voters added further nuance to this picture. They too pulled politics and public policy to the left in northern states, but in the South, suburban voters proved the most conservative in the region. In the South, rural areas were the centrists, and reapportionment only fueled a growing schism within the region: the division between conservative suburban Republicans and liberal urban Democrats.

Our argument so thoroughly breaks with the received wisdom on this subject that we must take care in developing each of its component parts. First, we reconstruct the distribution of voters' preferences across urban, suburban, and rural areas in the regions of the country and the states. Second, we gauge how much the median or average legislative district would have changed as a result of reapportionment. It is important to note that, in many states—especially in the South and West—metropolitan voters were not more liberal than rural voters on many issues, especially on government spending issues. Finally, we show that policy shifts in the form of increased spending generally and on social welfare and education *did* occur in the states where (1) metropolitan voters were more liberal than rural voters, and (2) the states were badly malapportioned pre-*Baker*, or changes in gerrymandering shifted the partisan balance sharply in a pro-Democratic direction pre- and post-*Baker*. Throughout the South and West—the states where it was conservative voters, not liberals, who were disproportionately underrepresented—no such shift to the left occurred.

14. Only Robert Erikson in "Malapportionment, Gerrymandering, and Party Fortunes in Congressional Elections," *American Political Science Review* 66, no. 4 (December, 1972): 1234–45, seems to have appreciated this important point. He offers no assessment of the relative ideological orientations of voters in the different areas.

WHAT DID VOTERS WANT?

Political differences between metropolitan and rural areas were palpably obvious to commentators at the time. Surprisingly little effort was made to document these differences at the time. It was a working assumption of the earliest research on this subject that voters in metropolitan areas were liberals and voters in rural areas were conservatives. The observation that malapportionment also devalued the relatively conservative suburban vote cast doubt on the simple interpretation of the politics of city versus farm. But even that observation masks important differences across the regions of the country.

As we shall see, the usual account of the preferences of urban, suburban, and rural voters follows an eastern stereotype. It was indeed the case that urban voters in the Northeast and Midwest were very liberal, rural voters were very conservative, and suburban voters lay somewhere in between. The South and West, however, were quite different. In the South, rural and city voters were, on economic matters, quite moderate, and suburban voters were among the most conservative in the country. And in the West, policy preferences of those in cities, suburbs, and towns differed little. This varied pattern of political preference would drive the policy consequences of reapportionment.

Piecing this picture together, however, proved quite difficult. Ideally, we would like to have a snapshot of the distribution of voters' preferences in each state in 1960. Today, political scientists use large-scale surveys, such as exit polls, to gauge the distributions of policy preferences in different areas of the country.[15] Unfortunately, these did not exist in the 1950s and 1960s. Exit polls began to appear in the mid-1970s, and large public opinion polls, such as the Cooperative Congressional Election Survey and the Annenberg National Election Survey, became affordable only in the past decade.

Lacking a single reliable indicator of the political orientation of the different areas, we will rely on multiple pieces of data to construct an overall picture. Fortunately, a number of different sorts of data are informative about the preferences of voters in urban and rural areas.

First, high-quality national survey data are available for the 1950s and 1960s. The American National Election Study provides a portrait of the American electorate for each presidential election from 1952 onward. Although the samples are not large enough to permit analysis of individual states, it is possible to gauge the preferences of urban, suburban, and rural voters across the regions of the nation. Specific survey-research projects did focus on the states in

---

15. See, for example, Robert Erikson, Gerald Wright, and John P. MacIver, *Statehouse Democracy* (New York: Cambridge University Press, 1993).

some years, most notably the 1968 Election Study of the Comparative State Elections Project (CSEP). This study covers thirteen states in detail—Alabama, California, Florida, Illinois, Louisiana, Massachusetts, Minnesota, New York, North Carolina, Ohio, Pennsylvania, South Dakota, and Texas.[16]

These surveys offer an invaluable portrait of the American electorate in this era. Similar questions about policy preferences and ideological orientations span a large number of elections and a large number of states. We have pieced these data together to provide a picture of individual states and each region of the nation.

Second, the roll-call voting records of members of the U.S. House of Representatives provides information about the preferences of different sorts of constituencies. U.S. congressional districts in the 1950s and 1960s also adhered to county and municipal boundaries, and most districts could be readily classified as urban or rural. Roll-call voting records, then, express the revealed preferences of different areas within each state; in fact, congressional behavior might give an even better indication of the likely differences in state legislators' policy preferences across urban, suburban, and rural areas. Like the survey data, congressional roll-call votes provide comparable measures for all states and all regions of the country.

Scattered studies of legislative behavior in individual states provide further confirmation of the patterns we see. One early survey of state legislators compares the attitudes of urban and nonurban legislators in four key states— California, New Jersey, Ohio, and Tennessee. Since the data and methods used vary widely from study to study, we only include those with clear findings based on roll-call data or surveys of state legislators.

Third, election returns for president and other statewide contests allow us to map the partisan and political orientation of the counties. These data provide a much finer level of detail than survey data or roll-call votes. Presidential elections in particular allow us to compare the ideological orientation of counties, as the competing candidates are the same everywhere and the races pitted Democratic New Deal and Great Society liberals against traditional Republican conservatives. In states that use initiative and referenda, votes on bond measures provide additional information about the fiscal conservatism of metropolitan and rural areas.

We begin at the coarser level of regions. At this level, we have the most extensive data covering the entire nation from the American National Election

16. A few early state polls conducted by Louis Harris and Associates exist for Colorado, Illinois, Indiana, Kentucky, New Hampshire, and Vermont. Polls conducted by the Field organization are available for California. Other state polls exist as well, but they do not include information about whether respondents live in urban or rural areas. See John C. Wahlke and Heinz Eulau, *Legislative Behavior: A Reader in Theory and Research* (Glencoe, IL: Free Press, 1956).

Studies of 1964 and 1968. Pooling the eight surveys conducted during this time yields a sufficiently large sample (of approximately 3,000 respondents) that we can measure with some confidence the party identifications and ideological orientations of different sorts of voters. We divide the data into four regions: Northeast, Midwest, South, and West.[17]

We focus on three summary measures of voters' preferences. We identified all questions in the surveys that pertained to issues generally, such as government regulation, taxation, and spending. We then aggregated the responses to the questions into a single scale the values of which run from very conservative to very liberal.[18] We also identified all questions that pertained to civil rights, racial policy, and racial tolerance, and we constructed a scale similar to the general policy scale. Racial politics deserve separate analysis as this was the great cross-cutting cleavage of the time.[19] We call these scales the General Ideology Scale and the Civil Rights Scale. The General Ideology Scale primarily covers economic issues, such as government spending and economic regulation. We orient this scale so that higher numbers represent more "liberal" positions. Similarly, higher numbers on the Civil Rights Scale represent more support for desegregation and other civil rights actions. The third measure is Party Identification, with higher scores representing greater identification with the Democratic Party. Party Identification and vote choice, although correlated, are not identical. The appendix provides further details about the scales and the actual survey items used.[20]

For ease of interpretation, we translated all three variables into a scale that runs from 0 to 100. The typical voter nationwide has a value of 50. A value of the scale of 50 percent means that the typical voter in this particular region and area expresses the same opinions as the typical person in the nation as a whole. A value of 0 would indicate the most conservative person, and a value of 100 would indicate the most liberal.

Using this metric, we can gauge the differences in ideological beliefs of urban, suburban, and rural voters within each region of the country. For each

17. The Northeast consists of Maine, Vermont, New Hampshire, Massachusetts, Rhode Island, Connecticut, New York, New Jersey, Delaware, Maryland, Pennslyvania, West Virginia, and Ohio. The South consists of Alabama, Arkansas, Florida, Georgia, Kentucky, Louisiana, Mississippi, North Carolina, Oklahoma, South Carolina, Tennessee, Texas, and Virginia. The Midwest consists of the states from Indiana and Michigan to the Dakotas to Nebraska. The remaining states constitute the West.

18. We used principal components factor analysis to make these scales.

19. See Edward Carmines and James Stimson, *Issue Evolution* (Princeton, NJ: Princeton University Press, 1989).

20. In an earlier study, we analyzed a large number of individual survey questions; see Stephen Ansolabehere and James M. Snyder Jr., "Reapportionment and Party Realignment in the American States," *University of Pennsylvania Law Review* 153, no. 1 (November 2004): 433–57. The findings here are qualitatively similar to those in our earlier study, but simpler to present and discuss.

TABLE 10.1 *Ideological and partisan leanings of urban, suburban, and rural voters in the Northeast, Midwest, South, and West at the time of reapportionment*

Region-area	Percentage of national population right of the typical respondent in the region-area		
	General Ideology	Civil Rights	Party Identification
Northeast			
Urban	*66*	*67*	*56*
Suburban	*50*	*52*	*40*
Rural	*45*	*57*	*33*
Midwest			
Urban	*61*	*58*	*56*
Suburban	*48*	*49*	*42*
Rural	*41*	*43*	*42*
South			
Urban	*52*	*52*	*62*
Suburban	*39*	*40*	*59*
Rural	*49*	*32*	*53*
West			
Urban	52	*62*	49
Suburban	48	*52*	46
Rural	50	*56*	63

Note: The triples in bolded italics are cases where an F-test rejects, at the .05 level, the hypothesis that the mean scores across urban, rural, and suburban areas are all equal.

Source: Compiled by the authors using American National Election Study data of 1964 and 1968.

region-area group, we computed the average value of the scale and the percentage of the national sample that expressed more conservative (or, in the case of party identification, more Republican) attitudes than the typical person.[21] Because the scale is the same throughout the nation, we may also draw comparisons across regions.

As Table 10.1 shows, on questions of general ideology, civil rights, and party identification a considerable gulf lay between urban and rural areas. Urban

21. First, we normalize all three scales to have a nationwide mean of 0 and standard deviation of 100. The ratio of the mean and standard deviation to standard deviations provides a z-score with which we calculate

voters everywhere were more liberal than their rural and suburban counterparts. The distribution of voters' preferences across urban, suburban, and rural areas, however, differed in important ways on either side of the Mason-Dixon Line.

Political preferences in the Northeast and Midwest exemplify the stereotype of the urban, suburban, and rural voters that holds to this day. Those in urban areas expressed much more liberal sentiments than those in rural areas, and the ideological orientation of suburban citizens lay somewhere between these two poles but closer to that of the rural voters. Northeastern urbanites—those living in Boston, Hartford, New York, Philadelphia, and other northern cities—were the most liberal voters in the nation in terms of general ideology and civil rights. Two-thirds of the country expressed more conservative attitudes than the urban dwellers in this region. Urban voters in the Midwest scored similarly high on the liberalism measures, expressing attitudes that were, on average, to the left of those of three out of five people in the nation as a whole.

Suburban voters in the Northeast and Midwest expressed the most moderate opinions. On general ideology, the suburban voter in states such as New York, New Jersey, Pennsylvania, and Massachusetts stood exactly at the center of the national electorate, with a score of 50. On civil rights, these voters were slightly to the left of center for the nation as a whole, but much more conservative than the voters in the cities that they neighbored. Suburbanites in the Midwest were slightly to the right of center, but only slightly, and the difference is statistically not distinguishable from 50. Northeastern and midwestern suburbanites, then, occupied the position of the median voters in the nation on general ideology and civil rights, a position shared by suburban voters in the West.

Rural voters in the North were fairly conservative. In New England and the Atlantic states, rural voters were noticeably right of center, with 55 percent of the electorate being more liberal. They were also the most strongly attached to the Republican Party. On the cross-cutting issue of civil rights, however, the rural northerners were pulled strongly to the left, a fact that made them very reluctant to join forces with the emerging Republican coalition under Nixon and Reagan. Rural midwesterners were among the most conservative people in the nation in 1960, and their conservatism ran across the board. They were among the most conservative when it came to questions of general ideology and matters of civil rights; they were also among the staunchest Republicans.

---

the probability that a respondent in the survey lies below that value. We use the normal approximation to the density function.

The political divide in the South looked quite different. Southern city dwellers were among the most liberal and Democratic in the region, but they were considerably less liberal than their northern counterparts. In fact, they expressed very moderate positions on questions of general ideology and civil rights.

The most conservative voters in the South lived in the suburban fringe around the cities. Indeed, these were the most conservative areas in the nation in 1960, and current polling data suggests that this pattern lives on. On general ideology and economics, the southern suburbs were the most conservative areas in the nation, and on civil rights only rural southerners took positions further to the right. The southern suburbanites, then, held quite different political beliefs from their counterparts in the Northeast, Midwest, and West. They anchored the conservative end of the political spectrum among the different areas.

Rural southerners were torn. They held moderate views on economics and general ideology, not too different from their urban counterparts. But on civil rights, the rural South was by far the most conservative area of the nation. Its conservatism on this issue matched the extreme liberalism found in northern cities. Both areas also leaned strongly toward the Democratic Party. The national Democratic Party through the actions of the Kennedy and Johnson administrations would take sides in this struggle, forcing rural southerners to make difficult choices regarding their partisan attachments. The moderation of rural southerners on questions of economic policy, however, would keep them close to the strong Democrats from the urban areas in their state governments, an affinity that helped sustain the Democratic Party as a regional party in the South well into the 1990s. Setting aside the issue of race, both economics and general ideology in the South divided the very conservative suburbs from the moderate cities and rural areas.

Therein lay a cautionary tale for the southern lawyers who spearheaded the reapportionment cases. On ideological politics, rather than distributive politics, they had much more in common with the overrepresented rural areas. To accommodate the Court's rulings in *Reynolds v. Simms* and subsequent rulings, the state legislators had to divide the metropolitan counties into single-member districts. The practice of respecting community boundaries led to the creation of separate urban and suburban districts. These new districts would add a conservative economic voice to southern state politics that had been absent. A similarly liberal urban voice would not, however, emerge, as the urban voters were on the whole quite moderate.

The West showed no differences across urban, suburban, and rural areas. The western region shows comparable scores on all of the measures in Table 10.1. City, suburb, and farm—in the West, all areas look moderate. That is not to say that all voters held similar views. Rather, within each type of area there was considerable heterogeneity. There were conservative and liberal farm areas in California, for example, as well as liberal and conservative cities, and considerable heterogeneity within these cities. In this respect, the West appears to be the most distinctive region politically, as the populace had not sorted itself geographically along political lines either because the rural areas were the most moderate, as in the South, or because voters in the metropolitan and rural areas held similar ideological views, as in the West.

It is clear from Table 10. 1 that in the Northeast and Midwest, a shift in state legislative representation from rural areas to urban and suburban areas would have moved the position of the median state legislator to the left, especially on the economic issues captured in the General Ideology Scale. Such an effect looks doubtful in the South and West.

State-level surveys, congressional and state legislative roll-call votes, and election results for ballot measures and other questions allow us to refine the regional analysis for approximately half of the states. These additional sources of information confirm the broad regional differences detected by the American National Election Surveys, but they also point to a few exceptions, especially in the West.

A more refined view of the regions comes from a special one-time study of the American states, the 1968 Election Study of the Comparative State Elections Project (CSEP). This study drew separate samples from each of thirteen states and asked questions similar to those of the American National Election Studies (ANES).[22] Using these data, we constructed measures of General Ideology and Party Identification for each of the states in the CSEP that are analogous to the measures of ideology and party from the ANES.[23] The results are shown in Table 10.2.[24] We group the states by regions.

Overall, the state surveys fit the general regional patterns well, with two important exceptions in California and Florida. In states in the Northeast and Midwest, urban areas were consistently more liberal and more Democratic than rural areas. The urban-rural differences on both scales were large—ranging

22. Additional state polls that identify respondents as urban or rural exist for New Hampshire, Vermont, Illinois, Indiana, Kentucky, California, and Colorado. The polls were conducted by Louis Harris and Associates and David M. Kovenock and James W. Prothro, COMPARATIVE STATE ELECTIONS PROJECT, 1968 [computer file] (Chapel Hill: University of North Carolina, Institute for Research in Social Science, 1970) [producer]; (Ann Arbor, MI: Interuniversity Consortium for Political and Social Research 1977 [distributor]. These polls lack sufficient questions to gauge the ideological orientations of different areas within the states.

23. We discuss the construction of the General Ideology Scale, including the actual survey items used, in the appendix.

24. The CSEP has four community types: urban, fringe, town, and rural. We grouped town and rural together into the "rural" category, and we relabeled the fringe category "suburb." This may bias the urban-rural and suburban-rural differences toward 0 for Massachusetts. The sample of suburban voters in North Carolina was too small, so they are dropped. South Dakota had no respondents classified as suburban.

from 10 to 20 points—and statistically significant. In the South, the differences were smaller and also more mixed. Suburban residents were the most conservative group in Alabama and Louisiana, and the most Republican group in Alabama, Florida, and Texas. Florida looked a bit more like a midwestern state than a southern state, exhibiting sharp ideological and partisan differences between urban and rural citizens. In fact, urban respondents in Florida were more liberal than those in Minnesota, while rural respondents were as conservative. South Dakota looked much like the overall western region in Table 10.1. In California, however, there were clear ideological differences

TABLE 10.2 *Ideological and partisan leanings of urban (U), suburban (S), and rural (R) voters at the time of reapportionment*

| | Percentage of national population right of the typical respondent in the state-area | | | | | |
| | General Ideology | | | Party Identification | | |
	U	S	R	U	S	R
Northeast						
Massachusetts	68	52	55	67	47	33
New York	67	55	53	54	36	25
Pennsylvania	64	50	45	51	36	25
Midwest						
Illinois	60	42	37	53	29	36
Ohio	63	43	50	58	41	36
Minnesota	55	44	39	45	46	44
South						
Alabama	48	30	47	59	46	57
Florida	58	49	50	63	50	57
Louisiana	52	42	46	60	63	69
North Carolina	53	*	50	58	*	58
Texas	53	47	48	61	50	63
West						
California	61	45	40	50	51	47
South Dakota	42	*	39	38	*	33

*Insufficient numbers of cases.
Source: Compiled by the authors using Comparative State Elections Project data, 1968.

among urban, rural, and suburban citizens, similar to the differences in northeastern and midwestern states. California's exceptionalism in the CSEP points to the great heterogeneity that existed in the West. The Pacific states had markedly different politics from the Mountain and Plains states.

To examine further the variability across regions and to confirm the results of the polling data, we drew on the congressional voting record and studies of individual state politics.[25] We discuss these various streams of information in detail in the appendix, but they clearly confirm the pattern revealed by the ANES surveys.

Legislative roll-call voting in the South, Northeast, and Midwest showed a remarkably similar pattern to public opinion. Urban legislators in the Northeast and Midwest had very liberal voting records, and urban southerners were moderates. Rural legislators from the Northeast were slightly right of center, and rural legislators from both the Midwest and the Plains states in the West anchored the conservative end of American politics. At a broad level, the consistency between the surveys and the roll-call voting records suggests that voters' preferences do translate into policy. Studies by congressional scholars routinely find that the voting records of members of Congress are correlated with the ideological preferences of their constituencies. Scattered studies of state legislatures find similar results.[26] The correlations are not enormous, and at any moment in time there are representatives who appear to be out of touch with their districts; but on average, the relationships are fairly tight. Liberal districts tend to be represented by liberals, and conservative districts tend to be represented by conservatives.

As with the survey data, we found substantial variability within the West. In Washington, Oregon, and California, urban legislators indeed voted much more liberally than their rural and suburban counterparts. Colorado followed a similar pattern. These legislative divisions more closely resembled those in the Northeast, although the differences are not as large. Elsewhere in the West, the legislative voting and voting on bond measures resembled the political divisions in the South or showed no differences among urban, suburban, and rural areas.

Finally, election results themselves confirmed the political leanings of

25. We used the DW-NOMINATE scores from Keith T. Poole and Howard Rosenthal, *Congress: A Political-Economic History of Roll Call Voting* (Oxford: Oxford University Press, 1997), to summarize representatives' roll-call "ideology." For each state, we compare the roll-call scores of urban and nonurban congressmen and congresswomen.

26. See, for example, Robert Erikson and Gerald C. Wright Jr., "Policy Representation of Constituency Interests," *Political Behavior* 2, no. 1 (1980): 91–106. Stephen Ansolabehere, James M. Snyder Jr., and Charles Stewart III, "Old Voters, New Voters, and the Personal Vote: Using Redistricting to Measure the Incumbency Advantage," *American Journal of Political Science* 44, no. 1 (January 2000): 17–34, comment on drawbacks, especially the difficulty of measuring true preferences of representatives and voters. See also James M. Snyder Jr., "Constituency Preferences: California Ballot Propositions, 1974–1990," *Legislative Studies Quarterly*, no. 4 (November 1996): 463–88, on California; Jeffrey Byron Lewis, "Who Do Representatives Represent? Estimating the Importance of Electoral Coalition Preferences in California" (PhD diss., Massachusetts Institute of Technology, 1997).

different areas. The presidential vote in counties and towns provides some sense of how strongly areas leaned toward the national Republicans and the national Democrats. At least at the national level in the 1950s and 1960s, the Democratic Party was clearly more liberal than the Republican, especially on economic matters. Within each state, we can compare the political orientations of urban, suburban, and rural areas. As with public opinion and legislative voting, the Northeast and Midwest exhibited a distinctly different pattern from the South. From Maine to Missouri, there is a clearly positive correlation between population density and Democratic vote. In the northeastern states, the correlations uniformly exceeded .5, a very strong relationship between Democratic voting and urbanization. In the Midwest, they were more moderate and averaged .2, but the most heavily urbanized areas cast the strongest Democratic vote. In the South, urbanization correlated less strongly with partisanship than in the North, but the correlations routinely ran in the opposite direction. Rural areas voted more Democratic for president than did more densely populated metropolitan counties. This was driven in part by the Black Belt counties; but even excluding the areas with large black populations, southern cities and suburbs voted somewhat more Republican than rural counties. Rural counties in the South, then, tended to support the national Democrats somewhat more than metropolitan counties in that region, indicating a more liberal tendency. But in the North, the cities and suburbs were much more Democratic than the rural areas, a pattern consistent with their liberalism expressed in surveys.

The West was mixed. California, Colorado, Oregon, and Washington resembled the Northeast; the more populous counties of New Mexico and Montana also leaned to the left relative to their states. The remainder of the Mountain West resembled the South.

This division portended the emergence of the current distribution of voter preferences across the cities and counties of the United States. Red and Blue America follow exactly the same lines that they did in 1960, at least in terms of ideology. The difference lay in the institutions for counting votes. Underrepresentation of the urban and suburban areas suppressed that schism. Reapportionment would allow it to emerge in elections and public policy, but the movement of the states and regions to the left and right depended very much on the composition of their electorates.

THE NORTH TURNS LEFT, THE SOUTH GOES RIGHT

The preferences of urban, suburban, and rural voters portended a great realignment after the Court handed down its reapportionment decisions, but it was a realignment that affected the regions of the country differently. How that shift unfolded depended as well on the distribution of legislative seats across areas before reapportionment and on the features of the districts created once the courts forced the states to redistrict.

Malapportionment treated urban, suburban, and rural areas differently across the American states. In most states, rural areas were overrepresented and both the cities and the suburbs were underrepresented. This owed to the dramatic population growth in these areas and the lack of change in district boundaries. It also stemmed from the nature of counties. Rural counties covered almost all rural areas in the nation. Cities and suburbs were a more complicated matter. Some metropolitan counties consist entirely of central cites, such as Manhattan. In these areas, malapportionment affected central cities and suburban counties differently. In fact, the five boroughs of New York City were reasonably well represented in Albany, but the immediate suburban counties of Westchester, Nassau, and Orange suffered under malapportionment. More commonly, though, metropolitan counties are a mix of city and suburb. Underrepresentation of the metropolitan counties hit both central cities and suburban communities equally. In either case, the Relative Representation Index reveals just how much cities, suburbs, and rural areas would gain with reapportionment.

The redistricting required to comply with one person, one vote sharpened the split among rural counties, central cities, and the suburban ring. Before 1964, states usually defined legislative districts as the counties, which became one of the primary means of overrepresentation of rural areas, as rural counties are more numerous. County districts also blurred the lines between the city and the suburb, at least as those areas were represented in state government. While many states did carve metropolitan areas into districts, states just as often used entire metropolitan counties as at-large districts. Davidson County, Tennessee, home of Nashville, was districted; Shelby County, which contains Memphis and its suburbs, elected its eight assemblymen at large. At-large or single county seats were used throughout the United States, but they were especially common in the South and West.

The courts, through a series of decisions in the late 1960s, eventually forced the states to use single member districts only. State legislatures proceeded to divide metropolitan areas into distinct spheres of representation—central city districts and suburban districts. Over time, those distinctions have become increasingly blurred, but most metropolitan counties to this day remain divided into city and suburban districts.

Metropolitan districts before *Baker* created a degree of moderation. They included both central cities and suburban communities, and the relative conservatism of suburban areas tempered the liberalism of the cities. Separating the cities from the suburbs created political divisions in many legislatures that had not previously existed. In the California senate, for example, the large counties, such as Los Angeles, San Diego, and Alameda, were very moderate districts. The figures in Table 10.2 suggest that they would have had a left-right score of 53. But creating city and suburb districts divided the county into very liberal and somewhat conservative districts, with scores of 61 and 45, respectively. The roll-call voting records of central city and suburban legislators are even more disparate. Suburban legislators tend to cluster near the center, while city legislators anchor the far left.

Malapportionment, by inflating the votes of some areas and devaluing others, skewed representation. But the pattern varied across regions and states. Using the Relative Representation Index and county populations as well as the survey data in Table 10.1, we can gauge who the median was in the legislatures before malapportionment and who became the median with the advent of equal population districting. In the Northeast, in both the upper and lower chambers, the median legislative district was a suburban seat. Some states such as Connecticut, Vermont, and Rhode Island were skewed even more heavily in the rural direction, but averaging across the states the suburban districts were pivotal to legislative politics in the 1950s and 1960s. The median voter in this region, however, was an urbanite. The larger cities in most states in the region contained a majority of the population. Reapportionment, then, shifted the center of gravity in state legislatures in this region from the suburbs to the cities.

The Midwest was a step further to the right, but it moved left with reapportionment. Rural areas held majorities of the seats in most of the midwestern legislatures. The ideological center of the electorate, however, resided in the suburbs. Although the midwestern cities and rural areas had more population than the suburban counties at this time, the suburbs held the pivotal position because they were more moderate than either the cities or the farms, and they had sufficient population to make the difference. Chicago, for example, fell just short of a majority in the Illinois legislature, and the suburban areas of Cook County as well as Lake County proved to be pivotal in the state's politics following reapportionment.[27]

In sharp contrast, little ideological change was expected in the South and West. In a large number of southern and western states, the majority of the population lived in rural areas in 1960. Florida was the exception in the South, as were California, Colorado, Oregon, and Washington in the West. Prior to

27. See Leo Snowiss, "Chicago and Congress: A Study of Metropolitan Representation" (PhD diss., University of Chicago, 1965).

Baker, the typical legislator in the South was a rural Democrat, and that re-mained the case after reapportionment even though reapportionment reduced the number of rural seats greatly. In addition, because most southern metro-politan areas used at-large districts, reapportionment merely added some dis-tricts on the left and some districts on the right without changing appreciably the ideologically central position of the rural areas.

Racial politics provided an interesting twist, however. On questions of race, rural southern areas expressed the most conservative views in the country. Reapportionment reduced the power of the rural voice in the southern state legislatures, although that bloc remained a majority most places. That shift, ac-cording to some, made the southern states more receptive to changes in their civil rights laws.[28]

The West exhibits the most complex pattern. Its counties are very large and heterogeneous, and the Pacific states differed ideologically from much of the rest of the region. In California, Colorado, Oregon, and Washington, the typical voter by 1960 lived in a suburban community, and the median in the lower chambers was usually in line with the electorate. Because of the use of county-based repre-sentation in the upper chambers, the pivotal state senators in these states came from rural districts. Throughout the rest of the West, the typical voter lived in a rural community, and the political center of the legislatures reflected that fact.

Reapportionment, then, changed the ideological center of state legislatures throughout the northern states, from Maine to Minnesota and Maryland to Missouri. Analysis of surveys and other voting information for individual states suggests that three other states should have shifted to the left ideologi-cally with reapportionment: Colorado, Kansas, and Nebraska. Figure 10.1 dis-plays the pattern and strength of change that resulted with reapportionment. Darker shades represent states that moved to the left. Note that changes do not equate to new ideologies. The western and Great Plains states transited from conservative to moderate in their political orientation.

The most dramatic and distinctive consequence was the ideological diver-gence of the northern and southern states.

Once reapportionment occurred in the mid-1960s, the handful of Republi-can state legislators in the South suddenly found themselves the leaders of real political parties. In Tennessee, ground zero for the reapportionment battles, Republicans held 21 of the 100 state house seats; by 1966, the first year after reapportionment, their numbers jumped to 39, and in 1968, they gained 10 more seats. Throughout the South, just 4 percent of all state legislators were

28. Erikson, "Reapportionment and Policy," studies the effects of reapportionment on civil rights law and finds that reapportionment contributed to the liberalization of civil rights laws in the South and West.

FIGURE 10.1. *Left shift states*

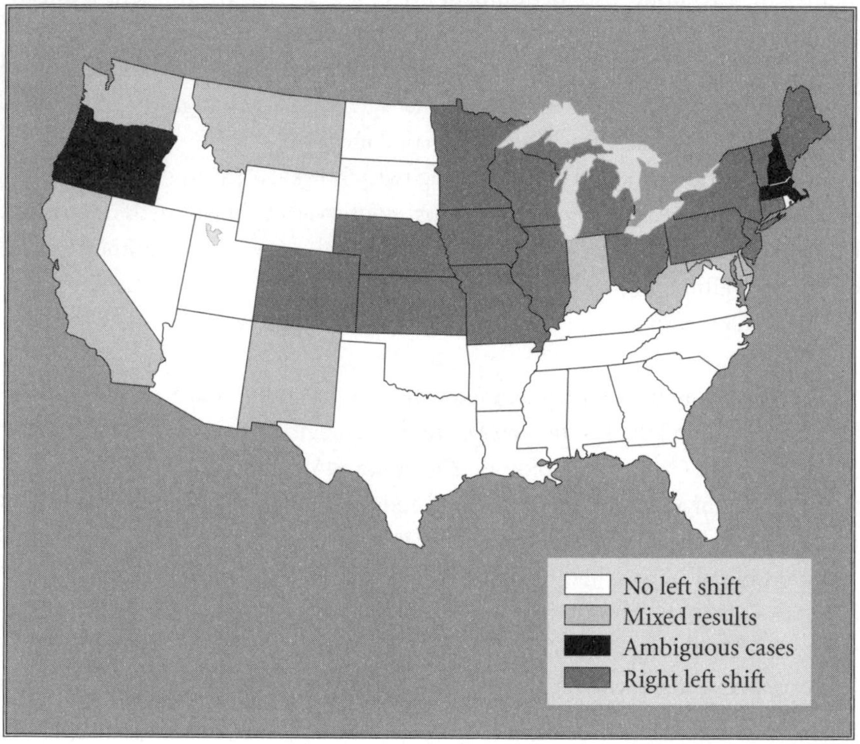

Republicans. That figure tripled by 1966 and quadrupled by 1972. Reapportionment created a pool of Republican politicians seeking to challenge the Democratic establishment, a new cohort that would feed the Republicans' Southern Strategy.[29] Partisan gerrymandering limited and slowed the Republicans' rise, as we discuss in Chapter 11, but reapportionment opened up the southern states to the party by creating urban and suburban seats that otherwise would not have existed.[30]

Reapportionment eliminated the devaluation of the Democratic vote in Northern states, just as it raised Republicans in the South. Perhaps the most dramatic change in the entire nation occurred in Connecticut's lower chamber,

29. This term comes from Kevin Phillips, *The Emerging Republican Majority* (New Rochelle, NY: Arlington House, 1969).

30. The civil rights movement and the economic development of the South drove this realignment. Malapportionment slowed its development, and reapportionment helped accelerate the change. See Jack Bass and Walter DeVries, *The Transformation of Southern Politics: Social Change and Political Consequence since 1945* (New York: Basic Books, 1976): 13–14, on reapportionment and the South generally, and 285–87 on Tennessee in particular.

which gave each town representation. Democrats won approximately one-third of the seats in the assembly before reapportionment, and two-thirds after reapportionment. Republicans won 184 seats in 1964 and were reduced to 60 in 1966, an otherwise good year for the GOP in that state and throughout the country. Democrats regularly won one-third of the seats in the Michigan lower house, regardless of their share of the statewide vote, and 45 percent of the seats in the upper chamber. After reapportionment, they routinely won 60 percent of the seats in both chambers. Across the North and Midwest, Democrats gained control of most state legislatures with the end of malapportionment. There were exceptions, such as New Jersey and Indiana, and those cases underscored the fact that partisan changes reflected the type of area that had been underrepresented. In these situations, the most underrepresented areas either were Republican suburbs, whose gains offset the gains of the Democratic cities, or contained Republican or divided cities, such as Indianapolis and Cincinnati. Although the pattern is less even than in the South, reapportionment certainly shifted the political balance in the North and Midwest. However, above the Mason-Dixon Line equalizing district population aided the Democrats, as it took seats away from rural Republican counties and redistributed them to the cities.

Reapportionment aided southern Republicans by increasing suburban representation, with the result that a new brand of conservatism arose in these state legislatures. The Republican suburbs, at least at the time, lacked numbers, but their newfound voice would provide a keystone in the foundation of the emerging Republican Party in that region. Throughout the Northeast and Midwest, the transformation resulted in the emergence of a new liberal majority. These state legislatures, long the home of moderate Republicanism, turned sharply to the left as the urban majority at last gained its fair share of representation.

THE LEFT SHIFT IN POLICY

A more tempered assessment of the effect of reapportionment on public policy is in order. The conclusion that equalization of district populations did not move policy to the left emerged out of a series of studies that assumed that reapportionment would affect all states in the same way. Clearly, that premise was wrong. Malapportionment distorted representation in every state, but it had markedly different consequences for the partisan and ideological orientation of the legislatures in different regions.

Reapportionment should have tilted the ideological balance in state politics to the left in the Northeast and Midwest, and perhaps in the Far West. The typical legislator was a fiscally conservative Republican before reapportionment.

After *Baker*, the center shifted in the northeaster and midwestern state legislatures toward the socially liberal Democrats. Rural political power thwarted New Deal economic liberalism in these regions of the country. In the South and Mountain West, however, the ideological center of legislative politics did not change much, and if anything it drifted to the right a bit. The ideologies of the typical legislators in the South and Mountain West were quite similar on economics issues before and after reapportionment. If anything, they became slightly more conservative and more Republican.

In those states where the typical legislator moved left, public policy ought to have followed suit. That result would seem to be commonsense. Indeed the reigning political science theory of legislative politics asserts that public policy tracks the preferences of the median legislator, a conjecture known as the Median Voter Theorem.[31] The fact that public policy did not move wholesale to the left raises some doubts about the veracity of this theoretical claim. It should not, however, have altered the public policies of every state. Only in the Midwest and Northeast should public policy have shifted to the left following the end of rural political power in those states. In the South and West, public policy should in fact have changed little, as the ideological orientation of the median legislator changed little in these regions.

The effect of reapportionment, then, was to bring states into alignment with the national economic policy agenda. Liberal Democrats nationally and in the states had long called for (1) state governments to address social ills and economic inequities directly by spending more on education, hospitals and health care, and welfare, and (2) a large expansion of the public sector generally. The national Democratic agenda also pushed for more favorable labor laws in the states. It was no accident that manufacturing unions funded reapportionment cases in the industrial northern states, or that the presidential candidates from the Northeast and Midwest embraced reapportionment. It was in these states that the great left shift would occur.

Once again, we turn to money to make our point. Conclusive evidence of the rise of liberal social policy is found in the *levels* of state spending overall and on social programs, including education, welfare, and hospitals. The distribution of expenditures across counties provides one of the cleanest metrics of the power of different constituencies and interests. Levels of spending, however, depend on whether or not the typical voter in the state is willing to pay higher taxes for public services and goods that benefit all. Such preferences reflect the economic liberalism of the typical constituency in the state legislature and may have little

31. This conjecture dates to the 1920s. For an excellent review of the idea and its application, see Kenneth Shepsle and Mark Bonchek, *Analyzing Politics* (New York: W. W. Norton, 1996).

to do with how well or poorly the state legislature represents the population. One state may be well apportioned but spend little money because the typical voter prefers lower taxes to more public goods or economic redistribution. Indeed, that is what early studies of the relationship between representation and liberalism found.[32] Levels of total spending and of social spending bore little correlation with malapportionment, and growth of a state's expenditures correlated only weakly with the degree to which the state reapportioned.

Such analyses, however, must take into account divergence between the preferences of the typical voter and that of the typical legislature caused by malapportionment. Our assessment of voters' preferences reveals that discrepancies between the typical legislature and the typical voter were not uniform; indeed, in some states they were not substantial. In the South and much of the West, unequal representation led to little disagreement between the policy preferences of typical voter and of the typical legislature because the rural areas held centrist policy preferences compared with urban and suburban voters. In the North and Midwest, on the other hand, urban and suburban areas were considerably more liberal than rural areas. The Northeast and Midwest, in fact, exhibited much faster growth in state spending due to reapportionment than did the South and West.

To gauge this, we contrast the growth in spending from 1957 to 1977 in left shift states with the growth in spending in other states. For each state, we define the pre-*Baker* period as the years 1957 to 1966. In most states the first major post-*Baker* reapportionment was in place for the 1966 elections, and the legislatures elected in 1966 took office in 1967 and probably had their first major impact on budgets and appropriations in 1968 or after. We define the post-*Baker* period as 1969–1977. We drop 1967 and 1968 because it is not clear whether spending in these years should have been affected by the reapportionment decisions. Every category of spending and measure of legislative professionalism is expressed in terms of percentage changes, or growth rates.

Analogous to the division of public spending, reapportionment serves as a natural experiment. Comparison of growth of spending in left shift and non–left shift states allows us to observe the extent to which policy responds to changes in the preferences of the typical voter. States where no left shift should have occurred serve as a control group or reference case. Spending might have grown or shrunk in these states, but any changes were not due to reapportionment. These states are shown without shading in the Figure 10.1. States where reapportionment raised the political power of the liberals and left serve as a treatment or experimental group. Reapportionment moved the median of these state legislatures sharply to the left. We do not have a direct measure of the decision making inside

32. See note 1, page 214.

the state governments or of the ideological preferences of the state legislatures, as we do with the U.S. House. The survey data suggest that the Northeast and Midwest should have experienced similar changes throughout these regions, while the South, with the possible exception of Florida, should have shown no movement to the left. We can observe directly how much the product of the legislature—its spending decisions—came to reflect the liberal agenda.

The measure of the effect is simply the difference between the treatment states and control group states in terms of changes in professionalism and spending. Government spending in general and on key social categories should have increased much more rapidly in the states where malapportionment made the legislature too conservative for the state and, thus, where we expect a left shift. The appendix elaborates on the details of the statistical analysis. Table 10.3 presents a summary of the results.

The results show a consistent and strong confirmation of the argument. More dramatic still were the changes in government spending. In the states

TABLE 10.3 *The Left Shift: Effects of reapportionment on state economic policy, 1957–1977*

Growth in state's . . .	Difference between left shift states and other states
Total spending	13.1%**
Overall social spending	13.0%**
Welfare spending	22.5%**
Education spending	13.0%**
Unemployment insurance average weekly benefit	2.3%*
State spending relative to local spending	16.2%**

Notes: All spending dependent variables are per capita, in real dollars, and logged. Overall Social Spending is total spending on education, welfare, housing, hospitals, and health care. The Unemployment Insurance Average Weekly Benefit is in real dollars and logged. All regressions include state fixed-effects, year fixed-effects, and the following control variables: (1) log of population, (2) log of per capita income, (3) log of percentage of population age 5–17, (4) log of percentage of population age 65 and over. The regression for Unemployment Insurance Average Weekly Benefit also includes the unemployment rate among covered workers as a control variable.
n = 935 in all regressions. Massachusetts, New Hampshire, and Oregon are not included.
*** = significant at the .01 level.*
**=significant at the .05 level.*

where malapportionment made the legislature more conservative than the public, reapportionment led to faster growth in public expenditures. Total state government spending increased by 13 percent more in left shift states than it did in other states. Similarly, welfare spending in the left shift states increased by nearly 22 percent more than in other states, and education spending increased by 13 percent; unemployment insurance rose 2 percent faster in the left shift states.

The last row of Table 10.3 reveals the increased importance of the state governments. Reform of government finance and provision of public goods depended on the credibility of the state governments. Concern about control of state legislatures prevented the federal government from devolving responsibility for programs to the states. One person, one vote scored a partial victory for such reforms. State spending relative to local spending rose 16 percent faster in states where reapportionment made the legislature more liberal than it did in states where the ideological balance did not change or moved to the right.

We are confident that these findings are not a spurious result of changes driven by the federal government. Total federal grants and federal grants to state and local governments did not follow the same pattern. In fact, there was no significant difference between the left shift states and the others in the federal transfers and grants.

We are also confident that the left shift was driven by changes in the weight of people's votes rather than by changes in voters' preferences. We tested whether the observed differences between the left shift states and other states reflect party control by holding constant the percentage of upper house seats controlled by Democrats, the percentage of lower house seats controlled by Democrats, and the party of the governor. The difference between the left shift states and other states remains of the same size and statistical significance; even controlling for partisan composition of the government did not explain the observed results. Also, similar to most previous studies, we find almost no significant effects of the three political control variables on any of the dependent variables.[33] The one exception is welfare spending, where we find a positive relationship between spending and the share of seats in the upper house controlled by Democrats.

33. See Warren Lee Kostroski, "Party and Incumbency in Postwar Senate Elections: Trends, Patterns, and Models," *American Political Science Review* 67, no. 4 (December, 1973): 1213–34; Barbara Hinckley, "Incumbency and the Presidential Vote in Senate Elections: Defining Parameters of Subpresidential Voting," *American Political Science Review* 64, no. 3 (September, 1970): 836–42; James E. Piereson, "Sources of Candidate Success in Gubernatorial Elections, 1910–1970," *Journal of Politics* 39, no. 4 (November, 1977): 939–58.

The findings are not an accident of incorrect classifications or other oddities. Even when we added or dropped various "doubtful" states, the patterns remained the same. The results are essentially unchanged if we add the three states—Massachusetts, New Hampshire, and Oregon—where a left shift is predicted but where the changes seem driven more by gerrymandering than by malapportionment. And the results are similar if we drop various states where the coding of left shift is difficult—California, Delaware, Florida, Indiana, Maryland, and West Virginia.

Reapportionment opened the way to a second sort of liberalization in the states, the professionalization of state legislatures. Progressive organizations, such as the League of Women Voters and the National Municipal League, had long pushed for the professionalization of state government. Their aims were not economic liberalism or redistribution; indeed, many of these organizations, such as the League of Women Voters, favored taxation. They wanted political reform in the form of full-time, well-paid, and well-staffed legislatures. Only a good government, the progressives argued, could tackle the problems of modern society. The New Deal and World War II had transformed the national government, but the state governments remained a backwater—part-time, underpaid, and understaffed. Fixing those problems would enable state governments to address other issues facing their states.

Reapportionment boosted the progressives' reform agenda, but especially in the left shift states. From the 1950s to the 1970s, almost every state legislature enacted reforms to improve its internal operations, including more staff, longer sessions, open-meeting laws, and higher salaries. The changes were especially pronounced in the states where Democrats and liberals gained the most as a result of reapportionment. The two most common indicators of legislative professionalism are salaries and days in session. Compared with state legislatures where reapportionment had no effect on the ideological balance, days in session grew 30 percent more in states where a left shift occurred and salaries rose by approximately $3,000 more.

The National Municipal League, the League of Women Voters, and other progressive groups had long fought for the end of malapportionment in order to push forward their good government agenda. Even the Eisenhower administration expressed this hope through the Advisory Commission on Intergovernmental Relations. That change indeed came about, but the reform did not occur across the board. It was felt strongly in the Northeast and Midwest and to a lesser extent in the West, and it seemed to have little consequence in the South. That was to be expected, as reapportionment boosted the progressives in the North and Far West but left them politically weaker in the South.

DEMOCRACY RESTORED

In its wake, reapportionment laid bare the plain value of the vote. *Baker* and its sister cases razed long-accepted inequities in representation and revealed the tremendous effect of the vote on the product of government and the contours of the laws of the land.

The lesson is manifest in two ways. The first is the ability of a constituency or its representatives to join coalitions inside the legislature to determine how resources are to be distributed—who gets what. As chapter 9 demonstrates, those who had relatively more representation had more bargaining power than their population deserved, and equal representation translated immediately into an equitable distribution of money.

The second is the balance of competing interests, ideas, or partisan platforms. Social liberals and progressives widely expected to come to power following reapportionment. That prediction proved too optimistic. It miscalculated the extent to which urban, rural, and suburban voters differed in their preferences about government and the magnitude of the changes that reapportionment would bring. Public policies changed relatively little in areas where those who gained representation held similar political beliefs to those whom they replaced. But across the Northeast and Midwest, reapportionment magnified the representation of the relatively more liberal cities and greatly reduced the number of seats selected by conservative rural counties and towns. It was there that the liberals ought to have triumphed, and they did. Reapportionment changed which party controlled large numbers of legislatures in the Northeast and Midwest; it moved the center of political gravity decidedly to the left; and it resulted in a large left shift in public policies.

The aftershocks of the reapportionment revolution, however, did not end with the guarantee of fair representation of urban, suburban, and rural areas inside the legislatures. Reapportionment removed one of the final barriers to the party realignment then under way in American politics. Overrepresentation of rural counties and towns preserved an old order in American state politics that reflected social and political divisions of another time. Southern Democrats and northern Republicans—the majority parties in these states' legislatures—were still firmly rooted in rural counties and towns. National politics, even the governors, had evolved with the changing society; the state legislatures and the state political parties had not, and they were the last line of defense of the old order.

Baker breached that line and began a rapid transformation in the American political landscape. The changes that it fostered varied across the country. In the Northeast and Midwest, reapportionment immediately changed control of state legislatures. Conservative rural Republicans had lost their majorities. In many states, Democrats ascended. In others, moderate suburban Republicans became the pivotal vote. In the South, the realignment would take more time. Reapportionment gave southern Republicans a foothold, especially in the suburban fringe, and it weakened rural dominance of the southern Democratic parties. Rural Democrats held on in most states, as the population was majority rural in most southern states even in 1970. Population shifts and successive rounds of redistricting subsequently facilitated the sweeping and long-overdue changes in the political parties, leading ultimately to the collapse of the southern Democratic majority in 1994.

These conclusions flatly contradict the received wisdom about the reapportionment cases. The initial forays into the field concluded that the greatest peace-time change in representation in the history of the United States, perhaps in the history of democracy, was of no consequence. That conclusion, though clearly incorrect, became part of the received wisdom about politics and the courts. It was a stray false fact that led generations of scholars and critics of the Warren Court to conclude that Earl Warren's greatest case left little imprint on American politics. Nothing could be further from the truth. *Baker* succeeded in its immediate aim of ensuring equal representation. That, in turn, resulted in enormous changes in the laws of the land. Where public resources were once highly inequitably distributed, their distribution was now equalized. Where legislatures were badly out of step with the preferences of their states' populations, they were brought back into agreement. *Baker v. Carr* stands as testament not to the futility of judicial influence but to the profound power that courts can wield.

11

A New Order

Reapportionment transformed American politics. It brought representation in line with population and, as a result, radically altered political power in the United States, ending rural dominance of the American legislatures and political parties. That transformation would prove lasting. The Justices changed not just the balance of power between urban and rural areas but the very process by which districts are created. With the dawn of each new decade, the revolution occurs again.

The Supreme Court broke the state legislatures' monopoly over the laws governing representation, and it did so by drawing on one of the most sacred tenets of the Constitution—the separation of powers.[1] *Baker* established the right and willingness of the courts to review legislative districts and, when necessary, declare them unconstitutional in order to protect individual voting rights. State and federal courts have since overturned hundreds of legislative district maps in order to protect individual rights. They have forced legislatures to draw fair plans, and on rare occasions, when the legislatures have failed, the courts have even required at-large elections of all seats or appointed independent experts, special masters, to draw the districts. Legislatures retain their authority over districting, but the courts now keep a watchful eye.[2]

1. The rationale comes directly out of *Federalist Papers* Nos. 10 and 51; see also Nathaniel Persily, "In Defense of Foxes Guarding Henhouses: The Case for Judicial Acquiescence to Incumbent-Protecting Gerrymanders," *Harvard Law Review* 116 (December, 2002): 649–83.
2. Gary Cox and Jonathan Katz, *Elbridge Gerry's Salamander* (New York: Cambridge University Press, 2002), demonstrate the effectiveness of the courts, especially when the federal judges are of the opposite party to the state legislatures.

The new districting process also changed the politics that occur within the legislature. *Reynolds* and subsequent cases require the states to adjust their electoral districts regularly in order to comply with the principle of one person, one vote. New districting plans, passed every ten years, are the product of the normal and noisy process of making laws. The committees and party leaders have their hand in drawing the boundaries, but any new plan must garner a majority in the chamber. Holding a majority together on a districting bill is no small feat. Districting cuts across every imaginable ideological, social, and economic cleavage in a state, and individual legislators are particularly sensitive to the details of districting legislature because equal population districting often requires changing every legislator's constituency. Self-preservation is a powerful motivation, leading even the most loyal partisans to bolt from the best-laid districting plans.[3] Bicameralism further complicates the negotiations over a new map, as it is devilishly difficult to resolve differences between the plans generated by each chamber and maintain equal district populations. Finally, any plan must gain the assent of the governor, who often has quite different objectives from and represents an entirely different constituency from the majority that hatched the legislature's plan.[4]

This was a uniquely American solution to John Locke's problem. The Court forced politics to happen, and to happen in the American mold. The reapportionment revolution has forced legislators to strike a new deal every ten years; it has brought scrutiny from the courts, and it has given the governors leverage that they had never before enjoyed. In such a fractured political process, it is difficult for any faction or interest to take hold. Any electoral plan that emerges out of the complicated and messy process, so the theory of the separation of powers prescribes, will be fairer than one dictated by the legislature alone.[5]

The advent of a new districting process provides social scientists with a further opportunity. Not only does the reapportionment revolution expose the value of the vote and representation, it allows us to put to the test some of the most fundamental arguments concerning the operations of American political institutions. Central to the American system of government lies the conjecture that a

3. Stories of such shifting coalitions are legion. See James Mills, *A Disorderly House* (Berkeley, CA: Heyday Books, 1987).

4. On the complexity of districting and its consequences for partisan gerrymandering, see Bruce Cain, "Assessing the Partisan Effects of Redistricting," *American Political Science Review* 79, no. 2. (June, 1985): 320–33; and David Butler and Bruce Cain, *Congressional Redistricting,* (New York: Macmillan, 1993).

5. Nathaniel Persily offers one of the most cogent and spirited defenses of this new system in "In Defense of Foxes Guarding Henhouses." For an excellent discussion of the districting process generally, see Butler and Cain, *Congressional Redistricting.* Cox and Katz, in *Elbridge Gerry's Salamander,* examine how the composition of the state and federal courts affects the behavior of legislators. Rational choice theories of judicial review have formalized this important power (see John Ferejohn and Charles Shipan, "Congressional Influence on Bureaucracy," *Journal of Law, Economics, & Organization* 6 [April 1990]: 1–20).

system in which the legislature, executive, and judiciary each have a say on any given matter leads ultimately to fairer political outcomes. The U.S. Constitution rejected the English notion of a supreme singular legislature. Legislative apportionment is one of the few areas in which the American legislatures were granted as much leeway as they enjoyed before *Baker*. *Baker, Reynolds,* and related cases not only equalized the voting power of people and transformed the balance of power between urban and rural areas; these Court rulings also moved the politics of apportionment from one of legislative supremacy to one in which courts and executives also have a say. If the theory behind the U.S. Constitution holds true, the result ought to have been a much fairer electoral system.

Today, four decades after *Baker,* the new districting process appears to be failing. It is fragmented, contentious, and widely disliked by the public and the political commentators alike.[6] The Court, many now feel, unintentionally unleashed an even greater abuse and injustice than the one it solved.

Frequent redistricting has allegedly opened the door to gerrymandering on an unprecedented scale. The politicians, it is widely argued, have learned to live with the constraints that the courts have placed on political cartography. Over the decades since *Baker,* politicians have adapted to periodic redistricting and allegedly now twist the process to their own benefit. They have figured out how to make district lines that work even more grandly to their personal and partisan advantage than was ever possible in the era of malapportionment.[7] As long as the legislatures still draw the lines, the problem of districting remains unchanged. Those in power will do what they can to stay there.

The new districting process has reputedly collapsed under the combined pressures of party gerrymandering, racial districting, and incumbent protection. Alan Ehrenhalt, one of America's leading political journalists, has offered the following succinct assessment:

> Decades of litigation and judicial activism have created a system in which bizarrely shaped districts exist to serve undisguised racial purposes. Partisan gamesmanship has brought us legislatures stacked

6. Mark DiCamillo and Mervin Field, "Voters Narrowly Back Governor's Legislative Redistricting Plan," Field Research Corporation, February 24, 2005, press release #2153, www.field.com/fieldpollonline/subscribers/RLS2153.pdf. The Cooperative Congressional Election Study found identical results. See note 8. Stephen Ansolabehere, Cooperative Congressional Election Study, MIT Content, Release 1, January 1, 2007, web.mit.edu/polisci/portl/data.html.

7. See, for example, Sam Hirsch, "The United States House of Unrepresentatives: What Went Wrong in the Latest Round of Congressional Districting," *Election Law Journal* 2, no. 2 (2003): 179–217, Samuel Issacharoff, "Gerrymandering and Political Cartels," *Harvard Law Review* 116 (December, 2002): 593–648. For a contrary view, see Persily, "In Defense of Foxes Guarding Henhouses"; Jeffrey C. Kubin, "The Case for Redistricting Commissions," *Texas Law Review* 75 (March 1997); Donald E. Stokes, "Is There a Better Way to Redistrict?" in *Race and Redistricting in the 1990s,* ed. Bernard Grofman (New York: Agathon Press, 1996).

with safe seats that preclude competition at election time. All of this has taken place under the auspices of a Supreme Court doctrine that virtually any political outrage is permissible as long as the census populations of the districts are mathematically the same—even though no such mathematical precision even exists.[8]

America suffers, according to Ehrenhalt's diagnosis, under "Frankfurter's Curse"—the great Justice's warning not to enter the political thicket. "Not only could the courts make things worse," he concludes, "they did."

This view stands in striking contrast to the optimism that accompanied the Court's decision in *Baker v. Carr* and the success of that case in achieving its immediate aim of equal population representation. The critiques, if true, amount to a stinging indictment not only of the new districting process in particular, but of the ability of the courts and executives to check legislative actions and the deeply held faith in the separation of powers.[9] These claims deserve careful examination.

The new districting process faces a triple threat—party, race, and incumbency.

THE DECLINE OF PARTY BIAS

The greatest threat to the new districting process today is perhaps the oldest—partisan gerrymandering. Throughout American history, the political parties and legislative factions have tried to chisel out of the political geography additional seats for themselves each time the opportunity arises to carve up the state into legislative districts. The new process may have allowed the legislatures to do even more damage. After *Reynolds*, the task of crafting new districts fell back to the legislatures. A few states opted to place that duty in the hands of independent commissions, as Britain and Canada and other nations have done. Most state legislatures chose to keep the responsibility and to redistrict every ten years. In all but a handful of states, then, the sitting legislatures get to draw the new district boundaries, and, as has been the case throughout history, they determine their own fates.

As compelling as the logic of the separation of powers seems, several very suspicious elections raise doubts about the integrity of current districting practices. In Indiana in 1982, a year after the Republican-dominated state

8. Alan Ehrenhalt, "Frankfurter's Curse" *Governing* (January 2004), www.governing.com/archive/2004/jan/assess.txt.
9. See Gerald Rosenberg, *The Hollow Hope* (Chicago: University of Chicago Press, 1993).

legislature drew new district lines, the Democrats won 52 percent of the vote statewide for the state house of representatives, but only forty-three of the hundred seats. In same year in California, the Democrats evidently got the edge. State senator Phil Burton drew what many consider one of the finest gerrymanders in the modern era. The total number of ballots cast for Republican candidates in California's U.S. House seats grew by 500,000 statewide from 1980 to 1982, but the party lost six seats.

Such abuses prompted new rounds of litigation. The Court, however, stayed out of the partisan morass as long as possible. Throughout the 1960s and 1970s, the Justices refused to hear such cases at all. They finally asserted in 1986 the judiciary's right to review allegations of partisan gerrymandering in the dispute over Indiana's district lines.[10] But they have failed to state a suitable standard or remedy, and they have since not overturned a single plan where partisan discrimination is alleged.

The legislatures, for their part, have increasingly challenged the judiciary's power. The most recent rounds of redistricting pushed the system perilously close to another breaking point, not unlike the situation in 1962.

Following the 2000 election, Republicans held majorities of both chambers of the Pennsylvania legislature as well as the governorship. Republican party leaders, with intervention by President Bush's chief political consultant, Karl Rove, eventually passed a plan that openly sought to squeeze thirteen Republican seats out of the states' twenty U.S. House districts.[11] The result, according to Democratic house minority leader William DeWeese, was an "unpalatable obscenity." The Democrats sued.

The bravado of the Texas Republicans overshadowed their Pennsylvania counterparts. A split Texas legislature failed to pass a plan in 2001, and the district court put in place a map that closely followed the lines drawn under unified Democratic government in 1991. That plan, however, returned Democrats to a majority of the state's U.S. House seats, even though the state trended strongly Republican. At last in 2002, Republicans broke the Democrats' hold on the state legislature. In the spring of 2003, now in complete control of state government, the Republicans drew and passed an electoral map to their liking. Texas Democrats, now in the minority, took the only action they could: they left. They fled the state, most going to Ardmore, Oklahoma, to prevent the Texas legislature from operating with a quorum and stopping the passage of any legislation. The tactic could only work for so long, and upon their return in the next session of the legislature, Texas passed the Republican map.

10. *Davis v. Bandemer*, 478 U.S. 109 (1986).
11. John M. R. Bull, "GOP Split over Congressional Districts," *Pittsburgh Post-Gazette*, December 13, 2001.

During the Texas Democrats' holdout, the Supreme Court issued its opinion in the Pennsylvania case *Vieth v. Jubelirer*. Here at last appeared a clear-cut case. The Republicans' intentions were never in doubt, and the new lines were widely thought to block Democrats from control of the House. Many observers expected the Supreme Court to use the *Vieth* case "to bring partisan gerrymandering under control."[12] Four Justices—Souter, Ginsberg, Stevens, and Breyer— laid out possible ways for the courts to tackle the matter. But four other Justices—Scalia, Thomas, O'Connor, and Rehnquist—concluded that courts have no authority over partisan gerrymandering because no "manageable standards" could exist. That left one pivotal vote—Justice Anthony Kennedy. April 1961 all over again.

Justice Kennedy, however, is both more decisive than Justice Potter Stewart and more demanding. He would not move forward without a workable standard, and if a solution could be found, he argued, "the courts should grant relief." But he remained unpersuaded that such a standard was in sight. Can the Court reasonably determine what is a partisan gerrymander and what is not? Lacking such a path forward, Kennedy chose to stay the Court's hand. He voted to deny Vieth's request that the judges overturn the Pennsylvania districting plan, but he could not support the resurrection of Frankfurter's principle. "A determination by the Court to deny all hopes of intervention," the Justice wrote in his concurring opinion, "could erode confidence in the courts as much as would a premature decision to intervene."[13]

Two and a half years later, the Supreme Court settled the issues in Texas. The decision was nothing short of byzantine, with different majority and plurality opinions for different parts of the case. Justice Kennedy wrote the opinion on the core questions in the case, and he reaffirmed his conclusion to the Pennsylvania controversy. The question of the Court's authority over partisan gerrymandering is settled; at issue is whether a remedy can be found. "That disagreement persists." Without a standard, the Court had no choice but to recognize that the Texas legislature acted within its powers, leaving the plan largely intact.[14]

The most recent round of litigation and political shenanigans is nothing new. Redistricting after each decennial census since 1970 has resulted in

12. Mitchell Berman, "Putting Fairness on the Map," *Los Angeles Times*, May 28, 2004, www.utexas.edu/law/news/2004/052804_berman.html.

13. *Vieth v. Jubelirer*, 541 U.S. 267 (2004).

14. Jeffrey Toobin, "Drawing the Line," *The New Yorker*, March 6, 2006, www.newyorker.com/printables/fact/060306fa_fact. Case materials available at Findlaw.com: news.findlaw.com/legalnews/lit/election2004/cases.html. Ronald Keith Gaddie, "Texas Districting, Measure for Measure," *Extensions, A Journal of the Carl Albert Congressional Research and Studies Center* (Fall 2004), www.ou.edu/special/albertctr/extensions/fall2004/Gaddie.html.

charges and countercharges of partisan gerrymandering. Those apparently on the losing side call foul, and those who had drawn the districts counter that they were merely fixing past discrimination. The U.S. Supreme Court has largely stayed out of these fights. The Justices have maintained that they have authority over these matters, but have failed to establish a simple standard analogous to one person one, vote that would clear up the controversies.

Baker v. Carr may have ended malapportionment. It did not, however, eliminate the enormous conflict of interest inherent in legislative redistricting. Many legal scholars and political observers now charge that the Court, lacking a standard for partisan fairness, has made matters worse. Unwittingly, the Justices may have uncaged Elbridge Gerry's monster.

Lacking malapportionment as an instrument of gerrymandering, legislators have reputedly turned to other techniques. The most important of these is packing. A simple example demonstrates the ease with which one can manipulate district lines to dilute the political strength of the opposition. Suppose three districts must be constructed in an area where half of the people are loyal to Party A and half are loyal to Party B. Suppose Party A gets to draw the new lines, subject to the constraint that the districts must have equal populations. Party A can secure two of the three seats permanently by packing one district with Party B's supporters. Party A can construct one district that consists entirely of Party B voters. This district will vote 100 percent for Party B, and it contains two-thirds of all of Party B's voters. The other two districts then can be drawn in such a way that Party A has a majority in each: split Party A's voters and the remaining Party B voters equally across the two districts. Party A's voters will outnumber Party B's voters three to one in these two districts. In this way, Party A can guarantee that it will win a majority of the new legislature.

Packing and other methods of partisan manipulations may distort the vote just as severely as malapportionment did. Consider again our hypothetical example. The vote distortion here is the discrepancy between the votes won and the seats won. In this electorate, the two parties split the votes evenly, 50-50. However, Party A has rigged the districts so that it can win two-thirds of the seats, or 67 percent—a distortion of 17 points.

Political scientists call this distortion the partisan bias in the electoral system. Specifically, the bias equals the surplus (or deficit) in the percentage of seats that a party would win were the parties to divide the vote equally. If Party A and Party B split the vote equally, each winning 50 percent, then an unbiased districting plan would give the two parties approximately half of the seats each. However, if the districts are skewed so that one party would win well over half of the seats when the vote divides equally between the parties, then the bias favors that party. The magnitude of the bias equals the difference between the percentage of seats that a party is predicted to win under the existing district-ing system and the percentage of the votes that a party *ought* to win under a fair districting map, which is 50 percent. Bias amounts to a permanent structural advantage that favors one of the parties.[15]

As legal dogfights suggest, gerrymander in the wake of *Baker* may have ac-tually magnified partisan biases. It is certainly easy to construct hypothetical examples, such as the one above, in which legislative districting readily creates severe partisan biases. Indeed, the journals of political scientists are rife with such theoretical exercises and hypothetical cases.[16] For their part, the judges have identified particularly ugly districts as indications that political cartogra-phers have attempted to rig the electoral system.[17]

But how bad is the current state of affairs? Has the courts' involvement exag-gerated these problems, or has the frequent districting required by one person, one vote made districts fairer for parties as well as for people? Is partisan bias worse today than before *Baker*?

The history of partisan bias before *Baker* and since leads to a striking con-clusion. As we show in the analysis to follow, electoral maps are much fairer now than before 1965. Although partisan biases remain, they are, on the whole, rather small today. That conclusion runs strongly counter to the conventional wisdom; it deserves a careful development.[18]

To gauge bias, we first examine how votes translate into seats. Specifically, we wish to measure what share of the seats a party wins as a function of the share of the vote that a party won in legislative elections throughout the state. As a practi-cal matter, there is an approximately linear relationship between votes and seats, so for each state we estimated the line that best fit the observed shares of seats and votes. Two characteristics determine that relationship—the slope and the inter-cept. These, in turn, allow us to assess the fairness of electoral systems and dis-tricts. First, the rate at which increases in the share of the two-party vote won by a party throughout a state translate into increases in legislative seats captures the responsiveness of the composition of the legislature to swings in the parties' elec-toral support. It is the slope of the line relating seats to votes. Empirically, the responsiveness of American elections tends to be around 2: a 1 percent gain in

15. Andrew Gelman and Gary King, "Estimating the Electoral Consequences of Districting," *Journal of the American Statistical Association* 85 (1990): 274–82.

16. Thomas W. Gilligan and John G. Matzusaka, "Structural Constraints on Partisan Bias under the Efficient Gerrymander," *Public Choice* 100, no. 1–2 (July 1999): 65–84; Kenneth W. Shotts, "The Effect of Majority-Minority Mandates on Partisan Gerrymandering," *American Journal of Political Science* 45, no. 1 (January 2001): 120–35.

17. See Justice O'Connor's opinion in *Shaw v. Reno,* 509 U.S. 630 (1993).

18. Andrew Gelman and Gary King, "Enhancing Democracy through Legislative Districting," *American Po-litical Science Review* 88 (1994): 541–59. They find declining partisan bias in the U.S. House.

vote share statewide translates into a 2 percent increase in seat share.[19] Second, partisan bias equals the division of the seats won when the vote shares of the two parties equal .5. The intercept of the line determines the bias. Specifically, bias equals the intercept plus .5 times the responsiveness.

We are further interested in whether the bias has changed over time. To examine those changes, we can estimate the relationship between seats and votes for different eras—in this case, before and after the reapportionment decisions.

The Connecticut assembly provides a particularly crisp example. Figure 11.1 displays the relationship between the share of the votes won statewide and the share of seats won in that body before reapportionment and over the decades since. The lower line shows the relationship between votes and seats for the earlier period, from 1946 to 1962, and the upper line captures the relationship since, from 1966 to 2006.[20]

Before reapportionment, elections to Connecticut's lower chamber exhibited an enormous bias in favor of the Republican Party. The parties divided the vote evenly in 1948 and 1950 during this period, but in those elections the Democrats won only about 30 percent of the seats. As a result, the estimated bias is approximately 20 points in the Republican direction. That bias was sufficient to guarantee Republican majorities in the state legislature, even in the face of Democratic victories in statewide elections. In 1954, 1960, and 1962, Democrats won slight majorities of the vote in statewide elections, but only 40 percent of the seats in the lower chamber. And in 1958, Connecticut Democrats rode a national landslide to overwhelming victories in the statewide vote, but that was only enough to win them slightly less than half of the seats in the assembly.

Redistricting in the wake of *Baker* virtually eliminated partisan bias in Connecticut's lower house. The upper line in Figure 11.1 shows the relationship between votes and seats from 1966 to 2006. Democrats appear to hold a slight advantage in this era, as the estimated bias in the relationship is about 5 points in their favor. Since 1966, when the parties divide the vote equally, the Democrats are predicted to win approximately 55 percent of the seats. That bias, however, is sufficiently small that it is not discernable from no bias at all, given the data at hand.[21]

At issue is whether the magnitude of the bias changed from the pre-*Baker*

19. Responsiveness was higher before the 1960s, around 2.5, and fell somewhat over the decades after. The decline appears to be due to the incumbency advantage. See Stephen Ansolabehere, David Brady, and Morris Fiorina, "The Vanishing Marginals and Electoral Responsiveness," *British Journal of Political Science* 22, no. 1 (January 1992): 21–38; and Gary Jacobson, "The Marginals Never Vanished: Incumbency and Competition in Elections to the U.S. House of Representatives, 1952–1982," *American Journal of Political Science* 31, no. 1 (February 1987): 126–41.

20. The 1964 state legislative elections in Connecticut were canceled.

21. The estimated slope in the post-1966 era is .97 with a standard error of .19, and the estimated intercept is .07 with a standard error of .10. The test of bias is whether intercept is statistically distinct from 0, which it is not.

FIGURE 11.1. *Relationship between seats and votes in the Connecticut assembly,*
1946–1962 and 1968–2002

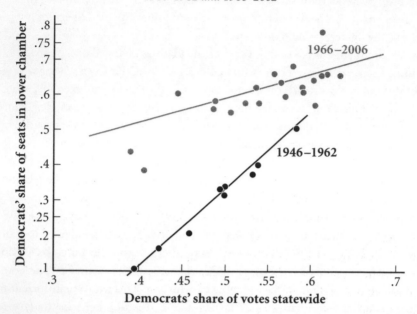

era to the present. At least in Connecticut, the answer is quite clear. The bias
was 20 points (in the Republican direction) before the Supreme Court intervened in districting question, and it shrank to 5 points (in the Democratic direction) after reapportionment. Court supervision, then, almost completely
eliminated partisan bias in the Connecticut assembly's electoral districts.

Connecticut exemplifies the trends in partisan biases throughout the country. For every state between 1946 and 2006, we estimated the partisan biases
before and after the reapportionment decisions. We first found the best-fitting
line to express how a party's share of legislative seats depends on the share of
votes won statewide. Using these estimates, we then computed the surplus
share of seats or the deficit. A few states could not be included in the analysis.
Nebraska has nonpartisan elections, as did Minnesota until 1973, making it
impossible to measure the shares of votes or seats won by the parties in these
states' elections. Also, Alaska and Hawaii did not enter the Union until immediately before the reapportionment cases. They had territorial elections, but
their status is sufficiently ambiguous that we chose to leave them out. We must
also omit from the analysis those southern states from before the 1970s that
had no Republicans at all, as it is impossible to estimate the relationship between seats and votes when the seat shares do not vary. The appendix contains
fuller details of our estimates of partisan biases.

TABLE 11.1 *Magnitude of bias in state legislative districts before and after* Baker

	Upper chambers	Lower chambers
Before (1940–1964)	15.5%	10.8%
After (1971–2000)	8.2%	6.6%
Difference	7.3*	4.2*
Margin of error	± 2.0	± 1.5

* = Statistically larger than 0 at the .01 level.

Patterns of partisan biases among the states speak to two essential questions about the fairness of the current districting process. First, has the magnitude of partisan bias shrunk since 1964? Critiques of the new districting process argue that biases have actually risen with more frequent districting, but frequent districting in a system of separation of powers ought to have reduced biases. Second, does the direction of bias depend on who controls the districting process? Divided government ought to yield the least bias in the electoral system if the separation of powers indeed weakens the ability of the majority party in the legislature to leave its mark on the districting system.

Let us turn to the first of these questions. Districts are certainly fairer in one sense: they now have equal populations. The relationship between seats and votes reveals that they are fairer in another sense as well: the new districting process has in fact lowered partisan biases. This has occurred even without a clear definition of what constitutes a fair map in partisan terms.

The relation between the share of seats won by a party and the share of votes won by that partly reveals the extent to which the district lines give that party an inherent or structural advantage or disadvantage. We estimated the partisan bias for every state legislature across the two decades before *Baker v.* (1940–1964) and the three decades since (1970–2002). The magnitude of the biases—rather than which party benefited—are of immediate interest and are displayed in Table 11.1.[22] The number 15.5%, for example, means that in the upper chambers before the *Baker* decision, the bias, either in the Republican or Democratic direction, averaged 15.5 percent. Thus in an evenly divided election, the party favored by the districting system would expect to win 65 percent of the seats!

22. The magnitude is the absolute value of the bias. This corrects for the fact that a pro-Democratic bias will be a positive number and a pro-Republican bias will be a negative number.

For each state, we also calculated the change in the magnitude bias from the pre-*Baker* era to the post-*Baker* era. The bottom row of the table displays the average change in the magnitude of bias; a positive number means improvement.

Partisan biases in state legislative districts were cut nearly in half over the forty-year period 1960–2000. In the upper chambers, the average bias was roughly 16 percentage points from 1940 to 1964. During this time, when the vote was evenly divided in the typical state lower house, the favored party would win 66 percent of the seats. The biases in the upper chambers averaged 8 percentage points over the decades since reapportionment, a 45 percent improvement. In the lower chambers, biases averaged roughly 11 percentage points before *Baker* and were reduced to nearly 7 points over the decades since.[23]

These figures reveal the broad success of the new districting process. The past sixty years of electoral history in the United States show a significant decline in the partisan bias in districting systems—not an increase, as has widely been claimed. Some states, most notably Massachusetts and Rhode Island, have seen biases increase, but these examples are uncommon. Nearly every state showed evidence of considerable partisan gerrymandering before *Baker*, and nearly every state has witnessed decreases in partisan biases. Bias has not been eliminated, but in the typical state it has been cut by 40 to 50 percent.

The pattern in state legislatures fits with what other scholars have discovered about the U.S. House. New district boundaries drawn in response to the Court's requirement that districts have equal populations reduced partisan biases considerably. Gary Cox and Jonathan Katz show that over the course of the 1960s, partisan biases in U.S. House elections outside the South shrank to 0.[24] Cox and Katz, however, remain critical of the manner in which the courts have handled districting since, especially the partisanship of the judicial process in some states. Setting aside problems in specific states, it appears that on the whole the new process has made elections much fairer.

Distortions in the American electoral system have not vanished entirely. In the typical state, the majority party gets an additional boost in seat shares of approximately 7 to 8 percentage points. Taken in isolation, the biases that

---

23. A few extreme cases emerged. In Massachusetts and Rhode Island, large pro-Democratic biases emerged in the 1970s, even though neither state had substantial partisan biases in the 1950s. At the other extreme, Vermont and Virginia witnessed huge improvements, with biases dropping by 30 and 40 points, respectively. Omitting these cases, however, does not change the picture. Without these outlying cases, biases in the upper chambers averaged 15 points before *Baker* and 8 points afterward; biases in the lower chambers averaged 11 points prior to *Baker* and 7 points afterward.

24. Gary W. Cox and Jonathan N. Katz, "The Reapportionment Revolution and Bias in U.S. Congressional Elections," *American Journal of Political Science* 43, no. 3 (July 1999): 812–41.

currently exist are not trivial. In a closely divided election, as many of them now are, partisan biases continue to help keep the sitting majority in power. Current reform efforts focus, rightly, on further reductions in partisan gerrymandering, and many reformers now propose that districting be taken out of the political process altogether, giving it to nonpartisan commissions (or, worse, political science and law professors).

The deeper question, then, is why the reductions in bias have occurred. We conjecture that the new process of frequent districting under court supervision has driven down the biases. It may, however, be the case that all of the reductions reflect gains made immediately after reapportionment. The courts, after all, have said little about partisan fairness and have repeatedly dodged the question. All of the gains that can be had may have already occurred; frequent districting may achieve little additional improvement.

The forty-year period since *Baker* counsels otherwise. Reductions in partisan bias continue to occur, long after reapportionment. Equalizing district population accounts for some of the declines, especially in the upper chambers. We can break down the post-*Baker* era further, into decades. Examining the biases a decade at a time reveals that each successive decade of districting has brought additional reductions in partisan gerrymandering. Biases have ratcheted down steadily, averaging 11 percent in the lower chambers before *Baker*, then 9 percent in the 1970s and 1980s, and 6 percent during the 1990s and 2000s.

Sharper evidence of our general argument emerges upon considering who controls the districting process. A party has the best chance of passing a highly favorable districting plan when that party holds majorities in both chambers of the legislature and occupies the executive office. When control of the process is divided, it will be difficult to pass a highly partisan plan. Today, a little over half of the state districting plans were drawn under conditions of divided control. The contrast between divided and unified party control further demonstrates the new process at work.

Over the decades since *Baker*, divided government, when it occurs, has virtually eliminated partisan biases in districting plans. Table 11.2 displays the average magnitude of partisan biases from 1946 to 2006, but this time we distinguish who controlled the districting process. The analyses include the four southern states for which we could estimate party biases (Florida, North Carolina, Tennessee, and Virginia) as well as the states of the Northeast, Midwest, and West. The top panel presents the result for upper chambers, and the bottom panel presents the results for lower chambers. The first column shows the average bias that existed before *Baker*; the second column shows the bias that existed after 1971. The rows indicate which party controlled the legislature at the time of districting—Republican, Democratic, or Divided. The entries in

TABLE 11.2 *Average bias in districting plans before and after* Baker, *by party in control of the districting process*

Party controlling districting	Upper chambers	
	Before 1964	After 1971
Republican	−12.7%	−5.5%
Divided	−11.9	−1.4
Democratic	20.8	13.6
	Lower chambers	
	Before 1964	After 1971
Republican	−10.4	−5.0
Divided	−3.3	−0.3
Democratic	14.6	11.1

the table preserve the partisan orientation of the bias. Positive values indicate a pro-Democratic gerrymander, and negative values indicate a pro-Republican map. A bias of 10 percent would mean that the Democrats won 60 percent of the seats when the parties each won 50 percent of the votes.[25]

The table reveals that divided control indeed reduces bias compared with unified control. In the years since *Baker*, the average partisan bias is just 1.4 percentage points in upper chambers and less than one-half of 1 percentage point when control of the districting process is divided. By contrast, where the Republicans have drawn the maps, they have subsequently enjoyed a 5 percentage point advantage in the upper and lower chambers. Where the Democrats have drawn the maps, the bias has averaged slightly over 10 percentage points in both chambers.

Over time, partisan biases have declined in every political circumstance from the 1940s through the current period. Before *Baker,* if neither party controlled the districting process, the lower chambers exhibited a slight Republican bias and the upper chambers had a strongly Republican bias. This reflects malapportionment and its tendency to favor the GOP outside the South. After *Baker*, districting in the context of divided government produced negligible partisan biases.

Even when one party controls the districting process, the biases in district maps have fallen. The biases when Democrats controlled districting are, on

---

25. Other work along these lines includes Janet Campagna and Bernard Grofman, "Party Control and Partisan Bias in the 1980s Congressional Redistricting," *Journal of Politics* 52, no. 4 (November 1990): 1242–57; and Richard Born, "Partisan Intentions and Election Day Realities in the Congressional Redistricting Process," *American Political Science Review* 79, no. 2 (June 1985): 305–19.

average, 3 percentage points lower now than before *Baker*. More dramatic still is the improvement when Republicans controlled districting. Then the amount of partisan bias shrank 8 percentage points, from 12 points on average in the pre-*Baker* days to an average of just 4 points today. Overall, the bias in the plans created by partisan state legislatures has fallen from 13 points to just 7 points. Outside the South, then, the new process has greatly reduced, though not eliminated, partisan biases.

The southern states have followed a different path, though they reflect the general trends operating elsewhere. So far, our analysis of partisan bias has ignored the changes that have occurred in the South since reapportionment. We are hamstrung by history. It is impossible to measure bias in the many southern states where Republicans had no representation at all before the 1960s or even 1970s. Nonetheless, the story of the South since the 1980s is instructive.

Democrats drew all of the southern districting plans before the 1960s, as they had a solid lock on the legislatures. For four states, Florida, North Carolina, Tennessee, and Virginia, Republicans won enough state legislative seats that it is possible to gauge the relation between votes and seats. These four states likely had less partisan bias in their districting plans than other southern states, as the correlation between Democratic share of the Presidential Vote and Relative Representation tended to be even stronger elsewhere in the South.[26] In Florida, North Carolina, and Tennessee, the partisan bias averaged a whopping 23 percent in the Democrats' favor during the 1940s and 1950s. In other words, under the hypothetical situation in which Republicans and Democrats split the statewide vote, the data analysis predicts that the Democrats would have won 73 percent of the legislative seats. Of course, this is quite hypothetical, as Republicans frequently did not even bother to run, let alone make for a competitive race.

The situation had changed markedly by the 1980s and 1990s, however. Republicans challenged and even toppled the Democrats in many states. Southern politics today is among the most competitive in the country, with state legislatures split evenly between Democrats and Republicans. The rise of the Republicans has decreased the electoral bias against them, but even today it remains high. During the 1980s and the 1990s, in the southern states where Democrats controlled the legislatures and drew the maps, the biases averaged 21 percentage points. However, where control was divided in this era, as it has increasingly become, the biases have fallen dramatically. In such cases, the biases are now below 10 percent.

26. In the lower chambers, the correlation between Relative Representation and Democratic Share of the Presidential Vote is .23 in Florida, North Carolina, Tennessee, and Virginia, and .41 across the rest of the South. In the upper chambers, the correlation is .73 in Florida, North Carolina, Tennessee, and Virginia and .52 elsewhere. See chapter 4, note 14, for details.

This picture of the southern states is striking. It speaks directly to the current controversies that have embroiled Texas, Georgia, and other state legislatures. Republicans have ascended in many southern states, in Texas in particular, but their success in legislative elections has lagged well behind their gains in party registration, party identification, and statewide elections. The reason, our findings suggest, is historic biases in legislative districting plans that remain even today. Democrats have controlled the electoral process in these states for well over a century. Many other institutions that protected the one-party South have fallen. Districting maps, it appears, are the one remaining legacy of the Solid South, but even they are slowly being leveled. Each successive round of redistricting in the South has whittled away at the Democrats' long-held advantage.

Political competition has risen throughout the nation. Few states today are dominated by a single party, the way Republicans reigned in the Northeast or Democrats in the South. Divided government has resulted in political gridlock on many areas of public policy, but in the area of legislative districting divided government has reduced sharply the amount of bias in the electoral system. Of course, without the requirement that the states periodically redistrict in the first place, many of the gains that have come about through mixed control would not have happened at all.

In the days when courts stayed out, the legislatures did not have to act at all. Divided control before 1964 was a recipe for stalemate, not compromise. And that was the true curse of Frankfurter's dictum.

RACE AND PARTISAN GERRYMANDERING

The most intense legal battles over districting since 1965 have not concerned party or population, but race. The judges resolved the great principle of population equality in a few short years; by 1965, there was little left for them to decide. The great majority of districting cases since have focused on representation of black and Hispanic communities. Racial districting has vexed the courts and Congress even more than questions of partisan districting.

Judicial decisions and government policy concerning racial districting proceeded on a track separate from equal population districting and its partisan consequences. But in the 1980s, the two strains of legal thinking about representation collided.

The Supreme Court took on the problem of racially discriminatory districts in 1960, two years before it tackled the question of fairness for the general population. A unanimous Court in *Gomillion v. Lightfoot* forbade states from using political boundaries to dilute the votes of African Americans. Felix Frankfurter penned the opinion of a unanimous Court, which found such activities blatant violations of the Fifteenth Amendment's guarantee of the voting rights of blacks.[27] Political boundaries were the least of the problems facing African Americans. Registration and polling place practices systematically excluded blacks from voting, and it would take an act of Congress—the Voting Rights Act of 1965—to outlaw the disenfranchisement of blacks.

The Voting Rights Act went into effect as the state legislatures began to redistrict under the reapportionment cases. The two pulled in opposite directions. The Voting Rights Act led to a massive increase in black voter registration and turnout throughout the South. In those states, only one in four adult African Americans were registered to vote in 1960. Thanks to the Voting Rights Act, two-thirds of African Americans in the South had registered to vote by the mid-1970s. Voter registration and turnout of blacks in the South approached those of whites.[28]

As blacks gained in registration and political organization, they lost in the apportionment process. Before *Baker*, blacks constituted a majority of the population in 18 percent state legislative districts in the South.[29] These percentages were roughly proportional to the composition of the region's population, of which 21 percent were black according to the 1960 Census. New district plans approved in 1971 left just 7 percent of the state lower house districts in the South with majority black populations and only 5 percent of state upper house districts with majority black populations. In many states, new district lines of 1971 provided for no majority black districts at all. Reapportionment caused some of the reduction in majority black districts through the elimination of rural Black Belt county districts, but more of the reduction appears to have occurred as a result of the nature of the new districts.[30] Southern state legislatures, dominated by white Democrats, drew new lines between 1965 and 1971 that blocked Republicans and blacks from winning legislative seats.

A legal firestorm ensued. Hundreds of state and federal lawsuits challenged the legality of the new southern districts; dozens reached the U.S. Supreme Court during the late 1960s and 1970s. Under the aegis of *Gomillion*, the Court

27. Here lies the great irony behind Alan Ehrenhalt's critique of *Baker*. Race, not population, set off most of the legal controversies since. Almost all of the litigation over districting since 1970 has concerned race, not party or population, and Felix Frankfurter led the vanguard.

28. James E. Alt, "The Impact of the Voting Rights Act on Black and White Voter Registration in the South," in *Quiet Revolution in the South: The Impact of the Voting Rights Act, 1965–1990*, ed. Chandler Davidson and Bernard Grofman (Princeton, NJ: Princeton University Press, 1994).

29. These calculations cover Alabama, Arkansas, Florida, Mississippi, North Carolina, and South Carolina. It is impossible to determine the racial composition of urban districts in the other four southern states in the 1970s. The racial composition of the legislative districts of the four other southern states before 1960 resembles that of the states for which we could assess the racial composition of the districts.

30. See William E. Bicker, "The Effects of Malapportionment in the States—A Mistrial," in *Reapportionment in the 1970s*, ed. Nelson Polsby (Berkeley: University of California Press, 1971): 151–201.

found cause to strike down some practices, most notably multimember and at-large districts.[31] Beyond that, the Court found no simple answers. Unlike malapportionment, the Justices struggled to establish any new standard. The Fifteenth Amendment to the Constitution, passed immediately after the Civil War, protects citizens' voting rights for blacks. Did that not mean proportional representation? The Court said no; but short of proportional representation, it was unclear how many seats a group ought to have.[32] Political science offered no clear answers either. How many majority black seats ought to exist depends on how responsive the electoral system is. If a system has high responsiveness, the number of seats that a minority party or group would elect falls far below proportionality.[33] The Court chose to approach the racial districting cases of the 1970s one at a time. The Justices required discriminatory intent as well as evidence of an effect. Vague language, such as "totality of circumstances," crept into the criteria for determining racially discriminatory districts. The Justices were headed into the same morass they had entered with the school desegregation cases.

The U.S. Congress, at last, weighed in. In 1982, it came time to renew the Voting Rights Act, and Congress decided instead to amend it to include districting. The amended act explicitly prohibited dilution of black and Hispanic votes and required that any state with past discrimination or sufficiently large minority populations first gain approval of its districts from the Department of Justice. The department has insisted on the creation of majority-minority districts wherever possible.

Majority-minority districting has been widely criticized. Large majorities in the American public disagree with this sort of districting practice on grounds of fairness.[34] The principle involved has angered many conservative politicians, as it sounds like affirmative action. In an odd twist, it has alienated many Democrats, who feel that this protected category greatly constrains

31. The most important decisions dealing with racial districting include *Allen v. State Board of Elections*, 393 U.S. 544 (1969); *Gaffney v. Cummings*, 412 U.S. 735 (1973); *Beer v. United States*, 425 U.S. 130 (1976); *United Jewish Organizations v. Carey*, 430 U.S. 144 (1977); *Mobile v. Bolden*, 446 U.S. (1980); and *Rogers v. Lodge*, 458 U.S. 613 (1982). In *Mobile v. Bolden*, the Court was clearly backing off from any sort of mechanical solution to racial voting, and it required evidence of intent. Congress imposed a mechanical solution in the 1982 Amendments to the Voting Rights Act, which the Court clarified in *Thornburg v. Gingles*, 478 U.S. 30 (1986). See also Daniel Lowenstein, *Election Law* (Durham, NC: Carolina Academic Press, 1995), chap. 5.

32. In one sense, blacks did better than expected. The relation of seats to votes predicts that blacks should have won less than 5 percent of all seats in a first-past-the-post single-member district system. This, of course, is the problem with a majoritarian system such as that used in the United States, the United Kingdom, and Canada, as opposed to proportional representation used in France and Germany, for example.

33. If the system is unbiased and highly responsive (e.g., responsiveness of 2 or 3), then a minority group with 20 percent of the population would expect to win 5 percent of the legislative seats or less.

34. Stephen Ansolabehere, Cooperative Congressional Election Study, MIT Content, Release 1, January 1, 2007, cl p.351, n6 web.mit.edu/polisci/portl/data.html.

what they can accomplish in districting and creates a bias against them. Even some black and Hispanic politicians express frustration, as their districts are "too liberal."[35]

The practice has further created a peculiar tension within the law. *Gomillion* expressed the protection of the right to vote for a particular group under the Fifteenth Amendment, and *Baker* expressed a right for all people to equal protection of the laws under the Fourteenth Amendment. While Brennan characterized this new right as the general form of that defined in *Gomillion*, it clearly is not. The Court has shielded blacks from gerrymandering because of the Fifteenth Amendment and now Hispanics under the Voting Right Act, but it has not extended the same protection to all social groups.[36] A highly unified community, such as a religious or ethnic enclave within a city, can be divided by districting and its vote diluted.

Many of these criticisms are matters of principle and philosophy rather than practice. But majority-minority districts are thought to have created a very real political problem.

Majority-minority districts led to an immediate crisis in the Democratic Party. The Department of Justice, the courts, the caucuses of black and Hispanic legislatures, and even many liberal Democrats insist on the creation of districts capable of ensuring representation of these racial minorities. Left to their own devices, white Democrats in states with large minority populations would rather distribute the minority vote so as to create a larger number of solid, but not overwhelmingly, Democratic districts. Black and Hispanic Democratic Party leaders and the Department of Justice have pushed for districts that contain at least 65 percent minority voters. In their quest to increase minority seats, black Democratic legislators have found a willing partner—the Republicans. Following the 1990 and 2000 Censuses, white Democratic legislators in many states with large minority populations failed to pass their own redistricting bills. They were rolled by an odd coalition of conservative white Republicans and very liberal black Democrats.

Such divisions have not been limited to the southern states. White flight and immigration have radically altered the face of America over the last three decades. States like New Jersey, Massachusetts, California, and Ohio have struggled over requirements to create majority-minority districts, as whites increasingly find themselves in the minority in central cities and even in many

35. See Alan Gerber, "African Americans' Congressional Careers and the Democratic House Delegation," *Journal of Politics* 58, no. 3 (August 1996): 831–45.

36. District boundaries in the 1980s divided a community of Hassidic Jews in New York City into two separate legislative districts. The intention was to break up the voting strength of this highly unified neighborhood, and the Supreme Court ruled that the legislature was allowed to do so. See *UJO v Carey*, 430 U.S. 144 (1977).

counties. State Democratic leaders have tried to minimize their losses by drawing districts that give the least possible representation to minority groups. Blacks, Hispanics, and other minority groups, they have argued, would be better off with a Democratic majority than with more minority representation and a Republican majority.

Democratic pols have found sympathetic ears among political scientists, election lawyers, and even some judges. The potential to pack the most Democratic voters into a few districts is undeniable, and critics of the creation of majority-minority districts argue that the practice creates a substantial partisan bias against Democrats in legislative district plans. Democratic leaders, armed with legal and social science expertise, have begun to attack racial districting in the courts.[37]

A compelling logic lies behind these arguments. Maps that concentrate Democrats in a few minority districts necessarily hurt the party. If the critics of racial districting are right, then we ought to observe strong biases against the Democratic Party in the states with large numbers of majority-minority districts. With this argument in mind, we took another look at the relation between votes and seats in the state legislatures during the 1990s. The 1990s are the first full decade in which the Voting Rights Act and the Department of Justice forced states to create as many majority-minority districts as possible. Is there a pro-Republican bias in states with large numbers of majority-minority districts?

The answer, surprisingly, is no. Democrats enjoyed favorable partisan biases in states with the highest numbers of majority-minority districts in the 1990s. In states where more than 10 percent of legislative districts contained a majority of minorities (blacks or Hispanics), partisan biases averaged about 4.6 percentage points in the Democratic direction in the lower chambers and 3.5 percentage points in the upper chambers. States varied around this average from a high of 25 points in the Democratic direction to a low of 12 points in the Republican direction, but over 60 percent had a pro-Democratic slant.

States with fewer minority districts, by contrast, tended toward the Republicans or neutrality. The biases were slightly pro-Republican (2 percentage points in the lower chamber and less than 1 percent in the upper chambers) in those states where racial minorities had a majority in less than 5 percent of the

37. Abigail Thernstrom, *Whose Votes Count? Affirmative Action and Minority Voting Rights* (Cambridge, MA: Harvard University Press, 1991); David Lublin, "Racial Districting and African American Representation: A Critique of 'Do Majority-Minority Districts Maximize Substantive Black Representation?,'" *American Political Science Review* 93 (March 1999): 1830–89; David Lublin and D. Stephen Voss, "The Partisan Impact of Voting Rights Law," *Stanford Law Review* 50 (February 1998): 765–77; David Epstein and Sharyn O'Halloran, "Trends in Minority Representation, 1974–2000," in *The Future of the Voting Rights Act*, ed. David L. Epstein, Richard H. Pildes, Rodolfo O. de la Garza, and Sharyn O'Halloran (New York: Russell Sage Foundation, 2006).

districts. The biases were slightly more Republican (1 percentage point on average in the lower chambers and 3 percentage points in the upper chambers) in states where 5 to 10 percent of the districts were majority-minority.

It was the Democrats who did better where large numbers of minority districts were created. Looking across states, there is a noticeable positive correlation between Democratic partisan bias and the proportion of districts that are minority-majority in the 1990s. The correlations equaled +.23 in the upper chambers and +.36 in the lower chambers. The correlations are hardly perfect, but they run counter to the widely maintained assertion that majority-minority districting has hurt the Democrats. Even in specific cases, the data do not conform to the critics' arguments. New Mexico, where approximately one-third of the districts were majority-minority in the 1980s and 1990s, has the highest percentage representation of Hispanics and blacks. That state exhibited a slight Democratic bias over these decades. At the other extreme are states with no majority-minority districts. These are Idaho, Iowa, Maine, Minnesota, Montana, North Dakota, South Dakota, Utah, Vermont, West Virginia, and Wyoming. These states have very few minority voters, and the partisan bias leans in the Republican direction.

None of this fits with the widely voiced complaints that majority-minority districting hurts the Democrats. These patterns sharply contradict a deeply held conviction that racial districting has hurt the Democratic Party, a conviction backed up by the simple logic of gerrymandering. What is going on? Are the critics wholly off base? No. They are right, but in a way that disproves their overall conjecture.

The creation of majority-minority districts has indeed made districting less favorable to the Democrats, but that change has followed an unusually high pro-Democratic bias in the states that have large minority populations. The states with the highest proportion of minority voters lie disproportionately in the South—where Democrats enjoyed electoral biases that averaged in excess of 20 percentage points before 1964. Under the Voting Rights Act and court order, the southern states created a large number of majority-minority districts during the 1980s and 1990s. Indeed, throughout the South, approximately 18 percent of all state legislative seats are majority-minority.

A tremendous bias against the Democrats should have surfaced. But that has not happened. Even today, the Democrats enjoy slight advantages in the districting maps of most of these states. By the 1990s, the partisan bias averaged about 8 percentage points in the Democratic direction across the South. Democratic legislators drawing lines are evidently clever enough to construct maps that produce a sufficient number of majority-minority districts and a pro-Democratic partisan bias.

The southwestern states, which have high Hispanic populations and less partisan bias historically, offer an even more telling picture. Consider California. Partisan biases in that state tended to favor Republicans somewhat before the reapportionment and Voting Rights Act revolutions, and it had large minority populations and almost no minority districts. Today, more than one in four California state legislative districts have a majority of their population that are Hispanic or black. If there were a hard trade-off between creating Democratic districts and minority districts, California today would have a strongly pro-Republican slant in its electoral districts. That state's districting plans now show a partisan bias that benefits the Democrats somewhat.

In 2006, Congress renewed the Voting Rights Act. That decision was telling. Republicans—not Democrats—expressed the most intense opposition to renewal in Congress. Were the Democratic Party suffering badly under the provisions of the Act, surely another alignment would have emerged and Congress would have let the law expire. The testimony of some scholars expressed the view that the majority-minority districts indirectly produced pro-Republican partisan gerrymanders. But others, upon looking closely at election returns, arrived at the conclusions that we have reached. Partisan biases resulting from pro-Democratic gerrymanders in the South have shrunk dramatically under the Voting Rights Act.[38]

There is, in the drawing of district lines, plenty of room to accommodate multiple goals. A districting plan that ensures minority representation does not necessarily create a pro-Republican bias. At least in the current setting, a well-drawn map can treat Democrats and Republicans fairly and counteract historical discrimination.

THE CARTEL

A third line of criticism of the new districting process is that it has created a wholly new form of political manipulation—incumbent protection.

One person, one vote is an elegant solution to a vexing problem. It achieves periodic reformations of the political process with very little direct intervention by the courts. It is up to the politicians to figure out how to comply with the dictum, and the courts give them wide latitude in doing so. The politicians remain central to the process, and their instincts for political self-preservation

---

38. Testimony of Professor Theodore Arrington, U.S. Senate Committee on the Judiciary, May 16, 2006, judiciary.senate.gov/testimony.cfm?id=1888&wit_id=5352. See also Delia Grigg and Jonathan Katz, "The Impact of Majority-Minority Districts on Congressional Elections" (paper presented at the annual meeting of the Midwest Political Science Association, Chicago, April 7–10, 2005).

remain as strong as ever. It is at this very personal level that the new process has allegedly broken down. Periodic reapportionment has reputedly only strengthened the hands of incumbents in determining their own fates because they now have the opportunity to draw district boundaries every ten years and sometimes more often.

The notion that redistricting and incumbency are linked emerges out of a historical observation. Sometime in the 1950s or 1960s (political scientists debate exactly when), a new phenomenon emerged in American politics—the incumbency advantage. For most of American history, party competition drove electoral politics. Over the past half-century, our politics have become more focused on individual politicians, and the politicians have increasingly become single-mindedly focused on their own reelection.[39] The average vote margins of incumbent politicians have crept slowly upward since the 1950s, and their reelection rates now routinely top 95 percent. The reapportionment revolution hit just at the time of the rise of incumbency. The coincidence between reapportionment and rising incumbency advantages has led many observers to see districting as a primary cause of incumbency advantages. Even today, we hear that incumbents win reelection at alarmingly high rates *because* district lines have been carefully drawn to protect those already in office.

The argument that redistricting caused the incumbency advantage is the Freddy Krueger of American politics. The claim has been repeatedly tested and disproven over the years.[40] But it just won't die. Robert Erikson and John Ferejohn published important articles in the 1970s disputing the claim that redistricting caused the incumbency advantage, but the assertion resurfaced in the work of Edward Tufte.[41] The argument seemed to die off following a series of comprehensive studies probing the source of the incumbency advantage, which pointed to casework, challenger quality, and campaign spending but not to districting as the explanation.[42]

Like the creature in a bad horror movie, the argument that districting causes incumbency advantages, seemingly vanquished, returns to haunt again and

39. Richard Fenno, *Home Style: House Members in Their Districts* (Boston: Little Brown, 1978); David Mayhew, *Congress: The Electoral Connection* (New Haven: Yale University Press, 2004).

40. See Robert S. Erikson, "Malapportionment, Gerrymandering, and Party Fortunes in Congressional Elections," *American Political Science Review* 66, no. 4 (December1972): 1234–45; John A. Ferejohn, "On the Decline of Competition in Congressional Elections," *American Political Science Review* 70, no. 1 (1977): 166–76; and Alan I. Abramowitz, Brad Alexander, and Matthew Gunning, "Incumbency, Redistricting, and the Decline of Competition in U.S. House Elections," *Journal of Politics* 68 (2006): 75–88.

41. Edward Tufte, "The Relationship between Seats and Votes in Two-Party Systems," *American Political Science Review* 67, no. 2 (June 1973): 540–54.

42. See Morris Fiorina, *Congress: Keystone of the Washington Establishment*, 2nd ed. (New Haven: Yale University Press, 1989); and Bruce E. Cain, John A. Ferejohn, and Morris Fiorina, *The Personal Vote* (Cambridge, MA: Harvard University Press, 1987).

again. Recently, Gary Cox and Jonathan Katz in *Elbridge Gerry's Salamander* argue that the partisan judges have allowed incumbents of their own parties to craft secure districts. Even their own evidence shows that districting could account for no more than a 2 to 3 percent of incumbents' vote margins. Nonetheless, Cox and Katz's work, we fear, woke the dead.

The simplicity of the argument that districting causes incumbency advantages has rekindled this old conjecture, even though the argument lacks much factual support. With this in mind, we try once again to lay to rest the conjecture that the legislative districting caused the rise of the incumbency advantage.

The observation that state legislators draw their own district lines is only suggestive that districting accounts for the rising reelection rates of incumbents. The legislators certainly have the motive, and the districting process gives them the opportunity. But that is only part of the story.

Meeting the standard of equal population districts is not easy. In areas where a large influx or exodus of people has occurred, the legislature must drastically alter district lines. The boundaries of neighboring communities must move as well, though less substantially, which in turn requires alteration of still other districts. Changes in any one district, then, ripple throughout the state.

The effects are felt at the most personal level. Almost every state legislator or U.S. House member sees his or her district altered with the decennial census. Legislators lose some communities where they have developed strong personal followings and gain new areas with unfamiliar voters. Shuffling district lines keeps politics in line with a changing society. It also exposes politicians to electoral risks. Changes in constituencies typically make legislators more vulnerable to defeat. They must redouble their service to voters and their campaign efforts simply to regain the personal connections with their constituencies that are lost at each districting.[43]

REDISTRICTING LEADS TO INCUMBENT DEPARTURES

The result is turnover. Periodic redistricting—more than any other force in contemporary American politics—turns incumbents out of office and brings in new people. Figure 11.2 displays the rate at which American state legislators have returned to office over the past half-century. From 1952 through 2000, the average state legislator's career has lengthened as voluntary retirements have declined. This has led to an upward trend in the rate at which state legislators return to office after each election.

Periodic downward spikes punctuate that trend, however. These spikes occur with each round of redistricting: in 1966 (immediately after the courts

---

43. An elegant account of such fears is Fenno, *Home Style*.

FIGURE 11.2. *Percentage of state legislators who return to office, upper and lower chambers, 1952–2000*

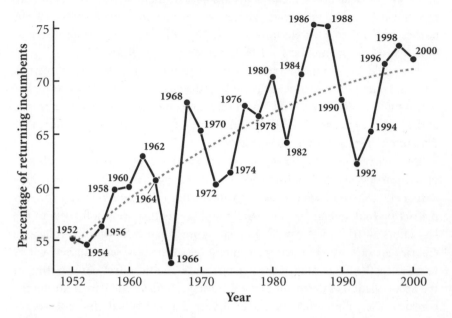

forced most states to reapportion) and then in 1972, 1982, and 1992. Even the tumultuous 1974 and 1994 elections did not cause as much turnover in the American states as has occurred in the elections immediately following redistricting years.

The same pattern holds in the U.S. House of Representatives. Reapportionment and redistricting cause the most turnover at the federal level as well as the state level. In a typical year, the relation rates of House members range from 80 to 90 percent, rates that advocates of term limits have likened to the those of Politburo of the Former Soviet Union. Following redistricting, retention rates in the House fall to 65 and 75 percent. In an era of high incumbency reelection rates, normal politics tend toward stability, even stasis, in American legislatures. Redistricting acts as one of the few forces in American politics today that turns incumbents out of office. Periodically drawing new boundaries has become a process of upheaval and renewal.

Still, redistricting is widely viewed not as a corrective but as a malignancy of modern American politics. The best plans of the Founders and the Justices have reputedly been twisted by sitting legislators to protect themselves from electoral defeat. According to the critics, we may have been better off with the stasis and distortions of malapportionment than the current mess.

There are really two distinct arguments. The first claims that somehow—and it is not clear how—incumbents are able to increase their personal vote through the districting process. The second alleges that incumbents of both parties have raised their electoral security by crafting safe partisan districts, with overwhelming numbers of Democrats or of Republicans.

The problem with the first form of the incumbency protection argument is a simple one. As we documented above, redistricting, in fact, leads to higher defeat rates of incumbents and lowers their personal vote margins. That is true at the highly aggregated level shown in Figure 11.2. It becomes even more evident upon digging down to the grassroots.

Redistricting produces a natural setting in which to observe its very dilution of incumbents' electoral advantages. Following redistricting, legislators' constituencies consist of some areas and voters whom they represented before redistricting (old voters) and some areas and voters that are wholly new to the legislators' district (new voters). In a study we conducted with our colleague Charles Stewart, we exploited the contrast between old voters and new voters to measure the magnitude of the personal vote and the effect of districting in the accumulation of the incumbency advantage. Redistricting, by shuffling the constituencies, diminishes the personal vote that individual officeholders receive. We contrasted incumbents' vote shares among their old voters and among their new voters. When they stood for reelection, U.S. House incumbents had vote margins that were 4 to 5 percentage points lower in the areas they had not represented before.[44] Changing district boundaries tends to lessen incumbents' personal vote and electoral advantages, not increase them.[45]

Perhaps the most compelling evidence that districting and the courts' interventions did not cause the rise of the incumbency advantage comes from the basic facts about incumbency. The incumbency advantage is a general phenomenon, not one limited to offices chosen from districts. While the incumbency advantage was first noted in U.S. House elections, early studies also documented its presence in U.S. Senate elections and gubernatorial elections—offices that are not districted.[46] Subsequent studies have found that the incumbency advantage exists in nearly every elected state office in the United States. Moreover,

44. See Stephen Ansolabehere, James M. Snyder Jr., and Charles Stewart III, "Old Voters, New Voters, and the Personal Vote: Using Redistricting to Measure the Incumbency Advantage," *American Journal of Political Science* 44, no. 1 (January 2007): 17–34.

45. See also Mark Rush, "Fair and Effective Representation," and Steven D. Levitt and Catherine D. Wolfram, "Decomposing the Sources of Incumbency Advantage in the U.S. House," *Legislative Studies Quarterly* 22, no. 1 (February, 1997): 45–60.

46. Warren Kostroski, "Party and Incumbency in Post War Senate Elections," *American Political Science Review* 67 (1973): 1213–34; James E. Piereson, "Sources of Candidate Success in Gubernatorial Elections, 1910–1970," *Journal of Politics* 39, no. 4 (November 1977): 939–58.

incumbency advantages rose in every office from 1940 to the present, including those not districted. The incumbency advantages for offices ranging from governor and U.S. senator to state auditor and state commissioner rose at the same time and at the same rate. In the 1940s, all offices had relatively small incumbency advantages, of about 2 percentage points. During the 1950s, those advantages began to grow; their growth accelerated in the 1960s, reaching about 7 percent by 1970. The incumbency advantage has continued to creep up, rising to about 10 percent in the 1980s and 1990s. The accelerated growth of the incumbency advantage during the 1960s leads many to identify reapportionment as the culprit. However, those offices not subject to districting saw the same pattern of growth. The coincidence between the rise of the incumbency advantage and the reapportionment cases appears to be just that, a coincidence.[47]

What of the second argument—that incumbents protect themselves by creating safe seats for both parties? Samuel Issacharoff, writing in the *Harvard Law Review*, offers the most cogent expression of this idea, which he calls duopolistic gerrymandering.[48] The two parties, he argues, have formed something of a cartel, a duopoly through which they decide to divide the political turf to suit each party's interest and fend off all potential entrants into their market. Most states are closely divided between the parties. Arbitrarily drawn districts would create a large number of districts that are split evenly between Democratic and Republican adherents, and with a good dose of Independent voters thrown in as well.[49] For politicians, this would be a terrible state of affairs as competitive districts are difficult to win and hard to hold on to. Democratic and Republican legislators, realizing this problem, may join forces and divide their state so that most seats are safe for one party or another, leaving only a handful of evenly split, competitive districts.

This is a nifty argument. Sitting legislators can improve their own political positions and reduce the risk facing their party. Duopolistic gerrymandering buys the support of the large majority of sitting legislators because the large majority of them are guaranteed safe (partisan) seats. Such a plan minimizes the

47. Stephen Ansolabehere and James M. Snyder, "The Incumbency Advantage in U.S. Elections: An Analysis of State and Federal Offices, 1942–2000," *Election Law Journal* 1, no. 3 (September 2002): 315–38. Consistent with the finding that districting hurts incumbents, the offices and seats that are districted and redistricted have smaller incumbency advantages than those that are not districted. More troubling still for the personal vote argument, the U.S. House incumbency advantage is at least as large in states with one seat (and thus no districting) as it is in states that regularly redistrict. Ferejohn, "On the Decline of Competition in Congressional Elections."

48. See Issacharoff, "Gerrymandering and Political Cartels"; and Samuel Issacharoff, Pamela S. Karlan, and Richard H. Pildes, *The Law of Democracy: Legal Structure of the Political Process* (Westbury, NY: Foundation Press, 1998).

49. See M. G. Kendall and A. Stuart, "The Law of Cubic Proportions," *British Journal of Sociology* 1 (1951): 1–31.

electoral uncertainty and electoral costs that the parties face since competition is limited to a few places.[50] It does not cause incumbency advantages, but it would have the side effect of protecting those incumbents who happen to be in safe Democratic and safe Republican seats.[51] It would, if real, deepen the partisan division among the constituencies that the legislators represent and further polarize the parties inside the legislature. Of course, it assumes that the members of the minority party would prefer to remain a permanent legislative minority, safe in their own seats but with little hope of gaining control of the house.

This is not just the stuff of academic debates. It is widely believed to be the new reality. Jeffrey Toobin, writing in *The New Yorker*, has called this "The Great Election Grab." Republican Congressman James Leach of Iowa said of Congress in 2003 that "a little less than 400 seats are totally safe."[52] Even those who had once defended the current process now think it is broken.

The sharp increases in incumbent departures following redistricting cast a shadow of doubt over this conjecture. Patterns of defeat increase those doubts still further. It is indeed true that in the typical election only one in ten seats is highly competitive, and the set of close elections varies from year to year— hardly what one would expect from a carefully crafted set of boundaries. Indeed, three years after Congressman Leach offered his assessment, the voters bounced Leach and thirty of his Republican colleagues, giving Democrats control of Congress for the first time in twelve years.

The districts themselves provide direct evidence that the politicians have not been able to capture the districting process in the ways that Issacharoff, Toobin, and others conjecture. It is not that they haven't tried, they just haven't succeeded wholesale.

Successive rounds of duopolistic gerrymandering over the past forty years should have created large numbers of highly safe Democratic seats and highly safe Republican seats. The result would be a small number of marginal districts in which the ratio of Democrats to Republicans is about even, and a very large number of districts where the proportion of Democrats far exceeds the proportion of Republican identifiers or vice versa. If one were to rank order the legislative districts in the country from most Democratic to most Republican and count the frequency of districts that were safely Democratic, marginal, or safely Republican, a two-humped shape would occur.

---

50. This view, however, has detractors. Most notably, Nathaniel Persily of the University of Pennsylvania Law School contends that incumbents do not have strong incentives to divide up the map just so. See Persily, "In Defense of Foxes Guarding Henhouses."

51. Issacharoff, "Gerrymandering and Political Cartels."

52. Jeffrey Toobin, "The Great Election Grab: When Does Gerrymandering Become a Threat to Democracy?" *The New Yorker*, December 18, 2003.

FIGURE 11.3. *Estimated density of the division of the two-party vote, state lower house legislative districts, 1984–1990*
Source: Data from the Record of American Democracy (ROAD) project.
Figure is kernel density.

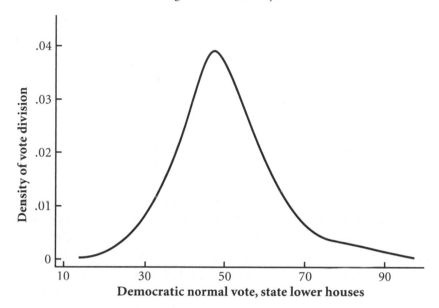

By contrast, the districts may be drawn with little regard for or opportunity to create safe seats or protect incumbents. The bargaining over districting across legislative chambers and with the executive may be so intense and subject to so many competing demands that it leaves little leeway for party. If the lines were drawn without regard to party, the typical district would reflect the division of the vote statewide, and the partisan division in most of the districts would deviate only somewhat from the division of the statewide vote. There would be a few highly Republican and highly Democratic districts. This principle has been conjectured, at least among statisticians, for over a century. The eminent nineteenth-century statistician F. Y. Edgeworth studied English parliamentary elections with just such a hypothetical district system in mind and predicted that if districting didn't matter we should expect a bell-shaped, or normal, curve.[53]

Which view is right? Figure 11.3 presents the distribution of the underlying (or normal) party division of the vote in the American state legislatures during the 1980s. This decade provides an ideal testing ground for the claims of

53. F. Y. Edgeworth, "Miscellaneous Applications of the Calculus of Probabilities," *Journal of the Royal Statistical Society* 61, no. 3 (September 1898): 534–44. See also Kendall and Stuart, "The Law of Cubic Proportions."

duopolistic gerrymandering. The 1980s represent the highwater mark for the incumbency advantages in U.S. House elections; furthermore, by the beginning of this decade, the questions about equality had been settled and the initial shock waves of the reapportionment revolution had damped down. Gary King and his colleagues at Harvard University developed a unique database of the precinct-level election returns for the years 1984–1990 for almost all state legislatures, called the ROAD database. We used these data to construct the partisan division in each state legislative district in the United States. For each district in each state in the 1980s, we calculated the average Democratic share of the two-party vote in all offices.[54] That resulted in fifty separate graphs. We laid each of the graphs over one another; that is, we centered all of the states at 50 percent and made a single graph of all state legislative districts. This allowed us to examine the distribution of the party division of the vote in all of the states at once. Figure 11.3 shows that distribution.

Pooling all of the states into a single graph might obscure the true pattern. The appendix presents the graphs for all legislative chambers. Only one state legislative chamber, the New York state senate, had two distinct humps, with the much larger lying on the Republican side of the ledger. About 30 percent of the state's districts are safely Democratic and half are safely Republican. Interestingly, New York's assembly has one hump, not two. A handful of other states had a smaller cluster of safe Democratic seats, likely the product of racial districting requirements. Otherwise, the distribution of votes among the states followed a bell-shaped curve.

The distribution of the vote across legislative districts is clearly unimodal. Most of the districts are near the center of the distribution, and the frequency of districts tails off as one moves away from the political center. To put matters bluntly, there is absolutely no trace of the bipartisan cartel. Rather, the distribution of the normal party vote in the legislative districts seems consistent with the notion that the parties can exert relatively little influence over the contours of legislative districts. They have some influence on the margin, but, consistent with our earlier findings on partisan bias, state legislative districts do not seem to reflect a strongly partisan tilt.

Finally, we turned our sights on the U.S. House. Nearly the same picture arises in the 1980s, 1990s, and 2000s. The distribution of the normal vote in the House follows a normal curve very closely. There is a slight asymmetry, a small cluster of extremely Democratic seats. These seats are created to ensure minority representation, and we will discuss them below. Otherwise, the distribution

54. We subtracted the incumbency advantage to arrive at a pure estimate of the normal party division in each district.

of the partisan division of the vote in U.S. House elections resembles that in the state legislatures. The large majority of districts are fairly evenly split between the two parties; they have partisan divisions that lie in the range between 40 percent Democratic versus 60 percent Republican to 40 percent Republican versus 60 percent Democratic. At least in their underlying partisan composition, most U.S. House and state legislative seats are competitive.

That is precisely the picture one would expect from a system in which legislators could not create safe seats for themselves. The division of the pie that duopolistic gerrymandering would have produced did not emerge, except in isolated cases such as New York's senate. The district maps do not polarize the electorate. Rather, they represent the typical voter in the state quite well. Most of the districts cluster near the average division of partisan preferences, which happens to be about 50–50.

Why, then, are there so few competitive seats in U.S. House elections? The answer lies with incumbency, but not districting. Incumbents win by larger vote margins than they would receive in open seat races, and open seat races are as competitive as ever. When an incumbent runs, even if he or she represents a district that leans toward the opposite party, the advantages that come from the office itself present a formidable hurdle to any challenger. Incumbents win at very high rates for reasons other than districting, such as campaign spending, constituent service, and simple name recognition. Districting has played little part.

The inability of incumbents to insulate themselves through the new districting process, as well as the electoral risk that the process exposes them to, underscore the basic workings of the new process. Districting only erodes the bulwarks that incumbents build up. Indeed, the new process acts as the strongest revolutionary force in legislative elections, more powerful than the occasional swings of national political sentiment such as those that swelled up in 1974, 1994, and 2006.

REVOLUTIONS

Politicians, if left to their own devices, do not act benignly in the public's interest. The history of legislative districting says otherwise. However, for all the hand wringing over current districts, the new process has blunted legislators' attempts to manipulate district boundaries for partisan or personal gain. Political cartography today results from struggles among the legislators themselves over many different objectives and goals. The new lines have become increasingly twisted as parties and incumbents, constrained by the courts and the governors, fight for any little gain that they can make. But their gains are just that—little.

Over the course of the last five decades, the political bargaining within legislatures and judicial supervision of the districting process has led to districting maps that are significantly fairer than what they replaced. Partisan biases, though they have not vanished, have fallen substantially. The Voting Rights Act and subsequent litigation have guaranteed a degree of minority representation that might have otherwise vanished, and contrary to Democrats' claims, that has not led to a systematic Republican advantage. And incumbents, even though they would seek even greater levels of security, are in fact made less secure with each periodic redistricting. Every decade brings a new census and corresponding shifts in the constituencies' boundaries.

These are small, periodic revolutions, but revolutions just the same. Incumbents must take on some new voters and lose some loyal constituents. They must reach out and form new loyalties. Parties must fight to make what gains they can, and the inevitable compromises tend to balance out the gains.

The process is a messy one. Even seasoned political observers such as Alan Ehrenhalt find it distasteful. But the overall consequences, at least as far as the tools of modern political science have taken us, have been beneficial. The contours of district maps more closely reflect the average voters' preferences than they did fifty years ago. With each new decade, the process of court-supervised districting has produced progressively more equitable election systems. The results are not perfect. Partisan biases have arisen from nothing in some states, notably Massachusetts and Rhode Island, and have persisted in others, especially the Old South and the Mountain West. In most states, however, partisan biases have fallen. For all the Sturm und Drang, the courts' involvement has made elections substantially fairer.

12

The Age of Fairness

In all walks of life, there occur moments of revelation when all that comes after is forever changed. Such was the case with *Baker v. Carr*. The decision opened a new age in American politics, an age of fairness. Equality of opportunity in our politics, as well as our society, became the new American ethos, and one person, one vote its defining principle.

Today, the broad right of equal representation is taken as the essence of American democracy. When asked to say what democracy means to them, most Americans reflexively assert "one person, one vote" and majority rule.[1] Looking back, it is hard to imagine how things could have been otherwise, how the public could accept and tolerate great political inequalities that meant that some people's votes counted more than others' and that a minority of people elected the majority of seats in every state legislature. Americans did accept gross inequalities for generations; yet when the Court issued its rulings in the Tennessee case, it became immediately clear that the Justices had changed forever the way we think of ourselves and our democracy.

THE VALUE OF THE VOTE

Baker changed more than abstract legal principles and public philosophies. The decision reshaped the most basic feature of practical politics—who wins

1. The changed idea of democracy became evident in survey data in the 1970s. See Herbert McCloskey and

and who loses. For decades, even centuries, unequal district populations had distorted the political process, greatly inflating the voice of the few and weakening the voice of many. State legislatures had little motivation to rectify the inequities; they were, after all, a product of the overrepresentation of rural towns and counties. *Baker* ended that old order suddenly. In the spring of 1962, the Court asserted the individual's right to equal protection in elections and its own power to intervene in cases involving legislative districts. Barely a year later, the Justices put forth a bold definition of what equal protection meant—one person, one vote. And in the summer of 1964, they swept aside dozens of state legislative districting maps. Within five years of *Baker,* every state legislature had complied with the requirement of equal population districting. Every district's boundaries changed as thousands of legislative districts shifted from rural counties to metropolitan areas. That shift in districts—from rural to urban and suburban—turned thousands of rural legislators out of office and brought into American politics a new generation of politicians who represented the interests of cities and the surrounding communities. The consequences for practical politics in the United States were far-reaching.

Equal representation brought the state legislatures in line with the political preferences of their populations. Originally, state constitutions had established towns and counties as the units of representation. In an agrarian society, that was not a bad approximation of the distribution of people across the landscape; yet with the rise of great cities and later suburbs, those boundaries became increasingly unrepresentative of the population. One person, one vote righted inequities that had grown by accretion. It allowed the country, at last, to embrace the idea of popular rule in the legislature.

Rural domination of American politics ended abruptly with the reapportionment of state legislatures. Overrepresentation of rural areas gave those constituencies control of the levers of legislative power. Legislators from sparsely populated towns and counties stacked the committees and controlled powerful chairmanships. They owned party hierarchies and leadership posts. Most important, they had the votes. In most state legislatures, rural towns and counties elected a majority of seats and could easily prevail over the cities and suburbs on any question that pitted "us versus them." They could determine which laws passed and which ones did not and the shape of public expenditures. Malapportioment clearly allowed rural-dominated state legislatures to steer state resources disproportionately toward their constituencies, towns and counties where increasingly few Americans actually lived. *Baker* eventually led to the

John Zaller, *The American Ethos* (Cambridge, MA: Harvard University Press, 1984); and Richard Reeves, *An American Journey* (New York: Simon & Schuster, 1982), especially chap. 7.

elimination of roughly half of all rural seats and brought down the hierarchies that governed state legislatures. In their place rose up new politicians elected from newly created urban and rural seats, but this transformation did not hand control over to the cities. The composition of the legislatures shifted from one in which over half of the seats were held by rural areas to one in which power was shared equally across rural, urban, and suburban constituencies; even the central cities were divided into many different constituencies, all of whom would compete with one another as equals.

Equalization of district populations sent shock waves throughout the party system, tipping the balance of power in many legislatures and spurring a realignment of the interests within the political parties throughout the country. Political parties drew their votes differentially from cities, suburbs, and towns. Reapportionment tilted the balance between the parties to the extent that partisans of one stripe tended to live in urban areas and those of the other tended to live in rural counties. The story varied across the regions of the country. In states like Michigan, Ohio, Vermont, and Connecticut, the Republicans benefited tremendously from malapportionment. Across the Northeast and Midwest, liberal urban Democrats replaced moderate and conservative rural Republicans. Here the edict of political equality accelerated the decline of rural Republicans and led to the emergence of large numbers of liberal urban Democrats. They would become the new core of the Democratic Party.

Changes in the South mirrored those in the North. Reapportionment eliminated large numbers of rural, conservative and moderate Democratic legislators. City Democrats posted noticeable gains in southern legislatures, but more impressive were the rising fortunes of suburban and urban Republicans in the South. Republicans from southern metropolitan areas gave rise to the core of the new Republican Party and its future legislative leaders, including Newt Gingrich and Tom Delay.

The deeper realignment occurred within the parties. Reapportionment shifted the balance between rural and metropolitan counties inside the Democratic and Republican parties. Both parties watched their rural bases shrink, and by the 1980s each emerged with their sights set on voters in the urban areas. Successive reapportionments ratcheted up the number of urban Democratic seats. Where a majority were rural in 1960, today better than two-thirds of the state and national Democratic legislators come from urban counties. Republicans also became somewhat more metropolitan, though they moved toward the suburban fringe. Over the long run, these shifts altered not just the cultural orientations of the parties but their ideologies as well. Urban northern and midwestern Democrats have become the foundation of that party, and they are much more liberal than the rural southern Democrats that were the bulwark of the party fifty years ago. Suburban Republicans in the West and South are similarly a much different breed than the stereotypical rock-ribbed New England and midwestern Republicans of the 1950s. These new Democrats and new Republicans have subsequently remade their parties to suit their political orientations. The Democrats, led by urban liberals, have turned sharply to the left, and the Republicans have stepped to the right.

It is tempting to chalk up the realignment of state politics to the old saw of "the law of unintended consequences," the unfortunate consequences of the judges meddling where they should not. Indeed, many critics in the legal arena today treat *Baker* as a great failing of the Supreme Court for precisely this reason. Echoing the words of Alexander Bickel, an early skeptic of the Court's ability to deal with such political matters, it has become sport among law professors, political scientists, and even journalists to take shots at the apportionment decisions. The political changes that have occurred since are now taken as evidence that judges should stay out of politics.[2]

This criticism is wrong, even dangerous. The political transformations following the reapportionment decisions were not unforeseen and uncontrollable side effects of a rashly made decision. These were in fact the changes reformers sought; indeed, most of those pushing the apportionment cases up the appellate ladder hoped for an even more extensive transformation of the political landscape. The Justices were fully aware of the political implications of their decisions. Earl Warren, William Brennan, and Hugo Black had all begun their political careers in elective office, and they knew full well what *Baker*, *Reynolds*, and other rulings would do.

The legal critics, we think, have it backward. The seismic shifts in our politics that followed directly from *Baker v. Carr* reveal the gross distortions to our politics caused not by reapportionment, but by malapportionment. Profound changes did occur, but they reflected the fact that the legislatures were badly out of sync with their publics. One person, one vote at long last brought the legislatures in line with the people. Election laws can enforce a strong norm of fairness, or they can twist and distort the public will as it is embodied in the legislature.

The reapportionment revolution stands as testament to the enormous, yet often indiscernible, importance of the rules that govern democracy. Fair rules

2. See Alexander Bickel, "The Supreme Court and Reapportionment, in *Reapportionment in the 1970s*, ed. Nelson Polsby (Berkeley: University of California Press, 1971); Gerald Rosenberg, *The Hollow Hope* (Chicago: University of Chicago Press, 1993); Samuel Issacharoff, "Gerrymandering and Political Cartels," *Harvard Law Review* 116 (December 2002): 593–648; Alan Ehrenhalt, "Frankfurter's Curse," *Governing* (January 2004), www.governing.com/archive/2004/jan/acess.txt.

and an equal voting right can yield a truly democratic and representative politics. Therein lies the powerful lesson of *Baker*, a lesson that speaks to the very nature of democratic politics.

Simply put, equal votes mean equal power.

Reapportionment of the American state legislatures provides a rare moment when we can see in clear relief the value of the vote. *Baker* pitted against each other two very different ideas of democratic politics. The first is the simple theory of democracy. The vote is the great leveler. It is the most powerful instrument in the polity, and it translates immediately and directly into influence over the collective decisions reached in the legislature. The history of representation in America from William Penn's Charter through the Help America Vote Act has been the progressive expansion and equalization of the franchise. Equal rights to the franchise, or so the theory goes, mean equal power in politics and equal outcomes in the public sphere. But against that view stands a second, darker image of democracy, one in which political power derives primarily from advantages in organization, wealth, and concentration of interests. Those are the assets held in metropolitan areas, and it was feared that further empowering the wealthy, the organized, the concentrated interests would only lead to greater inequities in society.

By tracing how these sudden and massive changes in the political geography of the nation translated into public policy, we are able to see the value of the vote. We view reapportionment as a tremendous natural experiment with which to observe how votes translate into public decisions and public policies. This historic moment allows us to assess the validity of the first and second images of democracy. *Baker*, *Reynolds*, and similar cases rapidly changed the electoral landscape from one of great inequality to one of equity and fairness, but to what effect? The striking result of that transformation is a resounding endorsement of the simple, indeed naïve, theory of democracy. Inequalities in representation translated directly into inequalities in the distribution of public funds and unequal influence over the public policies. Equal votes mean equal power.

That single finding carries a profound insight for the practical operation of democracy throughout the world today. Unequal representation, as is common in many upper chambers in the world today, creates inequitable political outcomes and distorts public policy. Unequal representation in a democracy usually reflects some sort of power-sharing agreement or compromise. Consider the U.S. Senate. Unequal representation in the Senate was a product of the political circumstances of 1780s America. Every state (not person) had equal representation in the original Congress, under the Articles of Confederation. The only way to get the sitting legislators to agree to create a representative institution was to create a legislative chamber that continued the practice of equal representation of states: the Senate. As another example, consider the Council of Ministers of the European Parliament. The allocation of seats in the European Union's legislature gives far too few seats to the most populous countries, such as Germany and France, and too many seats to the least populated countries, such as Luxembourg and Belgium. European social scientists have argued endlessly about the appropriate allocation of seats to countries and tried to justify giving small countries excessive representation. The debate mirrors many of the claims made in the United States—including the need to protect the small from the large and to represent places as well as people. Ultimately, these arrangements reflect the fact that the Europe Union and the United States began as agreements among equal states, and the deal that sustained their original social compacts gave excessive representation to the smaller states in order to bring them into these unions. The problem is that such inequalities in representation become lasting features of the legislatures, long after the differences that led to the original compromise have faded.

For nations, states, and other organizations that must choose how to represent interests democratically, the answer is simple. Provide equal votes to the different constituencies, and let the political negotiations that occur inside legislatures work. The result will be equitable distributions of the product of government. That lesson applies equally at the smallest levels of government, town and school councils, up to the grand democratic assemblies of nations and international organizations. Giving some constituencies, states, or (in international organizations) nations excessive representation in order to compensate for their supposed weaknesses invariably produces unequal results. To the extent that election districts and other procedures distort the ability of the legislature to reflect and represent the public as a whole, the legislature loses the legitimacy that emanates from the public, the legitimacy inherent in a truly democratic government. One might indeed desire greater economic redistribution, but it is a very bad idea to achieve that by distorting the fundamental laws that govern democratic elections. To attain truly democratic representation, we must protect the equal voting rights of all persons.

That is the singular discovery resulting from a careful reconsideration of the history of representation in the American states and the transformation set off by *Baker v. Carr*. It makes plain the value of the vote and the meaning of democracy. It should guide how the next generations of judges, legislators, and citizens understand the consequences of inequality and the proper functioning of a democracy in which all votes count equally.

POLITICS IS THE ANSWER

The value of the vote is the message that springs from the reapportionment revolution, but it is not the moral of our story. At the heart of the *Baker* decision lies a paradox whose consideration must guide those involved in the struggle today to improve further the workings of American democracy. We think this puzzle offers a way out of the doctrinal mess surrounding partisan and racial districting. The paradox is just this: politics is at once the problem and the solution.

For generations, normal legislative politics failed. Unchecked, state legislators allowed districts to become increasingly unrepresentative through inaction or manipulated district lines to gain political advantages for their constituents or parties. Old district boundaries were left in place for decades, even centuries; when legislatures drew new the lines, the boundaries often further magnified the rural areas' political advantages. The resulting malapportionment further distorted the representation of political parties and race and other social and economic interests in the United States. Therein lay the flaw in Felix Frankfurter's doctrine of judicial restraint.

The Warren Court did not intervene in a healthy political process; it fixed a broken one. Reapportionment succeeded because it enabled the noisy process of law making envisioned in the U.S. Constitution to proceed. Before *Baker*, state legislators who represented a small minority of the population had prevented any change from happening. They served their own purposes by failing to do their greater duty. Regular redistricting in compliance with one person, one vote necessarily leads the legislature to pass a law. Both chambers of the legislature must sign on, as must the governor. The courts can intervene if called upon, but they do not have to get involved in the nitty-gritty of the administration of the remedy, which they did with racial desegregation. This was an elegant solution to what could have otherwise been the disaster Felix Frankfurter portended. The courts played a definite and distinctive role in insisting on equal voting rights. Once the judges had discovered a principle—one person, one vote—they allowed normal politics to work.

Equal population representation forced the legislatures to come up with new maps; it empowered the governors in the bargaining over the formation of a new electoral map; and it granted the judiciary a check on the legislatures' actions. Ultimately, however, the judges were not going to draw new boundaries; the politicians had to. *Baker* insisted that the legislatures find a solution through normal politics—through negotiation, accommodation, and compromise. And herein lies the paradox.

Much fairer elections have resulted. Population inequalities have been eliminated, and as a byproduct of the new process, most states have reduced partisan advantages rooted in electoral maps. In the typical state, partisan biases have been halved since 1964. Certainly, more can be done to make elections more competitive and the electoral system more balanced; but by any accounting, the Court's intervention has not failed as Bickel, Rosenberg, and other critics claim. The Court forced the legislatures to engage in the normal politicking that goes into crafting any statute, with the sole constraint that districts have equal populations. Following the reapportionment cases, normal legislative politics quickly developed a more equitable and balanced electoral system. Even though the cases did not involve partisan districting, partisan biases have been greatly reduced.

Politics succeeded, we believe, because they are not simple. Legislatures bring together all of the interests and ideologies in a society and through their collective deliberations try to arrive at acceptable public laws. Indeed, every politician's preferences reflect many different and sometimes conflicting objectives, such as party, incumbency, race, and economic interests, and a body of one hundred or so state legislators reflects a great diversity of interests and personal objectives. When they are forced to find common ground, the bargaining among such disparate interests and cross-cutting coalitions appears sufficient to mute the power of any one interest and to lead to equitable outcomes. The process of law making involves the wide community of the state or nation coming together and finding common ground. It is wonderful to behold, but to the uninitiated it is also confusing, even alienating. For all of its flaws, legislative politics allows all people voice in the law-making process through their representatives. When the people's representatives are forced to negotiate, no single objective can rise to the fore, and that weakens the political influence of any one element such as party or economic interest.

The moral carries us a step further. Districting should not be taken out of the political process. One of the earliest commentaries on *Baker v. Carr* came from the editors of the *Yale Law Journal*.[3] They argued that to achieve true representation the U.S. Supreme Court should set down a standard that the district lines maximize the representation of all interests in the society, including social classes and income levels, ethnicities and races, and parties. William Brennan's clerks expressed their agreement with this broad theoretical approach but dismissed the idea as impossible to implement from the bench. From a purely technocratic or judicial view, such a solution is impossible.

---

3. "*Baker v. Carr* and Legislative Apportionments: A Problem of Standards," *Yale Law Journal* 72, no. 5 (April 1963): 968–1040.

Courts and commissions could not know all of the possible interests or how much weight to give to each. But the editors of the *Yale Law Journal* had described exactly what the legislature does in passing a law. It reflects the disparate interests of the society and forges an appropriate balance of those interests. In this regard, Felix Frankfurter was ultimately right. The act of drawing district lines is inescapably political.

The instinct today is to take districting out of the political arena entirely—put it in the hands of impartial technocrats, such as commissions and special masters (usually, law professors and political scientists). Many other democracies, including Britain and Canada, and even some states, have followed that instinct. Experts and commissions, however, are not devoid of partisanship. They are citizens as well as professionals. In fact, they may care even more intensely about politics than the average citizen because they have chosen to devote their careers to politics or election law. Experts and commissions lack an important aspect of the legislature: experts and commissions simply cannot represent. Only the legislature is designed to draw in all of the interests in the society and to engage in robust negotiations that (one hopes) find common ground around the form of representation desired by the public.

But normal legislative politics are not enough. Apportionment involves a question so fundamental to self-rule and with such an obvious conflict of interest for representatives that the legislature alone cannot be allowed to decide what to do or not to do. The great English philosopher John Locke saw this problem clearly in 1714 in Parliament, and it has dogged representative democracies ever since. England required the intervention of the king to force Parliament to act. In the American system, only the courts are positioned to impel the legislature to do its duty. The failure of politics before Baker does not mean that politics cannot succeed and that the responsibility for crafting districts should be taken out of the political sphere. When the courts insisted that the legislatures solve the problem, they did. Before *Baker*, the politics of apportionment failed because the legislatures usually did not engage in such negotiations, at least not successfully. When the courts forced legislatures to draw new boundaries in compliance with the simple stricture of equality, the resulting maps fixed the problem of population representation and lessened other problems, such as partisan and racial biases. Collective deliberation and decision making in the political arena, when it was thwarted, begat the problem; and when the courts required deliberation to happen, a solution emerged. This moral, we believe, can guide those grappling with the problems of representation today.

The debate over representation did not end in 1964. Brennan and Warren won their battle with Frankfurter over the apportionment question, but the liberals could not root out the problem that lay at the heart of the Tennessee case. The sitting legislature determines the rules that will govern elections in the future—their own elections—and, naturally, those in power will do what they can to stay there. Courts cannot eliminate the unavoidable conflict of interest that arises; they can only salve its symptoms. With time, the politicians have pushed back, and their actions have placed serious stresses and strains on the districting process. Party leaders, state legislators, and political consultants devise new tricks and use some very old ones to shape the electoral maps to their advantage. Those affected take to the courts to defend their interests and to forward their own visions of what ought to be.

With each new cycle of districting, new challenges arise, and new generations of men and women stand up to try to define and redefine the meaning of the vote. Equal representation of urban, suburban, and rural areas is now assured, and that problem has given way to questions about racial and partisan representation. On matters of race, five decades of litigation and legislation have given way to a solution of sorts. The debate today focuses increasingly on partisan gerrymandering. The courts have reaffirmed their authority, but the problem lacks a remedy. The same situation existed from 1962 to 1964, over the two years between *Baker* and *Reynolds*. Brennan and his clerks, drawing on the immense public debate and volumes of pending cases, arrived at a simple and ultimately successful remedy—one person, one vote.

Recent controversies arising out of the legislative districting fights in Texas, Pennsylvania, and elsewhere have sharpened the conflict over legislative districting. Partisan gerrymandering ignited the firestorm, which has subsequently engulfed the entire legal architecture constructed since *Baker* and threatens to lead the Court to withdraw from the political arena altogether. It is worth recounting these events. Following the 2000 election, Republicans controlled the legislature and governor's mansion in Pennsylvania, and they passed a districting map that many experts and the lower courts judged to advantage the Republican Party heavily. The same year, a divided Texas legislature deadlocked over a new apportionment plan, and the state courts imposed a slightly revised version of the 1991 plan. Two years later, Republicans had gained control of the executive and both chambers of the legislature. They took the extraordinary measure of writing a new law to replace the one put in place in 2001. Politics, it seems, failed. Legislative politics produced a highly partisan plan in one case (Pennsylvania) and no plan in another (Texas 2001) and thoroughly violated any sense of proper process in a third (Texas 2003). In all three instances, the legislatures tested the courts' resolve. If the courts passed, then the reigning party or faction might have a free hand in doing whatever it pleased. The Supreme Court issued quite complicated and fractured decisions in these cases, the upshot of which was that it had no basis to intervene as it lacked a "standard." We are left, as one lawyer involved in these cases recently stated, with a "doctrinal mess."[4]

The current chaos surrounding partisan gerrymandering was, in some sense, predictable. Political parties present the same sort of conflict of interest that legislators do. Parties are not like other interests, such as race and class. They originated as clubs and organized factions of legislators, and they remain integrally tied to the electoral and legislative arena. State election laws grant political parties unique access to the ballot, providing party labels for all candidates on the ballot and allowing the parties to control the nomination of candidates and qualification for the general election. After the election, the party caucuses organize the legislature and control the selection of leaders and committees. As a result of their special status in politics, parties are highly regulated by statute and legal rulings,[5] and the justification for such regulations stems from the peculiar conflict of interest that arises when parties, acting through the legislature, set down the rules that affect their own political fortunes.[6] This, of course, is the same conflict of interest that gave rise to malapportionment. The Court did not eliminate it; rather, it salved its effects by requiring equal population districting. The central question facing the polity today is whether the judiciary can do more to guard against partisan manipulation of electoral districts.

The current debate divides along familiar lines. Ironically, among law professors, the courts have few sympathizers.

One extreme echoes the words of Frankfurter and Harlan. Politics and only politics can produce adequate districts because districting, whether done by commission or the legislature, is unavoidably political. Daniel Lowenstein and Jonathan Steinberg offered perhaps the first defense of the Frankfurter view among modern legal theorists. As Lowenstein and Steinberg saw the situation in 1985, no legal standard analogous to one person, one vote could apply to party or race because party and race are group interests and *Baker* and *Reynolds* asserted individual voting rights. Any legal standard one could conceive of would necessarily favor one interest or one sort of interest over others. Courts protect individuals' rights, and politics provides the appropriate means to balance competing interests. "The mechanism for resolving political contests in our society," they wrote, "is the election."

4. Paul Smith, "A Conference on Elections and Democracy. Panel 2: Voter Representation" (Stanford Law School, April 7, 2007).
5. The U.S. Supreme Court has allowed regulation of party finance and membership that goes far beyond that of other sorts of organizations in the United States precisely because the parties serve a quasi-governmental function.
6. See, for example, Justice Breyer's opinion in *McConnell v. FEC*, 540 U.S. 93 (2003).

If we and those who share our views lose an election, we expect that our opponents will adopt policies that we oppose, including redistricting policies. We may not like it, but that is the price all of us must willingly pay, whether we are Republicans or Democrats, so long as we wish to remain republicans and democrats . . . [W]e do not accept the imposition in the name of "reform" or "neutrality" of arbitrary criteria that tilt the system in favor of one party. We do not accept the withdrawal of this most political issue from politics.[7]

Of course, politics was the problem, and the question remains as to whether partisan and racial gerrymanders, although aimed at group interests, also violate individuals' rights.

On the other side are those who see that the solution lies in apolitical and technocratic commissions. Sam Issacharoff, Pamela Karlan, and Richard Pildes have led this assault among the legal scholars, and a number of activist groups and reformers have pushed this agenda in the political arena. Their thinking begins with the observations that the politicians seem to have broken the system again and that the judges have been unable to resolve the matter. The central pieces of evidence are the high incumbency advantage and reelection rate of sitting legislators and the observation that the most recent rounds of districting (1991 and 2001) produced particularly bizarre maps and avowedly egregious gerrymanders.[8] The mainsprings of the partisan gerrymandering are the unavoidable conflict of interest that arises when legislators draw their own districts. No one has yet discovered a simple, objective standard analogous to one person, one vote that could apply to questions of party balance, in spite of several decades of intense consideration of these issues. The Supreme Court asserted its authority to review partisan gerrymander cases in *Davis v. Bandemer*, but the law professors conclude that the inability to find a simple remedy and standard means that the Court has "failed." The conclusion of this line of thought seems clear. Lacking the in-house expertise or any guidelines, the courts ought to leave the task to others. Because the legislatures cannot be trusted, the obvious alternatives are nonpartisan commissions, which have been used widely in the United States and elsewhere to draw district lines.

Both sides of this debate see little role for the courts. Those favoring a technocratic solution and those seeking a legislative one view as folly the quest for a legal standard analogous to one person, one vote. The judges, however, continue

7. Daniel Lowenstein and Jonathan Steinberg, "The Quest for Legislative Districting in the Public Interest: Elusive or Illusory?" *UCLA Law Review* 33 (1985): 30.
8. See, for example, Samuel Issacharoff and Pamela Karlan, "Where to Draw the Line? Judicial Review of Political Gerrymanders," *Pennsylvania Law Review* 153 (2004): 572–74.

that quest. The Supreme Court asserted its authority over partisan gerrymandering in 1986 and has repeatedly confirmed that authority, but the Justices have yet to say clearly what should be done.

After the most recent round of litigation, however, there are signs that the Court may follow the guidance of the law professors and avoid gerrymandering cases altogether. In *Vieth v. Jubelirer*, four of the Justices on the Supreme Court stated, in no uncertain terms, that such a standard does not exist and that, lacking a simple principle, the courts should once again show the self-restraint exhibited before *Baker*. Four other Justices have reiterated the need for judicial intervention and went so far as to state that the Pennsylvania case was a clear partisan gerrymander that needed to be fixed by the legislature. Justice Kennedy cast the pivotal vote. He showed restraint reminiscent of that of Wiley Rutledge. The Court had no clear rule in the Pennsylvania case that came out of precedent or that could apply in the future. Rather than close the door for future cases, he decided that the Justices should wait. Kennedy emphasized that precedent clearly holds for the Court's jurisdiction over the propriety of redistricting, but they are still not ready to declare a solution. And so we wait.

The difficulty that the Court has had in finding a remedy and standard lies in its success. One person, one vote succeeded well beyond any expectations—indeed, well beyond most other Supreme Court doctrines, including the rights asserted in the desegregation cases. Finding a similar standard is a lofty goal, perhaps too high to aim. The difficulty in finding such a principle does not, however, mean that the courts should stay out. The design of the U.S. Constitution gives the judiciary an important function in politics, a check on the legislature, and the prospect of judicial action affects how the legislatures negotiate a districting law. If the courts get out of the districting business because they have not found a principle as powerful as one person, one vote, then they will have given up for the wrong reason and perhaps done even greater damage in allowing new forms of manipulation and distortion to accumulate through new abuses of the districting process.

Short of a crisp standard, there are ways that the judges can keep a watchful eye. One approach is offered by Justice O'Connor in *Shaw v. Reno*. Her pivotal opinion is often taken to mean that the courts should hold gerrymandering to the same standard as pornography—one knows it when one sees it. Instead, her opinion holds a deeper wisdom. Absent a pithy principle, judges must now take individual cases based on the specific legal questions raised in each, but the courts cannot back off. Doing so would only strengthen the hand of those in the legislature who wish to push a particular partisan design. Many legal scholars and judges find that unappealing. It may lead to inconsistencies across states and even individual cases, and it only invites suits to be brought.

A second possibility was suggested by Justice Tom Clark in his memos on the *Baker* case and was echoed by Robert McCloskey in his 1962 *Harvard Law Review* assessment of the *Baker* decision. Clark and McCloskey both favored a procedural standard, one that allowed the Court to review whether proper procedures were followed. This is quite a bit weaker than an explicit fairness or equity criterion, but it allows the Court to review the details of the cases. During the 1970s, the Court was tending in this direction on racial gerrymandering cases, until the Congress set down its own rules for evidence in racial discrimination in districting in the 1982 extension of the Voting Rights Act.

A third possibility is that the existing legal standards are sufficient. One person, one vote allows the courts the power to review all manner of cases; additional criteria are not necessary. Most important, in order to keep district populations equal, the legislatures must pass a new law every ten years. They must negotiate among themselves and craft a law that satisfies both chambers of the legislature and receives the assent of the governor. That is the republican form of government envisioned in the Constitution at work. Our observation is that under the *Baker* regime, partisan biases have fallen dramatically and continue to do so, especially when control of state government is split between the two parties. If that trend continues, the practical concerns with partisan gerrymandering will, over the long run, become vanishingly small. That may leave a "doctrinal mess," but the mess may be of little political importance.

All three of these paths forward (and there may be others) point to the critical importance of the courts. It is undeniable that a rollback of the *Baker* decision and a retreat from questions involving districting altogether would be disastrous over the long run. History would surely repeat itself. Shifts in population would eventually render existing district lines obsolete, and the legislature would leave those lines in place as that path offers the greatest political security and the least resistance.

It is also clear that the possibility of judicial review exerts a pressure on the legislatures to behave. Court power manifests itself most clearly when judges scrutinize and overturn legislative districting plans, as they do regularly. Sometimes district maps lack population equality; sometimes they violate specific state statutes; sometimes they discriminate against racial groups; sometimes they fail to follow the right process. For these and other reasons, judges have found cause to force the legislature to go back to the drawing board. The potential for abuses in the future offers an equally compelling reason for keeping jurisdiction over partisan gerrymandering. If the U.S. Supreme Court today were to state that it did not have jurisdiction over partisan gerrymandering for want of a simple principle such as one person, one vote, then the Justices would set down a precedent that constrained judges in the future. Sometime in the future, perhaps in a decade or two, a legislature will perpetrate a truly egregious gerrymander. With a precedent in hand, judges would almost surely not take challenges to that plan. That was exactly the situation in the 1950s when judges throughout the country took Frankfurter's political-thicket doctrine as precedent, and that bulwark was breeched only after Archibald Cox convinced Justice Potter Stewart that Frankfurter's opinion in *Colegrove* did not have the standing of precedent. If a majority of the Court were to embrace the political-thicket doctrine in the area of partisan gerrymandering, that opinion would completely constrain the courts and would give the legislatures a free hand.

It is unclear, however, whether a stronger standard is needed. One person, one vote may be enough. The reapportionment cases did not address party manipulation of the process, but biases have fallen. Increased fairness of district maps since the 1960s resulted not from a change in the motivations of parties and politicians but simply from the periodic renegotiation of districting boundaries in a highly competitive and pluralistic political environment. A widely accepted principle like one person, one vote would certainly ease judicial decision making in the future, but it is not a necessary requirement to achieve fair elections.

Politics brought about fairer election rules, but it took the courts to force that to happen. Legislative politics alone could not break the vicious cycle that sustained unequal representation. It took the steady hand of the judges deeply committed to maintaining American democracy and the Constitution and their own power within that framework to enable bargaining and negotiation among the representatives to happen. In the American political system, it is the courts that must maintain their constitutional responsibility of checking the otherwise unfettered legislative authority. How they accomplish that may be less important than that they do accomplish it.

The story of *Baker v. Carr* carries one final lesson: the vote cannot be taken for granted.

Americans have become accustomed to the idea that all people have the right to be counted equally. One person, one vote—isn't that what democracy means?

As the history of the rise of malapportionment and the struggle to end it reveals, broad principles do not always translate into practice. Narrow self-interest triumphs just as often. Such was the case with the apportionment of representation in the American states. State legislators failed to correct gross inequalities in district populations, as correcting those inequities would invariably cost many legislators their own seats. Rural interests realized that reapportionment would increase the political power of their urban adversaries and even given urban areas a majority of legislative seats. The majority parties in the state governments—Republicans in the North and Democrats in the South—realized that correcting malapportionment would weaken them politically, even cost them their legislative majorities. And the worse malapportionment became, the more strongly narrow interests asserted themselves against the claims of broad principles of equality and democracy.

This problem is endemic to all democracies. Nearly every representative democracy has had to confront malapportionment and other inequities in its electoral system. And in nearly every democracy the solution must originate with the legislature, the very people elected under skewed and unequal districts. The United States, however, is fortunate. Its Constitution provides a potential corrective. The courts can check the power of the legislatures, and in the case of *Baker v. Carr* they did just that. Still, courts serve as an imperfect check. They are the least dangerous branch of government, one that can take action only when called upon. Courts merely serve as a vehicle through which to contest the meaning of the vote and the power of the legislature.

The true defense of equal voting rights must come from Americans themselves. As we searched back through the dust of history for the causes and consequences of political inequality in the United States, we encountered many of the men and women who fought against the established order and others who labored to keep things as they were. Equal protection of citizens' democratic rights came about because of their struggles and personal abilities—Tommy Osborn's doggedness, Archibald Cox's legal brilliance, and William Brennan's gift of finding compromise when it was necessary and seizing the opportunity when it was present. Although the liberals triumphed, those who preached judicial restraint also left their mark. Felix Frankfurter's words, as much as Brennan's, guide the courts today.

The Tennessee lawyers' victory was not an inevitable consequence of some underlying social force or natural law. It resulted from the deliberation and political struggles among many individuals. Their vision and their struggle transformed American democracy and made it what it is today. Each new generation inherits their mantle—the challenge to keep a healthy democracy.

Appendix

To Chapter 10

This appendix describes in detail the data analyses underlying Tables 10.1, 10.2, and 10.3 in Chapter 10, as well as the U.S. map showing the Left Shift variable in Figure 10.1.

ANES ANALYSIS (TABLE 10.1)

We study the 1964 and 1968 American National Election Study data (ICPSR Nos. 7235 and 7281, respectively).[1] The regions are defined as follows:

Northeast = CT, DE, ME, MD, MA, NH, NJ, NY, OH, PA, RI, VT, WV
  (n = 958)
North Central = IL, IN, IA, KS, MI, MN, MO, NE, WI (n = 717)
South = AL, AR, FL, GA, KY, LA, MI, MS, NC, OK, SC, TN, TX, VA
  (n = 883)

1. ICPSR 7235: Political Behavior Program, Survey Research Center, AMERICAN NATIONAL ELECTION STUDY, 1964 [Computer file]. Conducted by the University of Michigan, Survey Research Center. 3rd ICPSR ed. Ann Arbor, MI: Inter-university Consortium for Political and Social Research [producer and distributor], 1999.

ICPSR: 7281: Political Behavior Program, Survey Research Center, AMERICAN NATIONAL ELECTION STDY, 1968 [Computer file]. Conducted by the University of Michigan, Political Behavior Program. 2nd ICPSR ed. Ann Arbor, MI: Inter-university Consortium for Political and Social Research [producer and distributor], 1999.

West = AK, AZ, CA, CO, HI, ID, MT, NV, NM, ND, OR, SD, UT, WA, WY (n = 524)

The following questions are used to construct the General Ideology Scale:
Liberal-conservative thermometer index (640238, 640251, 680225, 680241)
Federal government support of health care (640074, 680064)
Federal government support of education (640066, 680060)
Federal government guarantee of jobs (640078, 680066)
Federal government too strong (640071, 680062)
People in government waste a lot of money (640402, 680503)
Labor union feeling thermometer (640246, 680235)

The following questions are used to construct the Civil Rights Scale:
Attitude on segregation (640127, 680088)
Federal government should integrate schools (640100, 680075)
Attitude on fair housing (640116, 680084)
Civil rights leaders push too fast (640105, 680081)
Federal government and fair treatment in jobs (640097, 680073)
Blacks feeling thermometer (640250, 680240)

The following questions are used to construct the Party Identification Scale:
Party identification (640146, 680120)
Democrats feeling thermometer (640242, 680230)
Republicans feeling thermometer (640247, 680237)
Net party likes and dislikes (640021–640024, 680028–680031)
In all cases, we orient the items so that higher scores are associated with more liberal, more pro–civil rights, or more Democratic attitudes.

Table A10.1 presents summary statistics for the factor analysis employed to construct the scales. We used principal factors. The "bottom line" is straightforward. In all cases, the variables appear quite one-dimensional, and there are no surprises in the factor loadings.

CSEP ANALYSIS (TABLE 10.2)

We use the Comparative State Elections Project, 1968 Election Study data (ICPSR No. 7508).[2]

2. ICPSR 7508: David M. Kovenock and James W. Prothro, COMPARATIVE STATE ELECTIONS PROJECT, 1968 [Computer file]. Chapel Hill: University of North Carolina, Institute for Research in Social Science,

TABLE A10.1 *ANES factor analysis results*

Item	Loading	Uniqueness
General Ideology Scale[a]		
Liberal-conservative thermometer index	.43	.81
Federal government support of health care	.64	.59
Federal government support of education	.56	.69
Federal government guarantee of jobs	.59	.65
Federal government too strong	.60	.63
People in government waste a lot of money	.30	.91
Labor union feeling thermometer	.29	.91
Civil Rights Scale[b]		
Attitude on segregation	.69	.52
Federal government should integrate schools	.71	.50
Attitude on fair housing	.61	.63
Civil rights leaders push too fast	.55	.69
Federal government and fair treatment in jobs	.62	.62
Blacks feeling thermometer	.55	.70
Party Identification Scale[c]		
Party identification	.81	.35
Democrats feeling thermometer	.67	.55
Republicans feeling thermometer	.58	.66
Net party likes and dislikes	.74	.45

[a] *(n = 2,968; eigenvalues = 1.80, 0.15, 0.04)*
[b] *(n = 2,972; eigenvalues = 2.34, 0.26, −0.02)*
[c] *(n = 2,969; eigenvalues = 1.99, 0.08, −0.11)*

The following questions are used to construct the General Ideology Scale:
   Liberal-conservative self-identification (099)
   Cut government spending (312)
   Increase Social Security benefits (335)
   Stop spending on poverty programs (354)
   Government should help labor unions (347)
   National government wastes a lot of tax money (480)

1970 [producer]. Ann Arbor, MI: Inter-university Consortium for Political and Social Research [distributor], 1977.

TABLE A10.2 *CSEP factor analysis results*

Item	Loading	Uniqueness
General Ideology Scale[a]		
Liberal-conservative self-identification	.43	.82
Cut government spending	.47	.78
Increase Social Security benefits	.25	.94
Stop spending on poverty programs	.46	.79
Government should help labor unions	.36	.87
National government wastes a lot of tax money	.37	.87

Note: The Party Identification Scale is simply the average of the two items (the correlation between them is .87).
[a] *(n = 6,875; eigenvalues = 0.93, 0.20, −0.01)*

The following questions are used to construct the Party Identification Scale:

National party identification (569)

State party identification (570)

In all cases, we orient the items so that higher scores are associated with more liberal or more Democratic attitudes.

Table A10.2 presents summary statistics for the factor analysis employed to construct the General Ideology Scale. We use principal factors. Again, the variables appear relatively one-dimensional, and there are no surprises in the factor loadings.

LEFT SHIFT ANALYSIS (FIGURE 10.1)

STATE POLLS

Table A10.3 presents the results from state polls. Scores on each item are normalized so that, for each state, the overall mean is 0 and the standard deviation is 100.

PRESIDENTIAL VOTING

Table A10.4 presents the results from county-level or town-level voting in presidential elections. For each state, we construct the variable Democratic Vote Percent by averaging the Democratic percentage of the two-party vote in the presidential elections of 1948, 1952, 1956, and 1960. We use town-level data for

TABLE A10.3 *Results from state polls*

State	Medicare		Federal school aid		Ideology		Party identification	
	Urban	Rural	Urban	Rural	Urban	Rural	Urban	Rural
New Hampshire	2	−3					16	−10
Vermont	−7	5					7	−5
Illinois					*13*	*−38*	*5*	*−15*
Indiana							6	−9
Kentucky	*−17*	*14*	*12*	*10*			−3	3
Colorado	8	−12					15	−22
California					3	−3	3	3

Note: Numbers in bolded italics are for cases where the t-test of no differences between Urban and Rural coefficients is rejected at the .05 level.

CT, DE, ME, MA, NH, RI, and VT, and county-level data for all other states. Urban counties are those with density in 1960 greater than 250 people per square mile, or counties that contain a city with population in 1960 over 100,000. If no county in a state meets these criteria, then we define the most populous county as urban. In addition, we define the following counties as urban because of their large population or density relative to their state: Palm Beach, FL; Black Hawk, IA; Linn, IA; Cascade, MT; Wake, NC; Washoe, NV; and Spartanburg, SC. Urban towns are those with population over 70,000 in CT, ME, MA, and RI, and towns with population over 20,000 in NH and VT.

VOTING ON BOND REFERENDA

Table A10.5 presents the results from county-level or town-level voting on statewide bond referenda. For each bond referendum in each state, we first compute the percentage of voters voting "yes" on each bond during the period 1950–1970. We then construct the variable Bond Support Score in each state by averaging these percentages. We use town-level data for RI, and county-level data for all other states. The urban definition is the same as in the Presidential Voting subsection above.

CONGRESSIONAL ROLL-CALL VOTING

Table A10.6 presents the results from congressmen's and congressman's roll-call voting scores. For each state, we regress the DW-NOMINATE scores on district population density (persons per square mile). We standardize the density measure so that it has a mean of 0 and a standard deviation of 1. We cluster the standard

TABLE A10.4 *Results from presidential voting*

State	Urban	Non-urban	Difference	State	Urban	Non-urban	Difference
Connecticut	59	46	13	Kentucky	47	52	−5
Maine	45	35	10	Louisiana	52	58	−6
Massachusetts	67	51	16	Maryland	48	43	5
New Hampshire	57	41	16	Mississippi	54	67	−13
New Jersey	44	37	7	North Carolina	51	61	−10
New York	47	32	15	Oklahoma	43	52	−9
Ohio	48	39	9	South Carolina	67	75	−8
Pennsylvania	49	39	10	Tennessee	52	53	−1
Rhode Island	65	55	10	Texas	49	56	−7
Vermont	53	33	20	Virginia	45	48	−3
Illinois	49	40	9	West Virginia	50	53	−3
Indiana	47	41	6	Arizona	42	47	−5
Iowa	47	42	5	California	47	46	1
Kansas	42	35	7	Colorado	48	43	5
Michigan	52	35	17	Idaho	35	44	−9
Minnesota	54	47	7	Montana	46	47	−1
Missouri	56	49	7	Nevada	48	45	3
Nebraska	43	35	8	New Mexico	44	50	−6
Wisconsin	50	40	10	North Dakota	39	39	0
Alabama	57	70	−13	Oregon	48	43	5
Arkansas	56	62	−6	South Dakota	38	41	−3
Delaware	56	45	11	Utah	44	44	0
Florida	46	52	−6	Washington	49	49	0
Georgia	59	75	−16	Wyoming	46	42	4

errors by congressman/congresswoman. One-district states are excluded. North Dakota is excluded because it has only 3 observations as a two-district state.

STUDIES OF STATE LEGISLATORS

New Jersey, Ohio, Tennessee, and California: Wahlke and Eulau's Legislative Behavior Study[3] surveyed state legislators in California, New Jersey, Ohio, and Ten-

3. John Wahlke and Heinz Eulau, LEGISLATIVE BEHAVIOR STUDY, 1957 [Computer file]. Nashville, TN: John C. Wahlke, Vanderbilt University, Department of Political Science [producer], 1958. Ann Arbor, MI: Inter-university Consortium for Political and Social Research [distributor], 197?.

TABLE A10.5 *Results from voting on bond referenda*

	Urban	Nonurban	Difference
Maine	71	61	10
Michigan	60	53	7
New Jersey	61	55	6
Rhode Island	65	60	5
New Mexico	69	66	3
North Carolina	62	64	−2
West Virginia	67	67	0
California	68	66	2
Oregon	54	51	3
Washington	63	60	3

nessee. The survey includes information on the urban-rural composition of each legislator's district, as well as the legislator's attitudes on several issue questions. The issue items were 5-point Likert scales regarding the following statements:

1. The government has the responsibility to see to it that all people, poor or rich, have adequate housing, education, medical care, and protection against unemployment.

2. Business enterprise can continue to give us our high standard of living only if it remains free from government regulation.

3. The most pressing problems which local governments face cannot be solved without new state taxes.

We scale Party Identification together with the three issue questions to construct a measure of "ideology," and we regress the Ideology measure on urbanization. Table A10.7 presents the results. In New Jersey and Ohio there is a significant positive relationship between the urban dummy and ideology, but in Tennessee and California there is not.

Colorado: Irvin[4] classified Colorado state legislators as shown in Table A10.8. The urban-rural differences are large and significant. Summing across both chambers, 55 percent of urban legislators were liberal, compared to only 13 percent of rural legislators. Conversely, only 20 percent of urban legislators were conservative, compared to 63 percent of rural legislators. Suburban legislators fell between these poles, with equal numbers of all types.

Connecticut: We factor-analyzed roll-call voting data taken from the state

4. William P. Irvin, "Colorado: A Matter of Balance," in *The Politics of Reapportionment*, ed. Malcolm E. Jewell (New York: Atherton Press, 1962), 78.

TABLE A10.6 *Results from congressional roll-call scores*

State	Coefficient	R^2	# Observations	State	Coefficient	R^2	# Observations
Connecticut	.02	.01	40	Georgia	−.03	.06	81
Maine	.06	.07	24	Kentucky	−.06	.08	65
Massachusetts	.09**	.15	109	Louisiana	.06*	.21	65
New Hampshire	.08	.34	16	Maryland	.14**	.32	54
New Jersey	.16**	.35	116	Mississippi	.06	.16	49
New York	.28**	.42	352	North Carolina	−.02	.04	95
Ohio	.12**	.13	182	Oklahoma	−.09**	.14	52
Pennsylvania	.18**	.28	253	South Carolina	−.06**	.22	49
Rhode Island	02**	.72	16	Tennessee	.05	.06	76
Illinois	.23**	.29	199	Texas	−.05	.06	169
Indiana	.04	.01	88	Virginia	.02	.03	79
Iowa	.10*	.12	64	West Virginia	−.04	.05	47
Kansas	.02	.01	47	Arizona	−.22**	.55	17
Michigan	.30**	.47	145	California	.10**	.06	236
Minnesota	.06	.02	72	Colorado	.12*	.18	32
Missouri	.13**	.15	91	Idaho	−.11	.07	16
Nebraska	.05	.04	32	Montana	.27*	.39	16
Wisconsin	.22**	.32	54	Oregon	.11	.12	32
Alabama	−.01	.00	63	South Dakota	.14	.23	16
Arkansas	−.08	.25	48	Utah	−.01	.00	16
Florida	.02	.01	64	Washington	−.01	.00	49

* = Significant at the .10 level; ** = significant at the .05 level.

Journal of the House of Representatives. We analyzed all roll calls taken in the 1957 sessions; see Table A10.9.

Urban legislators were noticeably more liberal than nonurban legislators in the state lower house (the difference is statistically significant at the .05 level). This is consistent with Lockard.[5] He finds a strong correlation between party and ideology (Democrats more liberal). Since urban areas were much more Democratic than rural areas, this would tend to make urban legislators more liberal as well.

5. Duane Lockard, *New England State Politics* (Princeton, NJ: Princeton University Press, 1959).

TABLE A10.7 *Results from legislative behavior study, 1959*

	New Jersey	Ohio	Tennessee	California
Urban Dummy	.37*	.48*	−.06	−.13
	(.18)	(.10)	(.13)	(.14)
Constant	−.29	−.39	.16	.16
	(.16)	(.06)	(.06)	(.11)
# Observations	79	161	118	109
R^2	.05	.14	.00	.01

Note: Robust standard errors in parentheses.
* = Significant at the .05 level.

Illinois: We factor-analyzed roll-call voting data from the League of Women Voters. The scores in Table A10.10 are standardized to have a mean of 0 and a standard deviation of 100 within each chamber, with higher scores denoting more liberal voting records.

Urban (Chicago) legislators were noticeably more liberal than nonurban legislators in both chambers, and much more liberal in the state senate (both differences are statistically significant at the .05 level).

Massachusetts: We analyzed "labor roll call support scores" constructed from the *Official Labor Record of the Massachusetts Legislature, 1955–1956 Session,* compiled by the Massachusetts branch of the American Federation of Labor; see Table A10.11.

Urban legislators were noticeably more prolabor than nonurban legislators in both chambers, and much more liberal in the state lower house (both differences are statistically significant at the .05 level).

TABLE A10.8 *Ideology of Colorado State Legislators, 1961–1962*

	Lower house			Upper house		
	Urban	Suburban	Rural	Urban	Suburban	Rural
Liberal	14	2	6	8	1	1
Moderate	8	2	6	2	1	6
Conservative	5	2	21	3	1	12

TABLE A10.9 *Ideology of Connecticut State House of Representatives, 1957*

	Urban	Nonurban
Average Ideology	67	−3

TABLE A10.10 *Ideology of Illinois state legislators, 1957–1965*

	Lower house		Upper house	
	Urban	Nonurban	Urban	Nonurban
Average Ideology	38	−24	90	−65

Michigan: Using the figures in Becker et al.,[6] we constructed Table A10.12 for the Michigan House of Representatives.

The urban-rural differences are large and significant. For example 58 percent (32/55) of the legislators from the highly urban districts were "very liberal" (90 percent or more liberal votes), while 0 percent of the most rural legislators were "very liberal." In contrast, only 16 percent of the legislators from the highly urban districts were "very conservative" (90 percent or more conservative votes), while 93 percent of the most rural legislators were "very conservative."

Minnesota: Although the Minnesota legislature was nonpartisan from 1913 to 1973, it was organized into clearly liberal and conservative caucuses at least since the 1950s. Mitau[7] gives the caucus affiliations of Minnesota state legislators in 1967, as shown in Table A10.13.

(Mitau classified three lower house and four upper house districts as Mixed. We drop these. He classified six lower house and two upper house districts as "Rural with City of 25,000." We classify these as Rural. He classified

TABLE A10.11 *Pro-labor voting by Massachusetts state legislators, 1955–1956*

	Lower house		Upper house	
	Urban	Nonurban	Urban	Nonurban
Average percentage prolabor	77	44	69	43

6. Robert W. Becker, Frieda L. Foote, Mathias Lubega, and Stephen V. Monsma, "Correlates of Legislative Voting: Michigan House of Representatives, 1954–1961," *Midwest Journal of Political Science* 6 (1962): 384–96.
7. G. Theodore Mitau, *Politics in Minnesota* (Minneapolis: University of Minnesota Press, 1970), 87.

TABLE A10.12 *Ideology in the Michigan House of Representatives, 1955–1961*

	Percentage urban in district			
	70–100%	50–70%	25–50%	0–25%
Cast 90% or more liberal roll-call votes	32	2	6	0
Cast 90% or more conservative votes	9	8	12	13
Total number of districts (legislators)	55	12	28	14

TABLE A10.13 *Caucus of Minnesota state legislators, 1967*

	Lower house			Upper house		
	Urban	Suburban	Rural	Urban	Suburban	Rural
Liberal	17	5	20	7	3	10
Conservative	18	23	48	8	13	23

four upper house districts as "Rural-Suburb." We classify these as Suburb.) The urban-rural differences are large and significant. Summing across both chambers, 48 percent of urban legislators were liberal, compared to only 30 percent of rural legislators and 18 percent of suburban legislators.

THE CONSTRUCTION OF LEFT SHIFT

We summarize the results above in Table A10.14. Columns 1–9 present each of the separate types of variables. Column 10 summarizes all of the information on each state with a prediction about whether or not we should expect a noticeable leftward shift in policy post-*Baker*. This variable is also shown in the U.S. map in Figure 10.1.

The symbols in the table are defined as follows: ++ denotes a substantively large positive relationship with urbanization that is statistically significant at the .05 level; + denotes a positive relationship that is significant at the .10 level; — denotes a substantively large negative relationship with urbanization that is significant at the .05 level; – denotes a positive relationship that is significant at the .10 level; and 0 denotes that the relationship with urbanization is not statistically significant even at the .10 level.

By and large, the results in columns 1– 6 of Table A10.14 are consistent with those in columns 7–9. In the states of the Northeast and industrial Midwest, voters, congressmen and congresswomen, and state representatives from urban

TABLE A10.14 *Summary of urban-rural differences*

State	1. Polls ideol.	2. Polls party	3. Votes bonds	4. Votes party	5. Cong. votes	6. State legis.	7. CSES ideol.	8. ANES ideol.	9. Party bias	10. Left Shift?
Connecticut				++	0	++		++	++	Yes
Delaware				++				0	−	Yes?
Maine			++	++	0			++	++	Yes
Maryland				++	++			0	0	Yes
Massachusetts				++	++	++	++	++	−	(Yes)
New Hampshire	0	0		++	0			++	++	(Yes)
New Jersey			++	++	++	++		++	+	Yes
New York				++	++		++	++	++	Yes
Ohio				++	++	++	++	++	++	Yes
Pennsylvania				++	++		++	++	++	Yes
Rhode Island			++	++	++			++	++	Yes
Vermont	0	0		++				++	++	Yes
Illinois	++	++		++	++	++	++	++	++	Yes
Indiana		++		++	0			++	+	Yes?
Iowa				++	+			++	++	Yes
Kansas				++	0			++	++	Yes
Michigan			++	++	++	++		++	++	Yes
Minnesota				++	0	++	++	++		Yes
Missouri				++	++			++	+	Yes
Nebraska				++	0			++		Yes
West Virginia			0	−	0			0	−	No
Wisconsin				++	++			++	+	Yes
Alabama				—	0		0	0	−	No
Arkansas				—	0			0	−	No
Florida				—	0		++	0	—	Yes?
Georgia				—	0			0	—	No
Kentucky	—	0		—	0		0	0	0	No
Louisiana				—	+			0	−	No
Mississippi				—	0		0	0	−	No
North Carolina			−	−	0			0	−	No
Oklahoma				—	—			0	—	No
South Carolina				—	—			0	−	No

State	1. Polls, ideol.	2. Polls, party	3. Votes, bonds	4. Votes, party	5. Cong. votes	6. State legis.	7. CSES ideol.	8. ANES ideol.	9. Party bias	10. Left Shift?
Tennessee				0	0	0		0	—	No
Texas				—	0		–	0	–	No
Virginia				–	0			0	0	No
Arizona				—	—			0	—	No
California			+	+	++	0	++	0		Yes?
Colorado	++	++		++	+	++		0	0	Yes
Idaho				–	0			0	0	No
Montana				–	+			0	+	Yes?
Nevada				+				0	0	No
New Mexico			+	—				0	0	No
North Dakota				0				0	+	No
Oregon			+	++	0			0	++	(Yes)
South Dakota				–	0		0	0	0	No
Utah				0	0			0	+	No
Washington			+	0	0			0	0	Yes?
Wyoming				+				0	+	No

Note: States with Left Shift=Yes? are states where the evidence for setting Left Shift=Yes is relatively weak. We checked the main analyses predicting policy outcomes (reported in Table A10.15 and Table 10.3 in the text) for robustness by dropping these states from the regressions. The results were largely unchanged.

areas were consistently more liberal than their nonurban counterparts, and in most cases the differences were large and highly significant.[8] In the South and West, the patterns were more mixed. None of the Deep South states show a significantly positive relationship between urbanism and liberalism, and some show a significantly negative relationship. In the West and border states, there are some cases where the pattern is clear (e.g., Kentucky, Arizona, and Colorado), but others are messier.

In two small northeastern states—New Hampshire and Vermont—the results are conflicting. The poll results suggest insignificant urban-rural differences. On the other hand, the poll data show that in both states Democrats were

8. There is, of course, a strong correlation between "ideology" and party affiliation among congressmen and congresswomen, especially in the Northeast and industrial Midwest. We do not want to control for party in our analysis, however. If urban voters are more liberal, then electing Democrats in these states is one way to ensure their representatives are also liberal.

significantly more liberal on Medicare. And in both states, malapportionment clearly favored Republicans (column 9). Moreover, the town-level presidential voting data show that the cities in both states were clearly more Democratic than the small towns and rural areas (column 4). So we set Left Shift = 1 for these two states.

A few southern and border states also have mixed patterns. Maryland and Delaware appear to be more like northeastern states than southern states. In Maryland, urban congressmen and congresswomen were noticeably more liberal than their nonurban counterparts. But malapportionment did not clearly favor either party, and it probably hurt suburban areas the most. In Delaware, urban areas were noticeably more Democratic than rural areas, but malapportionment hurt Republicans at least as much as Democrats because many suburbs were as underrepresented as the major city (Wilmington). The evidence is also mixed in West Virginia and Florida. The survey data in Florida indicate that the urban areas were noticeably more liberal than rural areas. On the other hand, the voting data and congressional roll-call data show either no differences or a pre-*Baker* malapportionment that was clearly pro-Democratic.

In the mountain and desert West, there is little evidence of urban-rural differences. One exception is Colorado, where urban voters appear noticeably more liberal and Democratic than rural voters. Colorado had the largest city in the mountain West—Denver, population 494,000 in 1960—and is probably not representative of the smaller mountain states such as Idaho and Wyoming. The congressional voting results suggest this as well.

California, Montana, New Mexico, and Washington are more difficult cases. Urban voters in California are more liberal, but not more Democratic, than other voters (see Table 10.2, p. 219). Also, California's urban congressmen and congresswomen were more liberal than their rural counterparts. On the other hand, there were no clear urban-rural differences among the state legislators. In New Mexico, the bond evidence suggests that urban voters were more liberal in their spending preferences, but other voting data show that they were not more Democratic and that malapportionment did not help Democrats more than Republicans.

Finally, there are three cases in which we expect to see a change post-*Baker*, but where the change appears to have come more from gerrymandering than from malapportionment. Massachusetts, New Hampshire, and Oregon were among the most well apportioned states in the 1950s and 1960s. Nonetheless, they all show strong signs that liberal voters gained representation post-*Baker*. The party bias terms all shift strongly in the pro-Democratic direction, and Democratic voters are clearly more liberal than Republican voters in these states.

ANALYSIS FOR TABLE 10.3

For Table 10.3, we conducted a panel analysis using all of the annual data, with state fixed effects, year fixed effects, and a battery of control variables. To deal with autocorrelation, we clustered the standard errors by state—this corrects the standard errors for autocorrelation of a general form. (This is one of the methods suggested by Bertrand et al.[9]) We also estimated models with a simple first-order autoregressive correction and found similar results to those reported below.) Table A10.15 shows the regression results.

TABLE A10.15 *Policy output regressions*

	Total spending	Social spending	Welfare spending	Education spending	Unemployment Insurance	State share
Left Shift	0.151***	0.130***	0.225**	0.130***	2.336**	0.162***
	[3.41]	[2.62]	[2.16]	[2.88]	[2.22]	[3.16]
Average	0.350*	0.529**	0.371	0.807***	15.143**	0.209
income	[1.86]	[2.21]	[0.82]	[2.93]	[2.05]	[0.93]
Population	−0.358***	−0.332***	−0.470	−0.411***	−3.503	−0.643***
	[−3.55]	[−2.78]	[−1.31]	[−2.68]	[−1.06]	[−4.56]
% Children	0.476	1.173**	2.844***	1.299***	−1.128	0.166
	[1.12]	[2.53]	[3.20]	[2.95]	[−0.14]	[0.33]
% Elderly	0.162	0.065	−0.232	0.058	−0.744	0.052
	[1.02]	[0.39]	[−0.61]	[0.29]	[−0.23]	[0.33]
Unemployed rate					1.295***	
					[5.69]	
Average wage					0.222***	
					[3.51]	
% Union					0.174	
					[1.38]	
# Observation	885	855	855	855	855	675
R^2	0.96	0.96	0.89	0.96	0.89	0.95

Note: All regressions include state fixed effects and year fixed effects. Robust t-statistics, clustered by state, in brackets.
* = *Significant at 10% level;* ** = *significant at 5% level;* *** = *significant at 1% level.*

9. Marianne Bertrand, Esther Duflo, and Sendhil Mullainathan, "How Much Should We Trust Differences-in-Differences Estimates?" *Quarterly Journal of Economics,* 2004, *119* (1), pages 249–75.

The key independent variable is Left Shift. This is equal to 0 for all states in the pre-*Baker* era. In the post-*Baker* era, it is equal to 1 for all states where (1) urban and/or suburban voters were clearly more liberal than rural voters on fiscal issues, and (2) malapportionment significantly overrepresented rural voters in the pre-*Baker* era, or a *Baker*-era redistricting caused a clear proleft shift (i.e., a pro-Democratic shift in a state where Democratic voters were significantly more liberal than Republicans).

Appendix

To Chapter 11

To measure the effects of racial districting on partisan bias, we examined how the relation between seats and votes varied with the racial composition of state legislative districts during the 1990s. Data on racial composition come from Lilley et al., *The Almanac of State Legislatures*.[1]

To measure partisan biases, we estimated the relationship between seats and votes among all state legislatures for the post-1990 period (i.e., 1992–2006). In each analysis, the dependent variable is the Democratic Share of Seats in the State Legislature and the independent variable is the Democratic Share of the Two-Party Vote statewide.

Two alternative measures of the vote were considered. The first measure, which is most commonly used in the literature, is the share of the vote that a party won in all state legislative elections statewide. The second, and the one favored here, is the average vote in all statewide and federal offices in that year or neighboring years. The problem with the first measure is that many state legislative races have no competition and thus record no "vote." One party wins an uncontested race with probability 1 (and a vote share of 100 percent), and the other loses. As a result, there will be simultaneity bias in seats-votes analyses, as the measure of vote will be affected by the number of uncontested seats won.

Statewide elections rather than the legislative elections offer a ready solution. The underlying and unobserved support for the parties in the legislative elec-

---

1. William Lilley III, Laurence J. DeFranco, William M. Diefenderfer, and William Lilley, *The Almanac of State Legistures*, 2nd ed. (Washington, DC: CQ Press, 1988).

tions throughout the state should closely follow the support for the parties in elections for statewide offices, such as governor and U.S. Senate. To measure the underlying division of support between the parties in a state and year, we computed the average of the votes for all offices elected statewide. This is the Expected Democratic Vote Share throughout the state in a given year.[2] By convention, we use the Democrats' share of the two-party vote, as that equals 1 minus the Republican's share. The Expected Democratic Vote Share in statewide offices measures the partisan leaning of the voters in the state in a given year. It avoids the difficulties that arise in using the state legislative vote directly, especially the sometimes large number of cases where no legislative vote is available because only one candidate stood for election. One objection to this method is that it does not separate the effect of having no candidates running, variable turnout, or the qualities of candidates. All of those factors, however, are consequences of the electoral system. Unfair districting lines can discourage competition, affect the intensity of campaigns and thus turnout, and make incumbents safe lowering their rate of retirement. The Expected Democratic Vote Share statewide is the input to the legislative election; seats are the output. An objection to Expected Democratic Vote Share is that it may contain measurement error, as it does not equal the votes cast for legislative races. The R^2 of regressions explaining legislative vote share as a function of Expected Democratic Vote Share and the net share of uncontested races range from .75 to .81. For example, among the lower chambers since 1970, the coefficient on Expected Democratic Vote Share is .62 ($SE=.04$) and the coefficient on the net share of uncontested races is .85 ($SE=.03$). Thus while the relationship between the two vote share variable is quite strong, it is clearly necessary to control for uncontested seats. This is why we prefer the Expected Democratic Vote Share variable.

Regression results differ somewhat depending on the measure, but the same overall picture emerges. Biases decline from before to after *Baker,* and by approximately the same amount under either model. Estimated biases are some what larger using Expected Democratic Vote Share.

The analysis allowed every state to have different intercepts (biases) but restricted all states to have the same responsiveness within a decade. We forced every state to have the same slope in order to gain efficiency. We tested for variation in responsiveness but found no statistical evidence that allowing the slopes to vary affected the estimated intercepts, which is the quantity of interest here. We further allowed for year effects.

2. We further adjust the data by subtracting out the incumbency advantage, which was growing in this period. Hence the statewide shares of the Democratic vote reflect party and not the popularity of individual incumbents. Expected Democratic Vote Share is the average in a given year and differs from the long-term average division of the vote in a state, called the Normal Vote.

TABLE A11.1 *Fixed-effects regression results estimating the relationship between seats and votes during 1992–2006 in upper and lower chamber state legislative elections*

	Linear model		Log-odds model	
	Upper chamber	Lower chamber	Upper chamber	Lower chamber
Democratic	1.016	0.842	1.111	0.952
vote share	(.161)	(.127)	(.188)	(.140)
# Observations	249	277	249	277
Adjacent R^2	.84	.84	.85	.89
F-test on state fixed effects	15.10	18.68	14.02	19.32
p-value	.00	.00	.00	.00

Note: *All regressions include state fixed effects. Robust standard errors in parentheses. Dependent variable – Democratic Share of Seats.*

We estimated a fixed-effect model for all states. The slope of the regressions is the same in all states, but the fixed effects vary around the common intercept. The fixed effects are then used to estimate the bias for each state.

We also allowed the functional form to vary, as some researchers prefer a linear seats-votes model, while others prefer an S-shaped curve implied by the log-odds transformation of the seats and of the votes.[3] Table A.11.1 presents the results of that regression analysis.

Tables A.11.2 and A.11.3 show the relation between racial composition of state legislative districts and partisan biases. Table A.11.2 presents the correlation between the partisan bias and the percentage of state legislative seats that are majority-minority districts (MMDs) for the upper and lower chambers, using each functional form. The positive correlations indicate that the more MMDs a state had, the higher the bias in the Democrats' direction.

Table A.11.3 presents the average state bias for states with 0 to 5 percent MMD, 5 to 10 percent MMD, and more than 10 percent MMD. The table also presents the number of states for which we have valid data and the standard

3. See Gary King and Robert X. Browning, "Democratic Representation and Partisan Bias in Congressional Elections," *American Political Science Review* 81, no. 4 (December 1987): 1251–73. See also Glendon Schubert and Charles Press, LEGISLATIVE REAPPORTIONMENT DATA, 1962 [Computer file]. Honolulu: Glendon Schubert, University of Hawaii [producer], 196? Ann Arbor, MI: Inter-university Consortium for Political and Social Research [distributor], 197? Also see Gary King, Bradley Palmquist, Greg Adams, Micah Altman, Kenneth Benoit, Claudine Gay, Jeffrey B. Lewis, Russ Mayer, and Eric Reinhardt, 1997, "Record of American Democracy, All Documentation and Miscellaneous hdl:1902.1/01959 Files," hdl:1902.1/01959 http://id.thedata.org/hdl%3A1902.1%2F01959 Murray Research Archive [distributor (DDI)].

deviation of the biases (variation in the estimated biases across states). Those states with few or no MMDs and those states with a modest number had biases slightly in the Republican direction on average. Those states with more than 10 percent MMD had a noticeable bias in the Democratic direction, contrary to those who claim that MMDs have led to a Republican advantage. T-statistics for the differences between the lower and upper categories are only slightly larger than 1, indicating that there are not strong statistical differences between states without MMDs and those with many MMDs; however, the sign of the difference suggests that more MMDs correlate with more pro-Democratic partisan biases.

Finally, Figure A11.1 presents kernel densities describing the distribution of the normal vote in each state's lower house districts. As noted in the text, these are constructed using data from the ROAD project.

TABLE A11.2 *Correlations between percentage majority–minority district and estimated bias*

	Linear model	Log-odds model
Lower chamber	.36	.35
Upper chamber	.23	.21

TABLE A11.3 *Average and standard deviations of estimated biases in relationship to percentage of state legislative districts that contain a majority of minority voters in 1992–2006*

	Linear model				
	Upper chamber		Lower chamber		
MMD Pct	Average bias	Standard deviation	Average bias	Standard deviation	# of states
0–5%	−.019	.14	−.021	.16	19
5–10%	−.026	.08	−.011	.10	9
10+ %	0.48	.11	0.45	.10	18

	Log-odds model				
	Upper chamber		Lower chamber		
MMD Pct	Average bias	Standard deviation	Average bias	Standard deviation	# of states
0–5%	−.020	.16	−.022	.16	19
5–10%	−.030	.08	−.013	.10	9
10+ %	0.47	.11	0.44	.11	18

Index

Page numbers in *italics* refer to illustrations, tables, and charts; *n* refers to footnotes.